Crisis Narratives, Institutional Change, and the Transformation of the Japanese State

Crisis Narratives, Institutional Change, and the Transformation of the Japanese State

Edited by

Sebastian Maslow
and Christian Wirth

SUNY
PRESS

Cover photo: iStock by Getty Images.

Published by State University of New York Press, Albany

© 2021 State University of New York

For information, contact State University of New York Press, Albany, NY
www.sunypress.edu

Library of Congress Cataloging-in-Publication Data

Names: Maslow, Sebastian, editor | Wirth, Christian, editor.
Title: Crisis narratives, institutional change, and the transformation of the Japanese
    state / edited by Sebastian Maslow and Christian Wirth.
Description: Albany : State University of New York Press, [2021] | Includes
    bibliographical references and index.
Identifiers: ISBN 9781438486093 (hardcover : alk. paper) | ISBN 9781438486109
    (ebook) | ISBN 9781438486086 (pbk. : alk. paper)
Further information is available at the Library of Congress.

10 9 8 7 6 5 4 3 2 1

For Hannah and Junko
and
Jérôme and Yukiyo

Contents

Part I
Narrating Japan's Social Crisis

Part II
Narrating Japan's Political and Economic Crises

Part III
Narrating Japan's National Security Crisis

Illustrations

Figures

Tables

Preface and Acknowledgments

The initial idea for this edited volume emerged in early 2016. At the time, we both worked at Tohoku University and witnessed firsthand the ongoing official and civil society efforts to reconstruct the physical and social infrastructure that the triple disaster of earthquake, tsunami, and nuclear meltdowns of March 11, 2011, had destroyed.

Large photo exhibitions at highly frequented public spaces in Sendai and Tokyo told the story of hope and successful common efforts of reconstruction. These local narratives resonated with the narratives of revitalizing Japan's rural areas, and clearly linked to long-standing debates about Japan's social, economic and political situation and trajectory. Soon after the tsunami struck, "3.11" had become imbued with meaning far beyond the disaster and the directly affected Tohoku region. It had become a catch-all frame for narrating Japan's most severe postwar crisis, including the possibilities and hopes for decisive change to end Japan's "lost decades." That is, the historical mission of reconstructing Japan as a whole—be it to make Japan "normal" again as conservative circles had long endeavored, or simply to return to economic growth and shared prosperity.

However, contemplating our personal experiences of witnessing the triple disaster in Sendai and Tokyo, respectively, we were intrigued by the contrast of decisive action taken in some areas, and the lagging responses we saw in others. Several years into the post-3.11 reconstruction effort, devastated areas had been cleared, partially rebuilt, and protected with new, massive concrete breakwaters. But while 3.11, not least due to deliberate official efforts, no longer served as frame for describing the state of the nation, the crisis continued in its localized form. News about radioactive leaks at Fukushima kept appearing; thousands still lived in temporary housing, and on the streets of Sendai volunteers kept collecting donations that would enable them to continue searching for missing people and assisting surviving disaster victims. Tohoku's major newspaper kept on listing the numbers of missing and dead people from the disaster on its frontpage. A decade after 3.11, these memories of personal loss, and of personal and national recovery, seem in danger of being eclipsed. Japan is battling the severe COVID-19 pandemic and the national crisis, social, economic and political, is far from over. Thus, it is timely to put the current and recent crises into a broader historical context.

Under the banner of the "lost decades," scholars and policymakers have long argued about the causes of and remedies for Japan's malaise. There is much excellent scholarship both on the causes of Japan's social and economic crises and on the politics of framing Japan's 3.11. But these accounts require updating. And as they usually cover specific issue areas, we also feel that there is a need for connecting them to broader historical and political developments. Thus, it is quite clear that no single perspective, disciplinary or in terms of issue area, can capture the multifaceted social, economic, and political transformations at hand. The remedy, we are convinced, lies in adopting a more critical and thus more incisive methodological perspective to cover a range of issue areas that are normally not considered as co-constitutive parts of an integral whole. Looking back at three decades of "national crises," how, then, has Japan been coping? Has this elevated sense of "crisis" resulted in fundamental change of the Japanese state?

In 2012, Abe Shinzō led his Liberal Democratic Party back to power, as he pledged to "take back Japan" from the prolonged crisis allegedly caused by the nation's postwar regime. In 2020, Abe became modern Japan's longest-serving prime minister before suddenly resigning after almost eight years in office. During this tenure, he had consistently called for decisive reforms to end the compound "national crises" in form of military weakness in international affairs, economic stagnation, and rapid demographic decline and labor shortage. Abe restored political stability and enabled Japan to play a proactive role internationally. Yet the 2020 Tokyo Olympics and Paralympics, in line with the 1964 Tokyo Olympics envisioned to become a powerful symbol for the national "rebirth," had to be postponed amidst the COVID-19 crisis. The impact of the pandemic also thwarted plans for the country's economic recovery, and ever-growing public debt further deepened concerns over the sustainability of social welfare institutions and social disparities. Moreover, spiking numbers of infected and deceased people have, once again, triggered debates over the political leadership's ability to manage national crises. Thus, ten years after the March 2011 triple disaster, the sense of "national crisis" and decline has not vanished from public debate. To the contrary, it has become more salient than ever. So has the urgency for scholarly debate. In this vein, we hope that this volume will stimulate deeper-going discussions about the many lessons Japan offers in addressing and mediating the manifold crises the world is facing to today.

We are grateful to the following institutions and individuals for their support, allowing us to pursue our research interest and to bring this project to fruition. Tohoku University's Tohoku Forum for Creativity provided generous financial and logistical support for a first workshop in Sendai in February 2018. We especially thank Maeda Yoshiaki for his encouragement at the early stage of this project. Juthatip Wiwattanapantuwong's professional work was decisive for the smooth preparation, holding, and administrative wrapping-up of the Sendai workshop. Misumi Taeko's continuous and generous support has been indispensable not only in arranging the workshop, but also for facilitating our earlier stays at Tohoku University. Moreover, we appreciate Bryce Wakefield's and David Leheny's valuable inputs and comments at this occasion. Providing further financial and logistical backing, Patrick Köllner from the German Institute for Global and Area Studies made the holding of the second workshop in Hamburg in October 2018 possible. We thank Kai Schulze for his incisive observations as a discussant of several draft chapters at that occasion.

Helpful, too, were Kei Koga, David Leheny, and Paul O'Shea's comments on an earlier version of the introduction. We are also grateful to Jon Morris for his careful reading of many earlier versions of this manuscript. At SUNY Press, we would like to thank Michael Rinella for his encouragement and for steering the manuscript through the peer review, and Diane Ganeles for smoothly managing the process of turning this manuscript into a book, during these trying times. The informed and very constructive feedback from the two anonymous reviewers, and James Harbeck's professional editing work, greatly improved the quality of the present text. The biggest thanks, however, must be reserved to the contributing authors, who have shown much patience when dealing with our requests for revisions. It is due to their dedication that we were able to complete this project in the way we had envisioned it from the outset, in 2016.

Finally, nothing of this work would have been possible without the support from our families. During the years of editing this book, we have moved between cities and continents multiple times. Providing us with a sense of stability and certainty, the patience and love offered by our families have helped us to overcome many difficulties. We dedicate this book to Hannah, Junko, Jérôme, and Yukiyo.

Sebastian Maslow and Christian Wirth,
Sendai and Hamburg, March, 2021

Conventions

Throughout this volume, Japanese names are given according to Japanese order (family name followed by given name). The exceptions are when Japanese authors state their names in Western order in English publications.

All chapters apply the Hepburn system in transcriptions from Japanese.

Introduction

Crisis Narratives, Institutional Change, and the Transformation of the Japanese State

CHRISTIAN WIRTH AND SEBASTIAN MASLOW

From Crisis to Crisis Politics

Crisis is a conjuncture in which the old simply cannot be preserved.[1]

Crisis is the moment in which the unity of the state is discursively renegotiated and, potentially, reachieved and in which a new strategic trajectory is imposed upon the institutions that now (re-)comprise it.[2]

While East Asia's and especially China's economic growth has become a major driving force of global change, many developed countries struggle to readjust their social, economic, and political institutions to the challenges of financial crises, shrinking populations, and the rising costs of social welfare. These contrasting trajectories led to the notion of a "power shift" and rekindled speculations about an impending "Asian Century." As an economically and technologically highly advanced society, Japan finds itself at the intersection and forefront of these regional and global transformations. Thus, understanding the challenges that Japanese policymakers face and the choices that they make is not only critical for understanding the future of East Asia, it also provides a clue about the post-modern future of the global economy and of international politics.

1

Converging with the abrupt end of Japan's economic miracle, drastic geopolitical changes rekindled public and elite perceptions that Japan was stuck in consecutive "lost decades."[3] This sense of crisis and decline was exacerbated when China replaced Japan as the world's second-largest economy in 2010; when the March 11, 2011, triple disaster shattered the belief in Japan's technological superiority; and when policymakers in Washington warned Japan that it would be downgraded to "second tier nation" status unless it stepped up "burden-sharing" in the US–Japan alliance.[4] Scholars articulated these anxieties not only by arguing that Japan was "in crisis,"[5] but increasingly also by noting that it had passed its "peak moment,"[6] and predicted a "precarious future,"[7] even collapse.[8]

These anxieties deepened over the course of the COVID-19 pandemic. Although the political leadership had been mobilizing the nation and centralizing executive power—ostensibly to prepare for such scenarios—for more than a decade, fears of the healthcare system's impending collapse and realization that Japanese research failed to play a role in the global race for vaccines added to the sense of national crisis. Thus, discussions about the COVID-19 response increasingly resembled the debates in the wake of the 2011 triple disaster. Once more, scholars and the public questioned the resilience and crisis management capabilities of the postwar state.[9]

To stop the slide toward the abyss, Prime Minister Abe Shinzō and his Liberal Democratic Party (LDP), upon regaining power in 2012, had renewed their pledge to create a "beautiful" and "new" Japan.[10] Strong leadership and an innovative political agenda promised to "take back Japan" (*Nippon o torimodosu*) from the constraints of postwar institutions and overcome the economic stagnation of the lost decades. Indeed, Abe's second stint restored remarkable political stability. His tenure coincided with the postwar era's second longest period of economic growth, and a series of electoral victories made him the longest-serving prime minister of modern Japan. However, electoral politics continued to reflect a deep sense of "national crisis" (*kokunan*). The crisis rhetoric suggested that there was "only one road" (*kono michi shika nai*) for bringing the nation back to prosperity and international standing: the neoliberal economic reforms known as "Abenomics" and the revamping of the national security system, including revising the constitution. Only these, LDP exponents argued, would enable Japan to play an active role alongside the United States in protecting the "rules-based international order" and lead to the country's "rebirth," "renaissance," and "rejuvenation."[11]

Yet academic debates about rising China, and declining and eventually rejuvenating Japan, remain imprecise if not contradictory regarding the questions as to what this decline actually entails, and which social and political institutions are in crisis. This ambiguity is deeply problematic. On the one hand, adequate policy responses depend on the clear identification of causal chains. On the other, the absence of clarity opens space for political entrepreneurs to promote their parochial interests by deliberately blurring and conflating "real" failures with subjectively narrated or entirely manufactured crises.

Therefore, the authors in this volume revisit the prevailing notions of "decline" and "crisis." For this purpose, they apply methodologies in line with the critical sociological approach that political scientist Colin Hay[12] suggested for the examination of state transformation. The authors analyze both the real failures of the Japanese social, economic, and political systems and the subjectively perceived and narrated interpretations of decline or crisis. This includes efforts on the part of political entrepreneurs to embed these various representations into politically actionable meta-narratives. Taken together, the chapters in this volume show how discourses of crisis and decline have been a crucial force for the restructuring of social, political, and economic institutions. Unlike much of the existing scholarship, which reverts to the conventional diagnosis of stasis, the contributors to this volume find that the state and society have been undergoing profound change. This suggests that research focusing on specific formal institutions has largely missed seeing and explaining the deep and incessant transformation of the Japanese state as a whole. A hundred fifty years after the Meiji Restoration, at the closure of the lost decades associated with the Heisei era (1989–2019), crisis narratives continue to spur policy lines that advance decisive social and economic restructuring. These aim to make Japan great again, ostensibly as great as it had been during its industrialization in the Meiji era (1868–1912).[13] Yet it remains to be seen which ideas ascribed to that period can serve as guides to peace and prosperity. And the actual outcomes of this agenda will likely differ from the envisioned future.

In the following section, we provide a brief overview of the political, social and economic changes as they have stimulated debates over national crisis and decline. We then build on this discussion and outline the theoretical approach for connecting crisis discourses to dynamics of institutional change and state transformation.

Debating Crisis and Change in Japan

The Socioeconomic Crisis: The Collapse of "Japan Inc."

Despite the impact of two global economic crises in the 1970s, Japan's political-economic institutions have shown considerable resilience. This is a consequence of the introduction and expansion of mostly corporate-based welfare systems for the broad redistribution of the benefits from the postwar industrial growth. While the Japanese state faced brief phases of contestation when conservative elites renegotiated the terms of the security alliance with the United States in the late 1950s and in the 1960s, the generally increasing affluence demobilized civil society and stabilized the LDP's position in power.[14] The political settlement of the "1955 system"[15] characterized by a powerful conservative one-party government, an interventionist state bureaucracy, and a highly protected corporate sector—influential observers traced the roots of this state back to wartime industrial modernization under the "1940 system"[16]—constituted the very fabric of "Japan Inc."[17] By the 1980s, three decades of sustained growth and prosperity had given rise to the hegemonic narrative of a Japan boasting an inclusive "one-hundred million people new middle class" (*ichioku sōchūryū shakai*)—the first and only East Asian country, and possibly the only non-Western country, with one.[18]

However, the end of the Cold War with the sudden collapse of the Soviet Union, and the simultaneous end of Japan's growth "miracle" with the equally sudden burst of the "bubble economy," intensified contentions about the present condition and the future of the economy, society, and the state. Consequently, debates about reform went far beyond questions of macroeconomic management.[19] In 1999, for instance, Prime Minister Obuchi Keizō set up the Commission on Japan's Goals in the 21st Century. With a sense of urgency in view of the nation "heading for decline," a group of eminent persons pointed out that the past "catch-up and overtake" paradigm that the country had been following since the Meiji era was no longer suitable, and that the world no longer offered any ready-made models.[20] Still feeling the impact of the state's dismal failure to respond to the devastating 1995 Kobe earthquake, the report embraced the neoliberal paradigm and called for the overhaul of the entire system of governance and the reform of social welfare, education, immigration, and science and technology policies. However, Japan's sluggish post-bubble economy, epitomized by the collapse of major credit houses under the heavy weight of non-performing loans, shattered public trust in the country's economic superiority and in the elites' capabilities to bring back sustained growth.

As David Chiavacci shows in this volume, among the numerous diagnoses of crisis in post-growth Japan, the notion of an economically "divided society" (*kakusa shakai*) has been most powerful in undermining the myth of an ever-expanding affluent middle class.[21] The emergence of a new cohort of young people who found it increasingly difficult to emulate their parents and enter the job market in positions promising life-long employment and steadily increasing wages amplified this narrative of widening socioeconomic discrepancy.[22] Following several rounds of labor market deregulations in the 1990s and 2000s,[23] precarity, poverty, and high suicide rates emerged as symptoms for "a society that lacked human bonds" (*muen shakai*).[24] In late 2008, Japan's social malaise was put into even starker relief after day laborers who had been disposed of in the aftermath of the Global Financial Crisis, were forced to camp *en masse* in Tokyo's Hibiya Park.[25]

Accelerating demographic decline and its ramifications for social welfare, particularly in rapidly depopulating rural areas, fueled concerns about a deep social crisis.[26] The Japanese population seemed to shrink unstoppably. Marking its peak of 128 million in 2010, it decreased to 126.4 million in 2017 and is projected to fall below the 100 million mark by 2040.[27] The working-age population is forecast to decline to 45 million by 2065, with the elderly composing almost 40 percent of the population. In what has prominently been labeled "a state on the brink" (*genkai kokka*),[28] recent reports suggested that the current Japanese pension system is unsustainable, that many villages and cities in Japan's countryside are bound to become "extinct" in the near future, and that corporations will struggle to sustain their productivity and employment levels in the face of global competition.[29]

Indeed, many municipalities lack the infrastructure required for taking care of their rapidly aging populations' welfare. And, as Jeremy Breaden illustrates in this volume, this social crisis both catalyzes and is catalyzed through the crisis of the education system. Japanese universities' international rankings deteriorate while many fail to attract sufficient tuition-paying students, and a growing number of students fall into debt. It is thus easy to see how the phenomena of societal and economic change, taken together, created the meta-narrative of Japan's "lost decades," of a nation in seemingly irreversible decline. The following chapters will show in more detail how these developments prompted a host of political leaders to come up with their own visions for an entirely new Japan.[30]

The Political Crisis: The Eclipse of the 1955 System and Failed Reforms

Academic studies have explained the above trends mostly as a recalibration of Japanese economic and political institutions in response to increasing pressures of globalization and post-Cold War international security problems. Sociologists such as Takahara Motoaki have convincingly shown how the crisis of Japan's welfare institutions bred anxieties that gave rise to new nationalisms among Japan's youth. Predominantly voiced on the internet, these currents contributed to the destabilizing of Sino-Japanese and Japan-Korea relations.[31] As Shogo Suzuki shows in this volume, conservative elites in particular embraced various cultural coping strategies. They increasingly harnessed idealized traditional values to bolster Japanese soft power and thereby underlined their nation's exceptional qualities. While officially mediated foreign threat perceptions also propelled incremental but deep-rooted changes in national security policies, it is Japan's political system that facilitated them.

Arguably, the revision of electoral laws and the decline of the political left represented by the Socialist Party played a critical role in opening new spaces for political discourse and overhauling policy-making processes, thereby altering the country's trajectory. Following the seeming collapse of the 1955 system in 1993 and the realignment of the party-political landscape, elites pushed for electoral reforms to end nearly four decades of LDP dominance. Hence, the introduction of a mixed single-member non-transferable vote/ proportional representation system was believed to nourish policy-oriented two-party competition and to resolve endemic corruption.[32] With the ideal of the British Westminster system in mind, political scientists have argued that Japan will, at the end of political realignment, witness a more policy-oriented and competitive democracy with the alternation of governing power between the LDP and the Democratic Party of Japan (DPJ), newly established in 1996.[33] However, despite a decade of electoral and administrative reforms and economic restructuring, observers have continued to lament policy stasis, going so far as labeling Japan "arthritic"[34] due to powerful veto players' obstruction of structural reforms.[35]

This seeming stasis notwithstanding, the ongoing economic and political crises, compounded by the deepening social crisis, have not only propelled the rise of authoritarian populism but also further entrenched patriarchal family politics, as Hiroko Takeda shows in this volume.[36] At the same time, it provided an opening for the epochal victory of the DPJ in the lower house election of August 2009, the first complete transfer of power since 1955. The success of the heterogeneous group of politicians was based on an election platform of comprehensive reform and breaking with basically everything that stood for the LDP-led 1955 system. The list of reform projects in their 2009 manifesto "Putting People's Lives First" resembled the Obuchi report of 2000. Rather than prioritizing certain policies, it was a call for the refashioning of the Japanese state and society as a whole.[37] Prime Minister Kan Naoto, in a January 2011 address to the World Economic Forum, promised an "opening" (*kaikoku*) reminiscent of Japan's modernization through the Meiji Restoration, and asked for reinventing "social bonds" (*kizuna*) to temper the impact of the Trans-Pacific Partnership free trade agreement.[38] As a consequence of the DPJ's ambitious agenda, however, struggles over a number of cardinal issues soon ensued not only between the ruling and opposition parties, but also within the DPJ. Moreover, the DPJ's offensive to curb bureaucratic influence backfired.[39] The national crisis became narrated as a crisis of leadership. And, as Paul O'Shea shows in this volume, influential US policymakers' general mistrust of the DPJ reinforced this narrative.[40] This was the state of affairs when on March 11, 2011, an earthquake of unprecedented magnitude occurred about seventy kilometers off the coast of Miyagi Prefecture.

The 3.11 Triple Disaster and the Resurgence of "Japan Inc."

Prime Minister Kan declared the tsunami's devastation and the subsequent nuclear meltdowns at the Fukushima power plant the worst crisis that Japan had suffered since its defeat in World War II.[41] Indeed, the Great Eastern Japan Disaster has, with reference to the disruptive impact of the "9/11" terrorist attacks, also become known as "3.11."[42] The catastrophe's impact on the national psyche certainly warrants this analogy. Most importantly, 3.11 disaster politics revealed how the postwar power structures, previously known as the "iron triangle" of bureaucrats, politicians, and big business—the elites at the heart of the developmental state, forged for and through the promotion of economic growth—have been operating.[43] As Koichi Hasegawa shows in this volume, these vested interests returned to the stage in the form of the "nuclear village" (*genshiryoku mura*).[44] And despite being widely seen as the prime source of the problems that caused the nuclear meltdowns and hampered crisis management, the establishment's overwhelming discursive power meant that the crisis narrative turned against the very people who sought to overhaul the failing institutions of the postwar state.

In a remarkable twist, vested interests managed to put the blame on Prime Minister Kan—ironically one of the few politicians without elite pedigree and known for his strong advocacy of public health issues during a stint as health minister in the mid-1990s—for deficiencies in the management of the unprecedented triple disaster.[45]

The DPJ subsequently changed prime ministers and, reminiscent of the Obuchi Report of the year 2000, came up with an innovative and comprehensive strategy to bring about the "rebirth of Japan,"[46] but it was to no avail. Hopes of establishing a functioning parliamentary representation akin to the United Kingdom's Westminster system quickly gave way to soul-searching diagnoses of a malfunctioning Japanese democracy.[47] When the DPJ-led government came to the brink of collapse in mid-2012, Ishiba Shigeru, bidding for LDP leadership and the office of prime minister, accurately framed the public mood as "national crisis."[48] The well-known ex-bureaucrat Koga Shigeaki noted the "collapse of Japan's center."[49] Others, such as the prominent historian and advisor to the Abe government Kitaoka Shinichi, went even further and saw a "collapse of Japanese politics" in the wake of "Japan's third defeat."[50] Facing a disillusioned and distrustful public, the "strong leadership" that the electorate and the establishment craved could only be provided by someone offering simpler, more convenient, and quicker fixes for restoring a "beautiful" (*utsukushii*) or "new" (*atarashii*) Japan. Prescribed by a politically resurrected Abe Shinzō, the recipe for bringing about Japan's "rebirth" (*saisei*) turned out to be a recalibration rather than fundamental rethinking of the policies which had produced the problems in the first place.[51] In other words, 3.11 exacerbated the already entrenched crisis narrative of the lost decades while betraying the hopes for fundamental change.[52]

Shortly after his election as head of the LDP and (re-)inauguration as prime minister, the hereditary politician Abe Shinzō traveled to Washington and assured the US that "Japan is back" in terms of both military and economic power.[53] The former would be achieved by overcoming the constraints of the pacifist constitution and making the "alliance of hope" "even greater" through allowing Japan to join the United States in its mission to uphold global security and stability.[54] The latter objective called for forceful macroeconomic interventions in what would, reminiscent of the Reagan presidency, become known as Abenomics.[55] Indeed, as Saori Shibata discusses in this volume, the subsequent introduction of an ultra-loose monetary policy combined with the annual dispersion of massive stimulus packages and neoliberal reforms of the labor market brought back some growth.[56] At the same time, as Iris Wieczorek shows in this volume, Abe's emphasis on science and technology innovation as national growth engines led him to promote structural change into the direction of an idealized Silicon Valley model. By way of referring to Japan's national crisis, moreover, Prime Minister Abe rekindled populist rhetoric that portrayed his reform approach as "the only possible way forward."[57] In his move to transform the Japanese state, Abe has been supported by a strengthened neoconservative movement around the Nippon Kaigi (Japan Conference).[58] Yet, despite occasional waves of purposeful optimism, the Abe administration's failure to implement significant structural reforms and tactical reluctance to steadily increase the consumption tax against the background of a ballooning public debt, soured people's confidence in the future. At the same time, the Abe government less and less subtly resorted to the China and the North Korea threats as tools for pushing constitutional revision and making Japan "normal" again. As Raymond Yamamoto shows in this volume, the China threat was mobilized to centralize decision-making on the crucially important Official Development Assistance foreign policy tool in the hands of the LDP. And Ra Mason and Sebastian Maslow illustrate in their contribution to this volume how Prime Minister Abe, in particular, had been fanning and successfully instrumentalizing North Korea–related threat perceptions throughout his political career. Embattled by several scandals, he explicitly referred to the October 2017 parliamentary snap elections as a means to renew his mandate in times of severe national crises, and pledged to "make sure the Japanese public is safe, and safeguard our nation [against the North Korea threat]."[59]

In other words, irrespective of the changes in government, most Japanese policymakers, bureaucrats, and analysts, and also a majority of the general populace, have been perceiving Japan as declining, and see no end to the general national crisis. These developments induced scholars like Kaneko Makoto and Kodama Tatsuhiko, who have been investigating the "dynamics of Japan's long-term decline," to diagnose a "Japanese disease."[60] Others such as Mikuriya Takeshi and Motomura Ryōji observed a "vulnerable Japan" that, in the absence of overdue course corrections, would be ultimately bound toward "collapse."[61]

Yet, despite the generally held view that there is something deeply wrong with the direction in which Japanese society, economics, and politics are moving, the participants in the crisis discourse disagree not only over what is going wrong, but, perhaps more fundamentally, also about what the crises' root causes are. Diverse perspectives and advanced scholarship notwithstanding, most analyses of the causes and remedies for Japan's lost decades remain hamstrung by their ontological and epistemological assumptions.[62] For instance, even studies that take into account the fundamental and predictable shrinking of the population rarely follow through with the discussion of the social, economic, and political consequences. And also authors who, rather narrowly, attribute much of Japan's doldrums to the fluctuating nature of policy-making leave us with the question of why a post-developmental consensus on how to advance society and state could not yet emerge.[63] What is more, analysts' preoccupation with GDP growth rates as indicators of prosperity often brings them close to advocating neo-authoritarian developmental policies. It is for these reasons that a geographically and theoretically broader perspective provides valuable insights.

Conceptualizing Crisis and Change in Politics

Global Change and Post-Modernity?

Where is the transformation of the Japanese state heading, and how does it relate to trends in Europe and elsewhere? In his seminal work, Manuel Castells argued that, in the Information Age, states were caught between and called into question by the opposing trends of globalization on the one hand and powerful expressions of local collective identity on the other.[64] According to him, this compels states to decentralize power to local and regional political institutions. Pointing to the negative social and environmental consequences of industrialization, as well as the dissolution of old certainties in the present times of the second modernity, the prominent sociologist Ulrich Beck argued that, paradoxically, states must denationalize and internationalize in order to fulfill their national interests.[65] Echoing Castells, Beck's reasoning boils down to recommendations for regional integration at supranational levels and simultaneous devolution of autonomy to subnational levels.

These views align with ideas that have been circulating in East Asia. The international relations scholar Amitav Acharya has highlighted processes of regional integration spurred by the Association of Southeast Asian Nations, and argued that diverse regional arrangements give rise to a multiplex world characterized by multiple modernities.[66] Albeit with a greater emphasis on culture and tradition, the historian and sociologist Prasenjit Duara also sees new sources of authority emerging from regional institutions and from networks of civil society such as campaigns for the protection of natural and cultural heritage.[67] These historicized conceptions are useful in describing and explaining social change in Northeast Asia.[68] The politics of 3.11, in particular, can be seen as an epitome of Beck's risk society and second modernity thesis. The Japanese sociologist Ōguma Eiji, for instance, understands nuclear power politics as a microcosm of the social structure of the 1960s, 70s, and 80s and symbol of the moribund "Japanese style industrialized society."[69] And, indeed, if the Fukushima crisis has not put in doubt the very purpose of the state and its institutions by undermining trust in the systems of modern governance, what else would? Yet the political consequences of profound socioeconomic change, and the conceptions of emerging network states and cosmopolitan states in particular, remain tenuous.[70] As the sociologist Zygmunt Bauman argued, new structures have yet to emerge from the "liquefaction" of earlier social, economic, and political certainties.[71] Accordingly, the findings of many chapters in this volume suggest a trend toward the accumulation of power in centralized state institutions. As Richard Samuels noted in his analysis of Japan's post-3.11 disaster politics, however, more often than not, the call has been "for recovery, not for change."[72]

Crisis as a Narrated Moment of Intervention

The questions of what precisely is being recovered and whether this recovery is sustainable remain to be answered. Here, Hay's conception of crises and their function in defining the state is insightful. He argues that the state, comprising "a diverse array of specific, but none the less interdependent, agencies, apparatuses and institutions," lacks a clear and substantive unity.[73] The modern state, he emphasizes, "displays, at best, a partial and latent unity."[74] The fact that state agencies and institutions "claim their authority and legitimacy to intervene within civil society and the economy" shows that the state itself has very little capacity to behave as a coherent, singular actor; its unity must first be accomplished. According to Hay, it is precisely in phases of institutional transformation that this relative unity is greatest. Hence, the very form of the state resides in "the crystallization of past strategies" of structural transformation.[75]

For students of Japanese society and politics, this conception and its consequences are not new. For one thing, political scientists have long observed the fragmented decision-making processes in the otherwise very strong postwar state, and lamented the silo-style structure of bureaucratic processes (*tatewari gyōsei*). Moreover, historicized critical accounts have consistently pointed to the roots of the modern Japanese state in the social mobilization of the Meiji period and found considerable institutional and ideational continuity between the pre- and postwar periods.[76] The phenomenon that contemporary conservative elites, despite the great success of postwar reconstruction and modernization, remain captive to the Meiji state ideal[77] confirms Hay's proposition that "the internal structure of the state reflects a series of formal/institutional boundaries defining a number of policy fields and corresponding policy communities" in ways that reflect former projects of structural state transformation.[78]

According to Hay, inertia due to fragmentation can be transcended to produce new directions in times when the territorial integrity of the state is threatened by war, or the social and political stability of the state is threatened by internal unrest, or the structural continuity and legitimacy of the state is threatened by state and economic failure.[79] In each of these scenarios, public perceptions of crisis are crucial for influencing the "trajectory imposed on the state in the post-crisis phase."[80] These perceptions are subjective constructions of the social reality, and the ways in which crises are narrated is decisive for determining the moment when an intervention can and must be made, by whom or on whose behalf it occurs with what objective, and how it will be implemented. The transformation of the state may succeed when a new projection of a future state regime is constructed, a single *agency* is forged from the collective agencies of its constituent institutions, and when a new trajectory is imposed upon the state *in transition*.[81] In this context, Hay also points to the necessity that not only the public but also those agents who are capable of responding have to see the need and opportunity to effect change. Moreover, these agents can only intervene at the particular "level at which the crisis is identified" through the crisis narrative.[82] Importantly, then, crisis is not only the property of a given system; it is lived experience.

In order to adequately assess the nature of a given crisis, including its root causes, severity, and effects for the designing of effective policy responses, it is crucial to analytically distinguish between "objective" failures—Hay defines these as non-reproductive properties of a system—and the "subjectively" felt and narrated crisis, that is, a widely perceived condition in which systemic failure has become politically and ideationally mediated.[83] In other words, the occurrence of crises presupposes the existence of certain failures or contradictions, but the ostensibly objective crisis narratives, more often than not, tell stories that misrepresent the actual nature of the problems and their root causes.[84] Consequently, not only may actions based on crisis narratives fail to address the underlying causes, they also have significant potential for worsening the contradictions while deepening perceptions of crisis.

These discrepancies stem from the fact that crisis narratives are a product of human efforts to make sense of a great variety of disparate policy and system failures. Crisis narration "operates through the discursive 'recruiting' of policy failures, and the lived experiences to which they give rise, as symptoms of a crisis of the state."[85] The discursive construction of a crisis can be understood as a process in which a number of contradictions become selected as being "newsworthy," are portrayed as a symptom of crisis through a primary narration, and finally become assimilated into a single meta-narrative.[86] The latter final move is only possible through the abstraction of the individual events or symptoms. Hence, the success of crisis narratives depends not on their accurate description of the underlying failures and their causes and effects, but "on their ability to provide a simplified account sufficiently flexible to 'narrate' a great variety of morbid symptoms *whilst unambiguously attributing causality and responsibility.*"[87] Crucially, crisis narratives serve to mark the political arena for the contest between those elites that are seen as incapable and the political leadership to be trusted in managing state transformation. This is particularly evident in the aftermath of the 2008 Global Financial Crisis when crisis narratives have become central in the rise of populism across advanced industrial nations.[88]

Importantly, the political battles over the future trajectory of the state are "won and lost *not* in the wake of the crisis moment, but in the very process in which the crisis is constituted."[89] These insights warrant asking the following questions: What structural—that is, "real"—societal, economic, "domestic" political, and international changes have been challenging what institutions of the Japanese state from the late 1980s onwards? How have these challenges become framed in crisis narratives? Who succeeded in pushing through their narratives? What institutional changes have these narratives provoked? If no change is to be found, who staged resistance with what counter-narrative? What is the potential of the (envisioned) institutional changes to alleviate the original causes of the crisis—the structural "real" challenges identified at the outset? Finally, what are the implications of these findings for the respective policy area, and for the future of Japan as a whole?

Taken together, lived experiences of decline, narrated in the form of the nation's lost decades, have deeply impacted politics, economy, and culture.[90] Yet, while Japan is not "number one" anymore, "decline" is also a "diversion," as not all is lost.[91] During the last decade Japan has seen sustained, though slow, growth. The country's living standards remain high, cities are run well, and crime rates are low. Higher education and businesses increasingly internationalize, civil society—though relatively weak—has flourished after 3.11, and political stability remains relatively strong.[92] Japan is setting new trends in consumption and fashion and remains an important site of technological innovation. Moreover, in what some have described as a "quiet social revolution,"[93] the country is (though slowly) opening up for migration. Narratives of crisis and decline are, therefore, justly accompanied by stories of hope informed by Japan's impressive postwar development as a source of optimism for the future.[94] Thus, the emerging "science of hope" (*kibōgaku*) and a "social science of crisis thinking" (*kikitaiōgaku*) have attempted to provide counter-narratives to the prevailing mode of decline.[95] Yet we argue that it is precisely the compound of narratives of hope and the politics of decline and crisis that reveal the transition of the Japanese state. Understanding this complex process is the aim of this volume. The evidence put forth in the following chapters will help us to identify the trajectory of this state-in-transition.

Organization of the Volume

The present volume is organized into three parts that move from the social to the economic and the political. The authors of the following chapters shed light on how competing narrations of crisis effect institutional change, and may co-constitute a transformation of the Japanese state.

In part I we account for socioeconomic developments and the pertaining discourses that, usually, display a loss of orientation and prescribe a return to Japan's postwar trajectory of economic growth and social stability. Looking at rising economic inequality (David Chiavacci), shrinking population (Hiroko Takeda), and structural problems of universities as leading institutions of higher education (Jeremy Breaden), the contributions problematize the idea of social crisis. These chapters illustrate the discrepancy between Japan's ostensibly ongoing *national* crisis and the reality of the relatively safe country, the increasing societal problems, and deepening individual hardships.

While economic doldrums have been continuing ever since the burst of the bubble in 1991, the fallout of the 2008 Global Financial Crisis created a "new normal" for the world economy, and the triple disaster of March 2011 created a "new normal" for Japan. Thus, the chapters in part II examine the societal and political responses to the 3.11 disaster (Koichi Hasegawa), efforts to restore scientific and technological leadership (Iris Wieczorek), and the deepening of contradictions in Japan's political economy (Saori Shibata). These accounts reveal how crisis narratives spurred reforms such as Abenomics that not only failed to resolve, but also entrenched, structural impediments to the decisive reforms that would remove systemic failures.

In part III, we shift our focus towards Japan's foreign and security politics and look at responses to the perceived crises caused by instability in the US–Japan alliance under the Democratic Party of Japan's rule (Paul O'Shea), the instrumentalization of fears about rising China for politicizing Official Development Assistance (ODA) policy-making (Raymond Yamamoto), the framing of the North Korea threat for restructuring Japan's national security system (Ra Mason and Sebastian Maslow), and the mobilization of ethnocentric nationalism to alleviate anxieties about Japan's declining status in international society (Shogo Suzuki). In summary, these chapters illustrate how defense strategists, alliance managers, and policymakers have used the meta-narrative of a national crisis to undermine political opposition and bring about incremental changes for moving Japan's foreign and defense policies away from their postwar pacifist orientation.

In the concluding chapter, we argue that Japan's various crises are in many respects not as severe as portrayed and often resulted from fears about unprecedented societal and economic changes in the context of irreversible global transformations. Yet, we also note that dominant crisis narratives often framed actual failures in ways that limited the range of politically acceptable interpretations and, as a consequence, precluded effective responses to the problems at hand. Thus, paradoxically, the strong leadership that the Japan-in-crisis meta-narrative demanded resulted in the deepening of the national sense of crisis. While the powerful leaders it produced effectuated more institutional change than is generally acknowledged, these entrenched elites also failed to think and act beyond their long-standing modes of doing politics. As a result, Japan is not heading toward a decentralization of power such as macro-sociological scholarship has been predicting, nor has the decidedly stronger center been able to steer the country toward an entirely new path into the future. In this vein, Japan, can serve as a basis for describing a Northeast Asian form of post-modernity, and as a reference for how developed countries struggle adjusting to post-modern conditions.

Notes

1. Colin Hay, "Rethinking Crisis: Narratives of the New Right and Constructions of Crisis," *Rethinking Marxism: A Journal of Economics, Culture & Society* 8, no. 2 (1995): 60–76, here 63.

2. Colin Hay, "Crisis and the Structural Transformation of the State: Interrogating the Process of Change," *British Journal of Politics and International Relations* 1, no. 3 (1999): 317–344, here 331.

3. Yoichi Funabashi and Barak Kushner, eds., *Examining Japan's Lost Decades* (London: Routledge, 2016).

4. Richard L. Armitage and Joseph S. Nye, "The U.S.-Japan Alliance: Anchoring Stability in Asia," Center for Strategic and International Studies, August 2012.

5. Bong Youngshik and T.J. Pempel, eds., *Japan in Crisis: What Will it Take for Japan to Rise Again?* (New York: Palgrave Macmillan, 2012).

6. Brad Glosserman, *Peak Japan: The End of Great Ambitions* (Washington, DC: Georgetown University Press, 2019).

7. Frank Baldwin and Anne Allison, eds., *Japan: The Precarious Future* (New York: New York University Press, 2015).

8. Saitō Takao, *Nihon ga kuzurete yuku* [Japan Heading Towards Collapse] (Tokyo: Chikuma Shinsho, 2018); Mikuriya Takashi and Motomura Ryōji, *Nihon no hōkai* [The Collapse of Japan] (Tokyo: Shodensha Shinsho, 2018).

9. Takenaka Harukata, *Korona kiki no seiji: Abe seiken vs. chiji* [The Politics of the Corona Crisis: The Abe Administration vs. Governors] (Tokyo: Chūō Kōronsha, 2020); Asia Pacific Initiative, Shingata Korona Taiō Minkan Rinji Chōsakai, *Chōsa/kenshō hōkokusho* [Survey/Investigation Report] (Tokyo: Discover, 2020); Murakami Yōichirō, ed., *Koronago no sekai o ikiru: Watashitachi no teigen* [Living in a Post-Corona World: Our Proposal] (Tokyo: Iwanami Shinsho, 2020); Osamu Tsukimori, "Why Japan is Largely a Spectator in the Coronavirus Vaccine Race," *Japan Times*, December 11, 2020, https://www.japantimes.co.jp/news/2020/12/11/business/japan-slow-corona-vaccine/.

10. Abe Shinzō, *Utsukushii kuni e* [Towards a Beautiful Country] (Tokyo: Bungei Shunju, 2006); Abe Shinzō, *Atarashii kuni e* [Towards a New Country] (Tokyo: Bungei Shunju, 2013).

11. Andrew L. Oros, *Japan's Security Renaissance: New Policies and Politics for the Twenty-First Century* (New York: Columbia University Press, 2017); Victor Teo, *Japan's Arduous Rejuvenation as a Global Power: Democratic Resilience and the US-China Challenge* (New York: Palgrave Macmillan, 2019); Mikio Sugeno, "Japan and Germany Must Unite to Protect the Western Order," *Nikkei Asian Review*, July 6, 2017, https://asia.nikkei.com/Politics/Japan-and-Germany-must-unite-to-protect-the-Western-order2.

12. Colin Hay, *Re-stating Social and Political Change* (Buckingham: Open University Press, 2016); Hay, "Crisis."

13. Ken Coates, Kimie Hara, Carin Holroyd, and Marie Söderberg, eds., *Japan's Future and a New Meiji Transformation: International Reflections* (London: Routledge, 2019); Robert Hellyer and David Leheny, "What Japan Can Teach Us About the Future of Nationalism: Lessons for the Future of the Nation-State on the 150th Anniversary of the Meiji Restoration," *Washington Post*, January 3,

2018, https://www.washingtonpost.com/news/made-by-history/wp/2018/01/03/ what-japan-can-teach-us-about-the-future-of-the-nationalism/.

14. Kent E. Calder, *Crisis and Compensation: Public Policy and Political Stability in Japan, 1949–1986* (Princeton, NJ: Princeton University Press, 1988); Margarita Estévez-Abe, *Welfare and Capitalism in Postwar Japan: Party, Bureaucracy, and Business* (Cambridge: Cambridge University Press, 2008); Nick Kapur, *Japan at the Crossroads: Conflict and Compromise after Anpo* (Cambridge, MA: Harvard University Press, 2018); Till Knaudt, *Von Revolution zu Befreiung: Studentenbewegung, Antiimperialismus und Terrorismus in Japan* (1968–1975) [From Revolution to Liberation: Student Movement, anti-Imperialism and Terrorism in Japan (1968–1975)] (Frankfurt a. Main: Campus Verlag, 2016).

15. On the historical process that has generated this political arrangement positioning the conservative LDP in power against an opposition led by the Japan Socialist Party, see Nakakita Kōji, *1955-nen taisei no seiritsu* [The Formation of the 1955 System] (Tokyo: Tokyo Daigaku Shuppankai, 2002).

16. Noguchi Yukio, *1940-nen taisei: Saraba senji keizai* [The 1940 System: A Farewell to Japan's Wartime Economy] (Tokyo: Toyo Keizai Shinposha, 2010).

17. "Japan Inc." was itself part of the "the postwar years are over" (*mohaya sengo dewa nai*) narrative that had originated in the 1956 Economy White Paper. See T.J. Pempel, "The Unbundling of 'Japan Inc.': The Changing Dynamics of Japanese Policy Formation," *Journal of Japanese Studies* 13, no. 2 (1987): 271–306.

18. Murakami Yasusuke, *Shinchukan taishū no jidai* [The Age of Japan's New Middle Class] (Tokyo: Chūō Kōronsha, 1984).

19. For example, T.J. Pempel, "Regime Shift: Japanese Politics in a Changing World Economy," *Journal of Japanese Studies* 23, no. 2 (1997): 333–361.

20. Prime Minister of Japan and His Cabinet, *The Frontier Within: Individual Empowerment and Better Governance in the New Millennium* (Tokyo: The Prime Minister's Commission on Japan's Goals in the 21st Century, 2000).

21. Yamada Masahiro, *Kibo kakusa shakai: "Make-gumi" no zetsubōkan ga Nihon o hikisaku* [Society of Divided Hopes: How the Disillusionment of "Losers" Will Tear Apart Japan] (Tokyo: Chikuma Shobo, 2004); Carola Hommerich and David Chiavacci, eds., *Social Inequality in Post-Growth Japan: Transformation during Economic and Demographic Stagnation* (London: Routledge, 2017).

22. Asahi Shimbun, *Rosujene Shuzaihan, Rosujenereeshon no gyakushu* [The Lost Generation's Revenge] (Tokyo: Asahi Shimbunsha, 2007); Mary C. Brinton, *Lost in Transition: Youth, Work, and Instability in Postindustrial Japan* (Cambridge: Cambridge University Press, 2011); Takahara Motoaki, *Gendai Nihon no tenki—"jiyū" to "antei" no jirenma* [The Transformation of Contemporary Japan: The "Freedom" and "Security" Dilemma] (Tokyo: NHK Books, 2009); Anne Allison, *Precarious Japan* (Durham, NC: Duke University Press, 2013).

23. See, for example, Steven K. Vogel, *Japan Remodeled: How Government and Industry Are Reforming Japanese Capitalism* (Ithaca, NY: Cornell University Press, 2006).

24. NHK Supesharu Shūzaihan, *Muen shakai* [Society Without Bounds] (Tokyo: Bungei Shunju, 2010).

25. Makoto Yuasa, *Han-hinkon—"suberidai shakai" kara no dasshutsu* [Anti-poverty: The Escape from the "Slide Society"] (Tokyo: Iwanami Shinsho, 2008).

26. Leonard J. Schoppa, *Race for the Exits: The Unraveling of Japan's System of Social Protection* (Ithaca, NY: Cornell University Press, 2006); Florian Coulmas, *Population Decline and Ageing in Japan: The Social Consequences* (London: Routledge: 2007); Wolfram Manzenreiter, Ralph Lützeler, and Sebastian Polak-Rottmann, eds., *Japan's New Ruralities: Coping with Decline in the Periphery* (London: Routledge, 2015).

27. Robin Harding, "Japan's Population Decline Accelerates Despite Record Immigration," *Financial Times*, April 12, 2019, https://www.ft.com/content/29d594fa-5cf2-11e9-9dde-7aedca0a081a.

28. Menju Toshihiro, *Genkai kokka—jinkō gensho de Nihon ga semarareru saishu sentaku* [State at the Limits: Japan's Last Options in the Age of Demographic Decline] (Tokyo: Asahi Shinsho, 2017).

29. Masuda Hiroya, *Chihō shōmetsu: Tokyo ikkyoku shūchū ga maneku jinkō kyugen* [The Extinction of Local Regions: Rapid Population Decline as a Result of a Concentration on Tokyo] (Tokyo: Chūō Kōron Shinsha, 2014); Nakahara Keisuke, *Nihon no kokunan: 2020-nen kara no chingin, koyō, kigyō* [Japan's National Crisis: Wages, Employment and Companies after 2020] (Tokyo: Kodansha Gendai Shinsho, 2018).

30. Best known are: Ozawa Ichirō, *Nihon kaizō keikaku* [A Blueprint for a New Japan] (Tokyo: Kodansha, 1993); Abe, *Utsukushii kuni e*.

31. Takahara Motoaki, *Fuangata nashonarizumu: Nikkanchu no netto sedai nikumiau hontō no riyū* [Nationalism of Anxiety: The Real Reason for the Mutual Hate Between the Japan-Korea-China Internet Generation] (Tokyo: Yōsensha, 2006); Higuchi Naoto, *Nihon-gata haigaishugi: Zaitokukai, gaikokujin senseiken, higashi-ajia chiseigaku* [Japanese Chauvinism: Zaitokukai, Voting Rights for Foreign Citizens, and East Asian Geopolitics] (Nagoya: Nagoya Daigaku Shuppankai, 2014).

32. Gregory Noble, "The Decline of Particularism in Japanese Politics," *Journal of East Asian Studies* 10, no. 2 (2010): 239–274; Amy Catalinac, "From Pork to Policy: The Rise of Programmatic Campaigning in Japanese Elections," *Journal of Politics* 78, no. 1 (2016): 1–18; Matthew M. Carlson and Steven R. Reed, *Political Corruption and Scandals in Japan* (Ithaca, NY: Cornell University Press, 2018).

33. For example, Yamaguchi Jirō, *Sengo seiji no hōkai: Demokurashii wa doko e yuku ka* [The Collapse of Postwar Politics: What is the Direction of Japan's Democracy?] (Tokyo: Iwanami Shinsho, 2004); Frances McCall Rosenbluth and Michael Thies, *Japan Transformed: Political Change and Economic Restructuring* (Princeton, NJ: Princeton University Press, 2010).

34. Edward Lincoln, *Arthritic Japan: The Slow Pace of Economic Reform* (Washington, DC: Brookings Institution Press, 2001); Aurelia George Mulgan, "Japan's 'Un-Westminster' System: Impediments to Reform in a Crisis Economy," *Government and Opposition* 38, no. 1 (2003): 73–91.

35. Aurelia George Mulgan, *Japan's Failed Revolution: Koizumi and the Politics of Economic Reform* (Melbourne: Asia Pacific Press, 2003).

36. See also Toru Yoshida, "Populism 'Made in Japan': A New Species?" *Asian Journal of Comparative Politics* 5, no. 3 (2020): 288–299.

37. Democratic Party of Japan, *2009 Minshuto no seiken seisaku* [2009 Manifesto of the Democratic Party of Japan].

38. Prime Minister of Japan and His Cabinet, "Speech by Japanese Prime Minister Naoto Kan Presented at the World Economic Forum, Davos, Switzerland 'Opening Japan and Reinventing KIZUNA,'" January 29, 2011, https://japan.kantei.go.jp/kan/statement/201101/29davos_e.html.

39. Ito Masami, "DPJ's Promise to Change the System Failed," *Japan Times*, December 1, 2012.

40. For an illustration, see also John V. Roos, "A/s Campbell, GOJ officials discuss PM Hatoyama's comments on U.S./China/South Korea," October 15, 2009, http://www.cablegatesearch.net.

41. Kan Naoto, *Tōden Fukushima genpatsu jiken sōridaijin toshite kangaeta koto* [Thoughts by the Prime Minister during the Tokyo Electric Power Company Fukushima Nuclear Power Plant Accident] (Tokyo: Gentosha Shinsho, 2012).

42. This analogy was made explicit on the cover of Japan's *Newsweek* issue of September 13, 2011; see https://www.newsweekjapan.jp/magazine/55630.php.

43. Chalmers Johnson, *Japan: Who Governs? The Rise of the Developmental State* (New York: W.W. Norton & Co., 1995).

44. Kainuma Hiroshi, *"Fukushima"-ron: Genshiryoku mura wa naze umareta no ka* [The "Fukushima" Debate: Why the Nuclear Village Emerged] (Tokyo: Seidosha, 2011); Sotooka Hidetoshi, *3.11 fukugō saigai* [3.11 Triple Disaster] (Tokyo: Iwanami Shinsho, 2012).

45. See also Koichi Hasegawa, *Beyond Fukushima: Toward a Post-Nuclear Society* (Melbourne: Trans Pacific Press, 2015).

46. Cabinet Office, "Comprehensive Strategy for the Rebirth of Japan— Exploring the frontiers and building a 'Country of Co-creation,'" July 31, 2012, https://www.cas.go.jp/jp/seisaku/npu/pdf/20120731/20120731_en.pdf.

47. See, for example, Yamaguchi Jirō, *Seiken kōtai to wa nan datta no ka* [What was the Meaning of Government Change?] (Tokyo: Iwanami Shinsho, 2012); Kobayashi Yoshiaki, *Seiken kōtai: Minshutō seiken to wa nani de atta no ka* [Government Change: What was the Meaning of the DPJ Government?] (Tokyo: Chūō Kōron Shinsha, 2012); Yoichi Funabashi and Koichi Nakano, eds., *The Democratic Party of Japan in Power: Challenges and Failures* (London: Routledge, 2017).

48. Ishiba Shigeru, *Kokunan: Seiji ni wa gensō ga iranai* [National Crisis: Politics Needs No Fantasies] (Tokyo: Shinchō Bunko, 2012).

49. Koga Yoshiaki, *Nihon chūsū no hōkai* [The Collapse of Japan's Centre] (Tokyo: Tokyo: Kodansha, 2013).

50. Kitaoka Shinichi, *Nihon seiji no hōkai: Dai-san no haisen o dō norikoeru ka* [The Collapse of Japanese Politics: How to Overcome the Third Defeat] (Tokyo: Chūō Kōron Shinsha, 2012).

51. For assessments of Abe and his politics, see Tobias S. Harris, *The Iconoclast: Shinzō Abe and the New Japan* (New York: Hurst, 2020); Steffen Heinrich and Gabriele Vogt, eds., *Japan in der Ära Abe: Eine politikwissenschaftliche Studie* [Japan in the Abe Era: A Political Science Study] (Munich: Iudicium, 2017).

52. Richard J. Samuels, *3.11: Disaster and Change in Japan* (Ithaca, NY: Cornell University Press, 2013): see also Jeff Kingston, ed., *Natural Disaster and Nuclear Crisis in Japan: Response and Recovery after Japan's 3/11* (London: Routledge, 2012).

53. Prime Minister of Japan and his Cabinet, " 'Japan is Back,' Policy Speech by Prime Minister Shinzo Abe at the Center for Strategic and International Studies (CSIS)," February 22, 2013, https://japan.kantei.go.jp/96_abe/statement/201302/22speech_e.html.

54. Prime Minister of Japan and His Cabinet, " 'Toward an Alliance of Hope': Address to a Joint Meeting of the U.S. Congress by Prime Minister Shinzo Abe," April 29, 2015, https://japan.kantei.go.jp/97_abe/statement/201504/uscongress.html; Paul O'Shea and Sebastian Maslow, " 'Making the Alliance Even Greater': (Mis-) Managing U.S.-Japan Relations in the Age of Trump," *Asian Security* (2020), https://doi.org/10.1080/14799855.2020.1838486.

55. Cabinet Office, "Program for Accelerating the Rebirth of Japan-Promoting Recovery of Japan's Economy and Reconstruction of the Disaster-Affected Areas," November 30 2012, http://www5.cao.go.jp/keizai1/2013/121130_accelerating_the_rebirth_of_japan.pdf; Cabinet Office, "Immediate Economic Measures for Extending Virtuous Cycles to Local Economies," December 27, 2014, http://www5.cao.go.jp/keizai1/keizaitaisaku/2014/141227_economic_measures.pdf.

56. See also Gene Park, Saori N. Katada, Giacomo Chiozza, and Yoshiko Kojo, *Taming Japan's Deflation: The Debate over Unconventional Monetary Policy* (Ithaca, NY: Cornell University Press, 2018).

57. Jimintō [Liberal Democractic Party of Japan], *Kōyaku 2014* [Manifesto], https://www.jimin.jp/election/results/sen_shu47/political_promise/.

58. On Nippon Kaigi, see Aoki Osamu, *Nippon kaigi no shōtai* [The Anatomy of the Japan Conference] (Tokyo: Heibonsha Shinsho, 2016).

59. BBC News, "Japan PM Shinzo Abe promises to handle North Korea threat," October 22, 2017, http://www.bbc.com/news/world-asia-41717219.

60. Kaneko Makoto and Kodama Tatsuhiko, *Nihon-byō: Chōkiteki Suitai no Dainamikusu* [Japan Disease: The Dynamics of Long-term Decline] (Tokyo: Iwanami Shinsho, 2016).

61. Mikuriya and Motomura, *Nihon no hōkai.*

62. McKinsey & Company, ed., *Reimagining Japan: The Quest for a Future that Works* (San Francisco: VIZ Media, 2011).

63. Keiichi Tsunekawa, "Japan: The Political Economy of Long Stagnation," in *Two Crises Different Outcomes: East Asia and Global Finance*, ed. T.J. Pempel and Keiichi Tsunekawa (Ithaca, NY: Cornell University Press, 2015), 185–215.

64. Manuel Castells, *The Power of Identity* (Oxford: Blackwell, 1997).

65. Ulrich Beck, *World at Risk* (Cambridge: Polity, 2009); Ulrich Beck and Edgar Grande, "Varieties of Second Modernity: The Cosmopolitan Turn in Social and Political Theory and Research," *British Journal of Sociology* 61, no. 3 (2010): 409–443.

66. Amitav Acharya, "After Liberal Hegemony: The Advent of a Multiplex World Order," *Ethics and International Affairs* 31, no. 3 (2017): 271–285.

67. Prasenjit Duara, *The Crisis of Global Modernity: Asian Traditions and a Sustainable Future* (Cambridge: Cambridge University Press, 2015).

68. Han Sang-jin and Young-hee Shim, "Redefining Second Modernity for East Asia: A Critical Assessment," *British Journal of Sociology* 61, no. 3 (2010): 465–487.

69. Eiji Ōguma, "Japan's Nuclear Power and Anti-Nuclear Movement from a Socio-historical Perspective," paper presented at the Institute of East Asian Studies, University of California, Berkeley, April 20–21, 2012.

70. Greg Calhoun, "Beck, Asia and Second Modernity," *British Journal of Sociology* 61, no. 3 (2010): 597–619.

71. Zygmunt Bauman and Carlo Bordoni, *State of Crisis* (Cambridge: Polity, 2014), 144.

72. Samuels, *3.11*, xiii.

73. Hay, "Crisis," 320.

74. Ibid., 321.

75. Jessop cited in Hay, "Crisis," 321, 322.

76. Chalmers Johnson, *MITI and the Japanese Miracle: The Growth of Industrial Policy 1925–1975* (Stanford, CA: Stanford University Press, 1982).

77. See Ministry of Foreign Affairs, "Meiji 150th: The Origin of the Fundamental Values of Japan," January 10, 2018, https://www.youtube.com/watch?v=E2e1kCuUu_E.

78. Hay, "Crisis," 322.

79. Ibid.

80. Ibid.

81. Ibid., 323, original emphasis.

82. Ibid.

83. Ibid., 324.

84. Ibid., original emphasis.

85. Ibid., 333.

86. Ibid., 334.

87. Ibid., 335, emphasis added.

88. Benjamin Moffitt, *The Global Rise of Populism: Performance, Political Style, and Representation* (Stanford, CA: Stanford University Press, 2016); also Murray Edelman, *Constructing the Political Spectacle* (Chicago: University of Chicago Press, 1988).

89. Hay, "Crisis," 336, original emphasis.

90. Tomoko Yoda and Harry Harootunian, eds., *Japan after Japan: Social and Cultural Life from the Recessionary 1990s to the Present* (Durham, NC: Duke University Press, 2006).

91. Gerald L. Curtis, " 'Japan's Decline': An Unhelpful Diversion," *East Asia Forum*, December 10, 2012, https://www.eastasiaforum.org/2012/12/10/japans-decline-an-unhelpful-diversion/; Takahiro Fukuda, "Looking Back at 'Japan as No. 1,' " *Japan Times*, November 11, 2010, https://www.japantimes.co.jp/news/2010/11/11/national/looking-back-at-japan-as-no-1/.

92. Hasegawa, this volume; Jeff Kingston, *Japan's Quiet Transformation: Social Change and Civil Society in the Twenty First Century* (London: Routledge, 2004).

93. Hiroshi Marutani, "Shinzo Abe's Quiet Social Revolution," *Nikkei Asian Review* (September 12, 2018), https://asia.nikkei.com/Spotlight/Cover-Story/Shinzo-Abe-s-quiet-social-revolution.

94. David Leheny, *Empire of Hope: The Sentimental Politics of Japanese Decline* (Ithaca, NY: Cornell University Press, 2018).

95. Both research projects were conducted by the University of Tokyo's Institute of Social Science. *Kibōgaku* was launched in 2005 (see https://project.iss.u-tokyo.ac.jp/hope/), and as a follow-up project *kikitaiōgaku* was initiated in 2016 (see https://web.iss.u-tokyo.ac.jp/crisis/). For a discussion of these projects see Leheny, *Empire of Hope*, chapter 6.

Part I
Narrating Japan's Social Crisis

Chapter 1

Japan's Melting Core

Social Frames and Political Crisis Narratives of Rising Inequalities

DAVID CHIAVACCI

Introduction

Over the last two decades, the rise of social and economic inequalities has been an integral part of public discourse and politics in Japan. Around the year 2000, the publication of several major academic studies stirred heated debates. Within a few years, these debates evolved into a new frame that described Japan as a "gap society" (*kakusa shakai*). The gap society frame became dominant and displaced the long-standing characterization of Japan as a "general middle-class society" (*sōchūryū shakai*).[1] According to the new frame, Japanese society was increasingly divided into winners and losers, and the formerly nearly all-encompassing middle classes are shrinking fast. In the 2007 and 2009 elections, Ozawa Ichirō and his Democratic Party of Japan (DPJ) used and connected it to a second frame of increasing regional disparities, according to which rural areas are decoupled from national economic growth and in a state of irreversible decline.[2] They turned these two social frames into a political "crisis narrative"[3] that depicted Japan as a society in which the social and political core is melting and political stability, along with people's livelihoods, is endangered. The DPJ government was short-lived and the Liberal Democratic Party (LDP) made a strong

25

comeback under Abe Shinzō in 2012. Nevertheless, social inequality and rural decline remained the dominant frames for defining the major political challenges, which Prime Minister Abe and his LDP chose to address with their so-called Abenomics—a series of economic policies that Abe's successors have pledged to continue.

In this chapter, I analyze the role and impact of the idea of rising inequalities in public debates and politics. Conceptually, I differentiate between social frames and political narratives. While social frames are simplified explanations that enable people to generate meaningful interpretations of their everyday lifeworlds, political entrepreneurs selectively emphasize elements of such frames and try to condense them into storylines that stress certain policies and prescribe specific reforms. In the next section, I will discuss the factors that led to the widespread acceptance of the gap society frame, despite its very thin empirical basis. In the subsequent section, the analysis will turn to the DPJ under Ozawa's leadership. It will show how the DPJ successfully used the resonance of these frames and developed a political crisis narrative that played a crucial role in the temporary but still historical change of ruling power from the LDP to the DPJ in 2009. In the final section, I will discuss the LDP's policies under Prime Minister Abe, as they aimed at leading Japan back onto a path toward shared growth through Abenomics and regional revitalization (*chihō sōsei*). I conclude that the current crisis is, on the one hand, much less severe than the dark picture that the rising inequalities frames and narratives paint. On the other hand, it is much more fundamental and cannot be solved by bringing back the good old days; Japan requires more radical reinvention.

The Gap Society Frame and Its Social Resonance

Around the turn toward the new millennium, a number of publications on social inequality, often written by social scientists for the general public, became bestsellers in Japan. Their messages, just to mention the most important publications up to the mid-2000s, encompassed widening income differences,[4] the social closure of the knowledge elite,[5] the stronger influence of social origin on educational attainments,[6] rising employment insecurity among younger workers,[7] the social polarization into winners and losers,[8] the transformation of Japan into an underclass society,[9] and the comparatively large share of people living in relative poverty.[10] These publications stirred heated public debates. Within a few years, they coalesced into the gap society frame that marked Japan as a society beset with rising social inequality and marked by social exclusion. This portrayal is diametrically opposed to the previous general middle-class frame that had presented Japan as exceptionally equal in terms of chances to advance in life, and the outcomes of income and wealth distribution.[11]

Measuring social inequality and its changing characteristics is highly complex. Results are sometimes strikingly different depending on the chosen data, time period, and method. For example, in the case of Japan, two large national government surveys are used to calculate income inequality: The Family Income and Expenditure Survey (FIES) and the Income Redistribution Survey (IRS). Depending on which of the two data sets is utilized, the results are contradictory, presenting Japan as a country with a mostly equal or mostly unequal income distribution in international comparison.[12] Hence, it is not surprising that a number of publications contradict the basic message of the gap society frame and criticize studies on the grounds of their methodological and theoretical weaknesses.[13] Overall, however, research shows a trend toward increasing inequality. Yet, it does not support the narrative of a comprehensive and rapid transformation from an outstandingly equal to a highly unequal society as suggested by the replacement of the general middle-class frame with the gap society frame. On the contrary, many studies on social mobility and social structure show surprising continuities and moderate changes, especially in international comparison.

Relative mobility, the widely accepted indicator for the openness of social structures, shows no significant alteration during the entire postwar era. Figure 1.1 uses levels of relative mobility in 1955 as benchmark, it shows that the openness has neither significantly increased nor strongly decreased since then, but remained highly stable within a narrow band over the next six decades. Accordingly, intergenerational income mobility has also remained stable over the last decades.[14] Though labor markets were marked by a significant expansion of non-regular employment, economic stagnation since the early 1990s has had no significant impact on the job stability of male middle-aged core workers. In their comparative analysis of micro data for Japan and the United States, Ryo Kambayashi and Takao Kato identify a widening gap between the two countries and conclude, "It is the US economy, with the longest economic expansion, not the Japanese economy, with the longest economic stagnation, in which employment stability and job security deteriorated."[15]

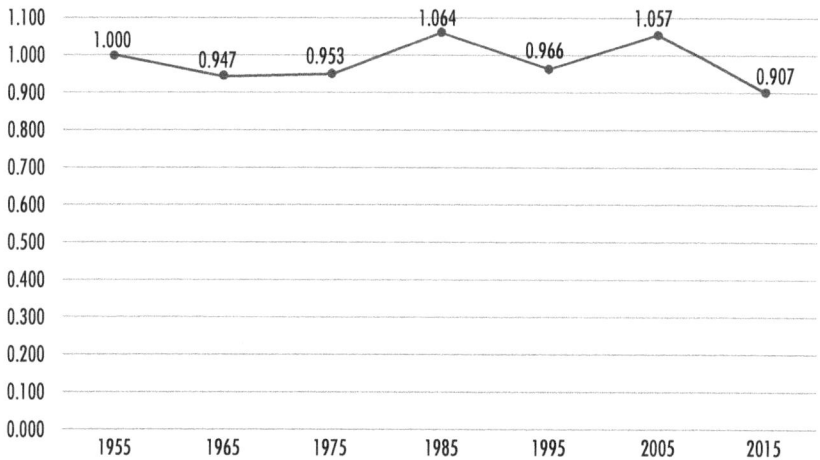

Figure 1.1. Relative mobility in Japan, 1955–2015. Source: *UTokyo Research*, "60 Years of Studying Society's Hidden Disparities: Sociologists Science People's Intuitions," June 2, 2017, https://www.u-tokyo.ac.jp/focus/en/features/f_00082.html.

Regarding the distribution of household income, national government surveys have shown a long-term trend of rising inequality in the distribution of gross income and disposable income after transfers and taxes between the mid-1980s and late 2000s.[16] Still, among advanced industrial countries Japan takes a middle position when it comes to the long-term trend measured by the Gini coefficient (figure 1.2). Moreover, the main drivers of Japan's increasingly unequal income distribution have been population aging and changing household structure.[17] From the mid-1980s to the late 2000s, the share of the elderly population (65 and older) more than doubled from about 10 percent to over 20 percent. This transformed Japan from an advanced industrial country with a young population into the oldest society worldwide.[18] At the same time, the average size of households and the share of elderly people living with their children decreased. This resulted in very high shares of single or couple households composed of retired people with small incomes. Comparatively, the increase of irregular employment among men as well as the increase of single households composed of non-regular employees and workers had much smaller effects on household income distribution.

Changes in labor market structures did not have a strong influence on wage inequality either. As early as the 1970s, wage inequality started to rise in many advanced industrial societies, but in Japan this trend has been very

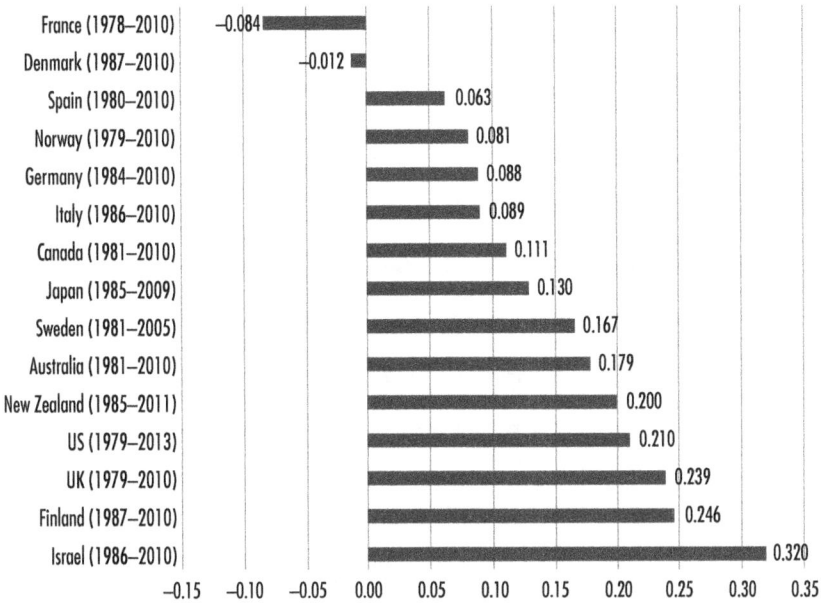

France (1978–2010)   −0.084
Denmark (1987–2010)   −0.012
Spain (1980–2010)   0.063
Norway (1979–2010)   0.081
Germany (1984–2010)   0.088
Italy (1986–2010)   0.089
Canada (1981–2010)   0.111
Japan (1985–2009)   0.130
Sweden (1981–2005)   0.167
Australia (1981–2010)   0.179
New Zealand (1985–2011)   0.200
US (1979–2013)   0.210
UK (1979–2010)   0.239
Finland (1987–2010)   0.246
Israel (1986–2010)   0.320

−0.15 −0.10 −0.05 0.00 0.05 0.10 0.15 0.20 0.25 0.30 0.35

Figure 1.2. Long-term average Gini coefficient change in advanced industrial countries. Source: Stefan Thewissen, Lane Kenworthy, Brian Nolan, Max Roser, and Timothy Smeeding, *Rising Income Inequality and Living Standards in OECD Countries: How Does the Middle Fare?* LIS Working Paper Series, No. 656 (2015): 16.

moderate until the mid-1990s (figure 1.3). Recent studies show that Japan's wage inequality also remained stable over the two most recent decades.[19] The newest available data even suggests a trend reversal. Since 2010, the distribution of household income started to become more equal again.[20]

Still, the gap society frame has become dominant and is taken as common sense in Japan's public debates. How do we explain this phenomenon, given that the gap society frame rests on a very thin empirical basis? Why did earlier publications with similar messages about Japan as an unequal society[21] have no such impact on public opinion? To answer these questions, we have to turn to the sociology of knowledge and the social resonance of frames.[22] The resonance of frames in society differs from academic research in its mode of verification and acceptance. In science, statements about social structures and changing inequality are tested on their accuracy by conducting empirical research and calculating complex indicators. However,

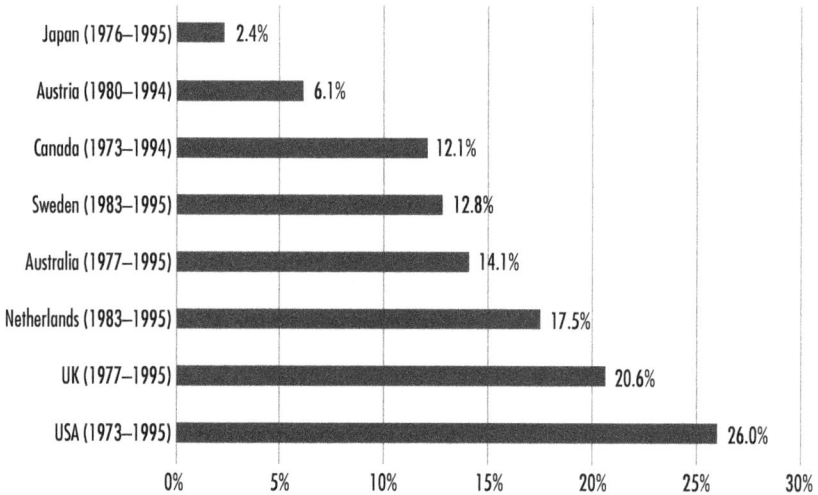

Figure 1.3. Wage inequality increase of top-10% versus bottom-90%. Source: David Rueda and Jonas Pontusson, "Wage Inequality and Varieties of Capitalism," *World Politics* 52, no. 3 (2000): 356.

the resonance of a frame in society depends on its ability to match and give meaning to everyday experiences. The question is not whether central statements of a frame are true or not, but whether they are convincing. At the micro level of everyday life, complex macro-social indicators of inequality like relative social mobility cannot be experienced at all, but people can relate frames of social mobility to their own life experiences—that is, whether they are advancing in society or not. Especially when change is experienced in everyday life, new frames become important for connecting these experiences meaningfully to overall social developments that are beyond one's immediate perceptual horizon.

Around the turn to the new millennium, many people in Japan, especially in large parts of the middle classes, started to experience fundamental transformations in their lifeworlds that matched the new gap society frame. In order to fully understand the scope of these changes, we must first return to the general middle-class society frame and explain briefly why it had such a strong resonance in daily life, and why it remained dominant from the mid-1960s until the late-1990s despite the very weak scientific evidence that Japan was an exceptionally equal society.[23] The main reason for the frame's persistence is that it had been based on shared growth as the social contract between the elites and the general population. This contract was established back in the early 1960s through the social embedding of the Yoshida Doctrine in the form of Prime Minister Ikeda Hayato's income-doubling plan. It was further strengthened with the establishment of Japan's employment model as a basic compromise between labor unions and employers.[24] Economic growth, which had been sustained even after several economic shocks in the 1970s, led to rapid structural changes, continuous upward mobility, and rising purchasing power. Put simply, as the cake grew bigger and (nearly) everybody received a bigger slice, the cake's distribution was of minor importance and regarded as fair. Through its general upward mobility, Japan became the prime example of Ernest Gellner's description of modern society: "Modern society is not mobile because it is egalitarian; it is egalitarian because it is mobile."[25] Yet social differences and exclusion did not completely disappear, and Japan did not become a paradise of equality. Instead, large segments of society were catapulted into mass consumerism and only knew rising living standards. The promise of shared growth had been realized in daily life.

By the late 1990s, however, the full impact on the labor market and society of the bursting of the economic bubble became discernible. The seemingly never-ending party came to a sudden end. Having risen over decades, the average worker's household income fell by over 10 percent between the late 1990s and early 2000s, and has been stagnating ever since.[26] This development is unique in the world. Household income trends in Japan are the exception among advanced industrial countries, as they did not rise at all over the entire period, even when including the high-income years during the 1980s bubble economy (figure 1.4). In order to maintain their living standards, people were now forced to use their savings. As a consequence, Japan's previously high household savings rate declined drastically to a level little above zero. This is a very low figure among OECD countries.[27]

Serious difficulties in maintaining living standards were not the only shock that affected everyday lives. The absolute mobility patterns fundamentally altered as well (figure 1.5). For decades, intergenerational upward mobility had been increasing and remained much higher than downward mobility. From 2000 onwards, however, not only did upward mobility diminish, but downward mobility grew. The ratio between the two began to fall starkly. This transformation had an enormous impact on young people, including university

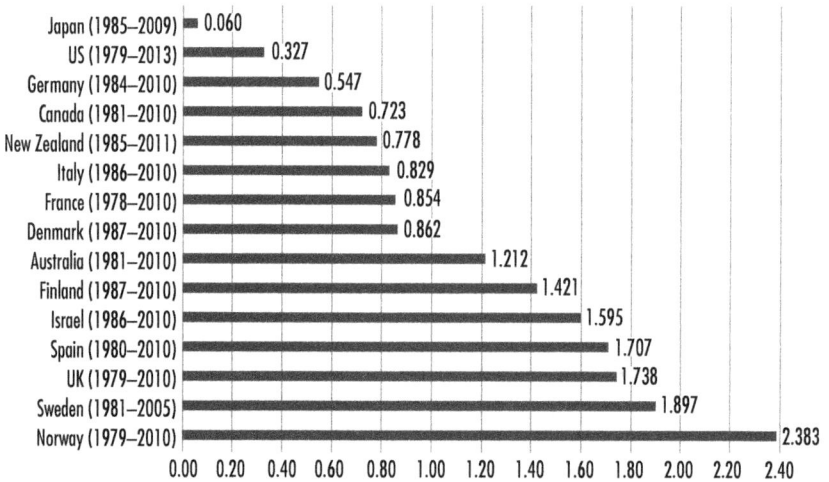

Figure 1.4. Long-term average growth of median real income in advanced industrial countries (in percent). Source: Stefan Thewissen, Lane Kenworthy, Brian Nolan, Max Roser, and Timothy Smeeding, *Rising Income Inequality and Living Standards in OECD Countries: How Does the Middle Fare?* LIS Working Paper Series, No. 656 (2015): 16.

graduates, whose job opportunities worsened dramatically. For example, in 1991, over half of the university graduates joining private industry found a good job in large corporations with more than 1,000 employees. However, by 2000, this share had dropped to about one quarter of those who left universities.[28] From the point of view of highly qualified graduates, and their parents and relatives, society began to enter a downward spiral.

In summary, income distribution and relative social mobility may have remained stable, but social upgrading grinded to a halt. The cake was shrinking, and many people started to worry about the size of their slice. Studies that diagnosed new and rising inequalities, and declared a fundamental turning point in societal development, hit the mood of the time perfectly. They were also meaningful with reference to the breakdown of the social contract of shared growth. Comparative research revealed the strength and prevalence of the social consensus on restricting competition and prioritizing social equality.[29] However, in view of Japan's continuing economic doldrums, proposals for structural reforms and neoliberal deregulation gained influence from the late 1990s onwards. Pundits and leading

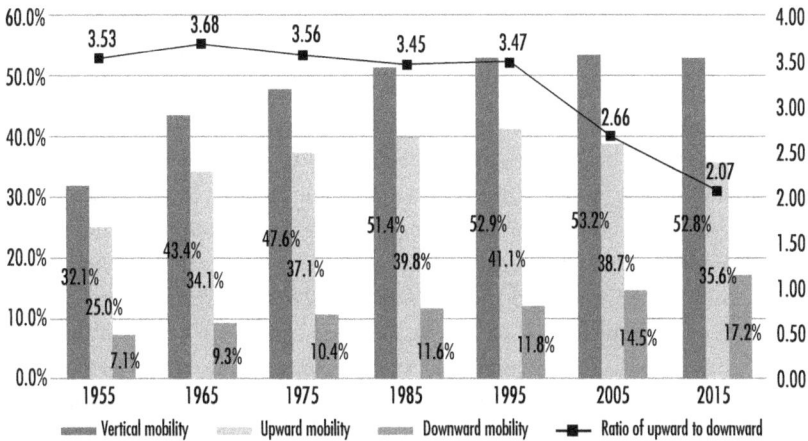

Figure 1.5. Social mobility in Japan, 1955–2015. Source: Hiroshi Ishida, "Long-term Trends in Intergenerational Class Mobility in Japan," in *2015-nen SSM chōsa hōkokusho, 3: Shakai idō—kenkō* [Report of the 2015 SSM Survey, 3: Social Mobility—Health], ed. Takashi Yoshida (Tokyo: 2015-nen Chōsa Kenkyūkai, 2018), 49.

politicians regarded social inequality not as a problem anymore, but promoted more competition as the solution for overcoming "evil equality" (*akubyōdō*) and to recover economic growth.[30] A prime example of this new thrust is Nakatani Iwao, an influential economist and member of key governmental advisory boards, who stated,

> Japan cannot be efficient and remain competitive in the world market if it continues to be preoccupied with the equality of outcomes seen in the overemphasis on the distribution of income. Egalitarianism, which long helped to increase demand, strengthen the spirit of cooperation among employees, and maintain the social order, has become a drag on creativity, competitive élan, and the desire to work and excel.[31]

The structural reform proposals put forward by important parts of the business and LDP establishments implied the cancellation of the social contract of equality and shared growth. The gap society frame explains the social outcomes of this new political agenda. Yet its resonance was also strongly class-based. In contemporary Japan, status anxiety is not confined to lower social classes; it reaches the upper middle class.[32] It was this class of salaried managers and professionals that experienced the most profound changes in their lifeworlds. Unlike the lower classes, which had already been confronted with insecurities and everyday worries due to structural inequality, the upper middle class had been living in a cocoon of life-course security.[33] Starting in the late 1990s, it was these segments of society that experienced rising within-group income inequalities[34] and falling career opportunities,[35] and thus became anxious about their children's abilities to maintain their privileged positions. Several high-profile cases of firms being restructured or even suddenly going bankrupt, such as Yamaichi Securities in 1997, demonstrated that secure lifetime employment and stable careers could no longer be taken for granted, even for those fortunate enough to have been employed by well-known large corporations. The members of the upper middle class were not only the main readers of new studies and reports on rising inequality, they also dominated the public discourse. Ironically, however, these people constituted postwar Japan's societal core that, while remaining very stable overall, suddenly saw their children confronted with new risks.

The Politicization of the Gap Society Frame and Political Crisis Narratives

From the mid-2000s onwards, the gap society frame became increasingly politicized.[36] The 2005 lower house election in particular was a clear triumph for Prime Minister Koizumi Junichirō with his neoliberal reform agenda. It enabled him to privatize Japan Post, the country's biggest employer and provider of postal, banking, and insurance services. Still, soon after the elections, criticism of the government and its structural reforms became more vocal. Not only the opposition, but also members of Koizumi's LDP started to make structural reform policies directly responsible for rising social inequality and exclusion.[37] Yet the prime minister and his cabinet remained committed to the neoliberal reform course. Koizumi replied to his critics that not creating an equal society but a vibrant society full of opportunities was important:

> Recently, I frequently hear from people that, "There is both light and shadow to the reform. The social disparity widened as a result of advancing structural reform." A certain level of disparity exists in any country at any given time. . . . However, I have been advancing reform bearing in mind the question of how to make Japan a society in which the people's vitality

could be exerted, and which provides abundant opportunities for each and every individual to realize their latent potential. I am convinced that we must advance reform to create a society where even those people who have failed on their first or second attempt can keep challenging themselves instead of giving up.[38]

However, the gap society frame continued to gain momentum. Although the years of the Koizumi cabinets seemed to mark a successful economic turnaround, with an average growth of around 2 percent,[39] household incomes and upward mobility continued to stagnate. Hence, the social contract of shared growth and general inclusion, in the eyes of many, definitely seemed to be a thing of the past. The gap society frame of an increasing bifurcation of the nation into winners and losers resonated all too strongly in light of stagnating living standards. Despite a return to national economic growth, the majority of the people seemed to be left behind as losers. In parallel, public opinion concerning Japan's ideal future shifted (figure 1.6). Up to

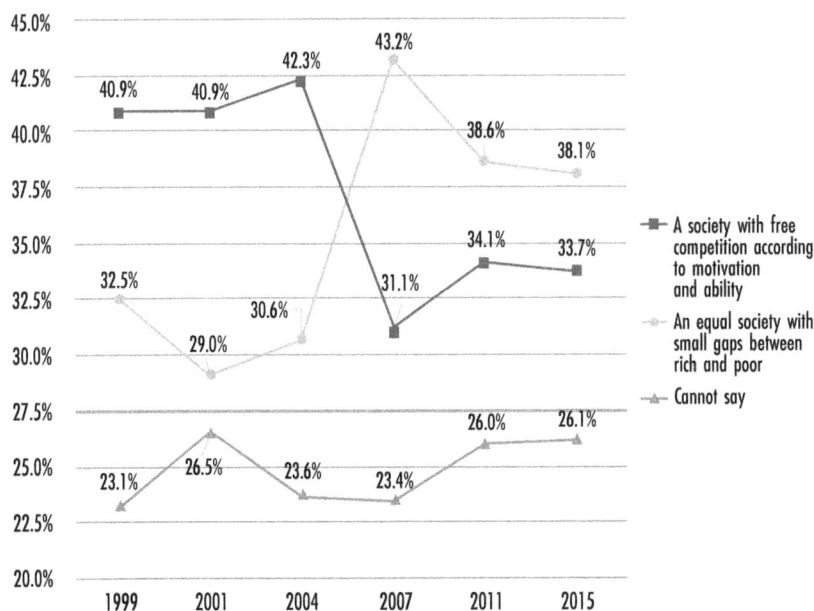

Figure 1.6. Japan's ideal society, 1999–2015. Source: The Japan Institute for Labour Policy and Training (JILPT), *"Dainana-kai kinrō seikatsu ni kan suru chōsa" kekka: Supesharu topikku "Zenin sankagata shakai' ni kan suru ishiki"* [Results of the "7th Survey about Working Life": Special Topic "Consciousness regarding an 'All-participation Society'"], September 23, 2017, press release, 8.

the mid-2000s, structural reforms and the deregulation leading to a society marked by free competition had enjoyed quite strong backing, but now a return of public support for an egalitarian society became discernible.

Koizumi stepped down in September 2006 and the LDP leaders who became prime ministers in rapid succession were weak figures in comparison. Facing increasing criticisms and shifting public opinion, they tried to change the LDP's image of a ruthless reform party through the introduction of more socially balanced policies. Prime Minister Abe, for example, during his first term in 2006–2007, promised in his inaugural speech a recalibration of policies:

> The kind of society that Japan should aim at is a society in which the efforts of people are rewarded, a society in which there is no stratification into winners and losers, and a society in which ways of working, learning, and living are diverse and multi-tracked—in other words, a society of opportunity where everyone has a chance to challenge again. If there are people who sense they are facing inequality, it is the role of politics to shed light on them. I will promote comprehensive "Challenge Again Assistance Measures" as an important task of my Cabinet.[40]

However, instead of steering the LDP into a truly new direction, the succession of short-term LDP prime ministers was hardly able to keep the government together. In short, the ground was laid for attacking the LDP. What was needed was a political entrepreneur who would exploit the gap society frame and turn it into a narrative of political crisis that would mandate decisive political intervention and bring in a new government that could stop Japan's society from declining and disintegrating.[41] This political entrepreneur was Ozawa Ichirō, who was elected DPJ president in April 2006.[42] Ozawa reinvented the DPJ in response to the politicization of the dominant gap society frame. This paradigmatic shift in the DPJ's basic policy orientation becomes apparent when comparing its manifestos for the lower house elections of 2005 and 2009.[43] While the DPJ had been pressing for even more comprehensive structural, that is, neoliberal reforms than the LDP in the 2005 campaign, Ozawa subsequently remodeled the party into a guarantor of social equality and promised to reestablish social systems that would guarantee good livelihood for the entire population. Buoyed by the LDP's failures, the DPJ came out of the 2007 upper house and the 2009 lower house elections with landslide victories. This was not only a change in power, but a political earthquake. Since its foundation in 1955, the LDP had been reigning almost without interruption; it had been ousted from power in national elections only for a brief ten months in 1993.

Still, the gap society frame per se would hardly have been sufficient for defeating the LDP and bring about a change of government. The DPJ under Ozawa's leadership introduced and politicized a second frame, that of increasing regional disparities. According to this frame, rural areas had become decoupled from national economic growth and were falling into irreversible decline. Touching on the long-standing issue of rural depopulation and rapid urbanization, this frame proved to be decisive, as it lent support to a political crisis narrative. Regional inequality, in contrast to social inequality, had been an important political topic throughout the postwar period when the general middle-class frame was dominant. The countryside had been the LDP's main power base. This resulted in a strong rural bias both in LDP policies and in the electoral system.[44] In most Western democracies, state intervention aims at the redistribution of wealth between social classes through welfare programs financed by progressive income and wealth taxation. In Japan, by contrast, tax money predominantly raised in urban areas is used for spending on infrastructure programs in the countryside, leading to inter-regional redistribution from economic centers to rural peripheries.[45] This incorporation of rural areas into the social contract of shared growth had been the foundation of the LDP's rural hegemony. It was a key element for its decade-long political dominance, thanks to the distortion of electoral representation in favor of rural voters. However, from 2000 onwards, when the LDP started to focus on structural reforms, redistribution to the countryside declined sharply, which negatively affected rural areas.[46]

At first, it seemed that the Koizumi administration had found the answer to the question of rural decline in the form of large decentralization programs. However, these reforms did not lead to a turnaround. To the contrary, rural areas were decoupled from national growth. Hence, increasing regional inequality became another topic that could be woven into the gap society frame. The LDP no longer seemed to be the champion of shared growth, especially for its traditional voters in rural Japan. Thus, the DPJ stressed rising regional inequalities in its 2009 electoral campaign.[47] It promised more redistribution to rural areas and became, for the first time for many rural voters, a valuable alternative. In the election victories of the late 2000s, the DPJ consequently defeated the LDP on its own turf, winning most of the rural electoral districts that had been LDP strongholds for decades.[48] Overall, the political crisis narrative about rising inequality did not lead to new social cleavages along class boundaries. To the contrary, the long-standing left–right orientation in politics further faded as the dividing lines among voters shifted and got blurred.[49] Yet, the political crisis narrative proved to be central for the dealignment of the rural–urban divide that had marked the political system for decades.

Abenomics: The Return to the Good Old Times?

The DPJ was unable to realize its agenda of welfare growth. To the contrary, internal conflicts and member secessions, the Fukushima nuclear catastrophe, and huge political mistakes before important national elections characterized DPJ rule.[50] This gave the LDP the opportunity to reclaim power under the leadership of Abe Shinzō, who ran a successful 2012 election campaign under the slogan "Take back Japan!" (*Nippon o torimodosu*).[51] Abe and the LDP propagated their own political crisis narrative and the party portrayed itself as the only political force capable of bringing back the old prosperous Japan, which it would do by reinstating shared growth and thereby overcoming the gap society of social and regional inequality. In fact, in the 2014 lower house election, that also resulted in an LDP victory, Abe campaigned with the unequivocal slogan "This [Abenomics] is the only way of economic recovery!" (*Keiki kaifuku, kono michi shika nai*).[52]

Under the "Abenomics" buzzword, Prime Minister Abe introduced a set of economic policies: monetary easing, fiscal stimulus, and structural reform. In essence, it was an adapted version of the LDP's former shared-growth model (see table 1.1).[53] Apart from the perfect public relations work that catapulted Abe onto the cover of the *Economist*,[54] where he was depicted as Superman, Abenomics' main innovation was to identify the inadequate monetary policy and resulting deflation as the principal causes for Japan's economic stagnation since the early 1990s. Through a new monetary policy in coordination with the Bank of Japan, the Abe administration promised to lead Japan back to a path of sustained growth. The creation of an inflationary monetary situation—and not the prioritization of redistribution—it argued, would result in renewed shared growth and social inclusion. Demand stimulation and supply-side reforms were also included, but much less emphasized. However, reestablishing shared growth proved to be a daunting task. It not only meant that Japan needed to achieve inflation and economic growth, but also that the macroeconomic turnaround would need to result in rising incomes and a higher purchasing power for the general population, also in rural areas.

Table 1.1. Japan's political-economic models of growth and equality

	Shared growth	Neoliberal growth	Welfare growth	Abenomics
Period	1960s to late 1990s	Late 1990s to late 2000s	Late 2000s to early 2010s	Since early 2010s
Main growth engine	Increasing productivity	Structural reforms	Consumption through redistribution	Overcoming deflation
Social contract of equality	National growth	Incentives through higher inequality	Reestablished equality through redistribution	Re-inclusion through regained national growth
Rural policies	Regional redistribution	Decentralization	Rural household support	Regional revitalization
Type of welfare state	Productivist	Liberal	Social-democratic	Mixed

Source: Author's analysis.

Prime Minister Abe was well aware of these challenges. Since coming to power, he and his cabinet had repeatedly and strongly called for salary increases. A senior commentator noted that Abe's "campaign for higher wages looks even stronger than [that of] the Japanese Trade Union Confederation, the country's largest labor organization."[55] This activism of a conservative politician and government, supporting the workers in negotiations between the labor unions and employers, is surprising. As wage increase negotiations are due to take place coordinately among many thousands of company unions in March every year, the mass media nicknamed it the "government spring offensive" (*kansei shuntō*).[56] Moreover, the Abe administration reacted swiftly to new challenges. In June 2014, the so-called Masuda Report made stark predictions about rural depopulation and decline.[57] This resulted in intense public debates about Japan's demographic situation and the future prospects of rural areas. In response, the Abe administration in September 2014 promptly appointed a Minister of State for the Promotion of Overcoming Population Decline and Vitalizing Local Economy (later renamed Minister of State for Regional Revitalization). The goal of this new cabinet

post and the accompanying policy of regional revitalization (*chihō sōsei*) was
to increase the competitiveness of rural areas in order to help them overcome
stagnation and participate in national growth. Although the policy proposals
were hardly convincing, these measures were enough to control the debates
about demographic and rural decline in the run-up to the December 2014
lower house elections.[58]

Still, the challenges remained. For example, a large national survey of
February 2015 revealed a clear gap in the support for Abenomics between
urban and rural areas.[59] Urban respondents favored Abenomics much more
strongly than rural populations. Also, an overwhelming majority—81
percent—felt no positive effect from Japan's economic recovery. What is
more, the year 2015 saw the rekindling of the public debate on old age
poverty.[60] Again, it did not take long for the Abe administration to react.
In September 2015, it presented an updated version of Abenomics. The
three original policies, or "arrows," were merged and supplemented with the
two new policies of "dream-weaving childcare support" and "social security
that provides reassurance."[61] The two new policies were clearly directed at
specific audiences, moving beyond economic policies into social welfare.
Saori Katada and Gabrielle Cheung accurately spoke of the "social turn" in
Abenomics.[62] The formulation of a new goal to achieve "lively and prosperous
retirement" directly addressed the problem of old age poverty.[63] Regional
revitalization was also stressed and given the tag of "local Abenomics."[64]
Thus, unlike earlier political-economic models of growth and equality that
could be assigned relatively clearly to one type of welfare state, Abenomics,
with this social turn, started to move toward the construction of a mixed
type of welfare state (see table 1.1).

Abenomics has not delivered shared growth. Up to the COVID-19
shock, the economy was growing, stock market prices were rising, and
companies were posting substantial profits. But economic expansion did
not translate into significantly growing household incomes, the real lit-
mus test for its success. Average worker household income continued to
stagnate.[65] Studies using different aggregate indicators unanimously show
increasing regional disparities, with rural areas still being decoupled from
the economic growth in urban centers.[66] Continuing income stagnation is
even more clearly visible in Japanese salarymen's average pocket money (see
figure 1.7). Fierce critics point out that Abenomics has not only failed to
reintroduce shared growth but also further increased social inequalities.[67]
While economic growth during the Koizumi era, up to the 2008 Lehman
shock, resulted in a 20 percent increase, the extra money that can be freely

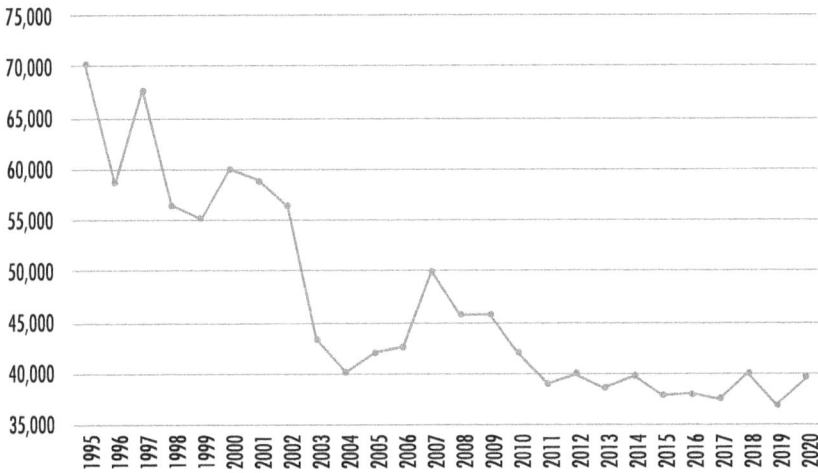

Figure 1.7. Average monthly pocket money of Japanese salarymen, 1995–2020 (in yen). Source: Shinsei Ginkō, *2020-nen sararīman no okozukai chōsa* [2020 Survey on Pocket Money of Salarymen] (Tokyo: Shinsei Ginkō, 2020): 5.

spent has not increased, even for the urban core group of salarymen, ever since Abe came to power in 2012. And it has remained far off the level reached in the late 1990s. Hence, it hardly surprises that in a survey of November 2017, still only a fifth of the respondents strongly or to some extent felt a positive effect from the recent economic expansion.[68] The gap society frame remained dominant in public debate. *Kakusa shakai* had not only been named one of the year's buzzwords in 2006. In 2013, it was also the only twenty-first-century term that made it on the list of the last thirty years' top ten buzzwords.[69] Moreover, a leading scholar's comprehensive analysis of Japan's new class society[70] not only became a bestseller, it also lead to another round of mass media reporting on increasing social inequality, polarization, and poverty.[71]

Thus, the political crisis narrative underlying Abenomics started to lose momentum. Public opinion polls documented that positive expectations for Abe's economic policies had significantly fallen.[72] Also, the frequency of key words used in newspaper reports about the lower house election campaigns shows that the LDP's control over the political agenda had become weaker.[73] In the 2014 election, "Abenomics" and "regional revitalization" were clearly the most important key words and reached nearly the same level of dominance as "structural reform" (*kōzō kaikaku*) and "postal privatization" (*yūsei mineika*) had in the 2005 elections. However, in the 2017 elections, the frequency of "Abenomics" decreased by nearly 65 percent, and "regional revitalization" by over 55 percent. Moreover, the use of the key word "poverty" (*hinkon*) in the election campaign reporting increased by nearly 75 percent in 2017, in comparison to eight years earlier. This shows that the gap society frame continued to be important for explaining the state of contemporary Japanese society. At the same time, critical voices became louder. Though Abe clearly won the LDP party presidency election of September 2018, this was only due to LDP parliamentarians' votes. His opponent Ishiba Shigeru, who in his new book likened Abenomics to a temporary shot of medicine instead of a proper focus on the solution to stagnating household income and rural decline,[74] was able to amass nearly half of the LDP member votes.[75] This showed that even inside the LDP not everybody was satisfied with Abe and his Abenomics. In September 2020, Suga Yoshihide replaced Abe, who had to retire as president of the LDP and as prime minister of Japan due to health issues. He will be forced to take up the unsolved issue of Japan's melting core.

Conclusion

Empirical research does not fully support the gap society frame, which seems to be blown out of proportion. We may even be tempted to speak of another "moral panic"[76] in Japan. However, since the late 1990s, people's lifeworlds have undergone fundamental transformations. This explains why the gap society frame superseded the general middle-class frame. The new frame, in combination with a second frame on rising regional disparities, was exploited by political entrepreneurs like Ozawa to achieve a historic victory over the LDP by turning it into a political crisis narrative. Nevertheless, the main factor behind this political earthquake was not a new class consciousness or a crisis of the middle classes, but the decoupling of rural areas from economic growth, and the LDP's ensuing loss of the monopoly as the only real electoral choice in the countryside.

Since 2012, the LDP has seemed to be comfortably back in the driving seat, with Prime Minister Abe's Abenomics controlling the political crisis narrative. However, the recent election success exaggerates the strength of the LDP. The party has yet to fulfill the basic promise of shared growth, with which it had regained power in 2012. This complicated task has been inherited from Abe by his successor Suga Yoshihide. Moreover, even in the best possible scenario where the LDP succeeds in bringing back a model of shared growth, it is unlikely that the party will ever return to a position as dominant as the one it held in the late 1990s. Like other advanced industrial countries, Japan has reached industrial maturity and the end to social upgrading. This means that upward social mobility will not return to previous levels (see figure 1.3).[77] The general middle-class society frame, due to structural factors, appears to be a model of the past.

Overall, the political crisis narratives of recent years are clearly overstating the social crisis. A decline of the middle classes as the core supporting element for Japan's open society, market economy, and democracy would augur ill. The good news is that, although social inequality is increasing and demographic change is a huge challenge, Japan and its democracy are still resting on a strong economy and an affluent society with solid middle classes. The bad news is that Japan's social, economic, and political crisis is much more fundamental and cannot be solved by trying to bring back the good old days. What is required is a much more radical reinvention of Japan.[78] Postwar Japan has been a work- and growth-oriented society. It needs to go beyond this framework.

Notes

1. David Chiavacci, "From Class Struggle to General Middle-Class Society to Divided Society: Societal Models of Inequality in Postwar Japan," *Social Science Japan Journal* 11, no. 1 (2008): 5–27.

2. David Chiavacci, "Divided Society Model and Social Cleavages in Japanese Politics: No Alignment by Social Class, but Dealignment of Rural-Urban Split," *Contemporary Japan* 22, no. 1–2 (2010): 47–74.

3. Colin Hay, "Crisis and the Structural Transformation of the State: Interrogating Process of Change," *British Journal of Politics and International Relations* 1, no. 3 (1999): 317–344.

4. Tachibanaki Toshiaki, *Nihon no keizai kakusa: Shotoku to shisan kara kangaeru* [Japan's Economic Disparities: Thinking from Income and Assets] (Tokyo: Iwanami Shinsho, 1998).

5. Satō Toshiki, *Fubyōdō shakai Nihon: Sayōnara sōchūryū* [Japan's Unequal Society: Goodbye General Middle Class] (Tokyo: Chūō Kōron Shinsha, 2000).

6. Kariya Takehiko, *Kaisōka Nihon to kyōiku kiki: Fubyōdō seisan kara insentibu dibaido e* [Education in Crisis and Stratified Japan: From Reproducing Inequality to Incentive Divide] (Tokyo: Yōshindō, 2001).

7. Genda Yūji, *Shigoto no naka no aimaina fuan: Yureru jakunen no ima* [A Nagging Sense of Job Insecurity: The New Reality Facing Japanese Youth] (Tokyo: Chūō Kōron Shinsha, 2001).

8. Yamada Masahiko, *Kibō kakusa shakai: "Make-gumi" no zetsubōkan ga Nihon o hikisaku* [Hope Gap Society: The Hopelessness of the 'Loser Group' Is Tearing Up Japan] (Tokyo: Chikuma Shobō, 2004).

9. Miura Atsushi, *Karyū shakai: Aratana kaisō shūdan no shutsugen* [Underclass Society: Emergence of a New Status Group] (Tokyo: Kōbunsha, 2005).

10. Organization for Economic Co-operation and Development (OECD), *Labour Force Statistics 1985–2005* (Paris: OECD, 2006).

11. Chiavacci, "From Class Struggle"; David Chiavacci and Carola Hommerich, "After the Banquet: New Inequalities and Their Perception in Japan since the 1990s," in *Social Inequality in Post-Growth Japan: Transformation during Economic and Demographic Stagnation*, ed. David Chiavacci and Carola Hommerich (London: Routledge, 2017): 3–26.

12. Chiavacci, "From Class Struggle," 18–19. Social scientists have been debating for decades which of the two surveys is more representative; even a recent interministerial working group could not reach a final conclusion. See Moriguchi Chiaki, *Nihon wa "kakusa shakai" ni natta no ka: Hikaku keizaishi ni miru Nihon no shotoku kakusa* [Has Japan Become a "Gap Society"? Japan's Income Inequality in a Perspective of Comparative Economy], RCESR Discussion Paper Series, No. DP17-4 (2017): 10–11; and Cabinet Office, Ministry of Internal Affairs and Communications, and Ministry of Health, Labour and Welfare, *Sōtaiteki hinkonritsu nado ni kan suru chōsa bunseki kekka ni tsuite* [Findings of Survey Analysis Regarding Relative Poverty Rate etc.], December 18, 2015, https://www.mhlw.go.jp/seisakunitsuite/soshiki/toukei/dl/tp151218-01_1.pdf. Unless otherwise stated, all online sources were accessed and available on October 12, 2020.

13. Hashimoto Kenji, *Kaikyū shakai Nihon* [Class Society Japan] (Tokyo: Aoki Shoten, 2001); Ishida Hiroshi and Miwa Satoshi, "Jōsō howaitokarā no saiseisan" [Reproduction of the Upper White Collar Class], in *Gendai kaisō shakai 2: Kaisō to idō no kōzoku* [Social Stratification in Contemporary Japan 2: Social Stratification and Mobility Patterns], ed. Hiroshi Ishida, Kondō Hiroyuki, and Nakao Keiko (Tokyo: Tokyo Daigaku Shuppankai, 2011), 21–35; Ōtake Fumio, *Nihon no fubyōdō: Kakusa shakai no gensō to mirai* [Inequality in Japan: Illusion of Gap Society and Future] (Tokyo: Nihon Keizai Shimbunsha, 2005); Kazuo Seiyama, "Chūryū hōkai wa 'monogatari' ni suginai" [The Collapse of the Middle Class Is Not More than a "Fairytale"], *Chūō Kōron* 115, no. 12 (2000): 84–91.

14. Arnaud Lefranc, Fumiaki Ojima, and Takashi Yoshida, "Intergenerational Earnings Mobility in Japan among Sons and Daughters: Levels and Trends," *Journal of Population Economics* 27, no. 1 (2014): 91–134.

15. Ryo Kambayashi and Takao Kato, "Long-Term Employment and Job Security over the Past 25 Years: A Comparative Study of Japan and the United States," *ILR Review* 70, no. 2 (2017): 383.

16. Moriguchi, *Nihon wa "kakusa shakai" ni natta no ka*, 29.

17. Ibid., 9–10; Ōtake, *Nihon no fubyōdō*.

18. Chiavacci and Hommerich, "After the Banquet," 6.

19. Hamada Koji, "Kinnen no chinkin kakusa no yōin bunseki: Koyō keitai, kakureki, keiken nensū, kinzoku nensū no kiyo" [Decomposition Analyses of Recent Wage Inequality in Japan, 2005–2013: Contribution of Type of Employment, Education, Experience and Tenure], *Seikatsu keizaigaku kenkyū* 43 (2016): 43–52; Daiji Kawaguchi and Yuko Mori, "Why Has Wage Inequality Evolved So Differently between Japan and the US? The Role of the Supply of College-Educated Workers," *Economics of Education Review* 52, no. C (2016): 29–50; Izumi Yokoyama, Naomi Kodama, and Yoshio Higuchi, *What Happened to Wage Inequality in Japan during the Last 25 Years? Evidence from the FFL Decomposition Method*, RIETI Discussion Paper Series, No. 16-E-081 (2016).

20. Moriguchi, *Nihon wa "kakusa shakai" ni natta no ka*, 29. Concurrently, in recent years, the income share of the top 1 percent has also decreased in Japan. See Brian Nolan and Luis Valenzuela, "Inequality and Its Discontents," *Oxford Review of Economic Policy* 35, no. 3 (2019): 401.

21. Kishimoto Shigenobu, *"Chūryū" no gensō* [Myth of the "Middle Class"] (Tokyo: Kōdansha, 1978); Ishizaki Tadao, *Nihon no shotoku to tomi no bunpai* [Japan's Income and Wealth Distribution] (Tokyo: Tōyō Keizai Shinpōsha, 1983); Tachibanaki Toshiaki and Yagi Tadashi, "Shotoku bunpai no genjō to saikin no suii: Kizoku yachin to kabushiki no kyapitaru gein" [Current Income Distribution and Recent Changes: Pure Rents and Equity Capital Gains], in *Nihon no shotoku to tomi no bunpai*, ed. Ishikawa Tsuneo (Tokyo: Tokyo Daigaku Shuppankai, 1994): 23–58.

22. Sarah Babb, " 'A True American System of Finance:' Frame Resonance in the U.S. Labor Movement, 1866 to 1886," *American Sociological Review* 61, no. 6 (1996): 1033–1052; Robert D. Benford and David A. Snow, "Framing Processes and Social Movements: An Overview and Assessment," *Annual Review of Sociology* 26 (2000): 611–639.

23. Chiavacci, "From Class Struggle," 10–17.

24. David Chiavacci, "The Social Basis of Developmental Capitalism in Japan: From Postwar Mobilization to Current Stress Symptoms and Future Disintegration," *Asian Business & Management* 6, no. 1 (2007): 35–55.

25. Ernest Gellner, *Nations and Nationalism* (Ithaca, NY: Cornell University Press, 1983): 24–25.

26. Chiavacci and Hommerich, "After the Banquet," 8. The same trend happened in salaries. Real wage rates were 2013 over 10 percent lower than in 2000 and had fallen back to the level of 1989; see Yokoyama et al., *What Happened to Wage Inequality*, 17.

27. Tokuo Iwaisako and Keiko Okada, "Understanding the Decline in Japan's Saving Rate in the New Millennium," *Japan and the World Economy* 24, no. 3 (2012): 163–173; Organization for Economic Co-operation and Development (OECD), *OECD Economic Outlook, Vol. 2014/1* (Paris: OECD, 2014).

28. Kosugi Reiko, "Gakkō to shūgyō no setsuzoku: Zōka suru furītā keiyu no idō" [Connections between School and Work: Increasing Transition via Freeter], *Kyōiku Shakaigaku Kenkyū* 70 (2002): 64.

29. James R. Kluegel and Masaru Miyano, "Justice Beliefs and Support for the Welfare State in Advanced Capitalism," in *Social Justice and Political Change: Public Opinion in Capitalist and Post-Communist States*, ed. James R. Kluegel, David S. Mason, and Bernd Wegener (Berlin: Walter de Gruyter, 1995): 81–105; Sidney Verba, Steven Kelman, Gary R. Orren, Ichiro Miyake, Joji Watanuki, Ikuo Kabashima, and G. Donald Ferree, *Elites and the Idea of Equality: A Comparison of Japan, Sweden, and the United States* (Cambridge, MA: Harvard University Press, 1987); Erik Olin Wright, *Class Counts: Comparative Studies in Class Analysis* (Cambridge: Cambridge University Press, 1997).

30. Ronald Dore, "Japan's Reform Debate: Patriotic Concern or Class Interest? Or Both?" *Journal of Japanese Studies* 25, no. 1 (1999): 65–89; Keizai Senryaku Kaigi, *Nihon keizai saisei e no senryaku* [Strategy for Japan's Economic Revitalization] (Tokyo: Keizai Senryaku Kaigi, 1999).

31. Iwao Nakatani, "A Design for Transforming the Japanese Economy," *Journal of Japanese Studies* 23, no. 2 (1997): 400.

32. Carola Hommerich, "The Gap as Threat: Status Anxiety in the 'Middle,'" in *Social Inequality in Post-Growth Japan: Transformation during Economic and Demographic Stagnation*, ed. David Chiavacci and Carola Hommerich (London: Routledge, 2017): 37–53.

33. See also David H. Slater, "The 'New Working Class' of Urban Japan: Socialization and Contradiction from Middle School to the Labor Market," in *Social Class in Contemporary Japan: Structures, Sorting and Strategies*, ed. Hiroshi Ishida and David H. Slater (London: Routledge, 2010), 161–164.

34. Ken Yamada and Daiji Kawaguchi, "The Changing and Unchanged Nature of Inequality and Seniority in Japan," *Journal of Economic Inequality* 13, no. 1 (2015): 129–153.

35. Toyonaga Kōhei, "Gakureki ga kyariani motarasu eikyō wa kawatta ka? Shoshoku, rishoku, kanrishoku ikō ni tai suru gakureki kōka no sūsei bunseki" [Has the Impact of Educational Credentials on Work Career Changed? Analysis of Trends in Educational Background Effects on First-time Jobs, Turnover, and Achieving Managerial Positions], in *2015-nen SSM chōsa hōkokusho, 5: Kyōiku II* [Report of the 2015 SSM Survey, 5: Education II], ed. Nakazawa Wataru (Tokyo: 2015-nen Chōsa Kenkyūkai, 2018), 191–218.

36. Chiavacci, "From Class Struggle," 22–23.

37. "'Kakusa ga ronten' tsuyomaru" ['Debate about Inequality' Becoming Stronger], *Asahi Shimbun*, January 27, 2006, morning edition, 3.

38. Junichiro Koizumi, "A Society with Disparity?" *Koizumi Cabinet E-mail Magazine* 224 (March 2, 2006), https://japan.kantei.go.jp/m-magazine/backnumber/koizumi/2006/0302.html.

39. Chiavacci and Hommerich, "After the Banquet," 5.

40. Shinzō Abe, "Policy Speech by Prime Minister Shinzo Abe to the 165th Session of the Diet," *Prime Minister of Japan and His Cabinet: Speeches and*

Statements by Prime Minister, September 29, 2006, https://japan.kantei.go.jp/abe-speech/2006/09/29speech_e.html.

41. For a fuller discussion of political crisis narratives, see Hay, "Crisis."

42. Maehara Seiji, as predecessor of Ozawa as DPJ president, had already attacked the LDP and Koizumi's reform policies as causes of social disintegration and increasing inequality; see "Shūin Yosani, kakusa ronsō mata hibana: Maehara-shi, shushō" [Disparity Controversy Inflames Farther in the Budget Committee of the House of Representatives: Deputy Maehara, Prime Minister], *Nihon Keizai Shimbun*, February 7, 2006, evening edition, 1. But Ozawa was the main driving factor in the comprehensive repositioning of the DPJ as the champion of social and regional equality.

43. Democratic Party of Japan, Minshutō (DPJ), *Manifesto 2005: Okuda seiken 500 hi puran* [Manifest 2005: 500 Day Plan of the Okuda Administration], 2005, http://archive.dpj.or.jp/policy/manifesto/images/Manifesto_2005.pdf; DPJ, *Manifesto 2009: Seiken kōtai* [Manifesto 2009: Change in Government], 2009, http://archive.dpj.or.jp/special/manifesto2009/pdf/manifesto_2009.pdf.

44. Sugawara Taku, "Nihon seiji ni okeru nōson baiasu" [Agriculture Bias in Japanese Politics], *Nihon no seiji kenkyū* 1, no. 1 (2004): 53–86.

45. Andrew DeWit and Sven Steinmo, "The Political Economy of Taxes and Redistribution in Japan," *Social Science Japan Journal* 5, no. 2 (2002): 159–178.

46. Yoshio Higuchi, "Circumstances behind Growing Regional Disparities in Employment," *Japan Labor Review* 5, no. 1 (2008): 14–16; Yamada Kyōhei, "Chiikikan kakusa to seiken kōtai" [Change in Government and Inequality between Regions], in *Seitō seiji no konmei to seiken kōtai* [Party Politics Confusion and Regime Change], ed. Hiwatari Nobuhiro and Saitō Jun (Tokyo: Tokyo Daigaku Shuppankai, 2011): 153–174.

47. DPJ, *Manifesto 2009*, 4, 10–11.

48. Chiavacci, "Divided Society Model"; Shiratori Hiroshi, ed., *Seiken kōtai senkyo no seijigaku: Chihō kara kawaru Nihon seiji* [Political Science of the Election Resulting in Change in Governmen: Japan's Politics Have Been Changed from the Countryside] (Kyōto: Mineruva Shobō, 2010); Sugawara Taku, *Yoron no kyokkai: Naze Jimintō ha taihai shita no ka* [Misunderstanding of Public Opinion Distortion: Why Did the LDP Have a Big Defeat?] (Tokyo: Kōbunsha, 2011).

49. Willy Jou and Masahisa Endo, "Ideological Understanding and Voting in Japan: A Longitudinal Analysis," *Asian Politics & Policy* 8, no. 3 (2016): 456–473.

50. Masanobu Ido, "In Search of a New Policy Regime: The Record of Democratic Party of Japan-Led Governments," in *Economic Crises and Policy Regimes: The Dynamics of Policy Innovation and Paradigmatic Change*, ed. Magara Hideko (Cheltenham: Edward Elgar, 2014): 240–262; see also O'Shea, this volume.

51. Liberal Democratic Party, Jimintō (LDP), *Nippon o, torimodosu: Jūten seisaku 2012 Jimintō* [Take Back Japan: LDP's Government Priorities 2012], 2012, https://jimin.jp-east-2.storage.api.nifcloud.com/pdf/seisaku_ichiban24.pdf.

52. LDP, *Keiki kaifuku, kono michi shika nai: Seiken kōyaku 2014 Jimintō* [This [Abenomics] Is the only Way of Economic Recovery: LDP's Government Promises 2014], 2014, https://jimin.jp-east-2.storage.api.nifcloud.com/2014/political_promise/sen_shu47_promise.pdf.

53. For comprehensive critical analyses of Abenomics, see Shibata, this volume, as well as Masanobu Ido, "Abenomics and Japanese Politics," in *Growth, Crisis, Democracy: The Political Economy of Social Coalitions and Policy Regimes Change*, ed. Hideko Magara and Bruno Amable (London: Routledge, 2017), 46–78; Sébastien Lechevalier and Brieuc Monfort, "Abenomics: Has It Worked? Will It Ultimately Fail?" *Japan Forum* 30, no. 2 (2017): 277–302; and Saori Shibata, "Re-packaging Old Policies? 'Abenomics' and the Lack of an Alternative Growth Model for Japan's Political Economy," *Japan Forum* 29, no. 3 (2017): 399–422.

54. "Is It a Bird? Is It a Plane? No . . . It's Japan! Abenomics, Nationalism, and the Challenge to China," *Economist*, May 18, 2013.

55. Hiroshi Marutani, "Shinzo Abe's Quiet Social Revolution: The Hawkish Prime Minister Is Opening Up Japan," *Nikkei Asian Review*, September 12, 2018, https://asia.nikkei.com/Spotlight/Cover-Story/Shinzo-Abe-s-quiet-social-revolution.

56. For example, Ōkubo Wataru, Tokaibayashi Satoshi, and Wada Kenji, "Bea saikō aitsugu: Chūshō hakyū, mitoosezu" [Continuing Payroll Increase: Impact Not Reaching Small and Medium Enterprises], *Mainichi Shimbun*, March 19, 2015, morning edition, 3.

57. Masuda Hiroya, NSK (Nihon Sōsei Kaigi—Jinkō Genshō Mondai Kentō Bunkakai), "Sutoppu 'jinkō kyūgen shakai': Kokumin no 'kibō shusseiritsu' no jitsugen, chihō chūkaku kyoten toshiken no sōsei" [Stop the "Society with Rapidly Declining Population": Realization of the "Desired Growth Rate" of the Population, Creation of Prefectural Core Cities in the Regions], *Chūō Kōron* 129, no. 6 (2014): 18–31.

58. Ken V.I. Hijino, "Regional Inequality in 2014: Urgent Issue, Tepid Election," in *Japan Decides 2014: The Japanese General Election*, ed. Robert J. Pekkanen, Steven R. Reed, and Ethan Scheiner (New York: Palgrave Macmillan, 2016): 183–198.

59. "Abenomikusu shintō nakaba: Toshibu to chihō hyōka wareru" [Abenomics Penetrates Halfway: Evaluation Divided between Cities and Countryside], *Nihon Keizai Shimbun*, February 23, 2015, morning edition, 2.

60. Fujita Takanori, *Karyū rōjin: Ichioku sōrōgo hōkai no shōgeki* [Underclass Elderly: Shock of the Decline of 100 Million General Old Age] (Tokyo: Asahi Shimbun Shuppan, 2015); Nippon Hōsō Kyōkai Supesharu Shuzaihan (NHK), *Rōgo hasan: Chōju to iu akumu* [Old Age Bankruptcy: The Nightmare of Longevity] (Tokyo: Shinchōsha, 2015).

61. Ichioku Sōkatsuyaku Kokumin Kaigi (ISKK), Shushō Kantei, *Ichioku sōkatsuyaku shakai no jitsugen ni mukete kinkyū ni jisshi subeki taisaku: Seichō to bunbai no kōjunkan ni keisei ni mukete* [Urgent Measures to Realize a 100 Million Active Society: Toward the Formation of a Virtuous Cycle of Growth and Distribution], November 26, 2015, http://www.kantei.go.jp/jp/singi/ichiokusoukatsuyaku/kinkyu_taisaku/hontai.pdf.

62. Saori N. Katada and Gabrielle Cheung, "Monetary and Fiscal Politics in the 2017 Snap Election," in *Japan Decides 2017: The Japanese General Election*, ed. Robert J. Pekkanen, Steven R. Reed, Ethan Scheiner, and Daniel M. Smith (New York: Palgrave Macmillan, 2018), 243–259.

63. ISKK, *Ichioku sōkatsuyaku shakai*, 10.

64. Ibid., 7.

65. Fukuda Shinichi, "Kōzō kaikaku toshite no 'shinsanbon no ya'" [The 'Third Arrow' of Structural Reforms] in *Kenshō Abenomikusu "shinsanbon no ya": Seichō senryaku ni yoru kōzō kaikaku he no kitai to kadai* [Verification of Abenomics "New Three Arrows": Expectations and Challenges for Structural Reforms by a Growth Strategy], ed. Shinichi Fukuda (Tokyo: Tokyo Daigaku Shuppankai, 2018), 220–223.

66. Takashi Hayashi, "Measuring Rural–Urban Disparity with the Genuine Progress Indicator: A Case Study in Japan," *Ecological Economics* 120 (2015): 260–271; Tachibanaki Toshiaki and Urakawa Kunio, *Nihon no chi'iki kan kakusa: Tōkyō ikkyoku shōchū kata kara Yatsugatake hōshiki e* [Regional Inequality in Japan: From an Overconcentration in Tokyo to a Yatusgatake Form] (Tokyo: Nippon Hyōronsha, 2012).

67. Shin Inoue, "Inequality and Precarity in Japan: The Sorry Achievements of Abenomics," *Asia-Pacific Journal: Japan Focus* 16, no. 6 (2018), https://apjjf.org/2018/6/INOUE.html (November 12, 2018); Okamura Natsuki and Yuji Masahiro, "Ijigen kanwa, saifu no himo yurumazu" [Another Dimension of Expansive Monetary Policy, Does not Loosen the String of the Purse], *Asahi Shimbun*, September 6, 2018, morning edition, 4; Shibata, this volume.

68. "Honsha seron chōsa: Shitsumon to kaitō" [Asahi Public Opinion Survet: Questions and Answers], *Asahi Shimbun*, November 14, 2017, morning edition, 4.

69. Chiavacci and Hommerich, "After the Banquet," 11.

70. Kenji Hashimoto, *Shin—Nihon no kaikyū shakai* [New Japanese Class Society] (Tokyo: Kōdansha, 2018).

71. For example, Kikkawa Tooru, "Gakureki to jinsei no kakusa" [Education Background and Life Gaps], *Nihon Keizai Shimbun*, article series of nine articles, morning edition, December 19–31, 2018; "Ichioku sōtenraku shin kaikyū shakai" [New Class Society of 100 Millions' Social Decline] *Shūkan Daiyamondo* 106, no. 4 (April 7, 2018): 32–63; "Renraku suru hinkon" [Continuing Poverty] *Shūkan Tōyō Keizai* 6785 (April 14, 2018): 16–49.

72. Yukio Maeda, "Public Opinion and the Abe Cabinet: Alternating Valence and Position Issues," in *Japan Decides 2017: The Japanese General Election*, ed. Robert J. Pekkanen, Steven R. Reed, Ethan Scheiner, and Daniel M. Smith (New York: Palgrave Macmillan, 2018): 133–137.

73. David Chiavacci, "Inequality and the 2017 Election: Decreasing Dominance of Abenomics and Regional Revitalization," in *Japan Decides 2017: The Japanese General Election*, ed. Robert J. Pekkanen, Steven R. Reed, Ethan Scheiner, and Daniel M. Smith (New York: Palgrave Macmillan, 2018): 232–237.

74. Ishiba Shigeru, *Seisaku shijōshugi* [Supreme Principle Politics] (Tokyo: Shinchōsha, 2018): 121–146.

75. "Ishiba-shi, mokuhyō kosu chihōhyō: 44.7% kakutoku, posuto Abe ni me nokosu" [Local Vote Exceeds Target of Ishiba: Gained 44.7%, Eyes Post-Abe], *Nihon Keizai Shimbun*, September 21, 2018, morning edition, 2.

76. Marshall McLuhan, *Understanding Media: The Extensions of Man* (New York: McGraw-Hill, 1964): see also Takeda, this volume.

77. See also Organization for Economic Co-operation and Development (OECD), *A Broken Social Elevator? How to Promote Social Mobility* (Paris: OECD, 2018).

78. In Hay's model, Japan's political crisis narratives have up to now resulted in conjunctural, but not structural, crises; see also Shibata, volume.

Chapter 2

Authoritarian Populism in Everyday Life

The Discursive Politics of Demographic and
Lifestyle Changes in Japan

HIROKO TAKEDA

Introduction

*Faced with a current situation that can only be described as a
national crisis, as exemplified by fertility decline and growing
tensions with North Korea, I show strong leadership. I stand at
the forefront of wrestling with this national crisis. To do so is my
responsibility as a leader, and it is my mission as Prime Minister.
The coming election may be bleeding, but it is time to hear the
Japanese people's voices, and in so doing, we all shall overcome the
national crisis. So I have decided.*

*This snap election is the election to overcome a national crisis. By
tackling the rapid fertility decline, we are going to open up the
future for our country. As for the security concerns posed by North
Korea, we protect the lives and the peaceful everyday life of the Japanese people at all costs. I am determined that I shall be absolutely
committed to breaking through this national crisis, together with
all of the Japanese people.*[1]

According to the government of Prime Minister Abe Shinzō, Japan had been facing severe crises. To start, in the campaign for running up to the 2012 lower house election, the Abe-led Liberal Democratic Party (LDP) challenged the incumbent Democratic Party of Japan (DPJ) by arguing that the DPJ's lack of competence had caused Japan to plunge into "a state of crisis."[2] After the LDP had comfortably won a parliamentary majority and formed a coalition government with the Komeitō, the Abe administration's crisis rhetoric continued to focus on two issues: security tensions in Northeast Asia[3] and fertility decline. The latter was described in the 2015 Outline of Countermeasures against Declining Fertility (*Shōshika taisaku taikō*) as "a state of crisis that may erode the bedrock of society and the economy."[4]

The Abe government certainly has made some efforts to resolve these crises. In August 2015, the postwar security system was radically revised, allowing Japan to exercise the right to collective self-defense. Meanwhile, a multitude of government initiatives were proposed and implemented to reverse demographic trends. These included a bill to promote women in the labor market, which passed the Diet approximately one month after the security-related bills. The government's rhetoric on these two crises intensified when Abe called a second snap election in September 2017. As the introductory quotation indicates, the prime minister named it "a breakthrough election for the national crisis" (*kokunan toppa senkyo*) and appealed for the electorate to equip the LDP with a mandate to resolve the nation's declining fertility and national security crises.

The Abe government's consistent use of "crisis" raises questions about how the term functions in the discursive politics of contemporary Japan. After all, the Abe government had been in office since December 2012. Thus, the claim that the 2017 lower house election had to be called due to a crisis facing the Japanese state would suggest that the government had been unable to effectively deal with long-standing problems such as fertility decline or North Korea. That is to say, the 2017 crisis claim contradicts the LDP's electoral strategy of stressing its achievements and competence as a governing party. Why then did Abe and his LDP intensify the crisis rhetoric? Did Japan face the crises as identified by the Abe government? And did the electorate accept the LDP's crisis claim? If so, why did the use of crisis rhetoric not backfire in the 2017 election and undermine the LDP-led government's legitimacy?

To consider these questions, recent theoretical discussions linking the rise of populism to crisis offer some useful insights.[5] Influenced by the work of Ernesto Laclau, scholarship on Latin American populism, for example, has viewed the link between populism and crisis "as a mode of organization and strategy."[6] Informed by studies of European politics, Paul Taggart also identifies crisis as one of the five central features of populism:

> Populism is not the politics of the stable, ordered polity but comes as an accompaniment to change, crisis and challenge. This crisis may well stem from a sense of moral decay but it always spills over into a critique of politics and into the sense that politics as usual cannot deal with the unusual conditions of crisis. . . . What is perhaps more important is that populism tends to emerge when there is a strong sense of crisis and populists use that sense to inject an urgency and an importance to their message.[7]

Benjamin Moffitt goes a step further and promotes "a view of crisis as a phenomenon that can only be experienced through performance and mediation, whereby a systemic failure is elevated to the level of perceived 'crisis.' "[8] Moffitt's constructionist discussion of populism indicates that evoking a sense of crisis is a political technique that populist political actors exploit. In this process, populist actors portray identified and perceived failures as crises. These performances then allow them to mobilize sets of narratives for presenting simple solutions and strong leadership to the public. The mass media replicate the performances of crisis, spreading the sense of "the people" pitted against those "responsible for the crisis."[9] "The performance of crisis," therefore, "should be seen as an essential core feature of populism itself."[10]

While these conceptions of populism appear to provide a useful perspective to understand the discursive politics of crisis in contemporary Japan, many scholars, political commentators, and journalists have argued that the Abe government, and Abe himself, were not populist. Analyzing polls conducted by major newspapers in Japan, Sugawara Taku has shown that support for the Abe government lacked a broad basis and was concentrated among core LDP voters. Initially high approval rates reflected voters' expectations for the Abe government's economic policy as much as their plunging trust in the DPJ as a political party.[11] In addition, voter turnout has remained low since the 2012 general election, consistently recording less than 60 percent, including the lowest rate since the World War II in 2014 at 52.7 percent. Furthermore, when the 2017 general election was called, political pundits portrayed the Abe government as a realist political force against the "populist" challenge led by Tokyo Governor Koike Yuriko,[12]

and saw the prime minister as being the quintessentially authentic establishment figure.[13] Political scientist Kinoshita Chigaya even argued that the
Abe government's political maneuvering was a reactionary response to the
"fear" that populist politics or movements might arise in Japanese society.[14]
Thus, suffice it to say that the Abe government and Abe himself did not
display the crucial features that the established literature has identified in
populist political forces, such as broad and enthusiastic popular support and
anti-establishment tendencies.[15]

That the Abe government and Abe himself cannot be qualified as
populist political actors based on the criteria set by extant studies, however,
does not imply that they had not exploited populist political strategies or
techniques. What the aforementioned theoretical discussions underline is
the operational and performative aspects of populism. Intensified debates in
the mass media and academia over the rise of populist politics in Europe
and the United States, particularly after the "Brexit" referendum in the
United Kingdom and the US presidential election in 2016, have provided
non-populist actors with opportunities to learn and use populist political
strategies and techniques as they seek to maintain, broaden, and consolidate popular support. Indeed, Cas Mudde directs our attention to the
use of populist rhetoric by William Hague, an unpopular Tory leader, in
opposition to Tony Blair's New Labour, as a sign of the mainstreaming of
populist politics in Europe.[16] The Abe government's political maneuvering
can be understood as an exercise of populist political techniques as in the
case of Hague, though with one crucial difference: Abe led the national
government, whereas Hague was in the opposition, challenging the popular
New Labour government. Why then did the incumbent government, holding
large parliamentary majorities in both the Houses of Representatives and
Councillors, resort to populist strategies and techniques? What is the nature
of the politics operating here?

To address this question, in this chapter I introduce the concept of
authoritarian populism, a particular type of populism first discussed by Stuart
Hall. The concept refers to the Thatcherite attempts to replace the Labour
government's corporatist politics rooted in the postwar consensus with a new
type of hegemonic politics based on neoliberal and neoconservative doctrines.[17]
Hall also examined the relationship between New Labour and authoritarian
populism and argued that New Labour promoted an updated version of
the neoliberal political project using authoritarian populism derived from
Thatcherism. In these processes, crises constitute an indispensable component
of authoritarian populism, offering opportunities to form a new hegemony,

and although Hall does not explicitly discuss it, gender norms function as pivotal referents that link individuals with the political system. Thus, the lens of authoritarian populism, not populism per se, helps to clarify the thrust of argument by reducing the level of conceptual ambiguity attached to "populism," while enabling us to better grasp the nature of the ongoing discursive politics under the Abe government as it trumpets demographic and family crises.

The rest of this chapter is organized as follows: In the next section, I outline the concept of authoritarian populism; after this, I explore the gender implications of authoritarian populism; then, having clarified the theoretical setting of the chapter, in the fourth section I apply authoritarian populism to the analysis of governmental discourses concerning fertility decline in Japan.

Authoritarian Populism

In September 2016, YouGov, in cooperation with the University of Essex, conducted a large-scale survey on the impact of authoritarian populism in twelve European countries. YouGov explained its motivation for conducting the survey with reference to the historical context: In the 1980s, the term "authoritarian populism" was used to discuss the politico-social attitudes of supporters of Margaret Thatcher and Ronald Reagan. It "moved to the fringes" as Tony Blair and Bill Clinton started "practising a different style of politics," but has now returned to the "forefront of politics," seen in the rise of far-right parties in Europe and in the electoral success of Donald Trump in the United States.[18] These developments prompted YouGov to wonder if they might need to go beyond the old "left vs. right" categorization and attempt to "quantify the layout of the political landscape from this new perspective."[19]

It was indeed Thatcherite politics that inspired Hall to coin the term "authoritarian populism."[20] At the same time, it is worth noting that Hall's discussion initially focused on examining the process through which a new hegemony was negotiated and formed when the Conservative Party was still in the opposition, fighting to retake office from the Labour government. Authoritarian populism, therefore, was not an established part of the political landscape at that time. Hall's seminal article on the subject, "The Great Moving Right Show," was published in *Marxism Today* in January 1979,[21] during the Winter of Discontent, and four months before the 1979 general election that opened the path to the Conservative Party's dominance of British politics for the next eighteen years.

In this article, Hall elucidated the mechanism through which popular support was shifting to the right, abandoning Labour's social democratic corporatist politics. The key to this process, according to Hall, are the contradictions within social democracy: "to win electoral power, social democracy must maximize its claim to be the political representative of the interests of the working class and organized labour," and "once in government, social democracy is committed to finding solutions to the crisis which are capable of winning support from key sections of capital."[22] Social democratic parties, therefore, are required to dismantle their "working-class-to-party" link with core supporters and redefine it as a "people-to-government" link when they take the position of the governing party and, more importantly, face crises necessitating "formative" changes, such as "new programmes and policies, pointing to a new result, a new sort of 'settlement.' "[23] The managing of these crises by instituting formative changes often involves the top-down imposition of unfavorable political decisions on party supporters, justifying them in the name of national interest, as observed in the negotiations over wage freezes under the Labour government in the 1970s. In sum, the notion of a social democratic party as a political representative of working-class people tends to be fundamentally challenged during crises, creating mounting frustration among core party supporters.

In contrast, Hall argues, the Conservative Party under the leadership of Edward Heath and Thatcher tried to present itself as the party of the British or "the people" and Labour as a corporatist political party representing the interests of specific groups. Such maneuvering by the Conservatives essentially portrayed Labour as a selfish, greedy political force that only protected vested interests, particularly those of bureaucratic trade unions, against the well-being of ordinary citizens as demonstrated in the Winter of Discontent as a "lived" crisis in British society at that time. In this discursive construction, Hall observed the redefinition of the "we" in British society. The process constituted two threads of discursive dynamics. First, through mobilizing a set of social values (e.g., efficiency, productivity, meritocracy, praise for a good work ethic, respect for social order, and an emphasis on family discipline and individual aspirations)—in other words, social norms rooted in neoliberal and neoconservative creeds—Conservatives presented the "we" through evoking a particular image of the British way of life closely tied with economic behavior in advanced capitalism. Second, the image of "we" was also projected by juxtaposing it to what Stanley Cohen terms "folk devils":[24] figures portrayed as outsiders or deviants to evoke the sense of abjection leading to "moral panics," as exemplified by the notion of the scrounger.[25]

What the Conservative Party strove to achieve was to mobilize voters in the name of the British people through reorganizing their sense of morality and arousing moral panics. To do so, the Conservatives projected from above an image of the authentic, respectable British people and British way of life while naming those to be excluded from British-ness. This process rearticulated the boundaries between good and bad citizens as well as between legitimate and illegitimate politics, and restructured the hierarchy of social values in a way that made the agenda set by the Conservative Party appear desirable for those who wished to break away from the present crisis and "make Britain 'Great' once more."[26] Differentiated from popular-democratic, this process, then, is called authoritarian populism. It is "an exceptional form of the capitalist state which, unlike classical fascism, has retained most (though not all) of the formal representative institutions in place, and which at the same time has been able to construct around itself an active popular consent."[27]

A crisis offers the opportunity for authoritarian interventions to constitute a new kind of common sense about the normative values set and promoted by the political elite. On this point, it is important to note that Colin Hay's exploration of the notion of crisis reminds us that, unlike what Gramsci argues, a crisis itself needs to be understood as a discursive construct narrated by political actors.[28] Hay, therefore, urges us to pay due attention to how the construction of crisis responds to structural contradictions/failures identified as the cause of crisis. This is because the links made by the political actors point to the political goal and objectives of the authoritarian intervention.[29] In this sense, according to Hay, a crisis is not a context in which discursive politics operates. Rather, the crisis itself needs to be recognized as part of the political process in which actors compete to tailor a political project that allows them to seize, maintain, and expand hegemonic power.

Once such hegemonic power was established in the UK, Hall argues, Thatcherite authoritarian populism left a long-lasting legacy of neoliberal understandings of and attitudes toward the Other and society, defining political legitimacy. Thatcherite influence was even detected well beyond the time of New Labour. It limited the range of policies Labour dared to offer due to a fear of discouraging aspirational and enterprising voters in the 2010s. Indeed, since neoliberal normative values and attitudes underlaid the

Third Way, and people were mobilized through "a more 'direct,' plebiscitary, referendum style of governance," Hall saw New Labour as an evolved version of the Thatcherite political project.[30] In his words:

> This is not the populism of Mrs Thatcher's neo-liberal Right but it is a variant species of "authoritarian populism" none the less—corporate and managerialist in its "downward" leadership style and its moralizing attitude to those to whom good is being done. It is also deeply manipulative in the way it represents the authority it imposes as somehow "empowering us"—another triumph for "customer services."[31]

As this statement suggests, authoritarian populism appears to be a highly effective and flexible political strategy, and a tool that, contrary to YouGov's analysis above, has consistently remained influential in British politics since the 1970s. However, Hall's and Hay's theoretical discussions on authoritarian populism and crisis do not address one crucial point: gender implications. If authoritarian populism requires a decisive intervention during a crisis to reformulate everyday common sense concerning work, the family, our own subjectivity, and way of life, then it inevitably touches upon the gender norms on which familial and social relationships are based. The next section addresses this question by reviewing literature on the relationship between authoritarian populism and gender.

Gendering Authoritarian Populism

Cas Mudde and Cristóbal Rovira Kaltwasser point out that gender has been a neglected topic in studies of populism, even though populist political actors often exhibit clear gendered traits.[32] In addition, support for populist politics is gendered. A series of analyses of voting behavior has demonstrated that more men than women vote for populist radical right parties across different countries.[33]

Authoritarian populism urges us to develop the discussion much further along the lines that Mudde and Rovira Kaltwasser suggest. As a political strategy and technique to form and maintain a new hegemony, authoritarian populism utilizes visions of desirable and undesirable everyday lives and good and deviant subjectivities. This ineluctably results in mobilizing gendered narratives about everyday life and subjectivity in ways to fit the overall political project that authoritarian populists attempt to achieve. In other words, populist political actors structure the relationship between populism and gender. Importantly, as Hall points out in the example of Thatcherite project of welfare reform, this process involves a careful reworking and readjustment of gender norms with reference to the politico-social environment and the underlying ideologies of the overall political objective. Hall puts this as follows:

> Women, mothers and the family have by no means been restricted, in the discourses of Thatcherite populism, to those themes which directly touch on questions of welfare. For women, represented as "guardians" of the family, are also, by the position, connotatively identified with the keeper of traditional wisdoms, and guardian of conventional popular morality; but this composite "she" is, at the same time, the "practical one"—the one who knows the "value of money" and the "impact of rising prices in the shops": that is, the figure through which the economic and monetarist themes of Thatcherism can be made to connect with the empirical experience of everyday life of ordinary folk.[34]

In concrete terms, the women posited by Thatcherite authoritarian populism can be, for example, "the housewife whom the state and the permissive educators would seek to detach from her traditional role and 'force' to 'abandon' her children and hearth and go out to work."[35] In other words, the portrayal of women mobilized by Thatcherite authoritarian populism embodies conventional gender roles and norms while simultaneously signifying competence and effectiveness as an economic actor in an advanced capitalist society. Through identifying themselves with this image, women became included in the "British" of Thatcherite Britain.

Angela McRobbie takes up and develops Hall's insights in her discussion of "post-feminism" in the 2000s. The term "post-feminism" refers to a social and cultural condition that encourages women to follow what she calls "a new sexual contract."[36] Women, in particular young women, are urged to become independent, autonomous, capable, economically and politically empowered subjects, and to organize their everyday lives to optimize their life opportunities, not only as workers but also as wives and mothers. This situation, which has become increasingly visible in Britain since the 1990s, can be superficially understood as indicating that women have been liberated from the old-fashioned regime that binds them to traditional gender roles.

Hence, it suggests that the feminist movement has achieved meaningful change in women's economic, societal, and political conditions. Angela McRobbie, however, presents a different interpretation: one typified by Bridget Jones. This female protagonist in a popular British series of newspaper columns, novels, and films of the late 1990s and 2000s seeks to build a respectable career, but constantly worries about her prospects for forming an intimate relationship leading to a family. That is, the new sexual contract still subjugates women to the status quo of the male-dominated, advanced capitalist society in the disguise of liberation. In this sense, post-feminism, as discussed by McRobbie, implies the reversal or undoing of feminism.

The regression of feminism observed in Britain since the1990s, McRobbie argues, has resulted from two processes. First, while becoming competent, enterprising, empowered subjects who lead meaningful and fulfilling lives, women are required to constantly check the state of their bodies, minds, and social and economic status vis-à-vis the mainstream neoliberal social values where the masculine gender remains hegemonic. In doing so, women form their subjectivities and organize their everyday lives. In other words, in a time of post-feminism, women are disciplined and made to live well by way of Foucauldian biopolitics.[37] Second, the image of women advocated in the era of post-feminism is that of an essentially rational actor who seeks to optimize individual utilities and benefits. This emphasis placed on individualized rationality, McRobbie observes, leads to the "disarticulation" of feminism—in other words, the loss of its capacity to be part of a collective movement through which a diverse set of actors cooperatively strive to create a better, more democratic society.[38]

McRobbie's discussion on post-feminism galvanized the scholarly debate about the nature of contemporary gender politics and feminism. However, it has rarely been acknowledged that her critical insights into feminist politics were informed by observations of contemporary party politics, particularly the rise of New Labour.[39] As pointed out by many scholars, during the 1980s and early 1990s, the British Labour Party, in the process of modernizing itself and regaining ruling power, made specific efforts to increase its shares among female voters. When Tony Blair's New Labour eventually won a parliamentary majority in 1997, these efforts resulted in a significant increase of female members in the Westminster Parliament.[40] Thus, New Labour was regarded as a political force signaling the empowerment of women: women became more visible as political actors with real decision-making power, while their votes were highly valued by the governing party.

McRobbie, however, categorically dismisses this general perception of the time. She contends,

> In the early days of the New Labour government, I even briefly held out some hope for the so-called third way agenda, never imagining that this government would prove to be hostile to feminists, and that it would in effect seek to reverse, or undo feminism, substituting for it the promise of seemingly more modern freedoms, along with ideas like the work-life balance, while at the same time introducing a kind of swaggering, resurgent patriarchalism, the political equivalent of the world of the lads' mags, where women had little choice but to fall into line, or risk the Siberia of feminism.[41]

McRobbie thus attempts to shed light on New Labour's recalibration of a hegemony in which active, capable, aspirational economic actors were highly valued, regardless of their gender, but the notion of a good life was still shaped in a gendered way based on models of an updated, standardized family performing a middle-class lifestyle. Crucially, these ideas of subjectivities and family lifestyles were closely intertwined with New Labour's main political agendas, which emphasized the aspirations of middle-class families. In this way, they formed the ground on which popular support for New Labour flourished and was consolidated. Simultaneously, however, feminism, as a radical political ideology advocating an alternative society, was marginalized to such an extent that a well-known female Labour activist advised "aspiring" female politicians in a newspaper article: "Don't use the F-word."[42] That is to say, the hegemonic understanding of subjectivities and family lifestyles under New Labour operated in ways that limited (the search for) alternate policy choices for both the political elite and the electorate, thereby bolstering support for the existing capitalist economic system and the lifestyles associated with it.

To summarize the above, the theoretical development from Hall to McRobbie points to the central role that gender plays when authoritarian populism operates to form, reform, and maintain the hegemony of "the people." The "people" is rendered an amalgam of gendered beings, and importantly, the way they are gendered is informed by the objectives and ideological orientation of the overall political project. Thus, through the operation of authoritarian populism, individuals perform their gendered everyday roles as legitimate members of the "people" in ways that lead them to support the very set of political choices and preferences that political forces are advocating. As such, the relationship between gender and populist politics is not just witting and context-dependent; it is structured by the political actor to successfully implement his or her political project, and in this sense, it is also, just like a crisis, part of the political process as discussed above.

The Discursive Politics of Demographic and Lifestyle Change in Japan

How does this gendered authoritarian populism help us understand the ongoing discursive politics that presents fertility decline as a national crisis? To tackle this question, it is useful to briefly review the ways in which fertility decline has been discussed and handled as a political matter in Japan.

In 1990, the Japanese policymaking elite—politicians, business leaders, and bureaucrats—flagged fertility decline as an imminent national political problem. This move was triggered by the release of the 1989 total fertility rate (TFR). The figure of 1.57 was the lowest ever recorded, and the news, as indicated by references to "the 1.57 shock," struck like a bombshell. This impact stemmed from the statistical fact that the TFR was lower in 1989 than in 1966, when many Japanese, including the policymaking elite, had expected it to be particularly low due to the superstitious belief that girls born in 1966, in the Chinese zodiac of the fire horse (*hinoeuma*), had been cursed with bad luck in their marriage and relationships with male family members.[43] In fact, Japan's TFR had shown a gradual downward trend since the mid-1970s (see figure 2.1),[44] but the 1.57 shock created the impression that fertility decline had reached an unprecedented scale and so became understood as a "problem that requires policy response."[45]

The sense of a demographic crisis, though, can be traced to a point prior to the release of the TFR in 1990. A report issued by the Advisory Council for the Future of the Household and Child-Rearing (*Korekara no katei to kodomo ni kansuru kondankai*) in January 1990, a few months earlier than the release of the 1989 TFR figure, begins with the following passages:

> Birthrates in our country have kept lowering in recent years, and the number of children who will shoulder society in the 21st century is decreasing. Such decreasing of birthrates may not only impact the healthy development of children but also

result in a situation in which the whole society faces worries, such as increased burdens of the elderly care and the decline of socioeconomic drive. . . . In the remaining short period of time in this century, we now have an imminent task to respond to this "serious and quiet crisis."[46]

In the following pages, the report presents an analysis that posits that fertility decline is caused by changes in the socioeconomic structure, particularly women's working patterns and family lifestyles. To cope with these changes, the report proposes introducing measures to "create an environment in which children are born and raised in a healthy manner."[47] The advisory council's to-do list includes measures to alleviate the costs of raising children and expand institutional support for working women (e.g., improved childcare services and maternal leave provisions). Interestingly, the report notes that each policy needs to be designed to make both men and women engage in child-rearing while bridging different policy areas and drawing on private-sector initiatives. It thus seems to already cover most policy ideas included in today's political debates.

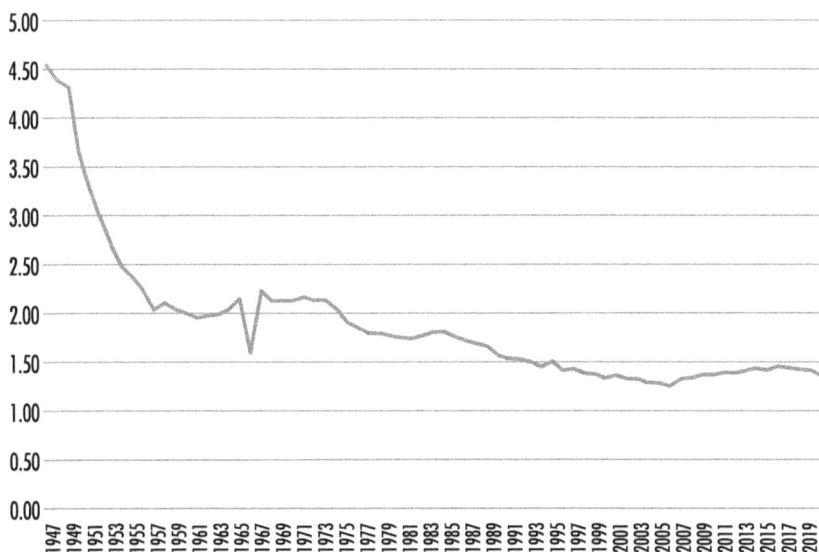

Figure 2.1. Development of Japan's total fertility rate (births per woman). Source: National Institute of Population and Social Security Research, Jinkō Tokei-shū (2019), http://www.ipss.go.jp/syoushika/tohkei/Popular/Popular2019.asp?chap=4&title1=%87W%81D%8Fo%90%B6%81E%89%C6%91%B0%8Cv%89%E6.

Table 2.1. The development of family and gender policies in Japan, 1990–2016

	Political Event	Family Policy	Gender Policy
1990	"1.57 shock" Kaifu government		
1991	Miyazawa government (November) Burst of the bubble economy (to 1993)		
1993	Hosokawa government (August)		
1994	Hata government (April) Murayama government (June)	Angel Plan Urgent Childcare Provision 5-year Plan	
1995	Keidanren report on the "Japanese management in the new era" Kobe earthquake		
1996	Hashimoto government (January) Aum Shinrikyō sarin gas underground attack		Vision of Gender Equality
1997	Asian Financial Crisis		Revision of the Basic Labour Law & EEOL
1998	Obuchi government (July)		
1999		Basic Policy to Promote Countermeasures to Birthrate Decline New Angel Plan	Basic Law for Gender Equal Society
2000	Mori government (April)		Basic Plan for Gender Equality

Table 2.1. Continued.

	Political Event	Family Policy	Gender Policy
2001	Koizumi government (April)	Countermeasures to Birthrate Decline Plus One Guidelines to Support Those Who Work While Raising Children (Cabinet Approval)	
2003		Basic Law to Tackle a Society with Birthrate Decline Act for Measures to Support the Development of the Next Generations	
2004		National Policy Guidelines for Birthrate Decline	
2005	Lowest TFR		Second Basic Plan for Gender Equality
2006	First Abe government (September)	A New Plan to Counter Birthrate Decline	
2007	Fukuda government (September) Global Financial Crisis (to 2008)	Major Strategies to Build Japan that Supports Children and the Family	Work and Life Charter
2008	Aso government (September) "Lehman Shock"	On the Operation for Zero Waiting List for Nurseries	
2009	Hatoyama government (September)	Vision for Children and Child-Rearing	
2010	Kan government (June)	Reviewing Council to Build a New System for Children and Child-Care	Third Basic Plan for Gender Equality
2011	Great East Japan Earthquake (March) Noda government (September)		

continued on next page

Table 2.1. Continued.

	Political Event	Family Policy	Gender Policy
2012	Second Abe government (December)	Act to Support Children and Child-Rearing	Japan Regeneration Strategy Operation Nadeshiko
2013		Urgent Measures to Breakthrough Birthrate Decline	Women's Notebook Three-Year Parental Leave
2014	The lowest number of childbirths GE (December)	National Policy Guidelines for Birthrate Decline (revised)	Policy Package to Make Women Shine
2015	Security-Related Bills (August)	Act for Measures to Support the Development of the Next Generations (extended)	Fourth Basic Plan for Gender Equality
2016		Act to Support Children and Child-Rearing (revised)	
		Policy package of Dynamic Engagement of All Citizens	

Source: Compiled by the author.

Japan's first framework laying out plans to support family-forming and childcare for the next ten years, the so-called Angel Plan, was issued in December 1994 by the coalition government of Social Democratic Party, LDP, and Sakigake. As table 2.1 shows, over the next twenty-two years, until the Abe government issued Japan's Plan for Dynamic Engagement of All Citizens (*ichioku sōkatsuyaku*)[48] in 2016, the government had been proposing and implementing a series of policy measures, including three laws: the Basic Law for Countermeasures to Tackle the Fertility Decline Society and the Act for Measure to Support the Development of the Next Generation in 2003, and the Act to Support Children and Child-Rearing in 2012. The primary objective of these laws and pertaining measures was, as we are told, to support family life among the Japanese, in particular family-forming and child-rearing, and in so doing, to reverse the downward fertility trend shown in figure 2.1.

Despite these government efforts, the demographic trends exhibited little improvement. The lowest TFR (1.26) was recorded in 2005. Since then, the trajectory has taken an upward turn but, in recent years, still hovered around 1.4. Most recently, in 2019, the TFR reached 1.36, far from the population replacement level of 2.08. Moreover, the actual number of annual childbirths set consecutive record lows. These suggest that the policies produced very few of the intended outcomes.

Although extant studies identified a number of reasons for the scant improvement despite the parade of government initiatives and legislative efforts,[49] it is the lackluster progress on institutional reform that is crucial. Take nursery shortages, for example. This issue was clearly acknowledged as a major problem contributing to declining fertility even before the 1.57 shock. However, the number of nursery places gradually decreased from 1,978,989 in 1990 to 1,927,536 in 1999.[50] Although the intake quota had never been met at the national level, the number of children who could not secure places and went on the waiting lists rose to 33,641 in 1999. The government's response to the problem in 2001, however, was to simply change the definition of "nursery shortage" by removing children who attended "non-approved nursery facilities," that is nurseries run without public subsidies, from the waiting list. This trick nominally shortened the waiting list from 35,144 to 21,201 but left the problem itself unsolved. The government at last embarked on more fundamental reforms and reorganized preschool education and childcare support. It set up a new institutional framework that allowed institutions to provide preschool children with both welfare and educational services. Overall, and despite the vociferous calls for change and ostensible legislative efforts, the implementation of reforms has been slow, while their scope remained limited. In other words, what the Japanese government has done to address the issue of fertility decline has mostly taken the approach that Hay, referring to Claus Offe, calls a "conjunctural mode of political rationality"—that is, "politics conducted within the limiting parameters of an accepted set of state structures."[51]

It is worth noting that institutional reform to tackle fertility decline in Japan has been burdened with a series of complications. The following three are particularly noteworthy. First, as is widely known today, the extent of demographic changes in Japan is much more profound than in the other industrially advanced countries of Europe and North America. Japan has one of the world's lowest fertility rates, coupled with one of the highest longevities, while the speed of change has been unprecedented. Second, throughout the postwar period, Japan's welfare state system has remained constrained by one of the lowest levels of public social spending among the Organisation for Economic Co-operation and Development (OECD) countries.[52] Even today, as aging pushes up levels due to rising pension and medical costs (which account for 84.8 percent of total public social spending),[53] public expenditures for families and social welfare remain the lowest in the OECD.[54] This limited level of public spending has traditionally been compensated by corporate welfare programs and family care provision, resulting in the strong familialist nature of the welfare state system.[55] With the economic downturn starting in the early 1990s, however, the familialist approach lost its foundations. Corporations reduced their welfare programs, while the number of irregular workers, who generally fall outside the scope of corporate welfare provision, significantly increased. Moreover, repeated economic setbacks, including the 1997 Asian Financial Crisis and the 2008 Global Financial Crisis, pushed more women in their thirties and forties into the labor market, mostly taking up part-time employment. Thus, the combination of these institutional and financial constraints with the above-mentioned socioeconomic developments rendered Japan's social security system even more precarious. Third, Japan is known internationally for its persistent gender inequality, especially in economic and political participation and empowerment. The 2019 Global Gender Gap Report ranks Japan at 121 out of 153 countries.[56] Despite the Abe government's loud calls for the promotion of women in the labor market, it slipped down from 110 in the 2018 Report.[57] One major reason for this poor performance stems from the low degree of female representation in the policymaking process.

In a book published in 2006, Leonard Schoppa highlighted limited input into the policymaking process from the female policymaking elite as one of the major reasons for Japan's inability to effectively tackle the issue of fertility decline.[58] To increase the number of female political representatives, the Basic Law to Promote Gender Equality in Politics was adopted in May 2018, though, by its very nature, the implementation of concrete measures was left at the discretion of political parties, and the scope of the law did not include enforceable sanctions. Indeed, the number of female candidates who ran for the 2019 House of Councillors election, the first national election since the introduction of the Basic Law, varied, while the share of female candidates for the LDP stagnated at 14.6 percent.[59] In other words, the effect of the Basic Law remains ambiguous. All in all, the Japanese state has been forced to deal with unprecedented demographic change with limited financial and human resources.

At the same time, Japan has not been alone in updating its social security system in response to socioeconomic structural changes as exemplified by financial constraints and the diversification of lifestyles. Many industrially advanced countries have carried out institutional reforms to cope with the new reality of family and work life in which women's labor participation draws level with that of men.[60] Yet, as I have discussed elsewhere,[61] the Japanese government's approach to institutional reform appears to be path-dependent, exhibiting a preference for the productivist paradigm and governmentality model while retaining familialist characteristics. Consequently, the model on which family policy has been based underwent only minor adjustments, shifting from the male-breadwinner model to the 1.5-adult-worker model,[62] with women still being responsible for most reproductive and domestic work while engaging in (often part-time) paid employment.

In sharp contrast to this insufficient, half-hearted process of institutional reform,[63] the Japanese government has been producing a wide range of publications projecting profiles of good, desirable families and their lifestyles versus problematic and deviant families. Visions of a good family and harmonious family life provided by the government are generally narrated in a concrete manner, and supplement major governmental policies and programs, such as observed in the case of the Abenomics structural reforms.[64] For example, the government food education campaign, initiated in 2005, offers practical advice on everyday food practice at home and displays idealized pictures of the family. Through exposure to discourses spread through a multitude of institutional channels such as nurseries, schools, sub-regional authorities, and retailers, individuals are led to recognize and encouraged to perform the Japanese style of neoliberalized food practice that aims to optimize each family's health and welfare, while firmly locating women as the main organizers and agents managing their homes.[65] These official discourses are often reinforced through the figures of folk devils that are circulated through the mass media for signaling threats to society. For instance, the food education campaign uses countless depictions that denounce as bad mothers those women who cannot perform the role of competent food managers.[66]

More broadly, terms signifying the malaise experienced by Japanese families (e.g., parasite singles, *hikikomori*, NEET, and recipients of public assistance, to name but a notable few), have continued to attract public attention since the 1990s. Like the British term "scrounger" under Thatcherite authoritarian populism, these terms identify those who do not follow the "normal" life course and exclude these individuals from the mainstream society. Contra these notions of problematic families and individuals, government documents present a vision of the ideal family lifestyle: a middle-class heterosexual couple with two or three children, striving hard to build a happy family life in a post-feminist era. This strategy is exemplified by the work of Yamada Masahiro, a family sociologist who coined the term "parasite singles" in the late 1990s and often engages in producing narratives of both the ideal and the deviant family.[67] Yamada was appointed to a governmental advisory council under the Koizumi government and provided a report that illustrated the governmental notions of "the new family in the era of structural reform" with concrete, detailed stories. What is striking is the homogeneity of the governmental notion of families. All members in the productive age appear sincere and hard-working, striving for the bettering of everyday family life, while fitting in the category of a Japanese heterosexual dual-income married couple with children (or with a plan of having children). Around the same time, Yamada published a book entitled *Family Risk* (*Kazoku to iu risuku*),[68] which argues that economically dependent family members such as housewives and parasite singles are risks to the welfare and happiness of the whole family.

The notion of the family has thus provided the central ground for building and maintaining a hegemonic discourse in which the post-feminist, standardized middle-class family lifestyle is closely linked with the neoliberal economic conduct and the neoconservative view of the Japanese nation. In this process, a sense of crisis is mobilized to envision the "Japanese people" as those who duly exercise their assigned gendered family roles in their everyday lives by managing the narrated "crises." Meanwhile, family problems are attributed to the individual traits of those excluded from normalcy, obscuring the slow, insufficient progress of institutional reforms. Here, we can observe how political strategies and techniques rooted in authoritarian populism operate in contemporary Japan.

Conclusion

The policymaking elite, and LDP-led national governments in particular, have long exploited notions of the family for encouraging the Japanese people to lead a particular type of life, for the purpose of smoothing the nation's economic and sociopolitical reproduction. In this political process, national economic prosperity has been conflated with the comfortable and happy life of the middle-class standard family. And the LDP's legitimacy as the governing party has been grounded on the delivery of such policy outcomes. Considering this historical trajectory, authoritarian populism mobilizing a

particular notion of family is rooted in the maneuvering of LDP-led governments since the early postwar era, and the Abe government's persistent
proclamations of demographic and family crises can be interpreted as the
latest but more cynical version of his party's long-standing political conduct.

At the same time, it is worth noting that the second Abe government has attempted to introduce a series of regulations and measures for
strengthening the moral framework of the family from the nationalist/statist
perspective. The LDP-proposed constitutional reform would substantially
change Article 24 on gender equality in marriage by emphasizing the duties
of care within the family. As well, the government in 2016 proposed the
Bill to Support Home Education, which has been criticized for applying a
state interventionist approach.[69] In addition, a series of administrative measures have been implemented to promote marriage and childbearing among
young people, especially women. These efforts have not only resulted in the
proliferation of matchmaking events offered by sub-regional authorities but
have also led to the political misconduct of publishing misleading scientific
data. In 2015, for instance, supplementary material for health and physical
education at the high school level issued by the Ministry of Education,
Culture, Sports, Science and Technology included a fabricated graph, giving
the strong impression that women's fecundity declines rapidly after 22 years
of age.[70] These developments suggest that the trend toward authoritarian
intervention into familial matters has increased under the Abe government.
As David Harvey argued in his seminal book on the history of neoliberalism,
ungovernability derives from contradictions between neoliberal creeds and
practices.[71] In this sense, the Abe government is certainly not "popular-democratic" but meets the condition of "an exceptional form of the capitalist
state which, unlike classical fascism, has retained most (though not all) of
the formal representative institutions in place"[72]—although, its exploitation
of authoritarian populism has not resulted in "an active popular consent."[73]

One insight for further consideration gained from the above discussion is the link between the operation of authoritarian populism and the
persistence of the LDP's dominance. At the end of the day, party politics
does not work in a vacuum and authoritarian populism is—as exemplified
by Thatcherite Conservatism and New Labour—a political program led by
elites, in particular the leadership of political parties, to nurture, expand, and
consolidate support among the electorate by popularizing a set of normative
values concerning the way of life. This suggests that challenges launched
against the LDP cannot succeed without the undoing of the long-standing
hegemonic structure that prioritizes certain views of the national economy,

the family, and lifestyles. Indeed, the lingering intimate link between the happiness of the family and national economic prosperity may explain the current lukewarm support rates for the LDP, which appear to be based on the electorate's expectations for economic prosperity. While support rates for the opposition parties remain in the one-digit region, popular support for Abe himself throughout his tenure remained parochial; in recent years, calls for the diversification of family and individual lifestyles can be observed at multiple societal levels.

Notes

1. Speech by Prime Minister Abe Shinzō, September 25, 2017, as translated by the author. The full manuscript of the speech is available at https://www.kantei.go.jp/jp/97_abe/statement/2017/0925kaiken.html. Unless otherwise stated, all online sources were accessed and available on October 15, 2020.

2. See O'Shea, this volume.

3. See Mason and Maslow, this volume.

4. Cabinet Office, *Shōshika shakai taisaku taikō* [Outline of Countermeasures against Declining Fertility], Tokyo, March 20, 2015, https://www8.cao.go.jp/shoushi/shoushika/law/taikou2.html.

5. For example, Benjamin Moffitt, "How to Perform Crisis: A Model for Understanding the Key Role of Crisis in Contemporary Populism," *Government & Opposition* 50, no. 2 (2015): 189–217; Benjamin Moffitt, *The Global Rise of Populism: Performance, Political Style, and Representation* (Stanford, CA: Stanford University Press, 2016).

6. Moffitt, "How to Perform Crisis," 191–192.

7. Paul Taggart, "Populism and Representative Politics in Contemporary Europe," *Journal of Political Ideologies* 9, no. 3 (2004): 275, emphasis in the original.

8. Moffitt, "How to Perform Crisis," 195.

9. Ibid., 197–198.

10. Ibid., 211.

11. Sugawara Taku, "Abe naikaku wa shiji sarete iru no ka: Naikaku shijiritsu o bunseki suru" [Do People Support the Abe Government? Analyzing Public Support for the National Government], in *Tettei kenshō: Abe seiji* [Exhaustive Study: The Abe Government], ed. Nakano Kōichi (Tokyo: Iwanami Shoten, 2016), 33–37.

12. Gregory Noble regards Koike's politics as "general-purpose pandering" rather than populist; quoted in Daniel Hurst, "Is Yuriko Koike Japan's Version of Political Populism," *Asia Times*, October 11, 2017, https://asiatimes.com/2017/10/yuriko-koike-japans-version-political-populism/.

13. Yoichi Funabashi, "Japan, Where Populism Fails," *New York Times*, February 8, 2017, https://www.nytimes.com/2017/02/08/opinion/japan-where-populism-fails.html; Nakakita Kōji, *Jiminto: Ikkyō no jitsuzō* [The LDP: The Actuality of One-Party Dominance] (Tokyo: Chūō Kōron Shinsha, 2017); Jonathan Silin, " 'What Gives: Why Hasn't Populism Reached Japan?" *Democratic Erosion*, October 23, 2017, http://democratic-erosion.com/2017/10/23/what-gives-why-hasnt-populism-reached-japan-by-jonathan-silin-brown-university/.

14. Kinoshita Chigaya, *Popyurizumu to "min'i" no seijigaku* [The Politics of Populism and Public Opinion] (Tokyo: Ōtsuki Shoten, 2017), 21.

15. See Taggart, "Populism"; Margaret Canovan, "Trust the People! Populism and the Two Faces of Democracy," *Political Studies* 47, no. 1 (1999): 2–16; Cas Mudde and Cristóbal Rovira Kaltwasser, "Populism," in *The Oxford Handbook of Political Ideologies*, ed. Michael Freeden and Marc Stears (Oxford: Oxford University Press, 2013): 494–511; John B. Judis, *The Populist Explosion: How the Great Recession Transformed American and European Politics* (New York: Columbia Global Reports, 2016); Jan-Werner Müller, *What is Populism?* (London: Penguin Books, 2017).

16. Cas Mudde, "The Populist Zeitgeist," *Government & Opposition* 39, no. 3 (2004): 541–563.

17. Stuart Hall, *The Hard Road to Renewal: Thatcherism and the Crisis of the Left* (London: Verso, 1988).

18. Joe Twynman, "Trump, Brexit, Front National, AfD: Branches of the Same Tree," *YouGov UK*, November 16, 2016, https://yougov.co.uk/news/2016/11/16/trump-brexit-front-national-afd-branches-same-tree/.

19. Ibid.

20. Hall, *The Hard Road to Renewal*, 151.

21. Stuart Hall, "The Great Moving Right Show," *Marxism Today*, January 1979: 14–20.

22. Ibid., 16.

23. Ibid., 15.

24. Stanley Cohen, *Folk Devils and Moral Panics* (London: Routledge, 1972/2011).

25. Hall, *The Hard Road to Renewal*, 46–56.

26. Ibid., 49.

27. Ibid., 42.

28. Colin Hay, "Narrating Crisis: The Discursive Construction of the 'Winter of Discontent,' " *Sociology* 30, no. 2 (1996): 253–277; Colin Hay, "Crisis and the Structural Transformation of the State: Interrogating the Process of Change," *British Journal of Politics and International Relations* 1, no. 3 (1999): 317–344.

29. Hay, "Crisis," 326–233.

30. Hall, "The Great Moving Right Show," 13.

31. Ibid.

32. Cas Mudde, and Cristóbal Rovira Kaltwasser, "Vox Populi or Vox Masculini? Populism and Gender in Northern Europe and South America," *Patterns of Prejudice* 49, no. 1–2 (2015): 16–36.

33. Niels Spierings and Andrej Zaslove, "Gendering the Vote for Populist Radical Right Parties," *Patterns of Prejudice* 49, no. 1–2 (2015): 135–62.

34. Hall, *The Hard Road to Renewal,* 145.

35. Ibid.

36. Angela McRobbie, "Top Girls? Young Women and the Post-Feminist Sexual Contract," *Cultural Studies* 21, no. 4–5 (2007): 718–737; Angela McRobbie, *The Aftermath of Feminism: Gender, Culture and Social Change* (London: Sage Publications, 2009).

37. McRobbie, *The Aftermath.*

38. Ibid., 24–30.

39. Angela McRobbie, "Gender and the Third Way," *Feminist Review* 64 (2000): 97–112.

40. Sarah Perrigo, "Women and Change in the Labour Party 1979–1995," *Parliamentary Affairs* 49, no. 1 (1996): 116–29; Sarah Childs, *New Labour's Women MPs: Women Representing Women* (London: Routledge, 2004); Harriet Harman, *A Women's Work* (London: Penguin Books, 2018).

41. McRobbie, *The Aftermath.*

42. Anna Coote, "It's Lads on Top at Number Ten: Feminism Just Doesn't Fit into Blair's Vision of a Pain Free Politics for Middle England," *Guardian*, May 11, 1999, p. 9.

43. Hiroko Takeda, "Power over Family Policy: Governing of or Governing through Individuals," in *Power in Contemporary Japan*, ed. Gill Steel (New York: Palgrave Macmillan, 2016), 93–107.

44. Hiroko Takeda, *The Political Economy of Reproduction in Japan: Between Nation-State and Everyday Life* (London: Routledge, 2005).

45. Naikakufu, *Shōshika hakusho* [White Book on Demographic Decline] (Tokyo: Shobi Insatsu, 2014), 33.

46. Korekara no katei to kodomo ni kansuru kondankai [Advisory Council for the Future of the Household and Child-Rearing], *Korekara no katei to kodomo ni kansuru kondankai hokokusho* [Report of the Advisory Council for the Future of the Household and Child-Rearing], January 1990, http://www.ipss.go.jp/publication/j/shiryou/no.13/data/shiryou/syakaifukushi/396.pdf.

47. Ibid., 107.

48. Cabinet Office, *Japan's Plan for Dynamic Engagement of All Citizens (Summary)*, June 2, 2016, https://www.kantei.go.jp/jp/singi/ichiokusoukatsuyaku/pdf/gaiyou_e.pdf.

49. Takeda, *The Political Economy*; Pricilla A. Lambert, "The Political Economy of Postwar Family Policy: Economic Imperatives and Electoral Incentives," *Journal of Japanese Studies* 22, no. 2 (2007): 1–28; Hiroko Takeda, "Structural Reform of the Family and the Neoliberalisation of Everyday Life in Japan," *New Political*

Economy 13, no. 2 (2008): 153–72; Margarita Estévez-Abe, *Welfare and Capitalism in Postwar Japan* (Cambridge: Cambridge University Press, 2008); Patricia Boling, *The Politics of Work-Family Policies: Comparing Japan, Germany, France and the United States* (Cambridge: Cambridge University Press, 2015); Shibata Yu, *Kosodate shien ga Nippon o sukuu* [Support Measures for Childrearing Save Japan] (Tokyo: Keisō Shobō, 2016).

50. These and the figures below in this paragraph are taken from the *Asahi Shimbun*'s "The Visualization Project of Nursery Shortages" project, http://www.asahi.com/special/taikijido/.

51. Hay, "Crisis," 329.

52. Mari Osawa, *Social Security in Contemporary Japan* (London: Routledge, 2011).

53. Tanaka Hideaki, "Bōchō suru yosan: Shakkin de makanau kōkyō sābisu" [The national Budget Expanding: Public Services Financed by Debts], in *Zaisei to minshushugi: Popyurizumu wa saimu kiki e no michi ka* [Financial Democracy: Is Populism a Path to a Financial Crisis?], ed. Katō Sōta and Kobayashi Keiichirō (Tokyo: Nippon Keizai Shimbunsha, 2017), 214.

54. Shibata, *Kosodate Shien*, 11.

55. Gøsta Esping-Andersen, "Hybrid or Unique?: The Japanese Welfare State between Europe and America," *Journal of European Social Policy* 7, no. 3 (1997): 170–189.

56. World Economic Forum, *Global Gender Gap Report 2020* (Geneva: World Economic Forum), http://www3.weforum.org/docs/WEF_GGGR_2020.pdf.

57. Hiroko Takeda, "Between Reproduction and Production: Womenomics and the Japanese Government's Approach to Women and Gender Policies," *Journal of Gender Studies* 21 (2018): 49–70.

58. Leonard J. Schoppa, *Race for the Exits: The Unravelling of Japan's System of Social Protection* (Ithaca, NY: Cornell University Press, 2006). He reiterates this point in a recent article, "The Policy Response to Declining Fertility Rates in Japan: Relying Logic and Hope over Evidence," *Social Science Japan Journal* 23, no. 1 (2020): 3–21.

59. Tsujimura Miyoko, Miura Mari, and Nukaduka Yasue, eds., *Josei no sankaku ga seiji o kaeru* [Women's Participation Will Change Politics] (Tokyo: Shinzansha, 2020), 210.

60. Gøsta Esping-Andersen, *The Incomplete Revolution: Adapting to Women's New Roles* (Cambridge: Polity Press, 2009); Janet C. Gornick and Marcia K. Meyers, *Gender Equality: Transforming Family and Divisions of Labour* (London: Verso, 2009).

61. Hiroko Takeda, "Reforming Families in Japan: Family Policy in the Era of Structural Reform," in *Home and Family in Japan: Continuity and Transformation,* ed. Ronald Richard and Allison Alexy (London: Routledge, 2011), 46–64.

62. Jane Lewis, "Work and Care," in *Social Policy Review 12*, ed. Hartley Dean, Robert Sykes, and Roberta Woods (Newcastle: Social Policy Association, 2000), 48–67.

63. Takeda, "Structural Reform."

64. Takeda, "Power over Family Policy;" see also Shibata, this volume.

65. Hiroko Takeda, "Delicious Food in a Beautiful Country: Nationhood and Nationalism in Discourses on Food in Contemporary Japan," *SEN: Studies in Ethnicity and Nationalism* 8, no. 1 (2008): 5–29; Hiroko Takeda, "The Governing of Family Meals," in *Changing Families, Changing Food*, ed. Peter Jackson (Basingstoke: Palgrave Macmillan, 2009), 165–84.

66. Iwamura Nobuko, *Futsu no kazoku ga ichiban kowai: Tettei chōsa, hametsu suru Nippon no shokutaku* [The Most Worrying Is Normal Families: Investigating Family Meals in Japan] (Tokyo: Shinchosha, 2007).

67. Yamada Masahiro, *Parasaito shinguru no jidai* [The Age of Parasite Singles] (Tokyo: Chikuma Shinsho, 1999).

68. Yamada Masahiro, *Kazoku to iu risuku* [The Family as Risk] (Tokyo: Keisō Shobō, 2001).

69. Ninomiya Shūei, "Katei kyōiku shienhō ni tsuite" [On the Bill to Support Home Education], in *Kokka ga naze kazoku ni kanshō suru no ka* [Why Does the State Intervene in Families], ed. Honda Yuki and Itō Kimio (Tokyo: Seikyusha, 2017), 25–56.

70. Takahashi Sakino, "Gurafu o mitara utagae: Senmonka ga yūdō suru hikagaku" [Question When You See a Graph: Anti-science Led by Experts], in *Monkashō/kōkō "ninkatsu" kyōzai no uso* [Lies Included in Pronatal Materials for High Schools Distributed by MEXT], ed. Nishiyama Chieko and Tsuge Azumi (Tokyo: Ronsōsha, 2017), 17–45.

71. David Harvey, *A Brief History of Neoliberalism* (Oxford: Oxford University Press, 2007).

72. Hall, *The Hard Road to Renewal*, 42.

73. Ibid.

Chapter 3

Save Our Students?

Shifting Subjects of Higher Education Crisis in Japan

JEREMY BREADEN

Introduction

Education is the crisis of choice in Japan. Concerns such as equality of access and academic achievement standards are habitual topics of public discussion and perennial targets of reform for politicians of all persuasions. These issues have been especially prominent since the 1990s, when, as part of the "lost decade" reassessment of social institutions, public discussions about the breakdown in discipline, decline in scholastic standards, and ivory-tower-ism in the university sector peaked. Portrayals of dysfunction in the education system prompted a number of policy interventions, which, in turn, occasioned new contradictions.

In this chapter I focus on those issues pertaining to universities (*daigaku*), the dominant type of higher education institution in Japan. Universities traditionally maintained a degree of separation from educational crisis narratives, threatened only by the products of school-level dysfunctions, rather than constituting problems in their own right. By the 1990s, however, they faced a number of critical challenges, including a dramatic decline in the university-age population and the implementation of new policy directions such as deregulation, corporatization, and the rise of an audit culture. Ongoing debates over the impact of and responses to these challenges underline the difficulty of decoupling university-related issues from more fundamental preoccupations of Japanese society, such as deepening economic disparities, the challenges to established ideas about life course, and the endpoint of neoliberal reforms.

A particular concern of this chapter is how problems in the university system have been framed and advanced using the student as a narrative subject. Students make compelling narrative subject matter because they can cultivate universal empathy and display symptoms—ranging from academic incompetence to motivational deficit to financial incapacity—that can be used to construct a convincing pathology of the problem at hand. However, the focus on treating these embodied symptoms also signifies a failure to answer important systemic questions about the relationship between universities and government, about public and private responsibilities for higher education, and about the interface between formal education and employment in an era of demographic change and economic disparity. A crisis, defined by Colin Hay as a "moment of decisive intervention,"[1] is averted as energy is channeled into piecemeal remedial actions rather than a search for common underlying causes. The process of abstraction and "discursive unification"[2] envisaged by Hay is thus short-circuited.

In this chapter I begin with an outline of the major structural changes occurring in Japanese higher education in the twenty-first century, the manifest contradictions arising therefrom, and some of the principal modes of their narration. Next, I look specifically at student-centered crisis narratives, noting the strong sense of public stakeholdership therein. To construct a point of reference for the following analysis of a particular student crisis in higher education, I briefly review one of the most long-standing issues in educational crisis narratives: declining scholastic abilities. This issue both forms part of the pre-history of current portrayals of university-level problems and exemplifies the peculiarly self-referential character of educational crisis narratives in general. I then turn to a more in-depth analysis of a crisis narrated at the time of writing: that of students unable to meet the costs of a university education and graduates deprived of the traditional benefits of a university degree. The current policy response, the establishment of a new system of financial aid, is an intriguing case study in how a variety of crisis symptoms can be treated so as to preempt accumulation into a meta-narrative of state failure. I also explain how the treatment has, unexpectedly, afforded an opportunity for the government to advance neoconservative proposals originally unrelated to the task of rescuing impoverished students.

The Changing Landscape of University Education

To borrow from Hay's lexicon, Japan's university system has a number of "unresolved contradictions" that result from dramatic changes since the 1990s. The first is the rise in the general participation rate in higher education. Japan exemplifies Martin Trow's 1970s model that describes the transition of higher education in industrialized societies from an "elite" system involving a small proportion of school leavers toward a "mass" and ultimately "universal" system, where advancement to university and other forms of higher education is the norm.[3] The entrance rate to all forms of higher education increased between 1990 and 2010, with the rates for university undergraduate education specifically going from around 25 percent to 50 percent (figure 3.1).[4] Almost three-hundred new universities were opened between 1985

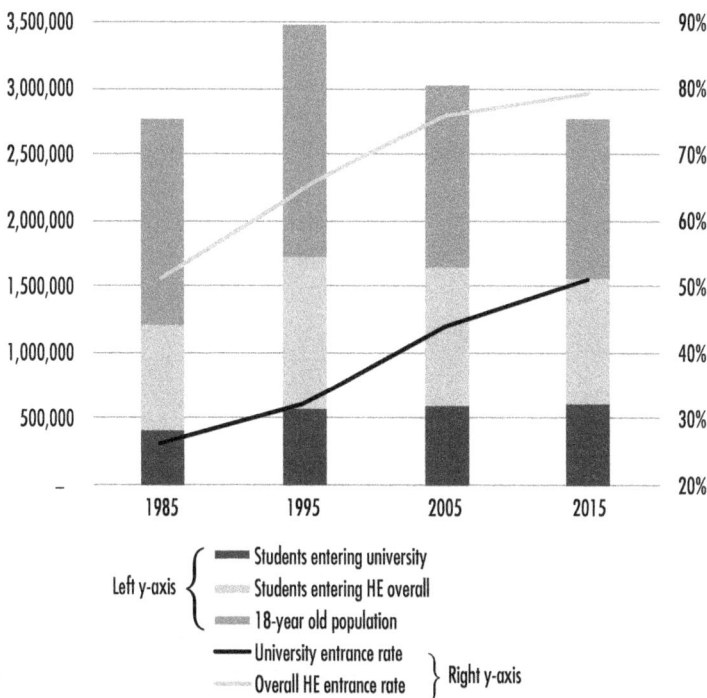

Figure 3.1. Higher education entrance rates, 1985–2015. Source: Created by the author from MEXT, *Kōtō kyōiku no shōraizō ni kansuru kiso dēta* [Basic Data on Future of Higher Education], April 11, 2017, http://www.mext.go.jp/b_menu/shingi/chukyo/chukyo4/gijiroku/__icsFiles/afieldfile/2017/04/13/1384455_02_1.pdf.

and 2005 alone. Thus, the categories of "university" and "university student" have expanded greatly, giving rise to contradictions I will examine later.

The relatively stable element in this process of "massification" (*taishūka*) is the degree of dependence on private funding rather than government spending. Historically, Japanese higher education has been overwhelmingly private, and today the private sector enrolls around 74 percent of all university students, with student fees making up around 77 percent of this sector's revenue.[5] An even higher proportion, more than 90 percent, of those studying at advanced vocational schools (*senmon gakkō*) are enrolled in private institutions. As a consequence, household spending accounts for more than half of all expenditure on higher education, and the rate of public spending is the lowest of all OECD countries. Put simply, the massification of higher education has been bankrolled by individual consumers.[6]

This private character of higher education is particularly significant because the massification has occurred at precisely the same time as the rise of insecure employment, decrease of disposable household income, growing wage disparity, and other hallmarks of the "gap society."[7] Contrary to the principles of supply and demand, higher education has not become more affordable as it has become more universally available. In fact, the opposite is true. The average wage in Japan declined by almost 20 percent between 1990 and 2010, whereas the average tuition fee at private universities doubled in the same period.[8] Unsurprisingly, participation rates rise in line with household income: there is a difference of as much as 35 percentage points in university entrance rates between the lowest annual income bracket (27.8 percent in 2012) and the highest (62.9 percent).[9]

One product of this development is the increasing reliance on student loans. The government, through the Japan Student Services Organization (JASSO), operates a large-scale program of higher education loans with low-interest and zero-interest options, repayable after graduation.[10] Since the turn of the millennium, the use of this program has ballooned to the point that, in 2015, it was accessed by more than 1.3 million students, or close to 40 percent of all students in higher education. Support from family remains the major source for students' livelihoods. But it has declined proportionally from around 75 percent in 1995 to 60 percent in 2016 as the dependence on loans has risen from 5 percent to over 20 percent. These figures show that the burden has shifted somewhat from up-front payment by parents and guardians to delayed payment by individual graduates.

The relatively steady expansion of the university sector conceals change in another crucial statistic: the university entrance age population. As shown in figure 3.2, through the 1970s and 1980s the number of 18-year-olds

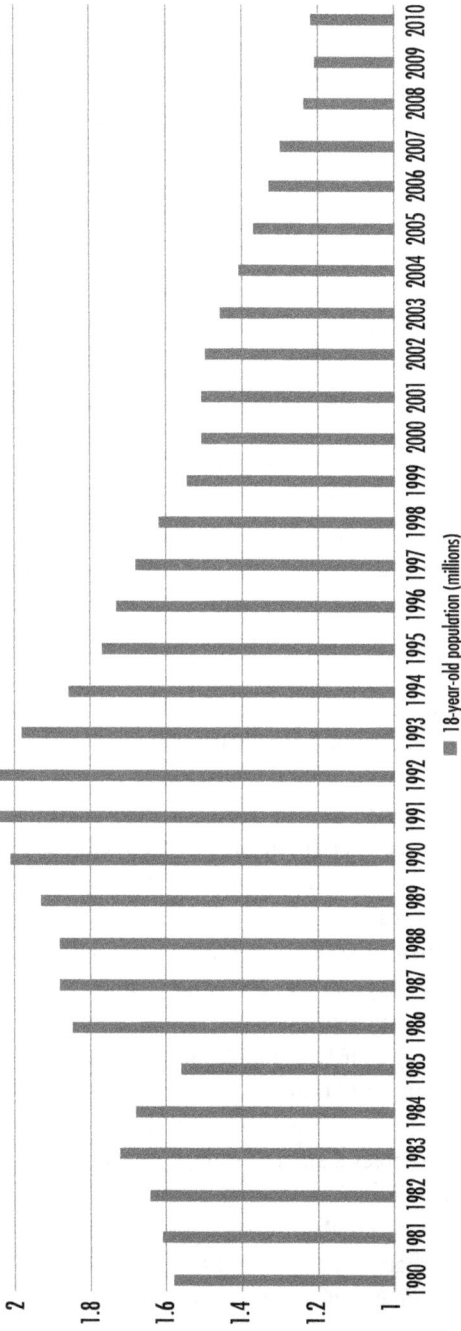

Figure 3.2. Eighteen-year-old (University Entrance Age) Population in Japan. Source: Created by the author from MEXT, *Kōtō kyōiku no shōraizō ni kansuru kiso dēta* [Basic Data on Future of Higher Education], Tokyo, April 11, 2017, http://www.mext.go.jp/b_menu/shingi/chukyo/chukyo4/gijiroku/__icsFiles/afieldfile/2017/04/13/1384455_02_1.pdf.

(who are the overwhelming majority of university entrants) increased roughly apace with the expansion described above. It shot up dramatically to a peak in 1992 and then entered a rapid decline through the rest of the 1990s and 2000s. The decline is forecast to continue, albeit at a less dramatic pace. Since the 1990s, a growing proportion of the shrinking population has been entering university. Japan's case thus upends the common assumption that higher education systems grow in parallel with population.

Although rising participation rates have softened the impact of demographic change significantly, universities are undoubtedly feeling the pinch. Most national and elite private universities have no shortage of applicants, but the same cannot be said for the rest of the private sector, which enrolls the great majority of students. Around 40 percent of private universities enroll less than their official student quota, and a similar percentage have negative revenue-expenditure balances. Around 20 percent fill less than 80 percent of their quota.[11] These alone may not be reliable indicators for institutional viability—very few universities have actually gone completely out of business as yet—but they mark a significant destabilization of what was once a very secure enterprise. This shift is evidenced in the proliferation of publications offering predictions on which universities will survive and which will fail in the coming years.[12]

The demographic squeeze also heralds changes in the character and function of university education, generating new contradictions. Until the changes of the 1990s described above, Japan had long been a credentialist society. A university degree was an asset for which students needed to compete through entrance examinations, but later enjoyed the rewards in the form of upward social mobility—or at the very least financial security.[13] This arrangement is now called into question. It is impossible to sustain the idea of university admission as the centerpiece of a system of meritocratic selection when virtually anyone can pass the exam. Hence, the orthodox university hierarchy breaks down and the sector polarizes into a few elite institutions that still enjoy a surfeit of applicants and can be genuinely selective, and a great many more that are happy to fill classrooms with virtually anyone. Not surprisingly, there is a growing consensus among parents that a degree no longer guarantees a stable future for their children. This can be seen in widespread dissatisfaction among students, rising withdrawal rates, and increasingly common extended leave from university.[14] That skepticism appears justified. More than 30 percent of 30-to-50-year-old higher education graduates in the workforce (not counting unemployed and homemakers) have annual incomes of less than 3 million yen. This is significantly lower than the private sector average of 4.22 million yen.[15]

Thus, there are at least two layers of inconsistency in Japan's higher education system. The first is a simple conflict of trends: expansion of supply in the context of contraction of demand (university entrance age population), and massification in times of declining affordability. The second type of inconsistency arises from the clash between these conflicting trends and the static operating logics of the university system. The system was developed in an era of high demand, limited supply, and economic stability. When entrance examinations were an effective means of filtering talent into universities, there was a clear place for university education within a predictable life course, and middle-class households were prepared to tolerate a burden that is exceptionally high by international standards. Previously, entering university was a reliable way to climb the socioeconomic ladder; now it is often little more than a way of avoiding a downward slide.

All these "real" changes are also a matter of narration, and coherent narratives are sometimes difficult to sustain as realities continue to evolve. For example, the reality of demographic change (fewer university-age students) is inseparable from the conjectured but yet-to-be realized outcomes thereof (widespread university collapse). The decline in both the affordability of university education and the anticipated returns from it belies the fact that demand for such education continues to rise. The dividing line between fact and narration is not a fixed one by any means.

More important for the discussion of Japan's perceived national crisis, these systematic contradictions are accompanied by an accumulation of contradictions in the role of the state in higher education. As noted above, the Japanese state has for many decades relied on a market-based solution to the problem of how to fund a growing higher education system. This reliance has become stronger since the 1990s. The national government has loosened controls on university establishment and expansion, promoted the transformation of national and municipal universities into more independent quasi-corporate entities, and introduced more competition into its funding systems. Processes such as corporatization of national universities and establishment of a third-party accreditation system in the early 2000s, for example, were originally held up as exemplars of the Liberal Democratic Party (LDP) government's neoliberal operating model for public institutions, in which the state, rather than "regulating," would simply "steer" healthy market competition.[16]

The official approach is far removed from market fundamentalism, however. Universities have been given prominence in policies for increasing economic competitiveness and productivity.[17] These policies have consistently involved high levels of administrative intervention. Thus, the state retains control over the processes for the establishment of new academic programs and alteration of enrolment quotas, oversees the third-party evaluation system, designs and administers competitively awarded funding schemes, and retains many mechanisms for micromanagement, especially in national universities. This includes competences such as the supervision of an annual budgeting processes and the control of personnel costs. The circulation of personnel, sometimes illegal (see discussion of *amakudari* below), sustains links between the education ministry and universities beyond the scope of formal regulation as well. The state's role is thus doubly contradictory: it is encouraging universities to take their future into their own hands, yet tying them to administrative controls and political priorities; it is also empha-sizing their role as economic drivers while denying them the resources to play that role effectively. The state is left in the curious position of being heavily *interested* in higher education while seeking to remain only lightly *invested* in it.

Narrating Crisis in Higher Education

Is there a crisis in Japanese higher education? Seemingly the only possible answer is "yes." The macro-trends noted above are debated intensely. The incongruity between the rapid expansion of the higher education and popu-lation decline, for example, has generated speculative discussion of a collapse of the private university sector. Dire predictions of waves of bankruptcies emerged in the early 2000s.[18] While the collapse has not yet eventuated on the scale expected, the debate continues under catchphrases such as *genkai daigaku* ("universities on the brink": chronically under-enrolled and financially stressed) and *2018 mondai* ("the 2018 problem," referring to the year when another major decline in 18-year-old population was expected to begin).[19] At the same time, policymakers are in the process of developing an elaborate system of early intervention for struggling institutions and safety nets for students left in the lurch by departmental closures.[20]

Almost as intensely debated are the contradictions between the growing political emphasis on universities' research productivity on the one hand, and evidence of a dysfunctional research system on the other. Domestic media and major international outlets plot the "slow decline of Japanese research" in both comparative and absolute terms.[21] Meanwhile, highly publicized cases of misconduct have tarnished the reputation of academic researchers themselves.[22] News reports and commentary by scientists themselves often put these problems down to government policies that fostered intense institutional pressure to produce high-impact research, but provided only limited funding amid growing global competition and resulted in less autonomy and security for scientists themselves.[23] As one commentator notes, "the more science and technology policy fills out and the further university reform advances, the more stifling it becomes for Japan's researchers."[24]

These paradoxical outcomes of state-driven university reforms are a recurring theme in discussions of research decline. But similar outcomes have also been noted in regard to other subject matter, most notably the frustratingly slow progress on internationalization despite an ongoing stream of high-profile policy interventions in this area.[25] The manifold structural (and sometimes "cultural") factors impeding internationalization are the subject of a burgeoning body of literature, both journalistic and scholarly.[26] But the lack of progress also points to a wider policy failure. Discrete project-based funding allocations with relatively short evaluation cycles foster a narrow view on outcomes and a hypersensitivity toward buzzwords, distracting from the fundamental, long-term institutional reforms that must precede the kinds of reforms the projects were originally designed to achieve.[27] The gaps between policy leadership, bureaucratic steering, and budgetary follow-through are once again exposed.

Other crisis narratives reveal different facets of the problematic relationship between universities and the state. The national education ministry (MEXT) has a long-standing culture of *amakudari*, whereby retiring officials find lucrative jobs in the higher education institutions they once supervised. The practice is widely frowned-upon in twenty-first-century Japan, and lobbying for *amakudari* positions has been illegal since 2007. Yet a 2017 probe by MEXT itself found seven senior bureaucrats involved in securing a top job for their colleague at the prestigious Waseda University. Ostensibly a straightforward corruption scandal, this case rekindled discussions about the extent to which universities are still tethered to state bureaucracy, leading some to conclude that the past two decades of university reforms have "fueled competition not for higher research and educational standards among universities, but for closer ties with the ministry."[28]

Problems in the educational bureaucracy have been compounded by political pressure on administrative decisions. Some of the most egregious cases occurred during the Abe administration, notably implicating the prime minister himself. Among the most well-known was the decision to approve establishment of a new veterinary faculty at a university run by the private educational corporation Kake Gakuen, which is headed by one of the Prime Minister's close confidants. Abe Shinzō denied applying direct pressure, but the implications of cronyism are unavoidable—as they are in the case of Moritomo Gakuen, another private academy which was offered low-cost public land to construct a school of which Abe's wife was honorary principal. These cases demonstrate that education policy, while central to Abe's claims of state transformation, also continues to yield familiar iterations of postwar LDP interest politics.[29]

The above are just a few prominent examples from a long list of recent policy failures in higher education. They are narrated not only in the popular media but also in the academic and institutional literature. Scholars of higher education have busied themselves identifying critical flaws in the structure and operations of Japan's university system for many decades.[30] There is also a long tradition of critique of Japanese higher education from abroad by academics who have worked in the Japanese system and from comparative researchers and international organizations.[31] These criticisms are sustained in recent analyses, most notably those of the internationalization of higher education.[32]

Crisis is business as usual in higher education. Yet if the question is whether there is a crisis in the sense used by Hay—a capital-C "Crisis," as it were—the answer is likely to be "no." While very real for those involved in them, crises such as deteriorating research environment, *amakudari*, and the imminent collapse of the under-enrolled private sector have failed to galvanize public opinion and have not generated the kind of political pressure required for a truly decisive transformation of state policy. The vital statistics of the university sector, for example, have changed surprisingly little since the turn of the millennium (see table 3.1). Regarding policy responses, it is difficult to identify anything more than "minor tinkering and failure management"[33] as the state continues to oscillate between laissez-faire and interventionist positions and remains committed to steering reform but reluctant to make long-term budgetary commitments to it. Borrowing from Gramsci, Hay terms this a state of "catastrophic equilibrium,"[34] in which symptoms are widely acknowledged but no decisive intervention has (yet) been made.

Table 3.1. Japan's universities, 2000 and 2018

		2000	**2018**
Number of universities		650	782
	% private	73.7	77.1
Number of students		2,740,023	2,909,159
	% private	73.3	77.4
Number of full-time academic staff		150,563	187,163
	student:staff ratio	18:1	15.5:1
Government funding of national universities (operating grants)		1,361.1 billion yen	1,066.0 billion yen
Government subsidies to private universities		269.1 billion yen	306.9 billion yen
Private university revenue from student fees		2,247.2 billion yen	2,535.5 billion yen

Source: Data on universities, students, and staff taken from MEXT, *Gakkō kihon chōsa kekka no gaiyō*, Tokyo, 2018, http://www.mext.go.jp/b_menu/toukei/chousa01/kihon/kekka/1268046.htm. Data on subsidies and revenue are from 2015/16 and adjusted to 2011 prices, from Research Institute on Higher Education, Hiroshima University, "Statistics of Japanese Higher Education," n.d., https://rihe.hiroshima-u.ac.jp/en/statistics/synthesis/.

Students and the Pathologization of Crisis

I suggest that narratives of higher education crisis in Japan have failed to mobilize one of the most powerful devices at their disposal: the student. In order for contradictions in the higher education system to become compelling markers of crisis—pathologized—they need to be connected to everyday life.[35] In the case of crisis in education systems, it is the experience of the student that furnishes this important element. Other possible subjects such as misbehaving university professors, beleaguered administrators, and corrupt bureaucrats may stir some voyeuristic interest, but they hardly foster engagement or empathy among a general audience. Students, on the other hand, not only embody educational dysfunction but also personalize it. The academically challenged student, the impoverished student, the unemployable graduate, the delinquent dropout: we may not identify personally with these images, but we intuitively appreciate them simply because they speak to the universal experience of being a student. Our experience not only allows us to empathize with the plight of students, but also confers expertise, as "each and every citizen feels entitled to act as natural expert' and 'stakeholder' in matters of education."[36] Debating student problems helps to anchor discussions about educational reform in experience common to all members of society.

Student-centered narratives, however, also have a number of specific features that tend to work against the progression into a full-blown Hayesian Crisis. One is that the tone of discourse can shift quickly from sympathetic to condemnatory as participants try to position the symptoms within their own personal experience of studentship. It is sometimes difficult to know whether the students are the victims or the perpetrators. Another feature is that narratives tend to be highly nostalgic, romanticizing a time in the past when things worked more satisfactorily—even if they never really did. This nostalgia makes for a peculiar articulation of forward- and backward-looking discourses and generates "solutions" that actually reference the very "problems" they sought originally to correct.[37]

In the late 1990s and early 2000s, for example, there was widespread concern over an apparent decline in children's scholastic abilities (*gakuryoku*) together with their attention span, motivation for study, and other factors once considered successes of Japanese education.[38] Critics pointed out the dubious statistical basis for such concerns and their one-dimensional focus on international scholastic test scores,[39] inviting parallels with "manufactured crises" of education observed in other countries,[40] but they largely failed to displace the growing panic. Declining scholastic abilities are a perennial topic of education system discussions everywhere, but they had particular consequence in the climate of post-bubble Japan.[41]

In this case, there was also a specific culprit: the *yutori kyōiku* ("relaxed education" or "room to grow") reforms of the school curriculum that were formulated in the 1990s and placed new emphasis on autonomous, exploratory learning to prepare children for the "knowledge-based society."[42] These reforms culminated in 2002 in some fundamental changes, including shorter instruction hours and streamlined subject content. In universities, the flow-on effect of the *yutori* reforms was framed as the "2006 Problem" (*2006-nen mondai*), a reference to the year in which universities would admit the first cohort of high school graduates taught under the full *yutori* curriculum.[43] By this time there was already a well-established narrative of academic decline, with popular writings expounding on the failure of university students to perform even simple arithmetic or label countries on a world map.[44] The *yutori* reforms drove this narrative to its peak.

The policy turnaround was swift. The education ministry had switched to a reemphasis on "solid academic abilities" (*tashika na gakuryoku*) already in the months leading up to the 2002 rollout of the *yutori* curriculum.[45] By 2004, the ministry had instituted a fresh set of curricular reforms including more rigorous standards, national achievement testing, and increased competition in schools. This turnaround was accompanied by an intensified neoliberal discourse, including emphasis on student employability and job-readiness (*shūgyōryoku, shakaijin kisoryoku*), and the universities' role in human capital development (*jinzai ikusei*), coupled with a revival of neoconservative themes such as patriotism and civic morality.[46]

Paradoxically, the *yutori* reforms themselves had been a response to a previously narrated failure of Japanese education, embodied in the image of the creatively stifled, over-pressured student. The reforms acted on a consensus that entrenched practices of rote learning and overemphasis on examinations was both smothering individual potential and causing harmful stress to students. The backlash against *yutori* partly rested on the nostalgic rediscovery of that system's merits of instilling foundational knowledge and sound study habits. International praise for Japan's schools was an important reference point. "Japanese-style education" (in traditional sense of orderly, disciplined schools delivering standardized curricular content) had been idealized in calls for reform to the US education system in the 1980s and 2000s, and was subject to "reverse importation" by conservative critics of *yutori*.[47]

This highly cyclical pattern conforms to Hay's crisis model, not in its full rendition but as a short-circuit thereof. Individual symptoms of dysfunction, as embodied in the student, are extrapolated into a wider narration of problems in the education system. These meta-narratives generate the momentum for "responses that directly address the crisis *as discursively constituted and mediated*, thereby resolving the 'crisis' as narrative without necessarily resolving the contradictions and failures that sustain such a narrative."[48] These responses can furnish opportunities for contradictions to be narrated afresh, which in turn demand further responses. The power of the student as a narrative subject is beyond doubt, but the question is whether or not the discrete failings of students can generate the "connotative resonance"[49] that enables a diverse landscape of crisis symptoms to be drawn into a single frame and abstracted into a meta-narrative of crisis that prompts decisive intervention.

The Destitute Student: Loans in Crisis and "Making Higher Education Free"

While underlining the cyclical character of education policy, the period of *yutori* reforms and counter-reforms was also one of sustained focus on the student, whether as victim of a stifling and depersonalizing classroom experience, as ill-equipped for the competitive demands of the working world, as lacking in moral fiber and social acumen, or as inward-looking and oblivious to the threats and opportunities of globalization. These student images are referenced in crisis narratives of university education too, but overwhelmingly they either index the problems of secondary education or stand for broader issues of youth motivation and morality that extend beyond education itself.[50] Students thus make compelling subject matter for educational crisis narratives, but the extrapolation of such narratives to the contradictions of the university system is rarely feasible.

The narrative of the student in dire financial circumstances, both while attending university and into the early years of working life, does appear as a case where such extrapolation occurs. Beginning as a relatively straightforward focus on economic disadvantage, the tale of the impoverished university student has gradually evolved into a narration of structural contradictions. It speaks to a crisis of higher education itself, articulating many of the contradictions discussed above. It is also the subject of a major policy intervention, inviting consideration of whether this particular "crisis" is actually evolving into a "Crisis."

The affordability of higher education has been a slow-burning issue for many years, but something closer to a full-blown conflagration arose in the mid-2010s. By then, terms such as "poverty" (*hinkon*) and "entrenchment of disparity" (*kakusa no koteika*) were already in widespread use. The application of these terms to the novel subject of university students in poverty (*hinkon daigakusei*) was a logical progression as universities became mass institutions. The news media produced a swelling stream of reportage on university students in dire financial straits, generally after having entered university under their own steam with little parental support (*jiriki shingaku*) and forced to rely heavily on loans and income from casual work.[51] Readers were told rather superfluously that "an easy-going campus life is an undreamt-of luxury"[52] for these students, who are often driven into exploitative casual jobs (*burakku baito*).[53] There were even reports of female students forced into prostitution as a way of making ends meet.[54]

These reports dovetailed with the release of alarming statistics on the use of the JASSO student loan program. Under the weight of public opinion, JASSO itself published increasingly detailed data on loan repayments, showing in 2015 that around 190,000 graduates were defaulting (failing to pay installments for more than three months). Around 80 percent of defaulters were in low-income households.[55] A widely reported 2016 survey found that almost 40 percent of those aged 34 and under said that JASSO loan repayments were a strain (*kurushii*), and significant proportions said that their loan debts had an impact on planning for their future (marriage 31.6 percent, home ownership 27.1 percent, work choices 25.2 percent, child rearing 23.9 percent, childbirth 21.0 percent).[56] Another authoritative survey found that three-quarters of current university students had concerns (*fuan*) about their capacity to repay their own loans after graduation.[57] In a popular monograph aptly titled *"Scholarship" Hell*, lawyer Iwashige Yoshiharu discussed the impact on students and their families in depth, including cases of parental guarantors being driven to bankruptcy and the "blacklisting" of defaulting graduates by credit agencies.[58] Picking up on Iwashige's critique, the popular media began labeling the JASSO system a form of "poverty business" (*hinkon bijinesu*), a term usually reserved for the practice of unscrupulous consumer credit providers.[59]

The inflation of the JASSO loan program, and especially its interest-bearing component, stemmed partly from a structural reform undertaken in the early-2000s. The program was originally conceived as a welfare initiative based on the guarantee of equality of educational opportunity in the Basic Act on Education, and in the Constitution. In 2004, however, the program was taken over by the newly-formed independent administrative corporation JASSO, and subjected to a performance evaluation regime that emphasized operational efficiency and financial autonomy. The loan program became classified as a "finance business" (*kinyū jigyō*) and JASSO shifted its emphasis from zero-interest (Type 1) to interest-bearing (Type 2) loans. By 2013, Type 2 had grown to 2.4 times as large as Type 1 in terms of user numbers, and 3.1 times in terms of total loans.

In response to the rising public concern that the loan program was creating a debt spiral, JASSO in 2016 produced a new guide to promote proper "understanding" of the program. In unprecedented manner, it emphasized the need to plan carefully before taking out loans and highlighted the (limited) provisions for reduced repayment in cases of financial hardship.[60] In late 2016, it launched a new grant-based scheme for students facing financial hardships. At the same time, packaged together as the "higher education advancement support plan," JASSO relaxed the eligibility conditions for Type 1 (zero-interest) loans and adopted a partially income-contingent scheme for loan repayments.[61]

This partial response, however, was soon overshadowed by the political momentum for a more fundamental intervention under the banner of *kōtō kyōiku no mushōka* or "making higher education free." It was part of a broader movement which began under the Democratic Party of Japan government in 2010 to reduce the cost of public senior secondary-school education with subsidies. In opposition, the LDP had labeled this a "hand-out policy" (*baramaki seisaku*).[62] But after regaining power, it began moves to extend it to preschool education and higher education as well. By the start of the 2017 general election campaign, virtually every political party was using the *mushōka* label to propose the direct subsidization of higher education student costs, albeit with differences concerning the degree of support and means to finance it. The incumbent LDP and its allies even considered including a guarantee of *mushōka* for pre-school and higher education in its package of constitutional revisions.[63] This inclusion ultimately became a crucial element of Prime Minister Abe's own strategy for achieving constitutional revision in 2020. A video message by Abe released on Constitution Memorial Day (May 3) 2019 places the constitutional enshrinement of *mushōka* directly alongside the revision of Article 9 as essential to creating a "constitution for a new era."[64]

While it is unclear whether the media discourse on the impoverished student was actually an independent force for the adoption of these *mushōka* policies or part of a process of consensus-building engineered by political actors, the resulting policy shift is notable. It not only reverses the general twenty-first-century trend of moving the financial burden further from public to private in a higher education system where the private burden is already very high, but also represents the prioritization of higher education in a time of great pressure on public resources. In such a context, the political support for *mushōka* was certainly enhanced by the pervasive student-in-crisis narrative that transposed rather complex and faceless arguments about revenue and funding structures into a familiar and empathetic mission to save our students.

Saving the Student, Fixing the System: Shifting Subjects

The discussion of the failing loans system and *mushōka* thus evolved into a narration of the aforementioned changes in the higher education landscape and contradictions resulting from them. Portrayals of the impoverished university student being set up for a life of debt and disadvantage called into question the ultimate purpose and value of a university degree and occasioned fresh scrutiny of the basic workings of university education.

The impoverished student became more than just another iteration of the "gap society" narrative, and opened up a wider reevaluation of the university reform agenda. This shift in subject from the student to the university becomes clear if we trace a few of the key questions raised in the search for a workable solution to the crisis.

What Kinds of Students Should Be Going to University?

As concerns over the JASSO loan program peaked in the mid-2010s, an argument commonly aired was that students should think more carefully about whether or not to go to university in the first place. Graduates defaulting on their loans were presented as evidence of a fundamental failure to acknowledge that, in an era of mass participation, a university degree is no longer any guarantee of income stability. This was in fact the position adopted by the JASSO director Endo Katsuhiro. He lamented the persistent "illusion" of a university degree as the foundation for a secure life course, and expressed his hope that students would "abandon the indulgent notion that as long as you can get a loan and go to university, everything will work out somehow."[65]

Endo came under heavy fire for attempting to deflect criticism of his own organization's role in the loan crisis and recasting the problem as one of naïve, overly optimistic students and families. But his ideas also found widespread support among those concerned with the products of massification of the university sector. Prominent political commentator Yayama Tarō exemplified the sentiment when he commented in regard to *mushōka*:

> It's fine if students have something they really want to study at university, but it's a problem if they can simply go to university to have a good time for four years, regardless of their family circumstances or academic performance. They will lose their sense of gratitude to their parents for paying their fees, and that's the real moral hazard.[66]

This discussion is not only a classic case of the aforementioned fluctuation between sympathetic and condemnatory discourse—these students are pitiable, but they really should have thought more carefully in the first place—but it also reflects a decidedly orthodox understanding of university education as something reserved for those who are highly motivated and academically talented and, moreover, have parents capable of paying for their education.

Others were more concerned about the hazard that subsidized students posed to educational standards at universities. The line of reasoning here was that *mushōka* in an era of open access to university education would lead to an influx of poorly qualified students, forcing universities to lower academic standards even further than they already had. While solving the crisis of affordability, *mushōka* would have the "negative side effect" of exacerbating the effects of massification, as it would "make higher education quality assurance even more difficult than it already is."[67] The contradiction between a contracting university-age population and an expanding university sector was once again brought into sharp relief.

What Kinds of Universities to Support?

These discussions also referenced long-standing concerns about the state's involvement in the university system. While the *mushōka* proposal was about alleviating the costs of university education, indirectly, it also represented a major allocation of public funds to universities and presented an opportunity to air a growing sentiment of the 2000s: that the government, through JASSO loans and other subsidies, may be artificially propping up poorly performing universities. Interest in this issue sharpened when it came to light that the proportion of students accessing loans and the rate of loan default by graduates were both highest in bottom-tier universities.[68] These were mostly private institutions established during the expansion of the 1990s and early 2000s, struggling to contend with the financial consequences of a shrinking pool of university entrants. The idea that such universities might gain a lifeline from the loan system fundamentally contradicted the government's market-forces approach to reforming the sector and was a common theme in news media editorials. The *Nihon Keizai Shimbun*, for example, admonished that "*mushōka* should not extend a helping hand to under-enrolled universities."[69] This view echoed the position of the Ministry of Finance that stated, "providing subsidies in the absence of reform activity . . . extends a lifeline to the management of universities that are unattractive to potential students."[70] The same concern was raised in the Council for Designing the 100-Year Life Society, a policy advisory body under the direct leadership of Prime Minister Abe whose members repeatedly stressed the need to impose eligibility standards on universities as well as students.[71]

From a more forward-looking perspective, the rollout of *mushōka* was an opportunity to push ahead with long-overdue university reforms. Epitomizing a common refrain in political manifestoes, Asada Hitoshi of the Japan Innovation Party asserted that "as well as cultivating talent for Japan's future, we want to reform universities into competitive entities."[72] Prominent business consultant Ohmae Kenichi took a similar stance, highlighting a whole list of fundamental reforms that must precede *mushōka* to address Japan's human capital needs.[73] And corporate Japan weighed in with strong arguments for enhancing universities' talent development functions in tandem with *mushōka*.[74]

Can We Help Students and Reform Universities?

Saving students and families from financial distress, saving universities from substandard students, saving public funds from wastage on undesirable universities—*mushōka* needed to be a multifunctional savior. In June 2018, the Abe government released a full-fledged higher education *mushōka* proposal for implementation in 2020.[75] The minutiae and form of this proposal clearly demonstrated an effort to achieve multi-functionality. Essentially, it is a system of tuition fee reductions and direct grants to cover basic living expenses for students from the lowest income bracket. Eligibility is linked to household income and phased out completely at the middle-income tier. The awarded amounts are to be differentiated depending on criteria such as whether students attend a national or local public versus a private university—the latter tending to have higher fees—or whether they live with parents or independently. The package represented a major budgetary commitment in the order of 760 billion yen per year,[76] to be funded through a consumption tax increase.[77]

The package has clearly been crafted to meet a number of political goals. It is framed heavily in terms of affordability and equal access to education, making it part of the LDP coalition's broader claim to build "a country overflowing with opportunities for everyone."[78] Prime Minister Abe himself had repeatedly explained the need to "create a society in which everyone with ambition can advance to vocational college or university, no matter how financially disadvantaged their family background."[79] These messages resonated strongly with other moves by Abe such as the promise during his first stint as prime minster (2006–2007) to provide people with opportunities to bounce back (*sai charenji*) from failure in the mainstream education and employment systems and the reform of national university entrance examinations to evaluate a wider range of twenty-first-century attributes.[80] Such moves seem calculated to mediate the public's fears and frustrations with the rise of the gap society. Nonetheless, the *mushōka* policy has also been subsumed within Abe's broader banner of the "human resource development revolution" (*hitozukuri kakumei*), positioning it as an investment in human capital in line with the demands of business and industry.

But the *mushōka* package is also a university reform initiative, seeking to address many of the contradictions advanced in the impoverished student narrative. Students are held to certain standards: initial eligibility is limited to those demonstrating motivation to enter university (*shingaku iyoku*); ongoing checks of credits, attendance, and grades are required, with a system of warnings and then disqualification in cases of underperformance. Universities, meanwhile, are subject to requirements regarding academic staffing, external input into university management, visibility of curriculum and assessment standards, and the disclosure of financial information. These ideas evoke the basic neoliberal model of university competition, public accountability, and alignment with the needs of industry and the market. The education ministry is responsible for administering the requirements and envisions a mechanism for disqualifying universities from the system in cases of ongoing poor financial performance and severe under-enrollment.[81]

Mushōka is thus being designed to help weed out the symptoms of contradiction in the higher education landscape: unmotivated, incompetent students and underperforming institutions. Because it is to be managed by the education ministry, the implementation of the package is also an opportunity for further indirect steering of the university sector, even as the deregulatory façade remains. It represents a compromise between the overarching and politically viable goal of rescuing the impoverished student and the equally pressing, but popularly less compelling, need to address other long-standing contradictions in the university crisis.

Mixing student welfare with university reform, however, may generate further contradictions of its own. The response from universities themselves has been overwhelmingly negative. A survey of national university leaders found 70 percent opposed and only 10 percent actively in favor of the proposed scheme, with many questioning the rationale for conflating the disparate themes of student financial aid and university quality assurance.[82] The President of Kyoto University denounced it as "meddling in university affairs" while the President of the University of Tsukuba labeled the use of *mushōka* as a pretext for further regulation "an exceedingly crude approach."[83] Private university leaders voiced similar concerns. The president of the Federation of Japanese Private Colleges and Universities Associations, while acknowledging the argument that poorly run universities should not automatically be propped up by government, bemoaned the imposition of standards unconnected with educational quality and the risk that the scheme would create an artificial split between "ministerially endorsed universities" and others.[84]

Even in the limited form under discussion at the time of writing, *mushōka* furnished yet another mechanism for state management and, at the same time, provided a pretext for abandoning those institutions which continue to underperform by disqualifying them from *mushōka* coverage. However, it is hardly the kind of "decisive intervention" required to end a Crisis, and instead seems more in the class of "responses that directly address the crisis as discursively constituted and mediated (as narrative) without necessarily resolving the contradictions and failures that sustain such a narrative."[85] The fundamental contradictions in the configuration of Japan's higher education system that produced the impoverished student and precarious university narratives remain in place.

Conclusion

Policy interventions precipitate crises; crises necessitate further interventions. A laissez-faire stance on the expansion of the university sector, combined with structural reforms that reframed a student welfare policy as a consumer credit business, led to the narrative of the impoverished student, which necessitated intervention in the form of *mushōka*. Emphasis on universities' productivity and competitiveness in the neoliberal era generated unprecedented pressure for research performance and led to more cases of academic misconduct. Acknowledgment of the stifling impact of rote learning led to a relaxation of the school curriculum, which in turn prompted the new narrative of students being unprepared for higher education. This cycle is both paradoxical and predictable. However, it can also be politically expedient. The academic achievement debate, for example, opened a window for further intervention in the school curriculum, including advancement of a neoconservative agenda not directly related to the problem at hand: a political dividend from a policy failure, as it were. *Mushōka* may be following the same pattern. A response to contradictions generated by two decades of neoliberal policymaking, the adoption of *mushōka* has actually bolstered the Abe/LDP human capital development agenda. It has proven electorally palatable, and even shown potential to be mobilized as a popular appendage to less attractive neoconservative proposals for constitutional revision. Other contributions to this volume identify similar cases in which victims of neoliberal reform have been mobilized in support of Abe's broader vision for transformation of the postwar state.

This analysis of university crisis narratives also revealed the mutability of students as a crisis subject. Their positioning varied from being a moral and academic hazard for a well-established system to being unfortunate victims of structural contradictions resulting from massification, demographic change, and deregulation. We are left wondering who exactly needs saving from whom. This problem is in a sense unavoidable in that students' issues are seen as *symptomatic* of educational crisis but not *constitutive* thereof. Interventions directed primarily at the student cannot actually resolve contradictions in the education system on their own; they are at best piecemeal and incoherent, and potentially just as disrupting as the original contradictions. Resolution is thus sought through a shift of emphasis from individual to institution—in the case of *mushōka*, from students in need of financial support to universities in need of quality enhancement—which, in turn, can generate new incongruities and call into question the logic of the intervention. And once the university becomes the primary subject of the narrative, the sense of stakeholdership is diminished, public opinion is difficult to capture beyond the voyeuristic level, and political momentum is lost. The use of the student as narrative subject therefore sustains the "relative autonomy of crisis narratives and crisis 'solutions' from the contradictions out of which they develop."[86] The conclusion, admittedly gloomy, is that the higher education system is likely to remain in small-c crisis mode indefinitely.

Notes

1. Colin Hay, "Narrating Crisis: The Discursive Construction of the 'Winter of Discontent,'" *Sociology* 30, no. 2 (1996): 253–277; Colin Hay, "Crisis and the Structural Transformation of the State: Interrogating the Process of Change," *British Journal of Politics and International Relations* 1, no. 3 (1999): 317–344.

2. Hay, "Crisis," 339.

3. Martin Trow, "Problems in the Transition from Elite to Mass Higher Education," in *Policies for Higher Education*, ed. Organisation for Economic Cooperation and Development (OECD) (Paris: OECD Publishing, 1973), 55–101.

4. MEXT, *Kōtō kyōiku no shōrai kōsō ni kansuru kiso dēta* [Basic Data on Future of Higher Education], Tokyo, April 11, 2017, http://www.mext.go.jp/b_menu/shingi/chukyo/chukyo4/gijiroku/__icsFiles/afieldfile/2017/04/13/1384455_02_1.pdf.

Unless otherwise stated, all online sources were accessed and available on October 15, 2020.

5. MEXT, *Gakkō kihon chōsa kekka no gaiyō* [School Basic Survey Summary of Results], Tokyo, 2018, http://www.mext.go.jp/b_menu/toukei/chousa01/kihon/kekka/1268046.htm; MEXT, *Shiritsu daigaku no keiei jōkyō ni tsuite* [Operating Conditions in Private Universities], Tokyo, 2018, http://www.mext.go.jp/component/a_menu/education/detail/__icsFiles/afieldfile/2018/02/16/1401001_7_1.pdf.

6. For an overview of Japanese private higher education in comparative perspective, see chapter 2 of Jeremy Breaden and Roger Goodman, *Family-Run Universities in Japan: Sources of Inbuilt Resilience in the Face of Demographic Pressure, 1992–2030* (Oxford: Oxford University Press, 2020).

7. See Chiavacci, this volume.

8. Japan Student Services Organization (JASSO), *Shōgakukin jigyō kanren shiryō* [Materials on the Scholarship Program], Tokyo, 2017, http://www.mext.go.jp/b_menu/shingi/chousa/koutou/069/gijiroku/__icsFiles/afieldfile/2016/02/23/1367261_7.pdf.

9. Kobayashi Masayuki, *Katei no keizai jōkyō/shakai jōkyō ni kansuru jittai haaku/bunseki oyobi gakuseitō no keizaiteki shien no arikata ni kansuru chōsa kenkyū hōkokusho* [Report of Survey Research on Economic and Social Conditions and Approaches to Financial Support for Students] (Tokyo: MEXT and University of Tokyo, March 2017), http://www.mext.go.jp/component/a_menu/education/detail/__icsFiles/afieldfile/2017/11/29/1398333_1.pdf.

10. These loans are known in Japanese as *shōgakukin* or scholarships, a rather misleading term that arguably contributes to the problems examined later in this chapter. Data related to this loan program are taken from JASSO, *Shōgakukin*, unless noted otherwise.

11. MEXT, *Shiritsu daigaku no keiei jōkyō ni tsuite* [Operating Conditions in Private Universities], Tokyo, 2018, http://www.mext.go.jp/component/a_menu/education/detail/__icsFiles/afieldfile/2018/02/16/1401001_7_1.pdf.

12. See, for example, Shimano Kiyoshi, *Abunai daigaku, kieru daigaku 2018ban* [Universities that Are in Trouble, Universities that Will Disappear—2018 Edition] (Tokyo: Yell Books, 2017); Shūkan Tōyō Keizai, *Hontō ni tsuyoi daigaku* [Truly Strong Universities] (Tokyo: Tōyō Keizai Shimpōsha, 2017).

13. For a general overview, see Ikuo Amano, *The Origins of Japanese Credentialism* (Melbourne: Trans Pacific Press, 2011).

14. See, for example, the surveys cited in pages 41–44 of Christian Galan, "From Youth to Non-adulthood in Japan: The Role of Education," in *Being Young in Super-Aging Japan: Formative Events and Cultural Reactions*, ed. Patrick Heinrich and Christian Galan (London: Routledge, 2018), 32–50.

15. JASSO, *Shōgakukin*.

16. Motohisa Kaneko, "Incorporation of National Universities in Japan: An Evaluation Six Years On," in *University Governance and Reform: Policy, Fads, and*

Experience in International Perspective, ed. Hans G. Schuetze, William Bruneau, and Garnet Grosjean (New York: Palgrave Macmillan, 2012), 179–95; Aya Yoshida, "The State and Private Higher Education in Japan: The End of Egalitarian Policy," in *Higher Education and the State: Changing Relationships in Europe and East Asia* (Oxford: Symposium Books, 2013), 109–216.

17. Wieczorek, this volume.

18. Well-known examples include Kawanari Yō, *Daigaku hōkai!* [University Collapse!] (Tokyo: Takarajimasha, 2000); Nakamura Chūichi, *Daigaku tōsan* [University Bankruptcy] (Tokyo: Tōyō Keizai Shimpōsha, 2002).

19. Ogawa Yō, *Kieyuku "genkai daigaku": Shiritsu daigaku teiinware no kōzō* [Vanishing "Universities on the Brink": The Framework of Insufficient Enrolment at Private Universities] (Tokyo: Hakusuisha, 2016).

20. Shiritsu daigakutō no shinkō ni kansuru kentō kaigi [Working Group on the Advancement of Private Universities], *Shiritsu daigakutō no shinkō ni kansuru kentō kaigi giron no matome* [Summary of Discussions in the Working Group on the Advancement of Private Universities], Tokyo, May 15, 2017, http://www.mext.go.jp/b_menu/shingi/chousa/koutou/073/gaiyou/1386778.htm.

21. Nicky Phillips, "The Slow Decline of Japanese Research in 5 Charts," *Nature Index* (March 27, 2017), https://www.natureindex.com/news-blog/the-slow-decline-of-japanese-research-in-five-charts; Hiramatsu Sawami, "Naze Tōdai wa 'sekai daigaku rankingu' ga hikui no ka" [Why the University of Tokyo is so Low in the "World University Rankings"], *Tōyō Keizai Online*, October 23, 2016, https://toyokeizai.net/articles/-/141598.

22. David McNeill, "In Japan, Research Scandal Prompts Questions," *Chronicle of Higher Education*, June 14, 2014, https://www.chronicle.com/article/In-Japan-Research-Scandal/147417/?cid=gn.

23. See, for example, Akira Arimoto, "Declining Academic Autonomy Under Neoliberal Reforms: Lessons from Japanese Higher Education After Incorporation," in *Higher Education Governance in East Asia: Transformations under Neoliberalism*, ed. Jung Cheol Shin (Singapore: Springer, 2018), 261–71; Ichiko Fuyuno, "What Price Will Science Pay for Austerity?," *Nature* 543 (March 22, 2017): S10–15, https://doi.org/10.1038/543S10a.

24. Uchimura Naoyuki, "Heisei no kagaku kenkyū to kagaku gijutsu seisaku no nejireta kankei" [Japanese Government's Science Push: Help or Hindrance?], *Nippon.Com*, January 24, 2019, https://www.nippon.com/ja/in-depth/d00464/.

25. MEXT, *Support for Internationalization of Universities*, n.d., http://www.mext.go.jp/en/policy/education/highered/title02/detail02/1373875.htm.

26. For examples in English, see Beverley A. Yamamoto, "The Internationalization of Japanese Higher Education," in *Japanese Education in a Global Age: Sociological Reflections and Future Directions (Education in the Asia-Pacific Region: Issues, Concerns and Prospects)*, ed. Akiyoshi Yonezawa, Yuto Kitamura, Beverley

Yamamoto, and Tomoko Tokunaga (Singapore: Springer, 2018), 221–239; Miki Tanikawa, "Japanese Universities Go Global, but Slowly," *New York Times*, July 29, 2012, https://www.nytimes.com/2012/07/30/world/asia/30iht-educlede30.html.

27. This point comes through most clearly in the analysis of Akiyoshi Yonezawa, one of the most prolific authors on Japanese universities in English. See, for example, Akiyoshi Yonezawa, "The Internationalization of Japanese Higher Education: Policy Debates and Realities," in *Higher Education in the Asia-Pacific: Strategic Responses to Globalization*, ed. Simon Marginson, Sarjit Kaur, and Erlenawati Sawir (New York: Springer, 2011), 329–342.

28. Sota Kato, "Getting to the Root of Amakudari: Sweeping Reform Needed to Close the Revolving Door," Tokyo Foundation for Policy Research, June 13, 2017, http://www.tokyofoundation.org/en/articles/2017/getting-to-root-of-amakudari.

29. Aurelia George Mulgan, "Scandals Starting to Stick to the Abe Administration," *East Asia Forum,* June 21, 2017, https://www.eastasiaforum.org/2017/06/21/scandals-are-starting-to-stick-to-the-abe-administration/.

30. See, for example, Ikuo Amano, *Kōtō kyōiku no Nihon-teki kōzō* [Structure of Higher Education in Japan] (Tokyo: Tamagawa Daigaku Shuppanbu, 1986); Ikuo Amano, *Daigaku kaikaku: Chitsujo no hōkai to saihen* [University Reform: Collapse and Reconfiguration of the Order] (Tokyo: University of Tokyo Press, 2004); Kazuyuki Kitamura, *Daigaku wa umarekawareru ka* [Can Universities Reinvent Themselves?] (Tokyo: Chūō Kōron Shinsha, 2002).

31. See, for example, Ivan P. Hall, *Cartels of the Mind: Japan's Intellectual Closed Shop* (New York: W.W. Norton & Co, 1998); Brian J. McVeigh, *Japanese Higher Education as Myth* (London: Routledge, 2002); Howard Newby, Thomas Weko, David Breneman, Thomas Johanneson, and Peter Maassen, *OECD Reviews of Tertiary Education: Japan* (Paris: Organization for Economic Cooperation and Development, 2009), https://www.oecd.org/education/skills-beyond-school/42280329.pdf.

32. For example, Elizabeth Stigger, Marian Wang, David Laurence, and Anna Bordilovskaya, *Internationalization within Higher Education: Perspectives from Japan* (Singapore: Springer, 2018); John Mock, Hiroaki Kawamura, and Naeko Naganuma, eds., *The Impact of Internationalization on Japanese Higher Education: Is Japanese Education Really Changing?*, Global Perspectives on Higher Education (Rotterdam: Sense Publishers, 2016).

33. Hay, "Crisis," 330.

34. Ibid., 327.

35. See Mason and Maslow, this volume.

36. Gita Steiner-Khamsi, "Reterritorializing Educational Import," in *Fabricating Europe: The Formation of an Education Space*, ed. António Nóvoa and Martin Lawn (Dordrecht: Springer Netherlands, 2002), 70, cited in Keita Takayama, "A Nation at Risk Crosses the Pacific: Transnational Borrowing of the U.S. Crisis Discourse

in the Debate on Education Reform in Japan," *Comparative Education Review* 51, no. 4 (2007): 423–46, here 425.

37. Takehiko Kariya, "Meritocracy, Modernity, and the Completion of Catch-Up: Problems and Paradoxes," in *Japanese Education in a Global Age: Sociological Reflections and Future Directions*, ed. Akiyoshi Yonezawa, Yuto Kitamura, Beverley Yamamoto, and Tomoko Tokunaga (Singapore: Springer, 2018), 302.

38. For detailed analysis of this crisis in English, see Ryoko Tsuneyoshi, "The New Japanese Educational Reforms and the Achievement 'Crisis' Debate," *Educational Policy* 18, no. 2 (2004): 364–94; Takayama, "A Nation at Risk."

39. See, for example, Iwakawa Naoki and Shiomi Toshiyuki, eds., *Gakuryoku o tou* [Questioning Scholastic Ability] (Tokyo: Sōdo Bunka, 2001); Katō Kōji and Takaura Katsuyoshi, *Gakuryoku teikaron hihyō: Kodomo ga "ikiru" gakuryoku to wa nani ka* [Critiquing the Discourse of Declining Scholastic Ability: Defining scholastic ability for children to "live" (Nagoya: Reimei Shobo, 2001).

40. David C. Berliner and Bruce J. Biddle, *The Manufactured Crisis: Myths, Fraud, and the Attack on America's Public Schools* (Reading, MA: Addison-Wesley, 1995).

41. A prime example of political mobilization of this post-bubble concern is former education minister Nakayama Nariaki's 2004 manifesto, *Yomigaere, Nippon!* (Arise, Japan!), which warns that Japan is becoming an antiquated irrelevancy in the globalized world, argues that the fundamental solution lies in developing Japan's human capital, and outlines the kind of rigorous education system required to do so, http://www.mext.go.jp/b_menu/shingi/chukyo/chukyo3/002/siryo/__icsFiles/afieldfile/2014/10/15/1265462_002.pdf.

42. OECD, *The Knowledge-Based Economy* (Paris: Organization for Economic Cooperation and Development, 1996).

43. "2006-nen mondai: Kōdai renkei tasūha seito e no shiten hitsuyō" [The 2006 Problem: High Schools and Universities Need to Work Together to Deal with Diverse Students], *Yomiuri Shimbun*, November 8, 2004.

44. Nishimura Kazuo, ed., *Gakuryoku teika ga kuni o horobosu* [Scholastic Ability Decline Will Drive Japan to Ruin] (Tokyo: Nihon Keizai Shimbunsha, 2001); Tachibana Takashi, *Tōdaisei wa baka ni natta ka* [Have University of Tokyo Students Dumbed Down?] (Tokyo: Bungei Shunju, 2004).

45. Takayama, "A Nation at Risk," 423–424.

46. Yuko Kawai, "Neoliberalism, Nationalism, and Intercultural Communication: A Critical Analysis of a Japan's Neoliberal Nationalism Discourse under Globalization," *Journal of International and Intercultural Communication* 2, no. 1 (2009): 16–43.

47. David C. Berliner and Bruce J. Biddle, *The Manufactured Crisis: Myths, Fraud, and the Attack on America's Public Schools* (Reading, MA: Addison-Wesley, 1995); Takayama, "A Nation at Risk."

48. Hay, "Crisis," 337, emphasis in original.

49. Stuart Hall, "Encoding/Decoding," in *Culture, Media, Language*, ed. Stuart Hall, Dorothy Hobson, Andrew Lowe, and Paul Willis (London: Unwin Hyman), cited in Hay, "Crisis," 267.

50. For in-depth treatment of these issues, see Roger Goodman, Yuki Imoto, and Tuukka Toivonen, eds., *A Sociology of Japanese Youth: From Returnees to NEETs* (London: Routledge, 2012).

51. Miwa Yoshiko, "Seikatsu hogo setai no hinkon daigakusei, shakkin/arubaito zuke no kurayami" [Impoverished Students from Households Receiving Welfare Aid], *Diamond Online*, May 26, 2017, https://diamond.jp/articles/-/129477; Yasuda Kenji, "Shōgakukin de 'oya ni shiokuri' o suru gakusei ga iru: Aratana hinkon o umu 'jiriki shingaku'" [Students Supporting Their Parents with Money from Their Scholarships], *Sankei Biz*, October 15, 2017, https://www.sankeibiz.jp/econome/news/171015/ecc1710151300001-n1.htm.

52. Kanda Keiichi, "Gakuhi no tame ni 'baitozuke' to naru hinkondaigakusei" [Impoverished Students Working Free Time to Pay Tuition Fees], *Nikkan Spa*, June 28, 2016, https://nikkan-spa.jp/1141049.

53. Maita Toshihiko, "Seikatsuku kara 'burakku baito' ni oikomareru Nihon no gakusei" [Japanese Students Taking On Exploitative Part-Time Jobs to Make Ends Meet], *Newsweek*, November 25, 2015, https://www.newsweekjapan.jp/stories/business/2015/11/post-4152_1.php.

54. Nakamura Atsuhiko, "Baishun de gakuhi o kasegu hinkon joshi daisei no kanashii genjitsu" [The Sad Reality of Female Students Engaging in Prostiution to Pay University Tuition Fees], *Tōyō Keizai Online*, April 12, 2017, https://toyokeizai.net/articles/-/166937. Parallels could be made here with coverage of the phenomenon of "compensated dating" by Japanese high school girls in the 1990s. See David Leheny, *Think Global, Fear Local: Sex, Violence, and Anxiety in Contemporary Japan* (Ithaca, NY: Cornell University Press, 2006).

55. See JASSO, *Shōgakukin.*

56. National Council for Workers' Welfare, *Shōgakukin ni kansuru ankēto chōsa kekka (gairyokuban)* [Survey Results on Scholarship Questionnaire], Tokyo, February 29, 2016, http://www.rofuku.net/network/activity_img/tottori20160301101822.pdf.

57. National Federation of University Co-operative Associations, "Dai53kai gakusei seikatsu jittai chōsa no gaiyō hōkoku" [Outline of 53rd Survey on the Conditions of Student Life], Tokyo, 2017, https://www.univcoop.or.jp/press/life/report.html.

58. Iwashige Yoshiharu, *"Shōgakukin" jigoku* ["Scholarship" Hell] (Tokyo: Shogakukan, 2017).

59. Sekita Shinya, "Shōgakukin ga 'hinkon bijinesu' to iwareru konpon gen'in" [The Real Reasons Why Scholarships are Called "Poverty Business"], *Tōyō Keizai Online*, January 26, 2016, https://toyokeizai.net/articles/-/102020.

60. JASSO, *Shōgakukin.*

61. MEXT, *Kōtō kyōiku shingaku sapōto puran* [Higher Education Advancement Support Plan], Tokyo, 2016, https://www.mext.go.jp/b_menu/houdou/28/12/__ics-Files/afieldfile/2016/12/26/1380888_1_1.pdf.

62. Liberal Democratic Party, "Kōkō jugyōryō mushōka no mondaiten" [Problems with Regard to Tuition Free High Schools], Tokyo, March 16, 2010, https://www.jimin.jp/news/policy/recapture/130395.html.

63. "Dōshō imu no kyōiku mushōka" [Living in Different Worlds of Tuition Free Education], *Nihon Keizai Shimbun*, February 17, 2017, https://www.nikkei.com/article/DGXLZO13019730X10C17A2PP8000/.

64. "Shushō '2020-nen, atarashii kempō no shokō o'" [Prime Minister Calls for 'New Constitution in 2020'], *Asahi Shimbun*, May 3, 2019, https://www.asahi.com/articles/ASM534RQ3M53UTFK005.html.

65. Nakagawa Masayuki, "Gakusei no shakkin 1-chōen ga utsusu kono kuni no yugami" [The Country's Distortion Seen in the One Trillion Yen Student Debt], *Nikkei Bijinesu Online*, March 26, 2015, http://business.nikkeibp.co.jp/article/report/20150325/279151/.

66. Sankei Digital, "Kyōiku mushōka 'Gakusei zen'in taishō ni wa hantai' vs. 'Kibōsha wa shingaku o kanō ni'" [Tuition Waivers: "Against Tuition Waiver for All Students" versus "Allowing Students to Advance to Higher Education"], *Sankei News*, October 14, 2017. https://www.sankei.com/premium/news/171014/prm1710140012-n1.html.

67. Asabina Nao, "Kōtō kyōiku mushōka ga maneku saidai no heigai wa nani ka" [What are the Biggest Obstacles caused by Tuition Free Higher Education?], *Tōyō Keizai Online*, 15 March 2018, https://toyokeizai.net/articles/-/212474; see also Editorial, "Make Education Free of Charge?" *Japan Times*, May 14, 2017, https://www.japantimes.co.jp/opinion/2017/05/14/editorials/make-education-free-charge/.

68. Sekita Shinya, "Dokuji shūkei! Zendaigaku shōgakukin entairitsu ranking" [Independent Survey! Scholarship Delinquency Ranking of all Universities], *Tōyō Keizai Online*, January 26, 2017, https://toyokeizai.net/articles/-/168512.

69. "Kadai ōi kyōiku/hoiku no mushōka" [The Many Problems of Free Education/Child Care], *Nihon Keizai Shimbun*, June 14, 2018, https://www.nikkei.com/article/DGXKZO31740600U8A610C1EA1000/.

70. University Journal Editorial Committee, "Abe seiken no daigaku kyōiku zenmen mushōka, zaimushō ga hantai o hyōmei" [Finance Ministry Expresses Opposition Against Abe Government's Plan for Free University Education], *University Journal Online*, November 6, 2017, https://univ-journal.jp/16667/.

71. Prime Minister of Japan and His Cabinet, Council for Designing the 100-Year Life Society, Meeting Minutes of the Council for Designing the 100-Year Life Society, Tokyo, 2018, https://www.kantei.go.jp/jp/singi/jinsei100nen/.

72. Sankei Digital, "Kyōiku mushōka."

73. Ohmae Kenichi, "Daigaku kyōiku no mushōka ni watashi ga hantai suru riyū" [Why I Oppose Tuition-Free University Education], *President*, December 14, 2017, https://president.jp/articles/-/23607.

74. " 'Shiritsu daigaku saihen kikō' o Keizai Dōyūkai ga teigen: Keiei kaikaku semaru" [Japan Association of Corporate Executives Promotes Plan for Agency to Restructure Private Universities: Need for Corporate Reforms], *Kyōiku Shimbun,* June 4, 2018, https://www.kyobun.co.jp/news/20180604_01/.

75. Cabinet Office, "Basic Policy on Economic and Fiscal Management and Reform 2018," Tokyo, 2018, https://www5.cao.go.jp/keizai-shimon/kaigi/cabinet/ 2018/2018_basicpolicies_en.pdf.

76. By way of comparison, the national government's overall annual spending on higher education prior to the *mushōka* package is in the order of 2 trillion yen.

77. "Kyōiku mushōka ni 1.5chōen: Seido no gutaisaku ryōshō" [1.5 Trillion Yen for Tuition Free Education: Agreement Reached on Concrete Institutional Measures], *Nihon Keizai Shimbun,* February 28, 2018, digital edition, https://www. nikkei.com/article/DGXMZO39488670Y8A221C1MM0000.

78. Prime Minister of Japan and His Cabinet, "Basic Policy (Cabinet Decision on November 1, 2017)," Tokyo, 2017, https://japan.kantei.go.jp/98_abe/decisions/ 2017/basic_policy.html.

79. Prime Minister of Japan and His Cabinet, "Press Conference by Prime Minister Shinzo Abe," September 25, 2017, https://japan.kantei.go.jp/97_abe/ statement/201709/_00011.html.

80. MEXT, *Daigaku nyūgakusha sembatsu kaikaku ni tsuite* [On University Entrance Exams], n.d., http://www.mext.go.jp/a_menu/koutou/koudai/detail/1397731. htm.

81. MEXT, *Kōtō kyōiku mushōka no seido no gutaika ni muketa hōshin no gaiyō* [Outline on Directions towards Institutional Implementation of Tuition-Free Education], Tokyo, 2018, http://www.mext.go.jp/a_menu/koutou/hutankeigen/ detail/__icsFiles/afieldfile/2018/12/28/1412286_001.pdf.

82. "Kōtō kyōiku mushōka seifu no yōken 7wari hantai: Kokuritsudai 'suji toorazu' " [70 Percent Oppose Government Requirements for Tuition Free Education: Public Universities say Requirements are "Illogical"], *Mainichi Shimbun,* May 17, 2018, https://mainichi.jp/articles/20180517/k00/00m/040/162000c.

83. "Kyōiku mushōka no jōken 'daigaku jichi e no kainyū' kokuritsu daigakuchōra ga hihyō" [National University Presidents Criticize Conditions for Tuition Free Education as "Meddling in Universities' Affairs"], *Asahi Shimbun,* January 27, 2018, https:// www.asahi.com/articles/DA3S13332400.html.

84. "Daigaku mushōka 'yōken' ni hanpatsu" [Opposing "requirements" for tuition-free university education], *Mainichi Shimbun,* February 19, 2018, https:// mainichi.jp/articles/20180219/k00/00m/040/133000c.

85. Hay, "Crisis," 337.

86. Ibid.

Part II

Narrating Japan's Political and Economic Crises

Chapter 4

A Crisis of Democracy

Civil Society and Energy Politics Before and
After the Fukushima Nuclear Disaster

KOICHI HASEGAWA

Introduction

In the aftermath of the March 11, 2011, earthquake and tsunami, the
Fukushima Daiichi nuclear power station's units Nos. 1, 2, and 3, and a
spent fuel pool in unit No. 4, lost their cooling capabilities. Subsequently,
hydrogen gas, which had been released from the melted cores and filled
the reactor buildings, caused explosions in units Nos. 1, 3, and 4. The
reactor core of unit No. 2 was also seriously damaged. Large quantities of
radioactive materials were released, and spread across Japan and beyond. In
terms of severity, the Fukushima nuclear disaster is second only to the 1986
Chernobyl disaster.[1] As such, it raised important questions for policymakers
and scholars in Japan and the world. Among the most important is the
question of why Japan, despite its confidence in technological development
and safety standards, failed to prevent such a disaster to occur. The multiple
nuclear meltdowns at the Fukushima site suggest that Japanese society had
failed to draw and implement lessons from the 1979 Three Mile Island
(TMI) and 1986 Chernobyl accidents as well as accidents in nuclear facilities
in Japan, including the so-called JCO criticality accident at the Tokaimura
plant in Ibaraki prefecture in 1999. They also imply that Japan had been

lacking effective regulatory measures for power companies and their nuclear power stations.

The Fukushima accident triggered deep anxieties in Japan. Then Prime Minister Kan Naoto declared it the "most severe crisis" (*mottomo kibishii kiki*) that his country had faced since defeat in World War II.[2] The nuclear meltdowns have not only undermined confidence in Japan's technological leadership and superior safety standards; as the incident revealed the crony networks among policymakers, regulators, and industry, and the civil society's inability to hold them accountable, the Fukushima accident has also signified a crisis of postwar Japanese democracy. Civil society in the form of local networks proved critical in enhancing communities' disaster resilience and greatly supported reconstruction efforts.[3] However, these networks failed to prevent the accident and to shape a crisis narrative that would have allowed for a "decisive intervention" to fundamentally change energy policy away from the reliance on nuclear (and fossil) power generation.[4]

In this chapter I revisit Japan's failing nuclear energy policy system and ask to what extent the Fukushima nuclear disaster has initiated change in Japan's energy policy. Essentially, what this analysis shows is that at the core of the crisis was a malfunctioning political system that lacked effective regulatory oversight. To be sure, the sociological problems that have resulted from this crisis and the lessons learned from this incident have been studied in great detail.[5] Yet, if we compare Japan's political culture and civil society with those of countries such as Germany, Taiwan, and South Korea, all of which have operated large fleets of nuclear power stations or are similarly exposed to the risks of earthquakes, Japan's traditional conservative political culture, and the relative weakness of its civil society, stand out as critical factors causing the Fukushima accident. In fact, as I will show in this chapter, in postwar Japan, the influence of independent critical voices at the national level has remained weak in the discourse on nuclear energy policy, while overall nuclear industry regulation has been insufficient. A prime factor in creating such a structure was the strong social pressure that muted opposition to nuclear power politics prior to March 2011. It was only after Japan witnessed the Fukushima calamity that antinuclear citizen protests began to spread. This indicates that perceptions of a social and political crisis propelled the emergence of a new political culture in which civil society challenges dominant narratives of energy security. And yet, the impact of civil society on policy-making remains limited at the national level. While civil society succeeded in causing significant delays in restarting Japan's nuclear power units, the administrations of Abe Shinzō and his successor, Suga Yoshihide, remained committed to nuclear energy and the export of nuclear power plant technology as a vital part of their governments' economic growth strategies.

The Fukushima Accident and Its Lessons

The word "Fukushima" consists of "fuku," which uses a character meaning "happy," and "shima," which uses a character meaning "land." This once happy and beautiful land abruptly became "the land of tragedy," reminiscent of Hiroshima and Nagasaki, where atomic bombs had been dropped in 1945. Peaceful family lives in homelands with fertile farmlands were suddenly destroyed by this nuclear accident. As such, the Fukushima nuclear accident is a historical incident marked by five major characteristics. First, it is the most severe accident of a nuclear power station, a complex disaster triggered by natural events in form of a large earthquake and tsunami. It is the first example of a "combined earthquake and nuclear power disaster" (*genpatsu shinsai*), of which the seismologist Ishibashi Katsuhiko had been warning since 1997.[6] Second, the four reactors were simultaneously endangered. A small number of workers had to operate under intense radiation exposure and very unstable conditions, in darkness due to the loss of electric power supply and under the impact of numerous seismic aftershocks. The Democratic Party of Japan (DPJ)–led government of Prime Minister Kan secretly estimated that in "a worst-case scenario" in which control over the situation would be lost entirely, all ten reactors of the Daiichi station and the nearby Fukushima Daini station would be abandoned. Consequently, the evacuation zone would have to be enlarged to cover an area within a 170-kilometer radius, and the seriously contaminated zone would be expanded to an area within a 250-kilometer radius, which would include the Tokyo metropolitan area with its 30 million inhabitants. In this scenario, almost half of mainland Japan would be radioactively contaminated. Third, stable cooling of the reactor cores resumed only four months after the accident, and the uncontrolled situation of the reactors' meltdown continued for more than nine months. In comparison, the situation at the TMI nuclear accident in the United States in 1979 was stabilized within six days. Even in the case of the 1986 Chernobyl accident, the leaking of large amounts of radiation could be stopped within ten days.

Fourth, in June 2012, the number of evacuees peaked at approximately 160,000 people. Forced to leave their homes near the nuclear site, either as a result of government orders or due to individual concerns about the possible effects of radiation contamination on their own or their children's health, they resettled within Fukushima Prefecture or moved to other parts of Japan. As of November 2020, nine and a half years after the disaster, and although both the national and the prefectural governments have stressed the safety of the Fukushima ruin and urged "an early return," more than 29,000 people are staying outside the prefecture. Another 7,500 people remain displaced within Fukushima Prefecture.[7] But these official numbers of evacuees provided by the Reconstruction Agency may underestimate the actual number of victims. People who have left their homes and moved into newly built housing in urban areas like Iwaki or Koriyama city are no longer counted as evacuees because their new homes are not considered temporary. In addition, some of the victims are still separated from their families. Many cases include a husband living in some city within Fukushima Prefecture keeping his job, while his wife and children have moved outside of Fukushima Prefecture due to concerns about exposure to radiation. Even today, no one can estimate exactly when these families will be able to reunite. Thus, many are still skeptical about the effectiveness and "safety" propagated by the central government's official "early return policy." Farmers in highly contaminated areas hesitate to grow crops, and fishermen are still reluctant to resume their work. They are left in despair and resent the fumbling of the electric power company and the national and prefectural governments.

Finally, the Fukushima accident is the first severe accident of a nuclear power plant on a coastal site. The TMI and Chernobyl nuclear power stations were both located inland. In Fukushima, by contrast, large amounts of contaminated water leaked into the ocean. With the continued uncontrolled release, scientists have voiced concerns about serious long-term contamination of seawater and damages to the ecosystem. Hence, the Fukushima meltdowns are extremely costly—also in monetary terms: the economist Ōshima Kenichi estimated that the loss from this catastrophe would amount to at least to 13 trillion yen.[8]

In light of the above, the Fukushima accident provides many important lessons. Policy makers, regulators, plant operators, and the public should acknowledge that absolute safety does not exist in relation to nuclear power stations and that society constantly faces nuclear risks. The trigger for the Fukushima nuclear accident was a huge earthquake and tsunami. But all three investigative reports that analyzed the accident have identified human error as the main cause, with the plant operator Tokyo Electric Power Company (TEPCO) and the national government bearing the responsibility for the catastrophe. In other words, post-disaster investigations have collectively concluded that what TEPCO has framed as a chain of "unexpected situations" (*sōteigai*) must be considered a series of "underestimations" and malfunctions on the part of the company and national government.

First, TEPCO and the Japanese Nuclear Safety Commission (JNSC) underestimated the height of a possible tsunami. Even though scholars had offered ample scientific predications and warned of a 15.7-meter-high tsunami wave as early as May 2008, both TEPCO and JNSC chose to neglect such reports. Instead, based on a 2002 estimation, the Fukushima Daiichi station was designed to withstand a 5.7-meter tsunami. On March 11, 2011, a tsunami with a height of an estimated 14 to 15 meters hit and flooded the plant.

Second, Japanese power companies and government agencies did not anticipate the possibility of sustained power outages caused by large-scale natural disasters. However, such a blackout occurred and led to a fatal disruption of all cooling functions at the Fukushima station. Authorities expected that in the case of a station blackout, external power would be recovered within thirty minutes. This optimistic estimation, which was not grounded in scientific research, dismissed the need to prepare for the possibility of a lengthy power outage. Thus, no manuals existed that could have provided guidance for crisis management in the case of a station blackout or a severe natural disaster beyond normal expectations. In comparison, in the United States, officials are prepared for station blackouts in the context of counter-terrorism measures and can access large amounts of water for cooling the reactors. After the Fukushima nuclear disaster, the Israeli government, wary of terrorist attacks, immediately decided to abandon its plan to construct a nuclear power plant. The German government's decision to end nuclear energy production was based on reasons that included the possibility of a station blackout caused, for example, by the impact of an airplane crash. More importantly, and in stark contrast to Japan, where nuclear safety continued to be framed as a technological problem, German decision-makers conceded that ethical and moral considerations were in fact paramount.

Third, local governments only planned for contingencies with twenty-four-hour-long evacuation periods of those living within a ten-kilometer radius around nuclear facilities. Despite recommendations from the International Atomic Energy Agency, the Japanese government, prior to the Fukushima disaster, neglected calls to enlarge the evacuation zone to thirty kilometers.

This is because the government and electric power companies had not seriously considered the possibility of a severe accident in which radiation would be released outside of a plant. Hence, regulators and operators failed to sufficiently prepare for large-scale and sustained evacuation scenarios, and for the zone outside ten kilometers no evacuation manuals existed. On March 11, the government declared a "nuclear emergency," but initially limited the evacuation zone to a mere three kilometers, which it later expanded to a ten-kilometer radius. When reports of the unfolding crisis reached Tokyo in the evening on March 12, Prime Minister Kan issued instructions urging people within twenty kilometers of the station to evacuate. However, due to a shortage of (reliable) information about the spread of radiation and a malfunctioning government, many people near the site actually rushed to even more highly contaminated areas.

The Making of Japan's Nuclear Energy Crisis

Why, then, did authorities fail to prevent the nuclear disaster from happing? Why did successive governments fail to amend the risky pro-nuclear-energy policy prior to Fukushima? The post-Fukushima media and public discourse combined the three narratives of the "nuclear power village," a "powerless civil society," and a "vicious circle of state subsidies" into a crisis as meta-narrative of a dysfunctional state. In this section, I focus on these three components of Japan's state crisis meta-narrative.

The Nuclear Village and the Malfunctioning of Japan's Regulatory Agency

A powerful explanation for the crisis is the prevalence of decision-making dynamics plagued by what some have termed "groupthink."[9] The members of an "atomic circle" composed of elites working on and advocating nuclear power generation, often termed a "nuclear power village" (*genshiryoku mura*), share similar professional and institutional backgrounds and are insulated from outside opinion while not bound to clear decision-making rules. Thus, this power elite dismissed sound scientific advice on the possibility of severe damage. Misconduct, malfunctioning, and delay of emergency actions meant that a "normal accident"[10] could lead to a human disaster at the Fukushima nuclear power station. Ever since Japan's development of nuclear power since the 1950s, the "nuclear power village" has been fostering close ties among politicians, government, academics, industry, and the media. This nuclear village consists of people with shared and vested interests in promoting nuclear energy. Its members are recruited from the nuclear industry, engineers of companies like Toshiba, Hitachi, and Mitsubishi that build nuclear plants, people working for the nuclear power divisions of the electric power companies, scholars of nuclear engineering, officers of governmental nuclear regulators, officers of the Agency for Natural Resources and Energy within the Ministry of Economy, Trade and Industry (METI), and politicians. The media have been implicated as well. For Japan's mass media, power companies have served as an important financial source paying for advertisements. After all, TEPCO is still the largest private electric power company in the world. Before the accident, it maintained very strong political influence on the government, politicians, academics, and the media. In particular, politicians of the conservative Liberal Democratic Party (LDP)—the party in power from 1955 to 2009 (with a brief interlude in opposition between August 1993 and June 1994)—have backed pro-nuclear policy in exchange for political funds. Even the DPJ, in power between 2009 and 2012 (and dissolved in March 2016), relied on labor unions that had strong links to the power companies that dominated local economies as well as to manufacturers like Toshiba and Hitachi, as their main support bases.

Thus, prior to Fukushima, the DPJ-led government did not change the pro-nuclear energy policy established under past LDP administrations or dismantle the nuclear village. Hence, no "real independent regulator" in overseeing nuclear issues developed. In fact, the Fukushima disaster revealed that the Nuclear Safety Commission and Nuclear and Industrial Safety Agency did not act as strict regulators. Even after the disaster, both organizations followed the prompting of power companies like TEPCO and Kansai EPCO and the cabinet. For many years, these regulators were in fact controlled by electric companies, and by METI, which has mainly worked to promote nuclear energy as part of its economic and industrial planning policies.

In the aftermath of the Fukushima accident, three investigative reports traced the chain of events that led to this disaster. The first report of 2012 was produced by a national governmental committee, the Investigation Committee on the Accident at the Fukushima Nuclear Power Stations of Tokyo Electric Power Company (ICANPS).[11] The second report, also released in 2012, was commissioned by the National Diet of Japan Fukushima Nuclear Accident Independent Investigation Commission (NAIIC).[12] A third report was published by a private investigatory committee called the Independent Investigation Commission on the Fukushima Nuclear Accident in 2014.[13]

The NAIIC report focused on regulatory and other organizational factors leading to the Fukushima accident. Its authors concluded that the Japanese regulators "stuck to their belief of infallibility so much that they were reluctant to improve safety regulations, and thus their mindset was structurally ill-matched for running a safety culture"; moreover, the safety culture "existed in name only, and as a result, the notion of safety and security was 'sold off,' cheaply and irresponsibly, to the whole nation."[14] This report also criticized the regulatory agencies' lack of independence, transparency, and expertise by using the term "regulatory capture," which refers to a condition in which "regulatory authorities become the 'captives' of nuclear operators as they are devoted to maximizing the interest of the nuclear operators that are supposedly placed under them."[15]

Scholars have also noted the role of the "iron triangle" or "triple control machine" in Japanese politics.[16] For example, the iron triangle at work in brokering the construction of hydropower dams consists of construction companies, LDP politicians, and bureaucrats.[17] However, the atomic circle is a much more tight-knit group and the power of the electric companies, due to their territorial monopolies on electricity, is much more pervasive than that of the typical iron triangle.

Such structures are not unique to Japan. In slightly varied forms, and to various extents and degrees, they can also be observed in other countries. In South Korea, for instance, the term "nuclear mafia" is used, and there are references to "atomic circles" in both the United States and France. In her book *La vérité sur le nucléaire* (*The Truth about Nuclear Power*), the former French Minister of Environment, Corinne Lepage, emphasized the similarities between the systems promoting nuclear power in France and Japan.[18] Published in June 2011, in the immediate aftermath of the Fukushima accident, the book is very critical of France, a major nuclear country. The problems pointed out by Lepage resemble those Japan has been facing in light of the nuclear meltdowns. They include frequent accidents and other problems both big and small; an inadequate nuclear safety regulatory system; a cozy, corrupt relationship between the supervisors and the supervised; one-sided advertisements of the myth of nuclear safety; underestimates of risks; covert activities of the nuclear lobby; the arrogance of those involved in nuclear power generation; direct and indirect government financial support; nuclear sector exceptionalism; secrecy; concealment; information manipulation; sophism; lost trust; resistance to renewable energies; risks associated with old reactors; high costs of dismantling decommissioned reactors; difficulties disposing of radioactive wastes; and using government funds to make biased investments in nuclear power.

Thus, what becomes clear is that nuclear industries across countries share a similar political culture. In turn, the imposition of change to this industry faces similar structural obstacles. The nuclear industry sector deals with "sensitive technology" that can also be used for military purposes. This creates veils of secrecy and exclusiveness, reliance on national policies, and enormous infrastructure requirements necessitating massive investments, often directly tied to a political party's electoral prospects. With nuclear policy and regulation enmeshed in such structures, accidents similar to the one at Fukushima can occur at any nuclear power unit in the world.

Powerless Civil Society

Because the iron triangle of big business executives, politicians, and bureaucrats was dominant, and political opportunities to change the course of Japan's energy policy was almost non-existent, Japan's civil society organizations have not functioned as an effective "countervailing power."[19] This was despite their eagerness to criticize pro-nuclear policies and shed light on the inadequacies of those in power, while trying to halt the further construction and operations of nuclear facilities. Consequently, local voices from civil society in areas hosting nuclear power station stopped activism after the operations of the unit commenced. At the national level, critical voices also declined in the early 1990s. More recently, civil society organizations such as Citizen's Nuclear Information Center (CNIC), World Wildlife Fund (WWF) Japan, Greenpeace Japan, Friends of the Earth Japan, Citizens' Alliance for Saving the Atmosphere and the Earth (CASA), the Kiko Network, and the Institute for Sustainable Energy Policies (ISEP) have advanced policy proposals for an alternative future that does not rely on nuclear energy. However, prior to the Fukushima accident, the national government and utility companies tended to neglect proposals from these environmental non-governmental organizations (NGOs).

A comparison with Germany, where the conservative government of Angela Merkel responded to Fukushima by revising its energy policy and decided to abandon all of the country's nineteen nuclear units by the end of 2022, puts the limited influence of Japanese NGOs into stark relief. There, a decisive policy shift had long been advocated by strong environmental NGOs, including BUND (Friends of the Earth Germany), with its 480,000 members, and Greenpeace and the World Wide Fund for Nature (WWF), which both have a membership of around 200,000 in Germany. In contrast, WWF Japan has about 35,000 members and Greenpeace Japan only counts 4,500 supporters. In addition, in Germany so-called green institutes had developed policy proposals for the promotion of renewable energy. Well-known organizations in Germany including the Wuppertal Institute, which was established by the federal government, and the Eco Institute, a large private research organization, have greatly influenced Germany's nuclear power, renewable energy, and global warming protection policies. No such organizations exist in Japan. As a result, Japan has not seen influential counterproposals that would have challenged dominant narratives about the necessity and safety of nuclear energy and could have helped to overcome the entrenched legacy of the postwar industrial growth model.

Japan's national policy for promoting nuclear energy has remained unchanged since the mid-1960s. Accidents failed to alter the trajectory, as did political changes such as the historical transfer of ruling power in 2009. Mapped along the dimensions of political opportunity structure, resource mobilization by citizen groups, and issue framing that constitute national political culture, Japan's nuclear energy policy can thus be characterized as follows: Firstly, a centralized political system in the form of a long-standing one-party LDP dominance has limited accountability and responsiveness to citizens' concerns. Under this system, utilities maintained a territorial monopoly over the energy markets for several decades. Secondly, antinuclear groups and civil society are relatively muted and weak due to lacking resources, finances, and professional staff. Thirdly, the national government and electric power companies' successful issue framing of Japan as "extremely dependent upon external energy supplies" have shaped postwar Japan's nuclear energy policy and forestalled change. Accompanying this framing was a strong faith in advanced technologies. It is also noteworthy that policy planners have skillfully applied different language, using the Japanese word for "atomic" (*genshi*) for commercial and the term "nuclear" (*kaku*) for military applications.

The Vicious Circle of Providing Subsidies for Siting Nuclear Power Stations

In 1974, the cabinet of Prime Minister Tanaka Kakuei introduced a package of Three Laws for Power Facility Development (*dengen sanpō*). The laws' purpose is to provide large grants to local communities who allow the construction of power plants—nuclear, hydropower, or geothermal. The prefectures and neighboring towns receive long-term grants proportional to the plant's electricity generating capacity from the utility company via METI. Because of these grants, communities have become increasingly dependent on their nuclear facilities. This dependence has been described as a "vicious circle" *(aku-junkan)*, because hosting one nuclear facility or unit has often led to the construction of additional units and nuclear facilities.[20] Typical examples of this practice are the Fukushima Daiichi Nuclear Power station, which has six units, and the Fukushima Daini Nuclear Power station, which has four. This has resulted in a total of ten units concentrated in this area of Fukushima Prefecture. Daniel Aldrich has shown that a relative lack of social capital in local fishing and farming cooperatives and decreasing population levels in remote and poverty-stricken areas (such as is the case in Tohoku) were key siting factors for nuclear power stations.[21] Studies have also illustrated that in such areas, NIMBY-like resistance to nuclear facilities is less likely to occur.[22]

Taiwan and South Korea introduced similar programs in 1988 and 1989, respectively. There, the power companies' revenues are used to fund financial benefits to communities who permit the construction of nuclear power stations. These programs are therefore different from the Japanese, which is funded through government tax revenues earmarked for this purpose. In Europe and the United States, various government subsidies, supplemented by contributions from electric power companies, are provided to site areas too, but there are no programs similar to those in Japan. Japan's policy, based on the Three Laws, is an outlier case, one that cannot be reconciled with a strong civil society and a system with well-developed watchdog organizations that enforce transparency and accountability. In fact, prior to the Fukushima accident, resistance against nuclear power stations in major regional cities like Sapporo, Sendai, and Fukuoka—coincidentally cities in which electric power companies are headquartered—was frequently suppressed. This becomes apparent when Japan is looked at in an international comparative context.

Energy Policy Shifts in Germany, Taiwan, and South Korea

Germany's Social Consensus on Denuclearization

Germany's swift shift toward denuclearization following the Fukushima accident was internationally identified as a model for policy change. In

June 2000, after reaching agreement with four major power companies, a governing coalition of the Social Democratic Party (SPD) and the Greens had introduced a new policy requiring all nuclear reactors to be shut down after thirty-two years of operation. This was a major policy shift in Germany's nuclear energy sector. Yet in September 2010, Chancellor Merkel decided to permit an additional eight years or fourteen years of operation.

On March 14, three days after the Fukushima accident, however, Merkel drastically revised her position and ordered a temporary three-month suspension of operations at eight nuclear reactors, including seven units that had started operating before 1980 and one trouble-prone unit that had started operating after 1980. Without ever resuming operations, these eight units were permanently shut down on August 6, 2011, the day set aside for remembering the atomic bombing of Hiroshima. This paradigmatic shift was facilitated through the Ethics Commission for a Safe Energy Supply. The commission consisted of seventeen members, including the late Ulrich Beck, a leading sociologist advocating the theory of risk society, and Miranda Schreurs, an expert in comparative studies of environmental policies. For two months, it engaged in intensive discussions over nuclear energy policy and hosted a public debate of more than eleven hours. The commission's report stressed the role of socially responsible decision-making before analyzing the technological and economic risks. "Sustainability," "human responsibility for nature," and "responsibility for future generations" were the key concepts guiding the commission's conclusions, and its recommendations can be regarded as best practices for "taming risks through dialogue."[23]

Eventually, based on the commission's 2011 report,[24] Merkel and her Christian Democratic Union–led governing coalition decided to shut down the operation of all seventeen of the country's nuclear units by the end of 2022. Although the report only focused on nuclear power plants in Germany, it is consistent with the view that, because a severe accident occurred in Japan, one of the most technologically advanced countries in the world, accidents could also occur in Germany. It does not provide an easy explanation for the Fukushima accident, as that had been caused by a combination of factors including an earthquake and tsunami of unprecedented scale coupled with geological conditions unique to Japan. But the report takes the view that similar accidents could occur if the cooling system for a nuclear reactor failed as the result of a prolonged loss of external power, which could result from an airplane crash, a terrorist attack, or any number of other events. Concluding the discussions, on June 30, 2011, the Bundestag passed a bill with majority support from four major parties.

The Bundesrat also approved it on July 8. These decisions brought an era in both energy and party politics to an end. Nuclear power had been one of the most contentious issues among Germany's major political parties (the Greens, the Social Democratic Party, the Christian Democratic Union, and the Free Democratic Party) since the 1970s. However, in less than four months after the Fukushima accident, a political and social consensus representing the prevailing public opinion was formed. In the 2013 and 2017 general elections, nuclear energy stopped playing an important role on the parties' political agendas.

Nuclear-Free Homeland Taiwan by 2025

In Taiwan, nuclear energy has long been a contested issue between the currently ruling Democratic Progressive Party (DPP) and the previously ruling Kuomintang (KMT). At the time of writing, three units are in operation and another three units were abandoned. Taiwan is smaller than Japan's Kyushu island, and is also an earthquake-prone country. Thus, for Taiwanese people, the Fukushima accident came as a shock.

The suspension of the construction of the Lungmen Nuclear Power Station, the fourth near New Taipei City, had been contested for years. Lungmen consists of two units. Construction work started in 1999 and was expected to be completed by 2004. However, the project was delayed for legal, regulatory, and political reasons. On March 9, 2013, falling together with the second anniversary of the Fukushima accident, more than 100,000 protesters gathered nationwide to demand an end to the station's construction. In March and April 2014, the sunflower movement of students and civic groups occupied the Taiwanese legislature to protest against the KMT's policies. And in April 2014, the government decided to halt the construction. Thus, in 2015, Taiwan's electricity demand was covered by coal (45 percent), natural gas (31 percent), nuclear power (14 percent), oil (5 percent), and hydrogen and renewables (5 percent). Notably, Taiwan's total energy import dependence was about 98 percent. Thus, the issue of energy security is even more severe than in the case of Japan. Against this background, the DPP's Tsai Ing-wen was elected as the new president in January 2016. In her campaign, Tsai pledged to phase out all nuclear units within nine years, following the examples of Germany, Belgium, and Switzerland. And in January 2017, the amended electricity act set the date for the complete phase-out by 2025. This is the first decision of denuclearization with a legally fixed target year in Asia. Although a referendum held in November

2018 resulted in a majority supporting nuclear energy, the government in January 2019 made it clear that there would be no life extensions for exiting units and no building of new nuclear units. Under the banner of a "Nuclear-Free Homeland," Tsai's government, supported by a network of scholars and environmental NGOs,[25] aims at establishing a low-carbon, sustainable, stable, and economically efficient energy system by 2025.

Toward a Post-Nuclear State in South Korea

In South Korea, President Moon Jae-in has been leading an energy transition since his presidency started in May 2017. South Korea has the sixth-largest nuclear energy sector—after the United States, France, China, Japan, and Russia—with an installed capacity of twenty-five nuclear units in operation as of 2019. In 2018, South Korea's electricity was generated by a mix of coal (40 percent), natural gas (26 percent), nuclear power (26 percent), and hydrogen and renewables (8 percent). Its total energy import dependence was about 95 percent. In his election campaign, Moon had promised that his government would take responsibility for people's lives and establish a "Nuclear Zero Post-Nuclear State" within forty years. This implies the closure of the country's aged nuclear power units and stopping the construction of new reactors. Moon also pledged to boost the share of renewable energy to 20 percent by 2030. In his speech marking the permanent shutdown of the Kori Station No. 1 unit on June 19, 2017, Moon announced a "paradigm shift for a safer Korea" and suggested a decision-making process based on social consensus. This new paradigm was called "Decision on Public Engagement Process."[26] After deciding to temporarily suspend the construction of the Shin-Kori units Nos. 5 and 6 on June 14, 2017, the government established the Public Engagement Committee, including 500 representative citizens, as a means to facilitate deliberation on nuclear energy policy. It decided to resume or abandon the construction depending on the majority within the group of the representative citizens. Despite pushback from conservatives and the nuclear industry, the political leadership of President Moon, supported by scholars and environmental NGOs such as KFEM,[27] has been pushing forward the country's energy transition.

In sum, the cases of Germany, Taiwan, and South Korea serve as good examples illustrating the critical roles of political leadership and political will in imposing a transition toward denuclearization. In all three countries, nuclear energy had long been contested among political parties. In Taiwan and South Korea, nuclear energy were top agenda items during presidential elections, especially so in the aftermath of the Fukushima accident. The differences in policy positions on nuclear energy in presidential elections are very visible to voters. In Japan's parliamentary system, however, Diet members elect the prime minister, and political parties tend to avoid energy issues in national election campaigns because they are deemed counterproductive for voter mobilization.

Japan's Changing Political Culture and the Possibility of an Energy Policy Shift

Will Japan follow these international examples of a major policy shift toward denuclearization? What impact did the Fukushima accident have on Japan's electricity supply? What strategies could antinuclear movements and civil society organizations employ to spur change? Who are their effective political partners in elections and in the Diet? What should the next steps be for Japan? These are the question addressed in the remaining part of this chapter.

Few Policy Changes in Post-Fukushima Japan

What concrete institutional and policy changes have occurred after the Fukushima accident? Nuclear power generation restarted in 2015, despite many unresolved questions about evacuation planning and safety measures. Following its return in late 2012, the Abe cabinet advocated a policy of gradually reducing Japan's dependency on nuclear energy, but these plans lacked a clear indication of when and how this would be achieved. In fact, the Abe government has expressed its intent to restart nuclear power units as soon as possible. Both the 2014 Strategic Energy Plan and the 2018 Strategic Energy Plan emphasize nuclear energy and coal as "'base-load power source(s),' which can be operated stably and at low cost."[28] For that purpose, "(the) restarting of nuclear power units that are recognized by the Nuclear Regulation Authority to conform with regulatory requirements which are at the most stringent level in the world" is a typical passage in government statements or government documentations; yet, many scholars and environmental NGOs remain highly skeptical of the claim that Japan's safety regulations are indeed "at the most stringent level in the world."

This suggests that Japan has witnessed few radical policy changes after the Fukushima accident. The most notable was the decision to abandon the troublesome Monju fast breeder reactor in December 2016. This plant cost more than 1 trillion yen but had, since 1991, been operating for a total of only 250 days. Other shifts include the establishment of a new regulatory agency in form of the Nuclear Regulation Authority (NRA) and the promotion of renewable energy resources by introducing a feed-in tariff system in July 2012.

The Current Status of Nuclear Power Plants and Electricity Supply

Before the Fukushima accident, as of 2010, a total of fifty-four units at sixteen nuclear power stations provided 31 percent of the country's electricity supply. Japan had the third-largest nuclear power capacity, after the US and France. However, as of the end of November 2020, only nine units at five nuclear power stations in the Kyushu, Shikoku and Kansai regions were still operating under the approval of the newly established NRA. Among the fifty-four units, twenty-one older reactors, including the ten units of the Fukushima Daiichi and Daini stations, were abandoned. Six reactors, including units six and seven of the Kashiwazaki-Kariwa Station in Niigata Prefecture, unit two of the Tōkai Nuclear Power Station in Ibaraki Prefecture, and unit two of the Onagawa Nuclear Power Station in Miyagi Prefecture are being prepared for a restart. At the time of writing, ten units are under review by NRA, but local governments have hesitated to provide their required approval. Another eight units' operations remain suspended by power companies themselves. No nuclear units at all were restarted in the eastern and northern parts of Japan where the 2011 earthquake and tsunami caused severe devastation. As a result, in 2018, nuclear energy provided only 4.7 percent of Japan's electricity supply. Following the Netherlands, that is the second-lowest rate among advanced countries using nuclear power.[29]

After the Fukushima accident, Japanese society experienced summer peaks in electricity demand with only two nuclear power units in 2012 and 2013, zero units in 2014, two units in 2015, and three units in 2016 operational, and winter peaks with two units in 2012, zero units in 2013 and 2014, two units in 2015, and one unit in 2016 operational. All nuclear units in Japan had been closed temporarily from September 15, 2013, to August 10, 2015, when the Sendai No. 1 unit in Kyushu was restarted. Due to the legal requirement for regular maintenance, a nuclear unit has to close temporarily after operating for at most thirteen months. Thus, before September 15, 2013, many units had to temporarily close on a one-by-one basis for regular maintenance. Some units along the Pacific Ocean had also been forced to close because of the direct damages sustained from the 2011 earthquake and tsunami.

Nevertheless, Japan experienced no electricity shortages. Saving electricity (*setsuden*) became a new commonsense practice for industry and daily civil life. Compared to the 2007 peak supply of 1030 billion kWh, electricity supply decreased 14.1 percent by 2015 and arrived at almost the same levels as it had been in 1995. Yet the NRA, established in September 2012 for replacing the Nuclear Safety Commission and the Nuclear and Industrial Safety Agency, has been under heavy pressure from the national government and the ruling LDP to accelerate the restarting process. Meanwhile, civil society organizations demand a new rigid regulatory framework. Thus, it appears that the largest challenge for civil society in Japan will be to lead the policy shift. Such a shift requires civil society protests to deepen the public discourse and to elaborate policy proposals in collaboration with scholars and NGOs. The objectives for civil society include strict and effective regulation for nuclear safety, reviewing of the nuclear fuel recycling policy and the safe handling of spent nuclear fuel, while promoting renewable energy, and energy efficiency, and examining possibilities for the separation of electricity distribution and generation, liberalizing the electricity market, and integrating climate change policies with energy policies. NGOs and scholars, including the author of this chapter, have served as advisory panel members and established the Citizens' Commission on Nuclear Energy in April 2013 to initiate discussion on these policy issues. To crystallize the voices of civil society into concrete policy proposals, this commission published the first draft report in October 2013 and the final report Framework for Nuclear Energy Phaseout Policy in April 2014.

Antinuclear Protests after the Fukushima Accident

The severe shock that resulted from the Fukushima accident, the sense of fear over the spread of radiation contamination, and anger and frustration toward TEPCO and the government changed the public's attitude toward nuclear power generation. Activism in Japan was supposedly a thing of the past, peaking in June 1960 when around 330,000 people gathered around the Diet to protest against revising the Japan–US Security Treaty. Since then, very few issues attracted more than 10,000 demonstrators, with the exception of the peaceful May Day rallies.

In the wake of the Fukushima accident, however, protest rallies began to exhibit a new energy. Buoyed by a sense of crisis and urgency, the number of participants increased rapidly. The "Goodbye to Nuclear Power Plants" rally, steered by a coalition formed by the Framework for Nuclear Energy Phaseout Policy of 1994 literature Nobel prize laureate Ōe Kenzaburō, the

Japan Congress Against A- and H-Bombs, and others, was held at Meiji Park in Tokyo on September 19, 2011, and drew 65,000 people, exceeding the 50,000 mark that the organizers hoped to mobilize. The previous attendance record for a nuclear protest rally held in Japan had been about 20,000 people who gathered at Tokyo's Hibiya Park in April 1988, two years after the Chernobyl accident.

The emergence of these protest movements must also be seen in the wider global context. Driven by new technologies such as Twitter and smart phones, a large-scale anti-government movement called the Arab Spring, erupted in Tunisia in January 2011. It spread rapidly to Egypt, Yemen, and Libya in the Middle East, triggered the collapse of long-standing despotic regimes in these four countries, and sent shockwaves throughout the world, as testified by *Time* magazine's choice of the protesters as Person of the Year in 2011. The Arab Spring reached Greece and Spain. Particularly in the latter, an occupy movement called the Indignados ("outraged") gained traction in May and June and drew large numbers of demonstrators ranging from 130,000 to 250,000 nationally. The Spanish movement subsequently inspired and informed the Occupy Wall Street movement, which began on September 17 in New York, and similar occupy movements spread throughout the United States.

Although *Time* magazine's feature on the protests failed to mention Japanese antinuclear rallies, based on my observation, a series of Fukushima-related protest actions in 2011 demonstrated synchronicity with those that spread from the Arab world to Europe and the US. They had the following common three characteristics: (1) use of communication technologies such as Twitter, SMS, YouTube, Ustream, and smart phones as new tools for mobilization; (2) spontaneous initiation of actions by individuals and small groups rather than established political parties, labor unions, or political organizations; (3) actions driven primarily by people's desire to voice their disapproval rather than a desire to achieve specific goals.

The Fukushima-related protests were expected to wane from the beginning of 2012. Yet, on March 11, 2012, the first anniversary of the Fukushima disaster, a total of 14,000 people formed a "human chain" around the Diet building and subsequently marched to a protest rally in Hibiya Park. Then, on March 29, 2012, the so-called *Kantei-mae* demonstration, a series of protests in front of the prime minister's official residence, began with about 300 protesters, who initiated gatherings held every Friday evening. The call was made by the Metropolitan Coalition Against Nukes, a loose network of activists with no official representatives or spokespersons.[30] The number of participants increased to about 2,700 people on June 1. After Prime Minister Noda Yoshihiko on June 8 announced the planned resumption of the Ōi Nuclear Power Station's No. 3 and 4 units, participation jumped to 4,000 on June 8, 12,000 on June 15, and 45,000 on June 22. Yet only when the number exceeded 40,000 did national television networks begin to widely report on the protests. Based on the organizers' announcement on the number of participants at each of these events, about 200,000 people were mobilized on June 29, shortly before the restart of Ōi's unit No. 3; 150,000 people on July 6, a day after the restart; 150,000 people on July 13; and 100,000 people on July 20, a day before the restart of Ōi's unit No. 4. The "Goodbye to Nuclear Power Plants" rally held in Yoyogi Park on July 16 attracted 170,000 people, exceeding the organizers' target of 100,000. The Human Chain Action Against the Diet Building for a Nuclear Free World on July 29 drew around 200,000 participants. In addition, about 40,000 protesters gathered every week during August and September, and a protest action in the Nagata-chō and Kasumigaseki districts, Japan's political and bureaucratic center, on Sunday, November 11, drew about 100,000 people. Although the number of participants have decreased, the weekly protests have continued for more than eight years.

It is important to note here that this was the first time in Japanese history when large-scale protest actions were held in local cities throughout the country as well as in metropolitan Tokyo on an ongoing basis for a duration of several years. Also, protesters were not mobilized by traditional organizations such as trade unions. Baby boomers, families, and young people voluntarily took part in these actions, individually or in small groups. Rally organizers tended to leave things to the spontaneity of the participants rather than providing an organized program. Still, at the time, in summer 2012, political messages other than criticisms of nuclear power generation and TEPCO were deliberately avoided. Many of the protesters had never attended a rally before and actions were akin to peaceful "walks" rather than typical demonstrations. As such, they highlighted the over-deployment of the police for security purposes.

Overall, five developments in terms of the history of Japan's antinuclear social movement and the political culture can be identified: (1) there has been a reliance on citizens' voluntary participation rather than organized mobilization by labor unions and other bodies; (2) "large-scale street protests" have successfully been held in the vicinity of the Diet building, where strict restrictions apply to many activities such as the use of loudspeakers; (3) the *Kantei-mae* protests have only produced few arrests and no stone-throwing or other violent behavior; (4) protests have been held not only in Tokyo but also in local cities throughout Japan. In Sendai, where the author of this chapter lives, antinuclear Friday protest marches are continuing, usually with more than thirty participants (more than 350 times thus far).

Rise of the Anti-Abe Protest Campaign

The 2012 antinuclear protests led to the emergence of another political campaign in the summer of 2015. On September 19, 2015, Prime Minister Abe and his LDP-led governing coalition passed a set of new bills that would allow the Self-Defense Forces (SDF) to operate alongside allies overseas, despite Article 9 of the Japanese Constitution restricting the SDF's role to Japan's self-defense. Unable to garner support for revising the constitution, the Abe government had altered the long-standing and pacifist legal interpretation of the passage and promoted new security legislation. Abe has been seeking to rid Japan of what he called the "US-imposed constitution" (*oshitsukerareta kenpō*) and replace it with a new one. These moves proved highly controversial within Japan, and the opposition criticized the legislation as a "war bill" (*sensō-hō*).

Challenging its envisioned agenda of a "departure from the postwar regime," the perception of the Abe administration itself representing a crisis of postwar democracy triggered the rise of the 2015 anti-Abe protest campaign, thus completing a crisis narrative circle where proponents of change are rendered part of the structural problem.[31] A student movement called Student Emergency Action for Liberal Democracy (SEALDs) emerged in May 2015 and started to campaign against Abe's security legislation. Quickly, SEALDs formed local branches to spread the protest. SEALDs Kansai, SEALDs Tohoku, SEALDs Okinawa, and SEALDs Tokai were established during May and September 2015. All of these protests were moderate and nonpartisan. Their activities included holding protest rallies, organizing study groups and talk events, and publishing of booklets, pamphlets, and videos. More than 2,000 professional academics and faculty supported these activities. This was the first large, nationwide student movement since the Anpo protests of the late 1950s and early 1960s. At the peak in September 2015, almost every night 30,000 to 120,000 protesters surrounded the Diet building. Some of the student leaders were clearly motivated by the 2012 antinuclear protests. This is evidence that Japan's civil society and political culture have undergone a deep transformation to a point where anyone can readily participate in demonstrations against government policy.

Nuclear Energy Politics after the Fukushima Accident

As opinion polls and protests have shown, Japan is "at the crossroads of energy and politics."[32] Some observers remain skeptical about the possibility of the energy policy shift.[33] Indeed, civil society supporting denuclearization failed to make significant inroads into national elections even after the accident. To be sure, the nuclear energy issue was discussed as one of the central issues in the 2012 general election when the new coalition government led by Abe returned to power, and again during the 2013 Upper House election. Though the policy positions on nuclear energy of the ruling LDP and its coalition partner, the Kōmeito, were ambiguous at each of these occasions, they nevertheless secured large majorities. In fact, maintaining an ambiguous position appeared to be an election strategy. The LDP-Kōmeito coalition won all five national elections in the aftermath of the Fukushima accident. These results mainly reflected voters' disappointment with the past three DPJ cabinets led by Hatoyama Yukio, Kan Naoto, and Noda Yoshihiko.[34] This does not mean that the majority of voters supported nuclear energy and hoped for a return to nuclear power. Still, the outcomes of these elections speak against an uprising of the broad public antinuclear power sentiment that could be readily observed in protests after March 2011. Why then did the antinuclear civil society fail to win national elections?

Usually, important issues of public concern become mobilized and contested during election campaigns. Yet, as they pushed for economic recovery, the ruling LDP-Kōmeito coalition succeeded in keeping questions of nuclear power generation from evolving into a top agenda item. The DPJ and other opposing parties joined in supporting denuclearization, but their positions were different and competed with a broad front of issues like economic development, welfare, and education. Especially under the single-seat constituency system at general elections, minor parties have to forge electoral alliances. This is a particular challenge in Japan. Within the DPJ, some politicians preferred a swift shift toward denuclearization. Yet others supported by the labor unions of private businesses, including utility companies and manufacturing firms, were eager to restart nuclear units on the condition that the NRA gave permission to do so. Although the Japan Communist Party and the Social Democratic Party explicitly supported denuclearization, at the time of writing, in the House of Representatives those parties held only twelve and two seats, respectively, and in the Upper House, thirteen and two seats, respectively. Thus, amid this fragmentation of policy positions and institutional constraints, civil society failed to find

an effective political partner and a political route to successfully promote
a denuclearization.

Another impact of civil activism and changing political culture has been
the increase of influential voices seeking denuclearization from right-wing
politicians like former Prime Minister Koizumi Junichirō and center-right
politicians such as former Prime Minister Hosokawa Morihiro. In Japan,
antinuclear issues have for many years been a platform mainly for the political left. This limited the number of participants in antinuclear movements.
In mid-December 2013, however, Koizumi urged Prime Minister Abe to
declare a policy shift toward denuclearization immediately, but Abe declined
to do so. Supported by Koizumi, Hosokawa ran for governor of Tokyo in
February 2014. Although he lost, it was noteworthy that two former prime
ministers used street-corner oratory during their election campaigns to discuss
requests for a policy shift away from nuclear energy toward the promotion
of renewable energy sources. In sum, civil society's impact on policy-making
at the national level is increasing, but still limited.

Conclusion

What happened in Japan after the Fukushima accident? In contrast to the
drastic energy policy shifts in Germany, Taiwan and South Korea, the Japanese government's position remained unchanged. With the return of Abe to
power in 2012, the nuclear energy status quo was prioritized, even though
previous crisis narratives of 3.11 had presented the Fukushima accident as
Japan's gravest crisis since defeat in 1945.

What, then, did the Great East Japan Disaster and the Fukushima
nuclear accident reveal? This is the most fundamental question being posed
by the people from the devastated areas. On one hand, there is a "system
of irresponsibility" (*musekinin no kōzō*)[35] represented by TEPCO, METI,
and the Abe government, who have evaded responsibility by claiming that
all outcomes were "unforeseeable" (*sōteigai*). The disaster is also framed in
terms of deficiencies in "science and technology." Thus, if more advanced
science and technology were employed, the mainstream argument goes,
the tsunami damage could have been predicted and therefore prevented.
According to such a typical "techno-centrist" view, any severe accident can be
prevented under a new regulatory regime. In this vein, the Abe government
has presented a blueprint for a push toward eroding the postwar pacifist
constitution while dazzling the public with the illusion of economic growth
generated by Abenomics[36] and successful suppression of critical voices.

This has forestalled the emergence of effective counter-narratives, such as that the Great East Japan Disaster is in fact challenging the old growth model and necessitates a radical shift away from the urban-centered, centralized economic policy that Japan has been pursuing since the Meiji era. Is Japan unable to change even after such an enormous tragedy? Helmut Weidner, a prominent German environmental policy expert, concluded a lecture in July 2014 by saying that "Japan became a laggard in many areas, and Germany a pioneer in some important areas of environmental and energy policy," and "not even the Fukushima catastrophe provided sufficient incentives to leave the high-risk path of nuclear energy."[37] Despite a deep sense of national crisis, the ability of Japanese politics and society to reason and transform itself is being questioned, thus leaving Japan with the task of exploring new routes to transform its postwar state and society.

Notes

1. Both accidents were rated seven on the International Nuclear Event Scale, which is the scale's highest level.

2. William Sposato, "Kan shushō, sengo saidai no kiki to uttae—Seiji jōsei ga ippen" [Prime Minister Kan Declares Most Severe Crisis in Postwar Era as Politics Changes Dramatically], *Wall Street Journal*, March 14, 2011, http://jp.wsj.com/layout/set/article/content/view/full/197766. Unless otherwise stated, all online resources were last accessed on November 30, 2020.

3. See Daniel P. Aldrich, *Building Resilience: Social Capital in Post-Disaster Recovery* (Chicago: University of Chicago Press, 2012); and Daniel P. Aldrich, *Black Wave: How Connections and Governance Shaped Japan's 3/11 Disasters* (Chicago: University of Chicago Press, 2019).

4. See the introduction to this volume and Colin Hay, "Crisis and the Structural Transformation of the State: Interrogating Process of the Change," *British Journal of Politics and International Relations* 1, no. 3 (1999): 317–344.

5. See, for example, Koichi Hasegawa, "Facing Nuclear Risks: Lessons from the Fukushima Nuclear Disaster," *International Journal of Japanese Sociology* 21 (2012): 84–91; Koichi Hasegawa, "The Fukushima Nuclear Accident and Japan's Civil Society: Context, Reactions, and Policy Impacts," *International Sociology* 29, no. 4 (2012): 283–301; Koichi Hasegawa, *Beyond Fukushima: Toward a Post-Nuclear Society* (Melbourne: Trans Pacific Press, 2015).

6. Ishibashi Katsuhiko, "Genpatsu Shinsai" [Combined Earthquake and Nuclear Disaster], *Kagaku* 67, no. 10 (1997): 720–724.

7. For detailed data see Reconstruction Agency, "Zenkoku no hinanshasu" [The Number of Evacuees], November 11, 2020, https://www.reconstruction.go.jp/topics/main-cat2/sub-cat2-1/20201127_koho1.pdf.

8. Citizens' Commission on Nuclear Energy, *Genpatsu zero shakai e no michi: Shimin ga tsukuru datsugenshiryoku seisakutaikō* [Framework for Nuclear Energy Phaseout Policy], Tokyo, 2014, 34 http://www.ccnejapan.com/20140412_CCNE.pdf.

9. Irving L. Janis, *Groupthink: Psychological Studies of Policy Decisions and Fiascoes* (Boston: Houghton Mifflin Company, 1983).

10. Charles Perrow, *Normal Accidents: Living with High-Risk Technologies* (Princeton, NJ: Princeton University Press, 1984).

11. Investigation Committee on the Accidents at Fukushima Nuclear Power Stations of Tokyo Electric Power Company, *Final Report*, Tokyo, July 23, 2012, https://www.cas.go.jp/jp/seisaku/icanps/eng/final-report.html.

12. National Diet of Japan, National Diet of Japan Fukushima Nuclear Accident Independent Investigation Commission (NAIIC), *The Official Report of Fukushima Nuclear Accident Independent Investigation Commission*, Tokyo, 2012, Tokyo, https://www.nirs.org/wp-content/uploads/fukushima/naiic_report.pdf.

13. Independent Investigation Commission on the Fukushima Nuclear Accident, *The Fukushima Daiichi Nuclear Power Station Disaster: Investigation the Myth and Reality* (London: Routledge, 2014).

14. NAIIC, *Official Report*, 12.

15. Ibid.

16. Jeffrey Broadbent, *Environmental Politics in Japan: Networks of Power and Protest* (Cambridge: Cambridge University Press, 1998).

17. Brian Woodall, *Japan under Construction: Corruption, Politics and Public Works* (Berkeley: University of California Press, 1996).

18. Corinne Lepage, *La vérité sur le nucléaire: Le choix interdit* (Paris: Albin Michel, 2011).

19. John K. Galbraith, *American Capitalism: The Concept of Countervailing Power* (Boston: Houghton Mifflin, 1952).

20. Koichi Hasegawa, *Constructing Civil Society in Japan: Voices of Environmental Movements* (Melbourne: Trans Pacific Press, 2004), 27.

21. Daniel P. Aldrich, *Site Fights: Divisive Facilities and Civil Society in Japan and the West* (Ithaca, NY: Cornell University Press, 2008).

22. Martin Dusinberre and Daniel P. Aldrich, "Hatoko Comes Home: Civil Society and Nuclear Power in Japan," *Journal of Asian Studies* 70, no. 3 (2011): 683–705.

23. Klaus Eder, "Taming Risks Through Dialogues: The Rationality and Functionality of Discursive Institutions in Risk Society," in *Risk in the Modern Age: Social Theory, Science and Environmental Decision-Making*, ed. Maurie J. Cohen (New York: Palgrave Macmillan, 2000), 225–248.

24. Ethics Commission on a Safe Energy Supply, *Germany's Energy Turnaround: A Collective Effort for Future*, Berlin, May 30, 2011, http://stophinkley.org/EngRevu/ENERGY%20TURNAROUND.pdf.

25. Founded in 1987, the environmental NGO Taiwan Environmental Protection Union (TEPU) has eleven local chapters and a total of 2,000 members. TEPU has sustained a strong influence on the environmental and energy policy of promoted by the DPP.

26. Remarks by President Moon Jae-In at a Ceremony Marking the Permanent Closure of the Kori No. 1 Nuclear Reactor, June 19, 2017, https://english1.president.go.kr/BriefingSpeeches/Policies/4.

27. Found in 1993, the environmental NGO Korean Federation of Environmental Movements (KFEM) has forty-seven local chapters and 85,000 members. KFEM is the largest and most influential NGO in South Korea and represents other NGOs such as the Friends of the Earth Korea.

28. Ministry of Economy, Trade and Industry, *2018 Strategic Energy Plan*, Tokyo, July 2018, 20, https://www.enecho.meti.go.jp/en/category/others/basic_plan/5th/pdf/strategic_energy_plan.pdf.

29. Natural gas (37.4 percent) and coal (28.3 percent) were the major sources of electricity supply in 2018. In contrast, hydrogen (7.8 percent) and renewables (9.6 percent) provided a total of 17.4 percent of electricity supply in 2018.

30. Noma Yasumichi, *Kinyō Kantei-mae kōgi* [Friday Protest in Front of the Prime Minister's Official Residence] (Tokyo: Kawade Shobō Shinsha, 2013).

31. Hay, "Crisis." See also Colin Hay, *Re-stating Social and Political Change* (Buckingham: Open University Press, 1996). A similar point is made by Mason and Maslow, this volume.

32. Daniel P. Aldrich, "Post-Crisis Japanese Nuclear Policy: From Top-down Directives to Bottom-up Activism," *Asia Pacific Issues* 103 (2012): 10.

33. Richard J. Samuels, *3.11: Disaster and Change in Japan* (Ithaca, NY: Cornell University Press, 2013).

34. See O'Shea, this volume.

35. See Maruyama Masao, *Gendai seiji no shisō to kōdō* [Thought and Behavior in Modern Japanese Politics] (Tokyo: Miraisha, 1964/2012).

36. See Shibata, this volume.

37. Helmut Weidner, "Kankyō seisaku no seisui" [About ups and downs in environmental policy development], *Kankyō to Kōgai* 44, no. 2 (2014): 67–69.

Chapter 5

From Leader to Laggard?

Crisis Narratives and Structural Reform
in Japanese Science, Technology,
and Innovation Policy

IRIS WIECZOREK

Introduction

During his tenure as prime minister, Abe Shinzō emphasized the role of innovation as a crucial growth engine and an important enabler for Japan's revitalization. Building on the US experience, high-tech start-ups were expected to stimulate innovation and to recover economic growth. Abe regarded the low number of start-ups relative to the United States as a major weakness of the country's innovation system. Their promotion thus became a pillar in his trademark "Abenomics" reform program. The goal was to double the number of start-ups between 2014 and 2020 to about 200,000. If the plan was successful, start-ups would make up 10 percent of the number of existing companies, elevating their share to the level of Silicon Valley.[1]

In line with the "national crisis" (*kokunan*) meta-narrative, the Abe government promoted the view that Japan had lost its global innovation edge. To raise optimism for restoring the country's technological and economic strength, the industrialization of the Meiji era (1868–1912) was frequently employed as a reference point for successful state transformation. Referring to historical examples of entrepreneurial accomplishments, including

Matsushita, Sony, and Honda, Abe promised to lead Japan toward economic recovery. Narratives of an innovation crisis and the importance of start-ups for economic growth are not new in Japan, and neither is the recognition of Silicon Valley as a success story. However, it was unprecedented for the government to convey a simple story centered on Silicon Valley as a blueprint for Japan to reform and to overcome economic crisis.

In this chapter I examine how discourses of crisis and decline have become crucial in the restructuring of political and social institutions. I illustrate how Japan's innovation crisis has been used to frame official policy since the 1990s, and how crisis narratives were adjusted over time, using start-ups[2] and the Silicon Valley model, to bring about change in Japan's innovation and entrepreneurship ecosystem. Crisis narratives were used to justify and accomplish a first transformation from an industrial policy to a science and technology (S&T) policy, followed by a second transformation toward an innovation policy. The embedding of policy frameworks in crisis narratives gave meaning to these paradigm shifts and made more radical change possible. These transformations imply the crafting and employment of new concepts, policy tools, and institutions to supersede the previous diffusion-oriented innovation system with its focus on large corporations. Entrepreneurship and start-ups became a central focus for realizing innovation and economic growth. Developments in the start-up scene therefore reflect major structural changes that the Japanese economy underwent since the 1990s. In this vein, I use discourses about the start-up scene as indications for a cultural shift toward favoring entrepreneurship. Features of the Silicon Valley ecosystem—availability of risk capital, a fluid and diverse labor market, industry–university interactions, and "open" innovation by large firms[3]—function as guidelines to analyze the status quo of Japan's contemporary start-up scene. In addition to scholarly and journalistic literature, this study is mainly based on S&T policy documents, as they reflect the results of intense discussions among the principal stakeholders from industry, academia, and the government. The analysis also includes data gained through interviews with actors of the start-up ecosystem and, where appropriate, participatory observations.[4]

Entrepreneurship in Crisis and the Shift Toward a Science & Technology Policy

Japan has a long tradition of entrepreneurship. During the second half of the Edo period (1603–1868), and despite the relative seclusion under the closed-country (*sakoku*) regime that limited international exchange, a rich entrepreneurial culture with increasingly sophisticated capitalist institutions dominated by merchants and traders had developed. After the forceful opening up of the country in the middle of the nineteenth century, Japanese entrepreneurs established so-called *zaibatsu*, large industrial conglomerates such as Mitsui, Mitsubishi, and Sumitomo, that primarily engaged in mining, trade, and banking. In the years before and after World War I, several corporations such as Toshiba, NEC, and Hitachi then laid the foundations for Japan's modern manufacturing sector. Another generation of entrepreneurs emerged in the 1930s. A prominent example is Toyota Corporation, which was established in 1937 as a garage company and later revolutionized automobile mass production with "just-in-time" manufacturing processes. After World War II, finally, corporations such as Sony and Nippon Telegraph and Telephone Corporation (NTT) followed.

Postwar economic growth has been attributed to the corporate groups (*keiretsu*) centered on large financial firms, the heirs of the prewar *zaibatsu*. These conglomerates relied primarily on in-house research and development and purchased various product-components and services from the outside. In this wealth-driven stage of corporate development, stewards replaced entrepreneurs in senior management positions, thereby reducing the drive to innovate.[5] As a corollary, in the 1970s and 1980s, small and medium enterprises (SMEs) were considered a problem for the national economy. Being too small, too many, and impediments to modernization, they were long treated synonymously with "subcontractors."[6] This view was most popular among the business and policy establishments. Accordingly, the political system was optimized to favor large firms. Only a few counter-narratives existed at that time. For example, a group of scholars who founded the Venture Business Association in 1971 argued that new types of research-and-development-intensive small companies managed by young entrepreneurs were on the rise. In order to distinguish this new type of small companies from SMEs, they used the term "venture business." At a time when start-up closure rates exceeded entry rates in most sectors, they proclaimed that venture businesses would enable Japan to enter a new era of economic growth.[7]

By the 1980s, Japan had moved from catching up to being a global leader. Yet when the global economy entered into a new phase, and even faster technological progress enhanced the crucial link to science, the Japanese system of innovation came under criticism. And when, at the beginning of the 1990s, the bursting of the asset bubble and stiff competition from the US computer industry hit the economy hard, actors in the Japanese innovation system had no choice but to reform.[8] The political leadership started to debate the long-term problem of how to design a "post-catch-up innovation system."[9] The government recognized that in the United States (and the United Kingdom), start-up companies had been providing valuable stimuli to the economy. It became obvious that the system that had been working well for large manufacturing firms in the electrical appliances and automobile industries did not meet the requirements of biotechnology and information technology, where start-ups and universities play a larger role. Moreover, the problem of the rapidly aging Japanese society and the challenges from Asian competitors, notably China and South Korea, added pressure to change. Silicon Valley emerged as a suitable model. By the mid-1990s, the pressure for a "decisive intervention"[10] to transform Japan's economic and political institutions increased, and policy makers formulated a new, comprehensive, government-wide policy in response.

The subsequent enactment of the Science and Technology Basic Law in 1995 marked a visible and significant turning point. The goal to become a "nation based on science and technology" had already appeared in a 1980 white paper, but had been pursued in piecemeal fashion by the various ministries. This time, however, the sense of urgency and crisis allowed for bold reforms. At the time the bill was formally introduced to the House of Representatives in October 1995, the Diet members who proposed it pointed out that, as a small, resource-poor nation facing a rapidly aging population, Japan had no choice but to restore its competitiveness in science and technology to remain a global leader in the twenty-first century. The bill's sponsors pointed to shortcomings of the existing system such as the deplorable research environments at universities and government laboratories, the low ratio of government-financed R&D as percentage of GDP (0.62 percent in 1994, compared to 0.91 percent in the U.S., 0.95 percent in Germany, and 1.10 percent in France), and limited collaboration among researchers across different disciplines, institutions, and sectors. Thus, they asserted that Japan had tried hard to "catch up" with other industrialized countries by importing advanced technologies, but that now, as a forerunner in global economic development, it was expected to show its own creative power to explore new frontiers in S&T.

The pertaining 1995 White Paper on Science and Technology entitled "50 Years of Postwar Science and Technology in Japan"[11] summarized the nation's evolving policy priorities as follows: From the end of World War II until the 1950s as "Science and Technology for Survival and Reconstruction and Recovery of Economy"; from the 1960s as "Science and Technology for

Economic Growth and Expanding the Socioeconomic Infrastructure"; from the 1970s as "Remedying the Strains of Rapid Growth and Responding to a Changing World"; from the 1980s as "Emphasizing Creative Science and Technology and Responding to New Issues"; and since the 1990s as "Striving to Become a Nation Based on Creative Science and Technology."[12]

The new Science and Technology Basic Law required the government to draw up "Basic Plans" for consecutive five-year periods. This policy-planning scheme forced the S&T community to periodically review the national innovation system. As such, the S&T Basic Plans reflect the mainstream debates in science policy. Crisis narratives have played an important role from the outset. For instance, the first Basic Plan (1996–2000) begins with the assertion that

> Japan is not only facing globalization and intensive economic competition with other countries, but is aging at an unprecedented pace. People are deeply concerned that Japan is heading towards a crisis where the hollowing-out of industry, lack of society's vitality, and a worsening living standard are highly evident. . . . To deal with these problems in Japan and abroad, science and technology is expected to play a larger role. . . . Many elements in the systems that have long supported Japan's development are turning out to be hindrances as society, the economy and the international environment changes.[13]

This framing enabled policy makers to double government R&D investment. Moreover, it contained a program for systemic changes in the R&D system such as strengthening cooperation between industry, universities, and government research organizations; increasing competitive research funds; creating a new system of peer review and evaluation; and promoting the establishment of "new ventures." In short, a new system, largely informed by US practices, was introduced. To converge with the Silicon Valley model, this also required the reinforcement of intellectual property rights, the liberalization of public universities, and the promotion of start-ups. In addition, the liberalization of the labor market was portrayed as imperative for increasing labor mobility. This policy change was well received among government agencies, industry, and the general public.[14]

Another important step in the promotion of start-ups and high-tech venture companies was the financial deregulation that started in 1996 and facilitated the creation of new stock markets. In November 1996, Prime

Minister Hashimoto Ryūtarō instructed the Ministry of Finance to fundamentally reform the Japanese financial system to create a "free, fair, and
global" market and put Tokyo on par with New York and London as a
world financial center.[15] Modeled after the Anglo-American securities-driven
system, the idea was to transform Japan from a bank-based to a capital
market–based economy. These reforms, also dubbed "The Big Bang," were
intended to reinvigorate the stagnating economy. Integral to the achievement
of these goals was the simplification of the process of initial public offerings
(IPOs). In 1983, JASDAQ had been established as an over-the-counter
market for small and medium-sized venture companies. And by 1999, with
a total 868 listings, JASDAQ's market capitalization grew to twice the size
of the Second Section of Tokyo Stock Exchange. Thus, in December 1999,
the Tokyo Stock Exchange reacted by launching its Market for High Growth
and Emerging Stocks (MOTHERS) to provide easier funding for emerging
companies with high growth potential. This move came in anticipation of
the opening in June 2000 of NASDAQ Japan at the Osaka Stock Exchange.

Changing Views on Small- and Medium-Sized Enterprises

The heightening pressure to spur economic growth through innovation fundamentally changed the view on SMEs, which constituted 99.7 percent of
all Japanese companies and employ 70 percent of the working population.[16]
During the 1999 "SME Diet" session, Prime Minister Obuchi Keizō strongly
underlined the "utmost importance" of SMEs and entrepreneurship for the
"rebirth of the Japanese economy."[17] Subsequently, the Ministry of Economy,
Trade and Industry (METI) began to promote a fundamental revision of
the 1963 SME Basic Law. SMEs, it argued, should no longer be treated as
"weak enterprises" dependent on large companies and trailing them in wage
and labor productivity. From now on, SMEs were to be seen as the source of
entrepreneurship, innovation, and job creation. Rather than protecting SMEs
from large firms, the new policy aimed at stimulating SME innovation and
promoting the vigorous growth of diverse and independent SMEs. The goal
was to raise the competitiveness of SMEs as a whole, so that they could rival
large firms. The measures included special R&D grants, greater tax incentives
than for larger firms, and special debt-guarantee insurances for innovative
activities. Moreover, METI aimed at doubling the number of start-ups within
five years,[18] to raise IPO levels to match those in the United States.

In the same year, Japan enacted the Industrial Revitalization Law. Since companies have long seen intellectual property rights as a sticking point in pursuing partnerships with national research institutes and universities, and in R&D consortia, it included a "Bayh-Dole" clause[19] to encourage the patenting of research results. Since then, Japanese universities and public research institutions, which receive most of their R&D funding from government, have been eligible to claim the ownership rights to most of their research outputs. In this environment, a new wave of start-ups gained momentum. By the end of the 1990s, a new breed of young entrepreneurs, who had been growing up in Japan's slow-growth era, emerged. For example, in 1997, Mikitani Hiroshi founded the global online shopping mall Rakuten, which, as of October 2020, had a market capitalization of about US$15 billion. More than ten other companies, so-called "Japanese unicorns,"[20] followed, including in 1998, Gung Ho (a game developer, US$4.5 billion); in 1999, DeNA (a game software developer for smartphones, US$2.1 billion); and in 1999, Mixi (a social networking service for smartphone games, US$4.4 billion). In the mobile internet domain, Japan became a global powerhouse. Most of these start-ups were concentrated in the Shibuya district of Tokyo. Because of its convenient location and low rents, the area had already been popular among young people for some time, and 300 entrepreneurs self-proclaimed it the "Bit Valley."[21]

Thus, 1999 marked the beginning of a fundamental transformation toward an entrepreneurism-driven economy. Nevertheless, many of the foreign policies used for inspiration were not properly evaluated before their implementation. This resulted in the impression of frenetic change for change's sake. According to Sébastien Lechevalier, by promoting the Silicon Valley–type system—which appeals more strongly to market principles, to entrepreneurship, and to intellectual property rights—the Japanese innovation system shifted toward a neoliberal approach.[22] This trend emerged before the advent of Prime Minister Koizumi Junichirō's idiosyncratic leadership, but accelerated under it.

Koizumi's Radical Structural Reforms and Advocacy of the Start-Up Scene

As Japan entered its second "lost decade," views favoring radical change continued to hold sway. In this climate, Prime Minister Koizumi, who took office in April 2001, started to implement decisive structural reforms of the bureaucracy to achieve Japan's "Restoration in a New Century." The public administration underwent its largest reorganization since World War II.[23] Executive power was strengthened through a range of measures, including the establishment of advisory councils in key areas chaired by the prime minister himself. Particularly noteworthy is the setting up of the Council of Science and Technology Policy (CSTP) in January 2001. It was meant to be a "control tower" ensuring joint policy-making and implementation, and therefore placed above the ministries in the new Cabinet Office. The twenty CSTP councilors, including fourteen politicians, seven bureaucrats, and seven members from the private sector (headed by Nobel Laureate Shirakawa Hideki), had a staff of sixty at their disposal.[24] Later, a special Minister for Science and Technology Policy was appointed. With its clearly defined role in the S&T budgeting process, the CSTP became a very powerful tool for overcoming the silo-style (*tatewari gyōsei*) structure of the bureaucracy.

The objective of Koizumi's reforms was to bring about a shift of responsibiltiy "from the public sector to the private sector" and "from the central government to the local governments."[25] In the new environment, the state would not only implement measures to foster techno-entrepreneurship in the business world, but also turn a critical eye on itself and become more efficient and competitive. Yet the problems had not been limited to bureaucratic sectionalism, but also resulted from lacking political leadership.[26] Unlike his predecessors, Koizumi adopted a populist approach. He spoke to the public in clear-cut, simple language, and he had a focused media strategy to promote the mantra of "no growth without structural reform." He displayed a penchant for casting issues into good and evil as he talked of crushing "resistance forces" that opposed his "reforms without sanctuaries." These battles between "reformers" and "anti-reformers" prompted the media to play up the 2005 snap election as if it were an entertainment show, resulting in a landslide victory for Koizumi. The binary "reformers versus resistance" narrative was so effective that many politicians such as Tokyo Governor Koike Yuriko and Prime Minister Abe continued to mimic Koizumi's populist approach for years to come.[27] Koizumi also used this strategy to promote admiration for entrepreneurship and embraced young businesspeople. He was a fan of the thirty-two-year-old entrepreneur Horie Takafumi (and vice versa). Horie, a former University of Tokyo student and founder of the successful web design start-up Livedoor, even ran in the 2005 general election as a poster boy for economic reform.[28] Although he failed to win a seat, Horie's campaign attracted much attention because it pitted him against former LDP politician Kamei Shizuka. The sixty-eight-year-old Kamei represented the LDP's old guard and thus personified politics that Koizumi's populism ventured to "destroy."

Koizumi strongly emphasized the fact that sustainable economic growth depended on the successful revival of Japan's depopulating rural regions and the revitalization of SMEs.[29] The Koizumi government thus used crisis narratives to justify a further increase of the S&T budget and a reorganization of the innovation system. According to these narratives, the prospects for economic growth were dire. Therefore, Koizumi's CSTP demanded to increase R&D to European and US levels to "reinforce industrial technology" for a "leading new industry generation" in order to "restore [Japan's] strong international competitiveness."[30] R&D expenditures were envisaged to reach 1 percent of GDP in 2005. Thereby, the government prioritized key national and social issues through investments into information technology, life sciences, environment, and new materials/nanotechnology sectors.

The second S&T Basic Plan strongly promoted an environment for activating high-tech venture enterprises. The plan promised deregulation of the labor market and reduction of financial hurdles for founding companies. For example, a *kabushiki kaisha* ("stock company") could now be founded with a base capital of a single yen. A few years ago, the minimum requirement stood at US$100,000.[31] Koizumi often referred to the success of these reforms, highlighting that "nearly 17,000 companies have been launched as a result of approving the minimum capital requirement for the start-up of business to one yen, which is at a rate of approximately 30 people starting a company per day."[32] In 2006, however, the start-up scene experienced a severe backlash. Horie was accused of fraud and money laundering, and was eventually sentenced to two and a half years imprisonment. Regardless of how valid the accusations were, newspaper reports and many in the start-up scene suspected politically motivated reasons behind this verdict. His fate was understood as resulting from the establishment's response to a young aspiring entrepreneur who had successfully been employing unconventional business methods while showing off his wealth. Hence, Horie's downfall was taken as a cautionary tale for how Japan's graying establishment would crush those who challenged its rules. As a result of the Horie scandal and the subsequent stock market crash of his Livedoor company, the risk capital market collapsed and subsequently reached its historic low in the aftermath of 2008 Global Financial Crisis.

The Shift toward an Innovation Policy

With the third S&T Basic Plan (2006–2010) formulated at the end of Koizumi's tenure, an explicit shift from the prior focus on S&T to "innovation" became apparent.[33] At the outset, the plan stated that "Japan intends to be a leading country in innovation" and that science and technology is "to be supported by the public and to benefit society."[34] Moreover, the Basic Plan put emphasis on fostering human resources and competitive research environments.[35] Continuing where Koizumi had left off, Prime Minister Abe, during his first short-lived one-year tenure in 2006–2007, pushed for more deregulation and developed his own "people-centered innovation" mantra.[36] But while all governmental documents included concrete examples of how people would benefit from innovation, the basic rationale for reform and deregulation remained unchanged: Japan's national crisis and international decline. Looking abroad to initiatives such as "Innovate America" and "Creating an Innovative Europe," the Abe administration considered innovation as "a key element in increasing productivity and underpinning industrial competitiveness," and for Japan to address the dual challenges of rapid demographic decline and globalization.[37]

In a departure from tradition, Abe therefore pledged to dramatically reform Japan's rigid structures of scientific education, funding, and decision-making. He appointed Kurokawa Kiyoshi as his science policy advisor—the first time a scientist held this position—and tasked him to lead the drafting of the Innovation 25 strategic guidelines, Abe's vision of how science and technology can contribute to Japan's economic growth throughout 2025. In March 2007, the newly established Innovation 25 Strategy Council, composed of intellectuals from industry and academia, presented their guidelines.[38] Directly referring to Abe's change of the narrative, the document begins with the statement,

> In order to realize the Abe Cabinet's new national image for Japan, known as "Beautiful Country," it is essential to ensure a vibrant economy and a society in which everyone can enjoy wealth. Even in the advent of a society with a declining population, we are able to incessantly generate innovative technologies, products and services, which are accepted by the people of Japan as well as of the world. This in turn creates economic and social energy, contributing to the realization of a society where people can have bright hopes and dreams for the future and live with peace of mind.[39]

In the strategy paper, one discovers many of the goals and plans that had already been announced in the plans of various ministries, and in the S&T Basic Plan before that. But the emphasis on the development of human capital was new. It asserted that the policies concerning the creation and promotion of innovation had to be drastically shifted from the conventional "industrial promotion type" or "government-led type" to an "infrastructure creation type" that supports ambitious and challenging efforts of individuals. Since the nature of innovation radically changes existing structures, the strategy notes, the circle of stakeholders should not be confined to the established organizations or systems. Instead, Japan must become a society where various stakeholders, such as venture businesses, SMEs, non-profit organizations, and entrepreneurs are deeply engaged in innovation processes. Otherwise, the group of experts feared that, in the face of intensifying global competition especially from China and India, Japan may not be able to continue to enjoy economic affluence. Notably, the Strategy Council's chairperson referred to innovation policies in other countries, among them the European Union (EU)'s New Lisbon Strategy of 2005, the Aho Report on Creating an Innovative Europe, and the EU's Seventh Framework Programme of 2006. He also pointed to the EU's attempt to revive society and economy through science and technology by increasing the ratio of R&D investments to 3 percent of the EU's gross regional product by 2010. Abe stepped down after a crushing defeat in the July 2007 upper house election, and Japan subsequently experienced a procession of six prime ministers in six years. While political instability did not allow for the formulation and implementation of cohesive structural reforms, however, S&T Basic Plans continued to function as general guidelines and provided orientation for the ministries.

Abenomics and the Promotion of Silicon Valley as a Blueprint for Japan

The leadership vacuum between 2007 and 2012, combined with the dramatic impact of the 3.11 triple disaster,[40] amplified the urgency to bring about Japan's "rebirth."[41] Strong leadership for restoring a "new" Japan was in high demand. Returning to power in December 2012, Prime Minister Abe was more than ready to take up the task to reform Japan. Besides continuing the 3.11 recovery effort, Abe prioritized a return to robust economic growth. To this end, his trademark "Abenomics" entailed the Japan Revitalisation Strategy to promote structural reforms.[42] Since fostering innovation as driver for economic growth played an important role, start-ups and universities became the central focus of this strategy.

Abe emphasized that Silicon Valley was to serve as a blueprint for Japan. This was an attempt to convey a clear and easy-to-understand message for driving reform. In 2013, he declared that he "would like to turn Japan into an entrepreneurial powerhouse brimming with entrepreneurial spirit, just like the United States."[43] In 2015, Abe officially visited Silicon Valley, where he announced the new policy initiative called "Bridge of Innovation between Silicon Valley and Japan," aiming at "capturing the dynamism of Silicon Valley."[44] In both his public addresses and private dialogues, Abe made references to Japan's tradition of entrepreneurial accomplishment, citing such examples as Matsushita, Sony, and Honda. He reminded his countrymen of the enduring strength of Japanese technology, technology that represented an enormous asset whose full potential might, once more, be unleashed through decisive changes in policies, institutions, and culture.

Unprecedented in Japanese politics, Abenomics introduced a range of key performance indicators (KPIs) with numerical targets, end dates, and periodic reviews of achievement levels. The effectiveness of the targets that favor quantity over quality, and the increasing number of KPIs, however, can be doubted.[45] Yet there was little criticism in the Japanese science-policy community, and so the setting of KPIs put the innovation system under increased pressure to adapt and produce outcomes. The need to contribute to the Revitalization Strategy also led to an enlargement of the CSTP's competences. Responsible for formulating science, technology, and innovation policy and ensuring its sound implementation, it was renamed Council for Science, Technology and Innovation (CSTI) in 2014. This change of vocabulary indicates that the role of government also changed from making "industrial" policy to pursuing "innovation" policy.[46] But while the overall system became better coordinated, the power of the CSTI still depended on the commitment of the incumbent prime minister. Therefore, the CSTI required a new policy-making tool to complement the five-year S&T Basic Plans. The subsequently annually updated Comprehensive STI Strategy serves as such. It entails a long-term vision as well as immediate action items. The 2014 issue explicitly stated that Japan will be "the most-innovation-friendly country," redistributing the fruits of economic growth to benefit peoples' lives, and that it will show this quality to the world. Frequent references to the 2020 Tokyo Olympic and Paralympic Games in various documents and discussions further testified to the urgency to credibly demonstrate that "Japan is back."[47]

Yet, after cracks in the Silicon Valley model had appeared, and Donald Trump's election to president in 2016 created frictions in US–Japan relations, references to Japan's capacity to adapt to the European innovation system increased. In particular, intense discussions about Germany's "Industrie 4.0" concept among stakeholders from the Japanese government and industry gave rise to the "Society 5.0" concept.[48] Thus, the fifth S&T Basic Plan set the primary goal of realizing a "world-leading 'super smart society' (Society 5.0)."[49] Despite these buzzwords, however, the plan's main thrust remains largely unchanged. It places strong focus on fostering "open innovation" and "diversity," and on the promotion of R&D-type start-ups. It also emphasizes the cultivation of an entrepreneurial mentality. Moreover, the plan puts high priority on unleashing the full potential of universities as engines of economic growth. Narratives of crisis now included clear references to Japan's "isolation" from the global (scientific) community. Increasingly, newspapers, scientific articles and governmental documents pointed out that Japan's innovative output is rapidly declining in international comparison, and that there is a great danger that Japan will be left behind.[50]

Again, these crisis narratives suggested an urgent need for increasing government R&D spending. Since the third S&T Basic Plan, a government R&D investment target of one percent of the GDP had been set, but still not achieved. Hence, the Japan Business Federation (Keidanren) urged the government to increase spending in order to bring about the "rebirth of Japan."[51] While it has to be seen whether such pressure will be effective, almost all ministries substantially increased their support programs for start-ups. The all-powerful Keidanren became a strong advocate of the "Society 5.0" concept as a way to resolve Japan's economic crisis.[52] Thus, Abe's statements also conveyed optimism about Japan's potential to transform in ways that would make the economy more adaptive, nimble, and innovative. His speech at the 196th Session of the Diet in January 2018 shows the same pattern of linking narratives of "national crisis" with the need for decisive change:

> Countless human resources were fostered in the new Meiji Era and they became the driving force for the rapid modernization of Japan, at a time when the country was being threatened by the technologically superior nations of the West in what could be deemed a "national crisis." Now, Japan is once again faced with an urgent issue that should be called a "national" crisis; a rapidly aging society and decreasing birthrate. . . . During the Meiji Era, Sakichi Toyoda started a small company that

made looms. "Be at the vanguard of the times through endless creativity, inquisitiveness and pursuit of improvement." . . . [H]is business grew into a large company [Toyota] that is matchless in the world. . . . As the world now moves towards Society 5.0, new innovations are being created in rapid succession. If we are not ahead of the wave of the productivity revolution, Japan's economy has no future. With 2020 as a major milestone, we will fully mobilize all possible measures.[53]

In order to achieve this goal, the Japanese government launched numerous financial support programs, initiated extensive structural reforms, and has been supporting various training programs for entrepreneurs at several universities. But what kind of "real" changes has Abenomics brought to Japan's start-up ecosystem?

Japan's Start-Up Ecosystem: The Silicon Valley Model Executed?

As shown above, political actors had long aimed at dismantling the developmental state to move Japan in the direction of the Silicon Valley model. Crisis narratives played a crucial role in justifying this transformation. Here, I examine the degree of convergence between Japan and the Silicon Valley model since the first big shift in Japan's science and technology policy of the mid-1990s. After an overview of the contemporary start-up scene, the key features of the Silicon Valley ecosystem serve as guidelines for an assessment of "real" changes.[54]

A "Brimming Entrepreneurial Powerhouse" like Silicon Valley?

Since around 2014, backed by the above-mentioned policy initiatives, the start-up scene has been recovering and developing quite dynamically.[55] The community considered Abe an ally and a symbol for the "power of failure"—Abe's first term in office as prime minister ended in failure, but given a second chance, he succeeded because he arguably learned from his mistakes. More important than increasing support from the establishment, the scene is now also backed by successful company founders of the 1990s, who are reinvesting in the system. Influential business "angels" entered the Japanese market and launched venture capital (VC) firms.[56] The start-up community became an incubator of new businesses where entrepreneurs exit one start-up to launch another, or where they make their ideas public to raise funds.[57] Nowadays, start-ups that generate substantial profits within a short period of time are no longer rare. While few high-tech start-ups become prominent, their numbers are increasing especially in the bio- and fintech sectors.[58]

Moreover, "Bit Valley" in Tokyo's Shibuya ward is reemerging as one of the centers of the start-up scene, and big companies like Google have announced plans to move back to this area.[59] This is a clear indication that times have changed and that start-ups have come to be regarded as important actors in the Japanese innovation system. However, it should be noted that "Bit Valley" is, in contrast to the Silicon Valley model, largely based on SMEs that already existed ten or twenty years before they entered the market. Experts call these companies "Startups Japanese Style."[60] In Japanese, they are called *dai ni sogyō* (second foundation businesses). But contrary to misinterpretations that label them as "restarters," these companies have not "renewed" themselves. Instead they have diversified into new business areas while maintaining their original activities. Nintendo is a prominent example.

The start-up scene also sought to mobilize support through a series of events. For example, in 2013, Rakuten CEO Mikitani launched the Global New Economy Summit (NEST), which has since convened annually. NEST invited prominent Silicon Valley entrepreneurs to Tokyo. The 2016 summit counted about seventy speakers and 3,000 attendees, including Premier Minister Abe. Whereas NEST is very much focused on Silicon Valley as the ideal model for supporting a vivid entrepreneurial ecosystem, another series of events, called Slush Asia, focuses on emerging markets in Asia. In 2015, it took place for the first time in Tokyo as the first branch event of the original Slush. Founded by Finnish entrepreneurs for networking purposes in 2008, Slush has become the "Woodstock" of the start-up and VC scene. In 2017, 4,000 people, including 360 start-ups, 100 investors, 200 journalists, and 60 speakers from 38 countries—among them Abe's wife Akie—attended. Slush Asia has a highly symbolic character, as Japan moved to position itself as a start-up hub in Asia. Parallel to this development, the Abe government has showcased start-ups that went through several rounds of pitch national competitions through the New Energy and Industrial Development Organization and its Technology Commercialization Program initiated in 2015.[61]

In line with the changing political mood, major newspapers such as the *Nihon Keizai Shimbun* started to focus on the start-up ecosystem. Over the last three years or so, they made a shift toward celebrating entrepreneurship. Featuring individual success stories, the influential business daily portrayed the start-up scene as vivid and brimming, and thereby created new models to be emulated.

Risk Capital Opportunities on the Rise

Since the inception of the new economic growth policy by the Abe administration in 2013, Japan's VC industry has been growing rapidly. The monetary policy of quantitative easing increased the amount of capital in the market and encouraged private-sector investment. Although VC investment is still small when compared to the United States,[62] Japan has seen a remarkable increase, from US$0.8 billion in 2013 to US$3.5 billion in 2018, surpassing the peak levels before the financial crisis hit in 2007.[63] Reflecting this trend, 50 percent of the start-ups that raised money in 2018 succeeded in attracting more than US$1 million, and "big checks" have been invested.[64] Moreover, we also see qualitative shifts that indicate changes in the innovation system, the most important of which is the rise of independent VCs. During the period from January 2013 to October 2014, new VC funds totaling approximately US$2.6 million were launched; 43 percent of this risk capital came from independent investors, 36 percent from the financial sector, and 19 percent from companies. Thus, the balance of power in the Japanese innovation system is shifting, with independent money available for start-ups. As a result, the start-up scene is becoming more independent from big companies and from the state, and is therefore able to gradually craft its own rules.[65]

Changes of the Japanese Labor Market and Social System

The environment for start-ups has become more positive the more corporate Japan has been in crisis. Japan's prolonged economic stagnation, with struggling companies such as Panasonic and Sharp, has threatened old corporate-welfare principles such as lifetime employment. This has caused many to reassess SMEs and start-ups more positively. Large companies are no longer considered a "safe harbor." More young people are joining start-ups or working freelance to enjoy flexibility in their working life. Part-time or contract workers now account for about 40 percent of Japan's workforce.[66] The crowdsourcing company Lancers estimates that freelancers, in particular, make up 17 percent of the country's working population, compared with 36 percent in the United States. The growth of online platforms such as CrowdWorks and Wantedly, a Japanese rival to the professional social network LinkedIn, is driven by the country's labor shortage. That has enabled corporations and even government ministries to tap into the pool of independent workers. Overall, Japan's labor market has become more "mobile."

Moreover, US start-ups have been expanding to Japan and have brought Silicon Valley culture with them, and several successful Japanese start-up founders have experience with working for US companies and/or in the Silicon Valley. Thus, different working cultures have evolved and helped to lower mental barriers to approach entrepreneurship in a nation that has traditionally emphasized seniority and corporate loyalty. Several Japanese deep-tech startups are now also open to global business; many are made up of of multinational teams.[67] Yet in Japan the "social stigma of failure" remains strong. Not only the fear of failure, but above all the consequences of failure—in particular the exclusion from the "Japan Inc." club—discourages young people from setting up start-up companies. Mothers and mothers-in-law are often opposed to their children and children-in-law forgoing the traditional path of striving for a secure career with the government or a large company. Yet, according to the Global Entrepreneurship Monitor 2018, there is much less "fear of failure" now than there was five years ago. While in 2013, 54.5 percent of those interviewed between the ages of eighteen and sixty-four feared failure, this rate has dropped remarkably to 41.2 percent in 2017.[68] Overall, Japan's corporate culture is gradually becoming more open for (and welcoming to) start-ups.[69] In 2008, 26 percent of those interviewed in the Global Entrepreneurship Monitor saw a good career option in the creation of a company; by 2017 this figure rose to 31 percent. In addition, company founders gained increasing social recognition. In 2008, 52 percent of respondents felt that company founders have a high social status; in 2013, 55.8 percent answered accordingly.[70] However, the fact that the ratio dropped to an internationally comparatively low 52 percent in 2017 shows that change is not guaranteed.

Large Corporations and "Open" Innovation

Large corporations have played a pivotal role in the innovation economy during most of the postwar recovery and growth eras, and today they account for 43 percent of national production. Moreover, they employ an important fraction of scientists and engineers working in innovation and development. However, over the past two decades, these same large corporations have increasingly struggled to keep up with the pace of innovation or to embrace new technological paradigms. As a consequence, since the late

1990s, large corporations in Tokyo have started to investigate new business models aimed at encouraging technological innovation, both within the organization and through new types of relationships with external actors such as universities and startups.

There is an increasing trend to facilitate cooperation and collaboration between large companies and start-ups to accelerate mergers and acquisitions. Networking events between startups and large companies are on the rise. Moreover, large companies are increasingly financing their own spin-offs in order to generate innovation and growth, as illustrated by the "intrapreneur-ship" in the Japanese service robot industry.[71] Sony and other IT companies have begun to promote "open innovation processes."[72] Corporations such as KDDI, NTT Docomo, and Recruit have launched incubator programs, following the example of mobile communication provider Softbank, to promote startups in their business area. In the manufacturing industry, many of the spin-offs are using crowdfunding. Fujitsu even established its own university to promote an entrepreneurial spirit internally.

The Changing Role of Universities

The role of universities within the Japanese innovation system has also been changing rapidly over the past two decades.[73] During most of the postwar period, universities' involvement in innovation and technological change has largely been informal and often limited to supplying students with a high level of general education. Individual universities building ties with emerging industries, such as the Keio University's Fujisawa Campus in the internet industry, have been rare. Yet, since the 1990s, the numbers of technologically sophisticated spin-off companies have increased. Japanese elite universities, formerly defining their success by placing as many of their graduates as possible into large companies and government, have begun to launch their own incubator programs and VC funds, as well as providing training for potential company founders. Moreover, since 2014, the Ministry of Education, Culture, Sports, Science and Technology has been promoting the development of an innovative ecosystem for the establishment of spin-offs at thirteen universities over a three-year period through its Enhancing Development of Global Entrepreneurs program. As a result, Entrepreneurship Education Centers have emerged at many universities.

Consequently, Japanese scientists are increasingly leaving the ivory tower. In 1990, there were only fifty-five spin-offs. By 2016, their number had grown to around 1,800.[74] Over the past five years the number of spin-offs at the University of Tokyo, the country's top institution, has doubled. For 2016, the university listed 216 spin-offs with a cumulative value of US$10.8 billion. This includes companies that are listed on the stock market, such as PeptiDream in the biopharmaceutical and Euglena in the bio-food industries. These success stories are the result of the private venture fund UTEC (The University of Tokyo Edge Capital), which was established in 2004 and subsequently launched three more funds with a total value of US$350 million. UTEC is spatially integrated with but legally independent from the University of Tokyo. This arrangement allows it to operate independently from the university's rigid administrative structures and to promote scientists at other universities—a novelty in Japan. Before the Internet bubble of the late 1990s, almost all graduates from the University of Tokyo preferred getting jobs at government agencies, big banks, or big manufacturers. Thus, this shift is significant and suggests that the innovation and start-up ecosystems are indeed in transformation.

Conclusion

From the mid-1990s onwards, Silicon Valley has been the success model to be emulated. Accordingly, successive governments have promoted a variety of structural reforms to lay the groundwork for substantial changes in the Japanese innovation and entrepreneurship ecosystem. Many of the measures and targets specified under Abenomics have emphasized the need for further development along these lines. The unambiguous commitment of the strategy's third arrow to promote a "brimming" start-up ecosystem, alongside with the "Society 5.0" concept, undoubtedly triggered dynamic change.[75] During his record-long term as prime minister, Abe Shinzō gave the start-up scene a powerful voice. Overall, support for innovation and entrepreneurship has increased considerably over the past decades. The accumulation of reforms has contributed to modifying the logic of the innovation system as a whole, and a new public architecture for innovation policies led to better coordination between its various actors and stakeholders. Crisis narratives have been decisive in driving these developments.

However, despite strong emphasis on Silicon Valley as a blueprint, we have not seen a convergence between the Japanese and US systems. The Japanese innovation and start-up ecosystem, in several aspects, differs significantly from Silicon Valley, and there has not been a comparable boom in technological entrepreneurship in Japan yet. As Lechevalier has pointed out, the reason for this missing convergence does not relate to a lack of change, but rather to differences in initial conditions. The Japanese innovation system follows the logic of the Japanese capitalism, and the evolution of the innovation system does not entirely result from technology.[76] After three "lost decades" and several reform initiatives, focusing on an underdeveloped innovation and start-up ecosystem, policymakers ironically still seem unable to cope with Japan's "economic crisis." The crisis narratives' focus on Silicon Valley as the ideal success model for innovation and entrepreneurship may be the major reasons why the Japanese ecosystem is regarded as unfavorable. As Robert Eberhart, director of the Entrepreneurship Project at Stanford University, put it, "If you look for entrepreneurship in the wrong places, you will not find it. In Japan there is a lot of entrepreneurship, but it is less visible than in the US."[77]

Notes

1. Data vary. Martin Hemmert, Ying Cheng, Florian Kohlbacher, Masahiro Kotosaka, Chang-Ti Loh, and Franz Waldenberger, "High-tech Start-up Ecosystems in East Asian Agglomerations: Are They Different from the West?" Deutsches Institut für Japanstudien, Working Paper 16, no. 1 (February 2016).

2. Startups differ from SMEs, but in the Japanese context both terms are often used with a similar meaning.

3. Richard Dasher, Nobuyuki Harada, Takeo Hoshi, Kenji E. Kushida, and Tetsuji Okazaki, *Institutional Foundations for Innovation-Based Economic Growth* (Tokyo: National Institute for Research Advancement), July 7, 2015, https://www.nira.or.jp/pdf/e_1503report.pdf. Unless otherwise stated, all online sources were accessed and available on October 10, 2020.

4. The author functioned as advisor to the Council for Science, Technology and Innovation (CSTI) during the period of the formulation of the fifth S&T Basic Plan. From 2014 to 2016, the author was also involved in the MIT Regional Entrepreneurship Acceleration Program as project manager of the participating Japan team.

5. Michael Porter, *The Competitive Advantage of Nations* (Basingstoke: Palgrave Macmillan, 1990); D. Hugh Whittaker, "Crisis and Innovation in Japan: A New Future Through Techno-Entrepreneurship?" MIT Japan Program, Working Paper Series 01.02, May 31, 2001, 6.

6. Whittaker, "Crisis and Innovation," 2. In reality, the SME sector has always been very mixed, with dynamic, entrepreneurial SMEs as well as static, livelihood businesses.

7. Kathryn C. Ibata-Arens, *Innovation and Entrepreneurship in Japan: Politics, Organizations, and High Technology Firms* (Oxford: Oxford University Press, 2009), 12–15.

8. See Marie Anchordoguy, *Reprogramming Japan: The High-Tech Crisis Under Communitarian Capitalism* (Ithaca, NY: Cornell University Press, 2005); Robert Cole, "Academic Entrepreneurship: A Comparison of U.S. and Japanese Promotion of Information Technology and Computer Science," Working Paper Series, Center on Japanese Economy and Business No. 324 (July 2013); Eichii Yamaguchi, *Innovation Crisis: Successes, Pitfalls, and Solutions in Japan* (Stanford, CA: Stanford University Press, 2019).

9. Kazuyuki Motohashi, "Innovation Policy Challenges for Japan: An Open and Global Strategy," *Asie.Visions* 45 (November 2011).

10. Colin Hay, "Crisis and the Structural Transformation of the State: Interrogating the Process of Change," *British Journal of Politics and International Relations* 1, no. 3 (1999): 317–344.

11. Kakagaku gijutsu-chō (Science and Technology Agency), *White Paper on Science and Technology 1995*, Tokyo, May 1996.

12. Ibid.

13. Government of Japan, *Science and Technology Basic Plan*, Tokyo, July 2, 1996.

14. This corresponds to Hay's argument that in phases of institutional transformation the unity of the state, comprising "a diverse array of specific, but none the less interdependent, agencies, apparatuses and institutions," is greatest; see Hay, "Crisis," 320–321.

15. Gillian Tett, "A Bang or a Whimper? An Inefficient System for Allocating Capital is the Issue at the Heart of Japan's Decision to Launch Today's Big Bang," *Financial Times*, March 31, 1998.

16. METI, *White Paper on Small and Medium Enterprises in Japan (Summary) 2019*, Tokyo, October 2019, 3, https://www.chusho.meti.go.jp/pamflet/hakusyo/2019/PDF/2019hakusyosummary_eng.pdf.

17. Ministry of Foreign Affairs of Japan, "Policy Speech by Prime Minister Keizo Obuchi to the 146th Session of the Diet," October 29, 1999, https://www.mofa.go.jp/announce/announce/1999/10/1029.html.

18. The target of the Japanese government's 2001 "Startup-Doubling Plan" was the doubling of startups from 180,000 in 2001 to 360,000 in 2006.

19. The 1980 Bayh-Dole Act gave universities the right to patent technology resulting from research funded by the federal government and is considered to have contributed to the success of US universities in generating and transferring technology to industry.

20. The term "unicorn" was coined in 2013 and describes innovative startups that are not older than ten years and have a market valuation of over US\$1 billion. "Japanese unicorns" usually take longer to mature than their counterparts in the United States.

21. "Bit Valley" is named after the computing term "bit," referring to software companies, as opposed to the term "Silicon Valley," which refers to companies in

the semiconductor and computer engineering field. In this sense, "Bit Valley" also derives from the fact that Japanese companies played a dominant role in the world market for gaming software until the 1990s, thus functioning as an equivalent success example to Silicon Valley; see Ito Shuichi, "The Changing Corporate Climate in Japan," *Journal of Japanese Trade & Industry* 19, no. 2 (2000): 31–34.

22. Sébastien Lechevalier, *The Great Transformation of Japanese Capitalism*, trans. J.A.A. Stockwin (London: Routledge, 2014), 131.

23. Kerstin Cuhls and Iris Wieczorek, "Changes in the Japanese Innovation System and Innovation Policies," in *Competing for Global Innovation Leadership: Innovation Systems and Policies in the USA, Europe and Asia*, ed. Rainer Frietsch and Margot Schüller (Stuttgart: Fraunhofer Verlag, 2010), 143–168.

24. Ibid.

25. Cornelia Storz, *Small Firms and Innovation Policy in Japan* (London: Routledge, 2006), 16.

26. Ibid., 22.

27. See Takeda, this volume.

28. Jonathan Soble, "Japan's Horie Faces Verdict in Livedoor Fraud Case," *Reuters*, March 16, 2007, https://www.reuters.com/article/businesspro-japan-horie-dc/japans-horie-faces-verdict-in-livedoor-fraud-case-idUSSP3491820070315.

29. Ministry of Foreign Affairs of Japan, "General Policy Speech by Prime Minister Junichiro Koizumi to the 161st Session of the Diet," October 12, 2004, https://www.mofa.go.jp/announce/pm/koizumi/speech0410.html.

30. Council for Science and Technology Policy (CSTP), *Science and Technology Basic Plan 2001*, Tokyo, March 30, 2001, https://www8.cao.go.jp/cstp/english/basic/2nd-BasicPlan_01-05.html.

31. David Corbin, "Meet Yoshiaki Ishii, the Government Official Who Can Save Startups in Japan," *TechinAsia.com*, July 30, 2014, https://www.techinasia.com/yoshiaki-ishii-meti-save-japan-startups.

32. Ministry of Foreign Affairs of Japan, "General Policy Speech by Prime Minister Junichiro Koizumi to the 161st Session of the Diet," October 12, 2004, https://www.mofa.go.jp/announce/pm/koizumi/speech0410.html.

33. Cuhls and Wieczorek, "Changes in the Japanese Innovation System," 145.

34. CSTP, *Science and Technology Basic Plan 2006*, Tokyo, March 28, 2006, https://www8.cao.go.jp/cstp/english/basic/3rd-Basic-Plan-rev.pdf.

35. Ibid.

36. See Breaden, this volume.

37. CSTP, *Basic Plan 2006*.

38. Government of Japan, *Long-term Strategic Guidelines "Innovation 25,"* Tokyo, June 1, 2007, https://japan.kantei.go.jp/innovation/innovation_final.pdf.

39. Ibid.

40. See Hasegawa, this volume.

41. Cabinet Office, *Comprehensive Strategy for the Rebirth of Japan: Exploring the frontiers and building a "Country of Co-creation,"* Tokyo, July 31, 2012, https://www.cas.go.jp/jp/seisaku/npu/pdf/20120731/20120731_en.pdf.

42. See Shibata, this volume.

43. Prime Minister of Japan and His Cabinet, "Address by H.E. Mr. Shinzo Abe, Prime Minister of Japan, at the New York Stock Exchange," September 25, 2013, https://japan.kantei.go.jp/96_abe/statement/201309/25nyse_e.html.

44. State initiatives to foster the internationalization of the Japanese startup ecosystem started about one decade ago; see Kent Calder, *Circles of Compensation: Economic Growth and the Globalization of Japan* (Stanford, CA: Stanford University Press, 2017), 161.

45. KPIs include the increase in the number of unicorns to twenty by 2030, and the doubling of the proportion of VC investments as a percentage of nominal GDP. While this does not address the quality of VC, it does provide explicit normative support.

46. Lechevalier, *The Great Transformation,* 122.

47. Council for Science, Technology and Innovation (CSTI), *The 5th Science and Technology Basic Plan,* December 18, 2015, https://www8.cao.go.jp/cstp/kihonkeikaku/5basicplan_en.pdf.

48. Observations by the author.

49. CSTI, *5th Basic Plan.*

50. Nicky Phillips, "Japanese Research Leaders Warn About National Science Decline," *Nature,* October 17, 2017, https://www.nature.com/news/japanese-research-leaders-warn-about-national-science-decline-1.22847.

51. Keidanren, "Chairman Sakakibara's Statements and Comments at His Press Conference," May 21, 2018, https://www.keidanren.or.jp/en/speech/kaiken/2018/0521.html.

52. Keidanren, "Toward the Establishment of a 'Venture Eco-system' in Japan," Tokyo, December 15, 2015, https://www.keidanren.or.jp/en/policy/2015/118_outline.pdf; and Keidanren, "The Keidanren Vision 2007: 'Land of Hope, Japan,' " Tokyo, 2007, https://www.keidanren.or.jp/english/policy/2007/vision.pdf.

53. For a translation of his speech, see Prime Minister of Japan and His Cabinet, "Policy Speech by Prime Minister Shinzo Abe to the 196th Session of the Diet," January 22, 2018, https://japan.kantei.go.jp/98_abe/statement/201801/_00002.html.

54. For a more detailed assessment see Iris Wieczorek, "Japans Alternativen zu Silicon Valley," *GIGA Focus Asia* 3 (July 2016), https://www.giga-hamburg.de/en/publication/japan's-alternatives-to-silicon-valley.

55. Since Abe took office, the start-up entry rates have increased, and the closure rates have decreased considerably. According to a Ministry of Health, Labour and Welfare report, the start-up rate in Japan increased to 5 percent in 2015 (for

the first time in twenty-three years), with the portion of entrepreneurs increasing to 19 percent, a number higher than in Europe and second only to the United States.

56. Tommy Goji, "Nihon no benchākapitarisuto gunzō" [Japan's Venture Capitalist Group Image], *Kigyō-ka kurabu*, June 2015, http://kigyoka.com/news/magazine/magazine_20160512.html.

57. This development is supported by the aforementioned "MOTHERS," which is an index at the Tokyo Stock exchange market that has been especially designed for start-ups with high growth potential.

58. Yusuke Asakura, "Current Trends Among Startups and How They Keep Momentum in Japan, Entrepreneurship in Asian High-Tech Industries," Stanford University, Entrepreneurship in Asian High-Tech Industries, April 7, 2015, http://asia.stanford.edu/us-atmc/wordpress/wp-content/uploads/2015/04/20150407_Entrepreneurship_in-Asian_High-Tech_Ind-final.pdf.

59. In the 2000s many of the big companies like Google and Amazon that were located in "Bit Valley" relocated to the more upscale Roppongi and other areas; they are now moving back.

60. Cornelia Storz, "The Diversity of Innovation Patters in New Industries: The Case of 'Cool Japan,'" in *New Economic Spaces in Asian Cities: From Industrial Restructuring to the Cultural Turn*, ed. Peter W. Daniels, K.C. Ho, and Thomas A. Hutton (London: Routledge, 2012), 102–117.

61. Kenji E. Kushida, "Abenomics and Japan's Entrepreneurship and Innovation: Is the Third Arrow Pointed in the Right Direction for Global Competition in the Digital Era of Silicon Valley?" Stanford University Working Paper 2018-1, 28.

62. Chiara Criscuolo, Peter N. Gal, and Carlo Menon, "The Dynamics of Employment Growth: New Evidence from 18 Countries," OECD Science, Technology and Industry Policy Papers, No. 14, 2014, http://dx.doi.org/10.1787/5jz417h-j6hg6-en. In Japan VC investments account for only slightly more than 0.02 percent of the GDP, which is one-seventh of the US capital market. The global top 8 VC investment markets in 2017, from top to bottom, are the United States (US$71.9 billion), China (US$40 billion), the UK (US$5.8 billion), Israel (US$3.9 billion), Germany (US$2.9 billion), Japan (US$2.5 billion), France (US$2.4 billion), and Sweden (US$1.7 billion). In terms of VC investment amount, Japan is ranked sixth in the world, behind Germany and ahead of France.

63. Based on the Japan Startup Finance Report published by Entrepedia. After the financial crisis, money raised for ventures in Japan was about fifty billion yen (US$450 million) annually, according to Japan Venture Research. Venture Enterprise Center, *Heisei 25-nendo sōgyō kigyō shien jigyō (Kigyōkaseishin to seichō benchā ni kansuru kokusai chōsa), kigyōka seishin ni kansuru chōsa hōkokusho* [2013 Entrepreneurship Founding Support Project (International Survey on Entrepreneurship and Venture Growth: Survey on Entrepreneurship Report)], Tokyo, March 2014, http://www.vec.or.jp/wordpress/wp-content/files/25GEM.pdf.

64. For example, Mercari, a start-up running a flea market app, raised US$160 million before it went public in June 2018.

65. Hiroko Nakata, "Startups Find There's Financing in Numbers," *Japan Times*, April 16, 2015, http://www.japantimes.co.jp/news/2013/04/16/reference/startups-find-theres-financing-in-numbers/.

66. Editorial, "Japanese-style Employment and Wages," *Japan Times*, February 6, 2020, https://www.japantimes.co.jp/opinion/2020/02/06/editorials/japanese-style-employment-wages/.

67. Examples include ispace, which operates an office in Luxemburg with a staff of twelve; Xtreme-D, a developer of plug-in computing for next generation high-performance computing, has opened an office in Silicon Valley; one of the co-founders of Ascent Robotics, a startup for automation algorithms, is from the US.

68. Global Entrepreneurship Monitor 2014 and 2018 respectively, https://www.gemconsortium.org; Jacqui Kew, Mike Herrington, Yana Litovsky, and Helen Gale, "Generation Entrepreneur? The State of Global Youth Entrepreneurship," September 2013, https://www.youthbusiness.org/wp-content/uploads/2013/09/GenerationEntrepreneur.pdf.

69. The evidence on how demographic changes affect entrepreneurial activity in Japan remains mostly anecdotal (and is mostly limited to certain corners of the internet and content industry) and more empirical data is needed to better understand how young Japanese perceive the position of an entrepreneur as a vocation.

70. Georg D. Blind, "Unternehmensgründer in Japan seit 1991: Evidenz zur Evolution gegensätzlicher Gründergruppen," 14. Deutschsprachiger Japanologentag 2009, Halle, 2012.

71. Sébastien Lechevalier, Junichi Nishimura, and Cornelia Storz, "Diversity in Patterns of Industry Evolution: How an Intrapreneurial Regime Contributed to the Emergence of the Service Robot Industry," *Research Policy* 43, no. 10 (2014): 1716–1729.

72. Cornelia Storz, "The J-system of Innovation: Continuity of the 'Intrapreneurial' Pattern of Innovation," in *Institutional Diversity and Innovation: Continuing and Emerging Patterns in Japan and China*, ed. Cornelia Storz, and Sebastian Schäfer (London: Routledge, 2010), 118–153.

73. J.S. Eades, Roger Goodman, and Yumiko Hada, *The "Big-Bang" in Japanese Higher Education: The 2004 Reforms and Dynamics of Change* (Melbourne: Trans Pacific Press, 2005).

74. Nomura Research Institute, *Heisei 27-nendo sangyō gijutsu chōsa jigyō (Daigakuhatsu benchā no seichō yōin tabi dai ni kansuru jittai chōsa)* [2015 Analysis of Industry and Technology: Survey of Growth Factors of University-affiliated Venture Businesses], Tokyo, March 2016. The share of university spin-off VC in Japan increased from 0 percent in 2014 to 4.1 percent in 2015.

75. Fukuda Shin'ichi, *Kenshō Abenomikusu "Shin sanbon no ya": Seichō senryaku ni yoru kōzō kaikaku e no kitai to kadai* [Verification of Abenomics "The New Three Arrows": Expectations and Challenges for Structural Reform by Growth Strategy] (Tokyo: Tokyo Daigaku Shuppankai, 2018).

76. Lechevalier, *The Great Transformation,* 129.

77. Richard Solomon, "Entrepreneurship in Japan: Separating Fact from Fiction," Beacon Reports, January 27, 2014, http://beaconreport.net/mythology-japans-failure-entrepreneur/.

Chapter 6

Contradiction and Discontent in Japan

Abenomics and the Failing Politics of Economic Reform

SAORI SHIBATA

Introduction

After a landslide victory in the October 2017 lower house election, Prime Minister Abe Shinzō successfully formed his third cabinet. This was possible mainly due to the lack of a strong opposition party and the effect of increasing security threats from North Korea. It did not reflect public support for his economic reform program, also known as "Abenomics." In fact, survey results repeatedly revealed high levels of discontent among Japanese voters toward both Abenomics and the Abe government.[1]

Following its introduction in 2013, Abenomics had attracted international attention, partly because of its reliance on fiscal stimuli. These came at a time when other advanced economies were implementing austerity measures as a means to cope with the fallout of the 2008 Global Financial Crisis. After the initial enthusiasm for the decisive fiscal and monetary political interventions abated, however, the lingering symptoms of Japan's economic malaise resurfaced. Wages and consumption stagnated, the inflation rate remained below target, investment was insufficient, the number of non-regular workers increased, and economic growth remained low. In response, the Abe administration revamped its economic reform agenda to support those left behind by previous policy changes. In 2016, the Liberal

Democratic Party (LDP)-led government pledged to initiate additional fiscal stimuli for alleviating the burden of low-income households through increases in welfare spending, extending post-3.11 disaster reconstruction, and continuing large-scale reflationary monetary policy.[2] Moreover, the Abe cabinet added three new "arrows" to the existing three, with a key aim to improve female labor participation.

The government began to emphasize the declining unemployment rates, increases in the number of employed persons, rising corporate profits, and steadily growing nominal gross domestic product (GDP),[3] alongside a gradual increase of annualized GDP from 2017 onwards.[4] The situation looked even more positive after the Cabinet Office revised the projected growth rate upwards to 2.5 percent in late 2017.[5] Regardless of whether these extra measures have worked or not, Abenomics was, as a consequence, received more positively. Does this mean that the government succeeded in generating sustained economic growth? If so, can Abenomics be considered an alternative growth model for Japan, overcoming the "lost decades"?

In this chapter I seek to answer these questions by unpacking the policies that are subsumed under the banner of Abenomics, including the newly added three arrows. As Abe and his LDP pledged to "take back Japan" (*Nippon o torimodosu*) and insisted that Abenomics was "the only way available" (*kono michi shika nai*) to achieve this goal, I will assess to what extent these policies amount to fundamental change and discuss their implications for the Japanese economy. Following the theme and framework of this volume, I build on Colin Hay's conceptualization of crisis and state transformation[6] to argue that Abe's consensus-building for promoting his economic reform agenda resembles in large parts earlier attempts to stimulate Japan's economic growth. Yet, in light of its contradictory economic policies—the Japanese economy ceased to be a coordinated market economy[7] and transformed into a neoliberalized[8] and increasingly disorganized market economy—Abenomics has created discontent among the public. We witness, I argue, policymakers' continuing inability to provide an alternative growth model, and Japan entering a vicious circle of neoliberalization, rising social antagonisms, and disintegrating societal and political consensus.

Unpacking Abenomics

Already before Abe's return to the prime minister's office in late 2012, various issues had been destabilizing the Japanese economy. The problem of non-performing loans, exposed after the bursting of the 1980s bubble economy, had not been adequately addressed, and it worsened in the course of the economic stagnation of the "lost decades." Furthermore, insufficient reforms of corporate governance structures heightened concerns over Japanese firms' overdependency on the government.[9] Observers widely agreed that the Japanese government, failing to recognize the seriousness of the country's economic problems, had mismanaged the post-crises market. For instance, Kenneth Kuttner et al. find that authorities tasked to design monetary and financial policies continued to make crucial mistakes from the mid-1990s onwards, while decision-makers failed to rectify previous mistakes and change their approaches.[10] In this context, the Abe government could present the drastic interventions under Abenomics as a necessary set of policies that would finally resolve long-standing problems and end the national crisis.

Numerous studies have examined the bundle of slogans and measures commonly summarized as Abenomics.[11] This chapter only provides a brief sketch of the original "three arrows" and mainly focuses on the adjustments that have been introduced in the subsequent stage that I call Abenomics 2.0.

The Three Arrows: Quantitative Easing, Fiscal Stimulus, Structural Reform

The first arrow in the form of expansionary monetary policy, sometimes called quantitative easing, was implemented from the onset of Abenomics in early 2013. The Bank of Japan (BOJ) purchased assets at an unprecedented level, including Japanese Government Bonds (JGBs), to increase the flow of money into the market and to achieve the proclaimed target of a 2 percent inflation rate. This included a promise to purchase 7 trillion yen of JGBs every month, and about 80 trillion yen of JGBs annually to boost market liquidity. However, due to the still stagnating inflation rate, the BOJ in 2017 announced further open-ended purchases worth US$660 billion (or 73 trillion yen) until Japan would achieve the 2 percent target. This amounted to the world's largest asset purchasing program, and some warned that this level of quantitative easing may harm Japan's banking system and potentially create speculative bubbles.[12] Despite an unprecedented amount of money injected into the market, however, the policy failed to bring about a return to growth.

Adding a second arrow, the Abe government in January 2013 initiated an economic recovery program. Out of the 20.2 trillion yen stimulus package, 10.3 trillion yen were spent directly by the government. However, even this large-scale spending proved insufficient to reenergize the economy. In December 2013, the Abe cabinet therefore decided to tie an additional package of 18.6 trillion yen, dubbed the "Virtuous Cycle" program. In April 2014, it added another 5.5 trillion yen, to be followed by yet another 28.1 trillion yen for "the investment for the future program" in August 2016.[13] These aggressive fiscal stimuli led to an increase of government debt from 215.4 percent of the GDP in 2012 to the record-high level of 232.4 percent in 2016.[14] In addition to the ballooning public debt, the lacking "soundness of the fiscal and economic situation and fiscal and economic policies"[15] and "heightened risks of the JGBs' devaluation"[16] raised concerns over these measures' long-term effects.

However, fiscal policies under Abenomics consisted not only of fiscal stimuli, but also included attempts at fiscal consolidation. For instance, in August 2013, the government announced that it would trim 17 trillion yen from the budget over the next two years. Thus, in 2014, it switched policies from fiscal stimulus to fiscal consolidation.[17] Fiscal policy as implemented under Abenomics has therefore been contradictory. It not only continued to rely on massive stimulus packages, but it also took recourse to austerity measures such as increases of the sales tax and pension contributions. Unsurprisingly, the latter have stirred considerable resistance.[18]

The third arrow of Abenomics consisted of a growth strategy comprising various structural reforms. Launched in June 2013, the program, entitled *Japan Revitalization Strategy: Japan Is Back*,[19] has been revised annually and flagged with different subtitles: *Challenge for the Future* in 2014, *Investment toward Future and Productivity Revolution* in 2015, and *Toward the Fourth Industrial Revolution* in 2016.[20] The strategy's proclaimed objective has been to revitalize the Japanese economy by increasing investments, exports, and labor flexibility; creating a more business-friendly environment; liberalizing the agricultural industry; and promoting technological innovation.[21] The establishment of the Headquarters for Japan's Economic Revitalization by the Ministry of Economy, Trade and Industry, in particular, highlights the importance that the government has attributed to the creation of wealth through GDP growth rather than through income redistribution.[22] And a statement by the chairperson of the Deregulation Committee, Ōta Hiroko, reveals that national prosperity clearly takes precedence over the alleviation of individual economic hardship: "day labor dispatching by temp agencies are banned under the current legislation. . . . This legislation is currently preventing people from working as day laborers, and this has been discussed as a problem."[23] In this vein, "Taking Back Japan,"[24] the LDP's manifesto for the 2012 lower house election, emphasized the need for the establishment of a business-friendly environment in Japan and the importance of improving corporations' competitiveness abroad. Intriguingly, the document said nothing about the improvement of labor and working conditions.

Thus, Abenomics bears the trademark of neoliberal reform in the sense that corporations benefit from the reduction of corporate tax, a more business-friendly environment, and a flexible labor market, whereas workers receive only slow wage increases while facing the continuation of job insecurity and long working hours. What is more, Abe's structural reform plans have also furthered neoliberal austerity politics. The flexibilization of labor often implied the reduction of welfare, and the liberalization of the agricultural sector meant that farmers in rural economies would likely have to cope with declining incomes due to an expected increase in imports and concomitant competition from abroad. Structural reforms have, therefore, faced strong criticisms and opposition.[25] Negotiations for joining the Trans-Pacific Partnership (TPP) free-trade agreement also prompted opposition from farmers' and consumer associations.[26]

In sum, two phenomena characterized the first stage of Abenomics: First, despite the decisive implementation of continuous large-scale monetary and fiscal policies, no fundamental shift toward strong economic growth could be observed. Second, the structural reforms, representing the third arrow, served to further neoliberal policies and consequently fueled discontent among large segments of the Japanese public. In this context, the rate of support for the Abe administration fell for the first time below the rate of non-support in July 2015.

Abenomics 2.0: Minor Tinkering, Failure Management, and Consensus-Building

In an attempt to address the growing discontent over its structural reforms, the Abe government in September 2015 began to make a number of concessions. In essence, however, these represented a revision and reinforcement of the Abenomics program. Abenomics 2.0 put forward three new arrows and in 2016 culminated with the announcement of a plan for "Promoting Dynamic Engagement of All Citizens" (*ichioku sōkatsuyaku shakai*).[27] This plan included the "urgent policies to realize a robust economy with GDP growth toward 600 trillion yen." Focused on the advancement of technology and work-style reforms, the initiative in many ways sought to revive the original three arrows. The new second arrow entailed policies directly linked to the target of achieving the "desirable birthrate of 1.8" by attempting to establish a stable and reliable childcare system.[28] The new third arrow, finally, introduced the objective of "no one forced to leave their jobs for nursing care" (*kaigo rishoku zero*),[29] which sought to improve the elderly care system in order to prevent people from resigning from work due to the need to take care of their aging family members. Thus, compared to Abenomics 1.0, the second salvo of arrows targeted Japan's labor shortage. I will now assess the degree to which these reforms have effectuated change and achieved their stated goals.

Appealing to the Youth, Women, and Non-Regular Workers?

The steadily growing number of non-regular workers and their experience of precarity have, over the last twenty years, developed into a serious social problem in Japan.[30] The low wages of non-regular workers and the increasing wage disparity between non-regular and regular workers, combined with an insufficient level of social insurance coverage, fueled impoverishment. This has triggered widespread anxieties and led to growing demands for change.

Public surveys show that the second Abe cabinet suffered from a gradual decline of popularity partly due to the stagnating economy. Despite the large amount of money pumped into the market, the majority of the population did not perceive an improvement in economic conditions. Support rates dropped from 50 percent in 2013, Abe's first year in office, to 45.1 percent in 2014, before slightly recovering to 48.1 percent in 2015 (see figure 6.1). The same poll revealed that the number of people who "do not support" (47.3 percent) the Abe cabinet rose above those who did (36.3 percent) for the first time in July 2015.[31] In response, the Abe administration in 2016 launched another round of fiscal stimuli totaling 6 trillion yen. This extra spending included 2.5 trillion yen for the welfare of pensioners and subsidies for childcare facilities, 1.7 trillion yen for infrastructure construction, and 0.6 trillion yen for small and medium-sized businesses that had been negatively affected by the announcement of Brexit.[32] It is noteworthy that these fiscal stimuli came at a time when structural reforms faced rising criticisms for facilitating the spread of precarious working conditions. And it is reasonable to argue that these measures were at least in part designed to offset the negative effects of Abe's structural reforms.

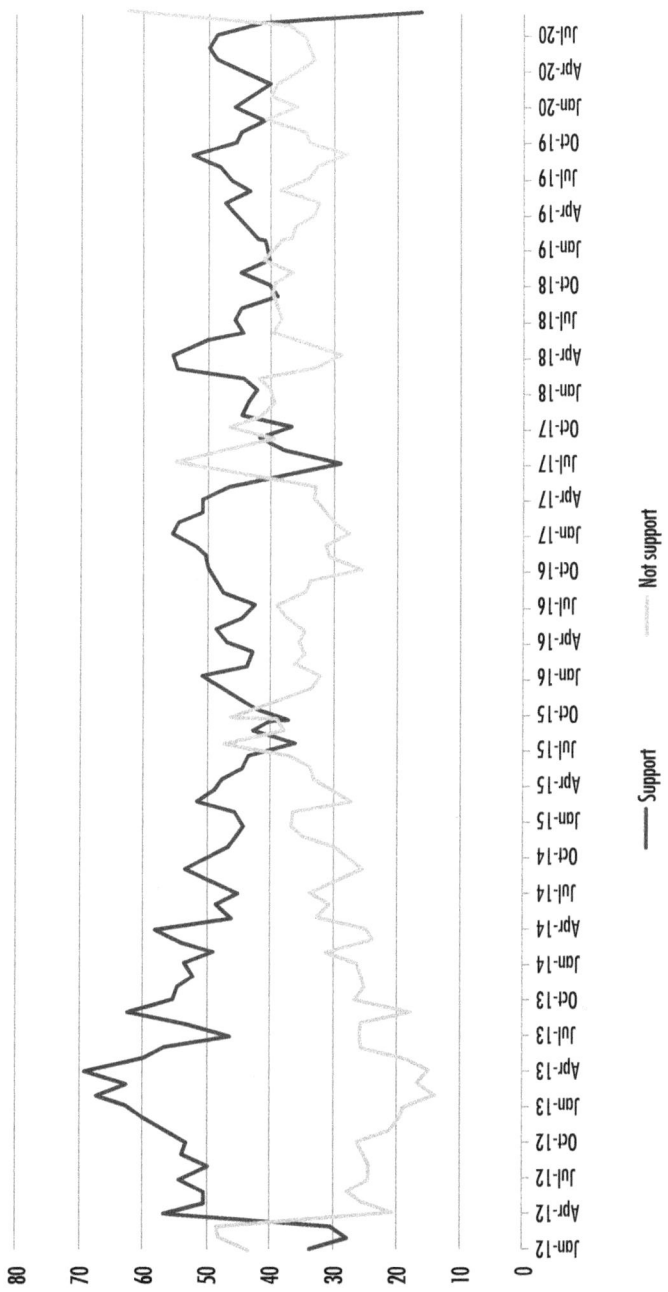

Figure 6.1. The popularity of the Abe government, 2012–2020 (in percent). Source: Compiled by the author based on TV Asahi Poll (various years), "Naikaku siziritsu no suii" [Change in approval rates of cabinets], http://www.tv-asahi.co.jp/hst/poll/.

Thus, to address growing public discontent and to solve the problem of sluggish wage growth, the Abe administration moved away from promoting the flexibility-focused policies of Abenomics 1.0 and started to advocate a new equal-pay-for-equal-work initiative. It remains unclear, however, whether this shift really was an attempt to help people stuck in precarious work conditions.

Whatever Abe's motivation, his government was successful in presenting itself as acknowledging the problem and attempting to reduce the wage disparity between regular and non-regular workers to the levels of other OECD economies. This had been achieved by highlighting the government's consideration of the plight of non-regular workers and the problem of their low wages. For instance, the LDP manifesto for the 2014 lower house election included a pledge to support those who wish to shift from non-regular to regular employment.[33] Further, in September 2016, Abe, in a speech to economists and fund managers in New York, asserted that he would launch "an expert group with a single mission, a mission to change the way we work," and promised to improve the pay and working conditions of non-regular employees, who then already made up roughly 40 percent of the Japanese workforce.[34] Soon after the LDP's victory in the 2017 elections, Abe also urged employers to increase wages by 3 percent in order to improve Japan's economy.[35]

In addition to focusing on non-regular (precarious) workers, the second arrow of Abenomics 2.0 also represented the government's attempt to convey its intent to improve childcare and elderly care facilities. In so doing, Abe promised to support young families by providing more affordable housing[36] and to create a better environment for women seeking to continue, or return to, work following career breaks for childcare. The policy package also claimed to provide more opportunities for female workers wanting to return to college and university, while encouraging men to take childcare and elderly care leave.[37] With these measures, the government sought to highlight its active approach to promoting gender equality. However, the policy to improve childcare facilities for enhancing female participation in the labor market has been long-standing.[38] It had already been set up in the 1990s. Thus, the recycling of this pre-existing and largely unchanged policy, somewhat ironically, illustrates that pertaining measures cannot by themselves improve gender equality in the labor market.

Wage Increase Appeals and the Postponement of Tax Hikes

Abe also appealed to the wider public by calling for wage increases and postponing tax hikes. The first sales tax increase, from 5 to 8 percent, implemented in April 2014, caused the Japanese economy to backslide into recession. Thus, to avoid the further deterioration of macroeconomic indicators and prevent the stifling of public consumption, Abe postponed the second hike from 8 to 10 percent until October 2019. In this way, the government responded in a timely manner to reverse an unpopular policy and regain public support. However, without realizing solid wage increases and improving working conditions first, this and prospective further increases of the sales tax would continue to dampen consumer confidence into the foreseeable future.

According to the 2015 Corporate Accounting Annual Report issued by the Ministry of Finance,[39] Japanese businesses had been able to significantly increase the volume of their internal reserves under Abenomics, while workers saw only small or no improvements of their pay. Abe subsequently sought to mask this disparity between employees and business owners by demanding higher wages. He had been calling on firms to increase salaries, including those of part-time workers, on many occasions.[40] Yet corporations had not followed through, prompting Abe to yet again urge companies to increase wages by 3 percent in 2018.[41] Abe's intention behind this political pressure on business was to boost consumer spending and to end chronic deflation. The Keidanren business association also made a similar call to its member corporations. This was the first time that Keidanren demanded a specific wage increase. Nevertheless, in 2019, average monthly wages fell 0.3 percent from the previous year.[42]

Voters First

Analyzing Abe's strategy of tempering public discontent, some argued that he had been following a "voter first" approach.[43] According to this view, Abe signaled to LDP policy experts (*zoku giin*) and government bureaucrats that his administration was serious about reforming Japan and ready to reach a compromise. He did this for the sole purpose of avoiding the kind of resistance that many former prime ministers had faced from bureaucrats.[44] In fact, former prime ministers, particularly Koizumi Junichirō, had employed similar tactics. Yet, compared to earlier attempts, Abe's approach to political communication proved extremely effective at highlighting his leadership and decisiveness, especially in the fight with the Bank of Japan over monetary policy.[45]

Likewise, Abenomics 2.0, introducing a "local Abenomics" scheme designed to address rural communities' concerns about an aging population, deteriorating agricultural sectors, and the heavy concentration of economic activities in Tokyo, helped to boost the popularity of Abenomics. Local Abenomics comprises a wide range of policies that aim to revitalize rural economies by increasing educational and training opportunities and by reforming local working practices.[46] This strategy and the positive narrative that accompanied Abenomics had contributed to the improvement of Abe's image as an effective leader demonstrating a credible commitment to reforming Japan. By 2016, Abenomics 2.0 had led to a rise in the prime minister's popularity to 51.8 percent.[47] Yet, in stark contrast to his rhetoric of "taking back Japan," little innovation had occurred. In fact, Abe simply enhanced the promotion of policies that had already been adopted by previous LDP administrations. His sustained popularity primarily stemmed from the ability to advertise policies.[48] Indeed, the launch of Abenomics 2.0 temporarily increased cabinet approval rates in 2016 and especially in 2017 (see figure 6.1).

Toward a Disorganized Model of Capitalism: Precarity, Insecurity, and Instability

Abenomics was a path-dependent policy choice "in that it strengthened pre-existing and largely unmodified structures of the state regime,"[49] rather than marking a fundamental break. Thus, as outlined above, Abe's recycling of previous policies maintained numerous unresolved economic contradictions. This section demonstrates how these policies acted to create and sustain precarity, insecurity, and instability, and thereby led to an increasingly disorganized model of capitalism.

Continuing Precarity and Insecurity in the Workplace

Seeking to legitimate Abenomics, the Abe administration in 2017 emphasized its policies' positive effects by pointing to Japan's lowest unemployment rate in 24 years,[50] increases in nominal GDP and employment, rising corporate profits, growing private investment, and higher tax revenues.[51] Despite these claims, however, we continue to see precarity grow. In stark contrast to the proclaimed achievements, the Abe administration failed to address problems in the labor market such as the continuing growth in the numbers of non-regular workers and the low availability of stable jobs and social security, as well as continuing widespread practice of workers taking on long working hours to make ends meet. The hourly wage gap between regular and non-regular workers remains at 30 percent.[52] Furthermore, suicides resulting from overwork cast doubts over the ruling elites' commitment to improve conditions through measures such as the Work-Style Reforms (*hatarakikata kaikaku*), which limits monthly overtime to a very high 100 hours per month. While *hourly* wages of part-time workers have increased as a result of the declining number of available working days, the *monthly* incomes of part-time workers remained at the levels they were at in the late 1990s.[53]

Unsatisfactory Work and Deteriorating Working Conditions

The Abe administration routinely highlighted its contribution to the increase of its demand, but labor policies remained insufficient. It claimed that the ratio of effective labor demand to effective supply had risen above 1.0, thereby contributing to an increase in the employment rate. This improvement, however, was restricted to the service sector, including elderly care, restaurants, food, and customer care, which face acute labor shortages.[54] Less precarious and therefore more popular positions such as general office work, however, remained hard to get.[55] This means that the labor market has not been able to offer jobs preferred by workers, thus creating a mismatch between the types of jobs people seek and those that are available. The selected narratives—increased effective labor demand and the lowest unemployment rate—therefore belie the persistence of underlying frustrations and unresolved problems.

In addition, the employment situation has shown few signs of improvement and continues to be unstable. The overall number of non-regular workers had significantly risen under the Abe government.[56] While the government had been keen to emphasize that the total number of employed people had increased under Abenomics, this is partly due to the large growth of those working on a part-time basis, with even people working for as little as one hour per day being counted as having employment status in the government's labor force survey.[57]

The Abenomics years have also seen a deterioration of the working conditions and a continuation of high levels of stress at the workplace. This is mainly a consequence of the Abe government's principal goal of creating flexible working practices. For instance, the number of reported harassment cases in the workplace increased from 25.3 percent of people surveyed in 2014 to 32.5 percent in 2016.[58] A majority of companies (73.4 percent) surveyed had systems in place to respond to complaints from workers, most frequently about instances of harassment.[59] Compounding the problem is the fact that the majority of workers who have experienced harassment also reported an increase of anxiety, discontent, anger, and a declining willingness to work.[60] This development partly explains the high levels of stress experienced in the workplace. For instance, according to a survey conducted by the Ministry of Health, Labour and Welfare, 68.5 percent of male workers and 71.5 percent of female workers reported experiencing stress, demonstrating a high level of pressure among a majority of workers.[61] The Abe government had largely failed to acknowledge this reality.

Deregulation and Liberalization of the Labor Market: Hidden Agendas

Seeking to revitalize the economy in the context of the declining population and aging society, the LDP-led coalition government, from 2013 onwards, implemented deregulation and liberalization measures.[62] This includes the introduction of the Work-Style Reforms in 2017. The policies' officially declared core goals are equal pay for equal work, reduction of long working hours, and employment promotion for elderly workers.[63] What these reforms implicitly aim at, however, is to make Japan a more business-friendly environment. Business elites who directly benefit from these reforms make up the majority of the advisory board members for Work-Style Reforms. Only one of the national labor union's associations, Rengo, was invited to the advisory board, and this only *after* the core features of the reforms had already been decided upon, thus preventing the genuine representation of workers.[64] As such, the Reforms tended to benefit employers rather than employees.

Abe's Work-Style Reforms pledged to abolish the term "non-regular worker," but this did not necessarily mean the elimination of precarious working conditions. While the Abe administration highlighted its own success in terms of increasing the number of jobs and reducing the unemployment rate, available jobs for non-regular workers were located mainly in the food sector, where employees are usually paid minimum wages with no prospect of improving their skills.[65] Further, while the principle of "equal pay for equal work" was introduced in a purported attempt to improve non-regular workers' employment conditions and increase wages, their situation has not changed significantly over the last ten years. The pledge to eliminate the term "non-regular workers" has therefore been a largely superficial and meaningless gesture.

The Work-Style Reforms also sought to shorten working hours by limiting legal overtime work to 45 hours per month, while allowing up to 100 hours per month in busy periods. This, however, attracted criticism from unions, citizens' groups, and bereaved families who lost members due to long working hours. According to critics, these reforms will effectively legalize death from overwork (*karōshi*).[66] Indeed, the average of the annual total working hours per full-time worker remains higher than in other advanced economies.[67] Commentators noted that it is impossible to achieve shorter working hours without reducing the absolute workload, and that this measure, therefore, paradoxically risks increasing unpaid overtime work.[68] At the same time, while the rate of people who work over sixty hours per week slightly declined, more than 10 percent of the working population, that is much higher than the OECD average, remain affected. Indeed, the practice of long overtime work remains a core employment strategy to reduce labor costs for many Japanese corporations.[69] Nevertheless, many have been defending Abenomics and praised the improved employment rate in terms that justify companies' pursuit of profits.[70] Seen in this light, the Abe government's claim to improve the long-working practice appears to be a policy designed as a "newsworthy" event to be recruited into an overall narrative, without addressing the actual problem at hand.

The Abe administration's introduction of more flexible working hours without employers' obligation to pay overtime corroborates this finding. This change came under the influence of the advisory board for Work-Style Reforms. After two failed attempts during his first tenure, Prime Minister Abe in 2017 tried again to institutionalize white-collar exemptions from overtime payments (the so-called zero overtime payment system). Similar reform efforts had already attracted criticisms, especially from labor unions, in the past. In June 2018, however, the Abe government succeeded in overcoming this resistance by first targeting higher income earners. The High-Level Professional Worker System (*kōdō purofeshonaru seido*), eventually introduced, sought to cap paid working hours through the introduction of unpaid overtime for employees whose annual salary exceeds 11 million yen. Opponents have argued that this new measure obscures actual working hours and leads to a further deterioration of working conditions, and, once normalized, could easily be expanded to the segments of lower salaried workers.[71]

It is in the context of these labor market reforms that citizens' groups, unions, and members of the public have resorted to acts of protest, voicing heightened frustration with the government's economic agenda.[72] For instance, in May 2016, 13,000 people went to the streets in Kyoto to criticize Abenomics for benefiting only large corporations and worsening the working conditions of non-regular employees.[73] In Hokkaido, 5,000 people rallied against Abenomics' insufficient measures for supporting declining rural economies.[74] In May 2018, 1,000 people gathered in front of the Diet building to protest the High-Level Professional Worker System.[75] People who had lost family members due to death from overwork also rallied against the system in June 2018.[76] Thus, the reality of working conditions for non-regular workers continues to differ considerably from the depiction provided by the government. As such, Abe's Work-Style Reforms remained superficial and focused on tempering dissent, rather than genuinely attempting to produce substantial improvement.

Gender Inequality

In 2013, the Abe administration announced "womenomics" as a key policy for economic growth. It sought to promote female participation in the labor market, in politics and management.[77] According to some observers, "womenomics" should be considered a success in that it contributed to an increase in the number of childcare facilities and employed mothers as well as a reduction of working hours for regular workers with infants.[78] On the other hand, gender-wage inequality remains significant.[79] In 2020, Japan ranked 115th in the Global Gender Gap Report, down from the 111th spot in 2016.[80] Japan also performed poorly in the ratio of female chief executive officers and board members: a shockingly low 2.6 percent.[81]

Similarly, Japan continues to see low female participation in politics due to prevailing structural barriers.[82] Policies similar to those adopted under Abe had already been implemented by former Prime Minister Koizumi between 2001 and 2006.[83] This suggests that Abe's proclaimed commitment to gender equality is neither new nor particularly strong. In addition, women's participation in business and politics has been considered important only to the degree that it contributes to economic growth, with neither the current Abe-led administration nor its predecessors valuing gender equality as being important in itself.[84] Instead, policies have been promoted in order to inject cheap female workers into the labor market.[85] "Womenomics" is, therefore, another example of what Hay refers to as "minor tinkering," a discursive construction designed to only superficially address the problem of gender inequality. Gender equality is "newsworthy" and "crisis-worthy."[86] The problem is selectively sampled to create the appearance that the lack of childcare and elderly facilities is addressed.[87] Yet these measures remain superficial and represent no more than an attempt at failure management. As such, "womenomics" acted to sustain gender inequality.

Poverty and Inequality

Economic growth under Abenomics remained low. Despite the government's continued dispersion of huge stimulus packages, Japan only achieved a real economic growth rate of 1.1 percent per year between 2013 and 2016. Importantly, this figure does not mark a significant improvement when compared to the 0.9 percent average real economic growth between the early 1990s post-bubble period and 2017.[88] While Abe sought to highlight the increase in stock prices as alternate proof of success, only 20 to 30 percent of Japanese households benefitted from this temporary effect.[89] Moreover, the number of rich people who earn an annual income of 20 million yen or more has been increasing, as has the size of their income, thereby widening inequality.[90] The majority of the people, therefore, do not benefit from one of the most-praised effects of Abenomics.

In addition, Japan has seen an increasing level of poverty among the elderly. The *2017 Analysis of the Labour Economy* reports that the proportion of elderly households with a low income increased from 13.7 percent in 2000 to 26.6 percent in 2015.[91] Particularly striking about elderly poverty is its severity. One shocking symptom thereof is the stark increase of incarceration rates.[92] Unable to make ends meet, elderly people have turned to committing crimes in order to secure food and shelter.

More recently, in January 2018, the Tokyo Metropolitan Government announced for the first time the number of "net café refugees" who sleep in internet cafés. According to the local government's own survey, Tokyo counts approximately 4,000 and reports that nearly half of those net café refugees (43.8 percent) are homeless.[93] Intriguingly, the majority of these people are not jobless but employed in precarious non-regular contracts: 38.1 percent are part-time workers, 33.2 percent temp agency workers, and 4.5 percent contracted workers. Many of them, currently in their fifties, had lost their jobs in the 2008 Global Financial Crisis and been unable to find steady income ever since.[94]

To be sure, the Gini index and the relative poverty rate show slight improvements for 2017. Yet, Japan still ranks sixth among the 34 OECD countries in terms of relative poverty. This situation partly explains Japan's fall in the happiness index from the forty-third spot in 2013 to the fifty-first in 2017. During the same period, the OECD also reported that Japan's rank for public spending on education dropped from fifty-third in 2013 to seventy-second in 2017.[95] This trend points to a situation where only the wealthy can afford to provide their children with high-quality education, thus further exacerbating a disparity between low-income and high-income households in the long term. The increase in poverty among the elderly and widening income inequality, therefore, all evince the opposite of what the current Abe government has been claiming as either its achievements or its intentions.

Suffering Rural Economies

One of the most significant agricultural policies introduced under the Abe administration is the reform of the once all-powerful Japanese Agricultural Cooperative Group (JA) and its affiliated organizations. Specifically, Zenchu, JA's umbrella organization, was transformed into an incorporated association, having its National Audit Body split off to be established as a third-party audit corporation.[96] While some observers saw these reforms a success in the sense that they weaken the political power of the JA,[97] others have raised concerns. For instance, farmers and consumers who considered foreign agricultural products unsafe in comparison to domestic products formed a coalition to oppose trade liberalization.[98] Also, local governments have often supported farmers in desperate attempts to support their ailing rural economies (with agricultural liberalization viewed as damaging rural economies).[99]

Regarding Japan's decision to join the TPP free-trade agreement, a key pillar of Abenomics, some local authorities feared that the trade deal would lead to a reduction in agricultural and dairy production. The Kumamoto prefectural government, for instance, estimated that agriculture, forestry, and fishery production would shrink between 8.3 billion and 15.1 billion yen annually.[100] Similarly, the Akita and Tottori prefectural governments foresaw a decline of around 4 billion yen[101] and 17 billion yen,[102] respectively. Echoing these concerns, JA warned that the deal would endanger Japan's already low self-sufficiency.[103] It argued that the government had underrated the impact of the Comprehensive and Progressive Agreement for Trans-Pacific Partnership, the TPP successor, as it underestimated the increase of imports.

Abe's JA reform has therefore been endorsed neither by farmers, nor by local politicians, nor by consumers. To the contrary, the iron triangle—an alliance among some in the LDP, JA representing farmers, and the Ministry of Agriculture, Fishery and Forestry—has been resisting the liberalization of the agricultural sector. Given the official objective to revitalize agriculture, it may be argued that the Abe government chose to reform the JA system to appeal to voters by "challenging JA and the iron triangle despite its traditional role as an important support base for the LDP."[104] Yet the Abe government decided to reform JA as a means to increase the power of the Prime Minister's Office. Rather than to "increase income in rural areas over 10 years and reorganize the JA to benefit farmers,"[105] it served to crush long-standing resistance from the iron triangle against trade liberalization through Japan's accession to bilateral and multilateral free-trade agreements.

Abenomics also included the promotion of entrepreneurialism in the agricultural sector as a means to increase national competitiveness.[106] In the same vein, efforts to integrate cutting-edge technology were made to transform agriculture into a more tech-savvy industry.[107] This agenda responds to the long-standing criticisms of Japan's agricultural protectionism and the pertaining view that its agricultural industry is uncompetitive and reliant on excessive government subsidies for its survival. Policymakers hope that the introduction of advanced technology, combined with a more targeted system of subsidies, will improve productivity of the declining and shrinking agricultural sector and make the rapidly aging Japanese farmers internationally competitive. Yet, these neoliberal policies bear the potential to create a situation where only those few farmers who are able to adopt such technologies will receive government subsidies and survive, while the majority of the poor and elderly farmers will be left behind.

The Abe government's agricultural reforms have therefore widely been viewed as a contradictory and unsatisfactory set of policies. This includes concerns over the reduction in the costs of machinery and other goods required for agricultural production. Farmers have been skeptical about how exactly the claimed cost reduction will contribute to a "strong agriculture." Local actors in the agricultural sector have consistently raised concerns that the neoliberal reforms will lead to a further deterioration of the rural economy.[108] As a result, rural communities continue to face serious questions about the sustainability of their local agricultural industries. Rather than resolving Japan's socioeconomic problems, therefore, the second stage of Abenomics risked exacerbating the economic and social problems in the forms of poverty, gender inequality, harsh working conditions, and the depopulation of rural areas.

Contesting Abenomics

The gap between the Abenomics' reform rhetoric and the socioeconomic reality generated a large amount of discontent. This discontent focused on the way that Abenomics furthered the process of capitalist disorganization and, in this sense, represented a response to the path-dependent nature of Abe's reforms. In contrast to the administration's pledges to fundamentally change postwar Japan for the better, Abenomics has produced the unfolding of a new "structural crisis of the state regime."[109]

Contesting Working Practices

Abenomics essentially represented the continuation of labor market flexibilization while falling short on its promises to improve working conditions for the majority of employees. This insufficiency generated dissatisfaction and contestation. According to a 2018 survey by the Rengo labor union, 44.7 percent of non-regular workers were employed as such because they could not gain regular employment status. Also, over 60 percent of those who found themselves unwillingly in a non-regular status were unsatisfied, and 67.5 percent of those expressed that they would like to achieve regular workers' status.[110]

Furthermore, gender inequality at the workplace continued to be widespread under the Abe-led government. Based on a survey of non-regular female employees conducted in 2017,[111] roughly 40 percent of those who worked over 35 hours per week stated that they could not find regular positions. Moreover, 44 percent of the surveyed felt that people only expect women to balance work and family-care duties. Many of the surveyed therefore viewed the Abe government's gender policies as inadequate. Nearly 35 percent thought that the government should pay more attention to the situation of female non-regular workers. As these examples illustrate, Abenomics lacked policies which could have proactively transformed Japan's economy. Instead, it recycled existing, largely unmodified neoliberal policies that were destined to exacerbate employment insecurity.

Contesting Inequality, Poverty, and Rural Economies

Abenomics has been contested on the basis of its limited positive effects on social and gender inequality, poverty, and rural economies. Inaba Tsuyoshi, an activist who has been working to eliminate poverty and to support people in poverty, points to "the increase in the rate of relative poverty over the last 10 years in Japan" and warns that "one of the main causes behind this is the increase of non-regular work."[112] The number of people employed under such contracts increased from 18,430,000 in December 2012, when Abe and the LDP returned to office, to 20,150,000 in December 2015.[113] The labor law expert Wada Hajime similarly points to this as cause of the increasing number of people in poverty, saying that

> it is unusual for advanced economies to have 40 percent of non-regular workers. Japan has enhanced deregulation (in the labor market) without providing adequate measures (to protect non-regular workers). This led to an increase in the number of unstable and precarious employees. We will further witness the dualization of Japan's labor market.[114]

This increase, combined with insufficient protection for non-regular workers who do not benefit from either employment security or social security insurances, exacerbated the inequality and poverty. Poverty among households with children has become a particularly serious problem.[115] In response, Japan saw a series of union-led May Day protests in which Abenomics was routinely criticized for increasing inequality and worsening working conditions. For instance, 6,000 people joined a rally against Abenomics and demanded improved employment security in April 2014.[116] One of the participants asserted that "from the perspective of ordinary citizens, I do not feel any effects from Abenomics."[117] Likewise, three major labor union associations, Rengo, Zenrōren, and Zenrōkyo, held a rally and street demonstration in May 2015 to oppose the labor policies of the Abe administration.[118] For three national organizations to act together is highly unusual and demonstrates the seriousness of the situation.

Many in rural areas have also consistently expressed discontent regarding their economic condition. This could be seen during the 2014 May Day event, when protesters alerted the public about the fact that Abenomics had only benefited large corporations and big cities.[119] This trend continued in 2015. Many labor unions based in rural areas opposed the austerity measures, and in demonstrations criticized the Abe-led government on the grounds that its policies increase inequality. For instance, protesters gathered in front of the Aomori prefectural government and blamed Abenomics for the continuing poverty in rural areas. These grievances are no mere subjective perceptions. In March 2015, the Cabinet Office announced the result of its own survey, reporting that increased inequality and disparity between the urban and rural areas was a core concern.[120] Similarly, a 2019 *Nihon Keizai Shimbun* opinion poll revealed that 78 percent of the surveyed did not feel that the Japanese economy has improved.[121]

Conclusion

The second stage of Abenomics aimed to appeal to people "left behind" from Abenomics 1.0, including non-regular workers, low-income households, households with children, and workers in small- and medium-sized companies, and residents of rural areas. It did so by selecting certain narratives that include "equal pay for equal work," "local Abenomics," support for agriculture, "womenomics," wage increases, and an increase in effective labor demand. As neoliberal policies imposed on the agricultural sector appeared as tool for securing executive control over policymaking, they also failed to adequately address deteriorating and depopulating rural economies. Thus, Abenomics 2.0, too, failed to alleviate the fundamental problems facing workers, including wage disparity, inequality between regular and non-regular workers, long working hours, and employment insecurity. Likewise, little progress has been made in achieving gender equality.

Prime Minister Abe and his government presented Abenomics as an attempt to introduce path-breaking policies. They claimed that Abenomics addressed Japan's fundamental socioeconomic problems and revitalized the country's stagnating and deflationary economy after a number of "lost decades." However, as I have shown here, a more adequate view of Abenomics is that of a set of recycled, repackaged policies of minor tinkering, all of which exacerbated Japan's unresolved socioeconomic contradictions. Thus, returning to the framework of this volume, Abenomics should be considered a policy that illustrates Japan's "inertial and re-active system," one that merely testifies to system failure, and not as a reform "through reflexive, strategic and decisive transformation."[122] Japan remains stuck within a path-dependent neoliberal policy framework that has led, and continues to lead, to economic failure, exacerbating social instability, and deepening the crisis of Japan's capitalist state. In doing so, it has acted to generate further contradictions and ongoing discontent, especially among workers and women. The cabinet approval rates plummeted from 52 percent in September 2019 to 16.3 percent in September 2020 (see figure 6.1), indicating discontent among population. This represents a further move toward a crisis that is turning Japan into a disorganized market economy.[123] The legacy of Abenomics looms over the still-ailing Japanese economy as it has been battered by the COVID-19 crisis with further waves of redundancies and job losses. Upon coming to power in September 2020, the Suga administration took over the Abenomics policy line. The failures of Japan's economic system are therefore unlikely to come to an end.

Notes

1. TV Asahi yoron chōsa [TV Asahi Poll], "Naikaku siziritsu no suii" [Change in Approval Rates of Cabinets], https://www.tv-asahi.co.jp/hst/poll/graph_naikaku. html. Unless otherwise stated, all online sources were accessed and available on October 10, 2020.

2. Larry Elliot, "Japan PM Launches Spending Programme to Boost Economy," *Guardian*, August 2, 2016, https://www.theguardian.com/business/2016/aug/02/japan-pm-shinzo-abe-launches-spending-programme-to-boost-economy.

3. The Government of Japan, "Abenomics: For Future Growth, for Future Generations, and for a Future Japan That is Robust," Tokyo, 2017, https://www.japan. go.jp/abenomics/index.html.

4. Leo Lewis and Hudson Lockett, "Japan Posts Longest Unbroken Growth Streak in More than a Decade," *Financial Times*, August 14, 2017, https://www. ft.com/content/848dad38-809e-11e7-a4ce-15b2513cb3ff.

5. Edward White and Robin Harding, "Japan's Growth Rate Revised Upwards to 2.5%," *Financial Times*, December 8, 2017, https://www.ft.com/content/32f019ac-dbbb-11e7-a039-c64b1c09b482.

6. Colin Hay, "Crisis and the Structural Transformation of the State: Interrogating the Process of Change," *British Journal of Politics and International Relations* 1, no. 3 (1999): 317–344.

7. Yasuharu Aoki, "How Does the Largest Shareholder Affect Dividends?" *International Review of Finance* 14, no. 4 (2014): 613–645; Jonathan Morris, John Hassard, and Leo McCann, "The Resilience of 'Institutionalized Capitalism': Managing Managers under 'Shareholder Capitalism' and 'Managerial Capitalism," *Human Relations* 61, no. 5 (2008): 687–710; Teranishi Jūrō, *Nihongata shihonshugi* [A Japanese Model of Capitalism] (Tokyo: Chūkō Shinsho, 2018).

8. Sébastien Lechevalier, *The Great Transformation of Japanese Capitalism*, trans. J.A.A. Stockwin (London: Routledge, 2014).

9. Keiichiro Kobayashi, "The Two 'Lost Decades' and Macroeconomics: Changing Economic Policies," in *Examining Japan's Lost Decades*, ed. Yoichi Funabashi and Barak Kushner (London: Routledge, 2015), 37–55, here 44–52.

10. Kenneth Kuttner, Iwaisako Tokuo, and Adam Posen, "Monetary and Fiscal Policies During the Lost Decades," in *Examining Japan's Lost Decades*, ed. Yoichi Funabashi and Barak Kushner (London: Routledge, 2015), 17–36.

11. Sébastien Lechevalier and Brieuc Monfort, "Abenomics: Has it Worked? Will it Ultimately Fail?" *Japan Forum* 30, no. 2 (2017): 277–302; Tina Burrett, "Abe Road: Comparing Japanese Prime Minister Shinzo Abe's Leadership of his First and Second Governments," *Parliamentary Affairs* 70, no. 2 (2017): 400–429; Saori Shibata, "Re-packaging Old Policies? 'Abenomics' and the Lack of an Alternative Growth Model for Japan's Political Economy," *Japan Forum* 29, no. 3 (2017): 399–422; Naoyuki Yoshino and Farhad Taghizadeh-Hesary, "Effectiveness of the Easing of Monetary Policy in the Japanese Economy, Incorporating Energy Prices," ADBI Working Paper, No. 503 (Tokyo: Asian Development Bank Institute, 2014).

12. James McBride and Beina Xu, "Abenomics and the Japanese Economy," Council on Foreign Relations, March 23, 2018, https://www.cfr.org/backgrounder/abenomics-and-japanese-economy.

13. Takashi Ito, Kazumasa Iwata, Colin McKenzie, and Shujiro Urata, "Did Abenomics Succeed? Editor's Overview," *Asian Economic Policy Review* 13, no. 1 (2018): 1–22.

14. Ibid., 2.

15. Ibid.

16. Haruo Shimada, "Abenomics: The Second Arrow and Fiscal Reconstruction," *Huffington Post*, February 26, 2016, https://www.huffingtonpost.jp/haruo-shimada/abenomics-second-arrow_b_9322686.html. The quote is my translation.

17. Ito et al., "Did Abenomics," 6.

18. David J. Bailey and Saori Shibata, "Austerity and Anti-Austerity: The Political Economy of Refusal in 'Low-Resistance' Models of Capitalism," *British Journal of Political Science* 49, no. 2 (2019): 683–709.

19. Prime Minister's Office, *Japan Revitalization Strategy: Japan is Back*, Tokyo, June 14, 2013, https://www.kantei.go.jp/jp/singi/keizaisaisei/pdf/en_saikou_jpn_hon.pdf.

20. Kantei, *Kore made no seichō senryaku ni tsuite* [Growth Strategies So Far], Tokyo, 2014, https://www.kantei.go.jp/jp/singi/keizaisaisei/kettei.html#saikou2014; Ito et al., "Did Abenomics," 2.

21. Kantei, *Seichō senryaku;* Ito et al., "Did Abenomics," 2.

22. Karube Kensuke, *Kanryōtachi no Abenomics* [Abenomics by Bureaucrats] (Tokyo: Iwanami Shoten, 2018), 39.

23. Cabinet Office, "Dai 37kai kisei kaikaku suishin kaigi shūryōgo kisha kaiken giji gaiyō" [Summary of Press Conference after the 37 Deregulation Committee Meeting], Tokyo, October 12, 2018, 5, https://www8.cao.go.jp/kisei-kaikaku/suishin/meeting/committee/20181012/interview1012.pdf.

24. Liberal Democratic Party, *Manifesto*, Tokyo, 2012, https://jimin.jp-east-2.storage.api.nifcloud.com/pdf/seisaku_ichiban24.pdf.

25. Bailey and Shibata, "Austerity."

26. Aurelia George Mulgan, "To TPP or Not TPP: Interest Groups and Trade Policy," in *The Political Economy of Japanese Trade Policy*, ed. Aurelia George Mulgan and Masayoshi Honma (New York: Palgrave Macmillan, 2015).

27. Kantei, *Nippon ichioku sōkatsuyaku puran* [Promoting Dynamic Engagement of All Citizens], Tokyo, June 2, 2016, https://www.kantei.go.jp/jp/singi/ichiokusoukatsuyaku/pdf/plan1.pdf; see also Takeda's chapter in this volume for further discussion of this problem.

28. Ibid., 4; see also Takeda, this volume.

29. Kantei, "Urgent Policies to Realize a Society in Which All Citizens are Dynamically Engaged: Toward a Positive Cycle of Growth and Distribution," August 18, 2015, http://japan.kantei.go.jp/97_abe/Documents/2015/__icsFiles/afieldfile/2016/01/22/urgentpolicies_20151126.pdf.

30. See Chiavacci, this volume.

31. TV Asahi Hōdō Station poll (n.d.), http://www.tv-asahi.co.jp/hst/poll/graph_naikaku.html.

32. Elliot, "Japan PM."

33. Liberal Democratic Party, *Manifesto*, Tokyo, 2014, 16, https://jimin.jp-east-2.storage.api.nifcloud.com/2014/political_promise/sen_shu47_promise.pdf.

34. Ben McLannahan, "Shinzo Abe Aims to Raise Pay for Japan's Part-time Workers," *Financial Times*, September 21, 2016, https://www.ft.com/content/31afa254-8015-11e6-bc52-0c7211ef3198.

35. Robin Harding, "Abe Demands 3% Pay Rise to Drive Japan's Economy," *Financial Times*, October 26, 2017, https://www.ft.com/content/0061a6a2-ba25-11e7-8c12-5661783e5589.

36. Kantei, *Nippon ichioku*, 14–15.

37. Ibid., 13.

38. See Takeda, this volume.

39. Ministry of Finance, *Zaisei kinyū tōkei geppo* [Corporate Accounting Annual Report] (Tokyo: Ministry of Finance Policy Research Institute, 2015), https://www.mof.go.jp/pri/publication/zaikin_geppo/hyou/g774/774.htm.

40. Robin Harding, "Abe Calls for Wage Rise to Boost Japanese Economy," November 16, 2016, https://www.ft.com/content/2ed90f76-abfc-11e6-ba7d-76378e4fef24.

41. Ibid.

42. JIJI.COM, "Meimoku chingin, rokuneburi mainasu = paato zouka de 0.3% gen" [Nominal Wages Down for the First Time in 6 Years = 0.3% Decline Due to Increase in Part-time Work], https://www.jiji.com/jc/graphics?p=ve_eco_company-wage.

43. Burrett, "Abe Road."

44. Ibid., 423.

45. Ibid., 421.

46. Kantei, *Machi, hito, shigoto sōsei kihon hōshin 2015: Rookaru Abenomikusu no jitsugen ni mukete* [Basic Plan for Revitalization of Town, People, and Work: Realizing Local Abenomics]," Tokyo, June 30, 2015, http://www.kantei.go.jp/jp/topics/2015/20150630hontai.pdf; see also Chiavacci, this volume.

47. TV Asahi Hōdō Station poll (n.d.), http://www.tv-asahi.co.jp/hst/poll/graph_naikaku.html.

48. Burrett, "Abe Road."

49. Hay, "Crisis," 329.

50. Robin Harding, "Unemployment in Japan Hits 24-Year Low," *Financial Times*, December 26, 2017, https://www.ft.com/content/31473500-ea01-11e7-bd17-521324c81e23.

51. The Government of Japan, "Abenomics," 2017, https://www.japan.go.jp/abenomics/.

52. Ito et al., "Did Abenomics," 11.

53. Ministry of Health, Labour and Welfare (MHWL), *Kōsei rōdō hakusho* [White Paper on Health, Labor and Welfare] Tokyo, 2017, 7, https://www.mhlw.go.jp/wp/hakusyo/kousei/17-1/dl/gaiyou.pdf.

54. Rōdō Sōken, "Abenomikusu to taiketsushi, ōhaba chinage de keizai kaikaku o" [Oppose Abenomics: Towards an Economic Reform through Wage Increases], January 18, 2018, 4, http://www.yuiyuidori.net/soken/ape/2018/data/180119_01.pdf.

55. Ibid.

56. MHLW, *2017 Analysis of the Labour Economy*, Tokyo, 2017, ii, https://www.mhlw.go.jp/english/wp/l-economy/2017/summary.pdf.

57. Hattori Shigeyuki, *Itsuwari no keizai seisaku: Kakusa to teitai no Abenomikusu* [False Economic Policies: Abenomics of Inequality and Stagnation] (Tokyo: Iwanami Shoten, 2017), ix, 72–73.

58. MHLW, *Analysis of the Labour Economy: 2016*, 2016, 1, https://www.mhlw.go.jp/english/wp/l-economy/2016/summary.pdf.

59. Ibid., 3, 5.

60. Ibid., 12.

61. MHLW, *2017 Analysis*.

62. Kantei, *Promoting Dynamic Engagement of All Citizens* (2016), http://www.kantei.go.jp/jp/singi/ichiokusoukatsuyaku/pdf/plan3.pdf.

63. Public Relations Office, Government of Japan (n.d), *Promoting Dynamic Engagement of All Citizens*, https://www.gov-online.go.jp/tokusyu/ichiokusoukatsuyaku/plan/.

64. Kuhara Yasushi, *Hatarakikata kaikaku no uso: Darega toku o shite, darega kurushimu no ka* [Work-Style Reform: Who Benefits and Who Suffers?] (Tokyo: Shueisha, 2018), 57–58.

65. Akagi, cited in Yōhei Tsunemi, "Hatarakikata kaikaku no zuremakurina giron ni monomousu," *Tōyō Keizai*, May 2, 2017, https://toyokeizai.net/articles/-/169640.

66. Kuhara, *Hatarakikata*, 85–87.

67. Ibid., 84–85.

68. Ibid.

69. Kuhara, *Hatarakikata*.

70. Noguchi Asahi, *Abenomics ga kaeta Nihon keizai* [The Japanese Economy Abenomics Has Changed] (Tokyo: Chikuma Shinsho, 2018), 164.

71. Kuhara, *Hatarakikata*, 36–53; Ninomiya Atsumi, *Shūkatsukino Abe seiken: Posuto Abe seiji e no pureryūdo* [Towards the end of the Abe Administration: A Prelude to Post-Abe Politics] (Tokyo: Shin Nihon Shuppansha, 2017), 223–224.

72. Saori Shibata, *Contesting Precarity: The Rise of Nonregular Workers and the New Policy Dissensus in Japan* (Ithaca, NY: Cornell University Press, 2020).

73. "Hirogaru kakusa, fuenai kyouryou: Atoshimatsuha korekarada. Abenomikusuno mayakashi" [Widening Inequality and Not-Increasing Salary: Fake Abenomics], *Asahi Shimbun*, May 2, 2016.

74. Kakusazesei/Han-anpo-ho nado uttae: Sapporode Meidei shukai" [Rasing Voice on Inequality/Anti-Security Treaty: May Day Rallies in Sapporo], *Asahi Shimbun*, May 2, 2016.

75. "Koupuro tekkai motome kokkaimaeni 1-sennin" [1,000 People Rally in Front of the Diet Against the High-Level Professional Worker System], *Asahi Shimbun*, May 20, 2018.

76. "Hatarakikata kaikaku, 'munashii' bouchyou no izoku ikidoori: Sanini kaketsu" [Work-Style reform, angry bereaved family: Passed by the Upper House], *Asahi Shimbun*, June 29, 2018.

77. Nobuko Nagase, "Has Abe's Womenomics Worked?" *Asian Economic Policy Review* 13, no. 1 (2018): 68–101.

78. Ibid., cited in Ito et al., "Did Abenomics," 10–11.

79. Kobayashi Yoshiaki, "Abe-seiken no 5-nen, kibishi kokusai hyōka mesaki no 'seika' kyōchō suru ga, shōrai nani kangaeteru?" [5 years of Abe government and critical evaluation: 'The Abe emphasized the outcome, but what is his future plan?'], *Mainichi Shimbun*, December 22, 2017, https://mainichi.jp/articles/20171222/dde/012/010/002000c.

80. World Economic Forum, *The Global Gender Gap Report 2020*, 2020, 12, http://www3.weforum.org/docs/WEF_GGGR_2020.pdf.

81. Marcus Noland, Tyler Moran, and Barbara Kotschwar, "Is Gender Diversity Profitable? Evidence from a Global Survey," Working Paper Series, February 2016, https://www.piie.com/publications/wp/wp16-3.pdf.

82. Emma Dalton, *Women and Politics in Contemporary Japan* (London: Routledge, 2015).

83. Ibid., 58, 65.

84. Ibid., 65–66.

85. Kobayashi, "Abe-Seiken."

86. Hay, "Crisis," 333.

87. See Takeda, this volume.

88. Kobayashi, "Abe-Seiken."

89. Noguchi, *Abenomics*, 12.

90. Hattori, *Itsuwari*, 171.

91. MHLW, *2017 Analysis*, 5.

92. Leo Lewis, "Japan's Elderly Turn to Life of Crime to Ease Cost of Living," *Financial Times*, March 27, 2016, https://www.ft.com/content/fbd435a6-f3d7-11e5-803c-d27c7117d132.

93. "Netto kaffe nanmin, tonai ni 4000-nin, to ga hatsu no chōsa" [Net Café Evacuees, 4,000 Evacuees in Tokyo, the First Survey], *Nihon Keizai Shimbun*, January 29, 2018, https://www.nikkei.com/article/DGXMZO2625622029012018CC0000/.

94. Ibid.

95. Kobayashi, "Abe-Seiken."

96. Masayoshi Honma and Aurelia George Mulgan, "Political Economy of Agricultural Reform in Japan under Abe's Administration," *Asian Economic Policy Review* 13, no. 1 (2018): 135.

97. Ibid.

98. Ito et al., "Did Abenomics," 17.

99. Ibid., 18.

100. Ōhata Shigeo, "Nōrinsuisanbutsu e eikyō: Saidai 151 oku en no shisan [Effects on Agricultural Products: Maximum 15.1 Billion Yen]," *Asahi Shimbun*, February 27, 2018, 33.

101. Kanai Nobuyoshi, "Nōrinsuisanbutsu no seisangaku: Saidai 38–41 oku en" [Production Values of Agricultural Products: Maximum 3.8 to 4.1 billion yen], *Asahi Shimbun*, March 7, 2018, 25.

102. Yanagikawa Jin, "TPP11 taisaku" [TPP11 Measures], *Asahi Shimbun*, February 2, 2018, 25.

103. Japan Agriculture, "Jikyū ritsu sara ni teika kenen [Concerns over the declining self-sufficiency rate]," July 10, 2018, http://www.jacom.or.jp/nousei/closeup/2018/180710-35749.php.

104. Honma and Mulgan, "Political Economy," 135.

105. Ibid., 136.

106. The Government of Japan, "Abenomics: Smart Regulations and Laws" (n.d.), https://www.japan.go.jp/abenomics/regulatory/.

107. Kaori Kaneko, "Tech-Savvy Farmers a New Hope for Japan's Shrinking Agriculture Sector," *Reuters*, August 9, 2017, https://www.reuters.com/article/us-japan-farming-transformation/tech-savvy-farmers-a-new-hope-for-japans-shrinking-agriculture-sector-idUSKBN1AP0JF.

108. "Genba ni genba no koe o" [More Voices from Farmers], *Asahi Shimbun*, November 3, 2016, 29.

109. Hay, "Crisis," 330.

110. Rengo, *Survey on Workers with Limited Contracts 2018*, Tokyo, June 28, 2018, 13–14, https://www.jtuc-rengo.or.jp/info/chousa/data/20180628.pdf.

111. Rengo, *Survey on Female Non-regular Workers*, Tokyo, August 25, 2017, 21, https://www.jtuc-rengo.or.jp/info/chousa/data/20170825.pdf.

112. "Senkyosen de mietamonoha" [What Have We Seen in the Election?], *Asahi Shimbun*, July 23, 2019.

113. Kujioka Jin, "Koyō, sūji wa kaizen shita kedo" [Employment, the Numbers Have Improved], *Asahi Shimbun*, February 19, 2016, 2.

114. Quoted in "Kakusa to hinkon Nihon no genjitsu Abenomikusu wa nani o motarasu no ka" [Inequality and Poverty: Reality in Japan, What Will Abenomics Bring About?], *AERA*, February 23, 2015, 17.

115. Ibid.

116. Ogata Yūdai, "Meidei kakusa No [May Day, No to Inequality]," *Asahi Shimbun*, April 27, 2014, 31.

117. "Nenkin, zouzei, saninsen ni tou: Kokkai heikai, 'Nisenmanen busoku' kanteimae demo" [Pension, Sales Tax Hike, Before the Upper House Election: Diet Closed, 20-Million Yen Problem, Demonstration in Front of the Diet], *Asahi Shimbun*, June 27, 2019.

118. "Rōdōhōsei kaikaku, hantai demo: Rōso 3dantai ashinami" [Work Regulation Reform and Protests: Three Unions in Solidarity], *Asahi Shimbun*, May 15, 2015, 7.

119. Furuta Hiroya, "Meidei ni 7000nin" [May Day 7000 People], *Asahi Shimbun*, April 27, 2014, 23.

120. "Jūzei hantai uttae: Zenrōren nado shukai [Against Heavy Tax: A Rally by Zenrōren]," *Asahi Shimbun*, March 18, 2015, 29.

121. "'Sengo saichō no keikikaifuku,' hachi wari ga jikkan sezu honsha seron chōsa" ["The Longest Economic Recovery": 80% Do not Feel the Economic Recovery], *Nihon Keizai Shimbun*, February 17, 2019, https://www.nikkei.com/article/DGXMZO41385010X10C19A2PE8000/.

122. Hay, "Crisis," 320.

123. Shibata, *Contesting Precarity.*

Part III

Narrating Japan's National Security Crisis

Chapter 7

"Failures" and "Crises" in Japanese Foreign Policy

The Democratic Party of Japan's Rule 2009–2012

PAUL O'SHEA

Introduction

Seen in the rear-view mirror, the three years of Democratic Party of Japan (DPJ) rule appear as not much more than a blip against the Liberal Democratic Party's (LDP) seemingly eternal dominance of Japanese politics. And yet, in the summer of 2009, as the DPJ rode a wave of popular support to victory in the lower house election, it seemed that Japan's idiosyncratic "one-party democracy" was over and an open and competitive party system was to take its place.[1] Only three years later, however, commentators and scholars were defining the DPJ by its policy "failures," at home and abroad. These "failures" not only helped delegitimize the DPJ and return the LDP to power, but also formed the basis of the "crisis" declared by Prime Minister Abe Shinzō upon taking office for his second stint in 2012: "the security of Japan is not someone else's problem; it is a crisis that exists right here and now."[2] Hence, Abe went on to announce the formation of a "crisis breakthrough cabinet" (*kikitoppa naikaku*), which, among other problems, would address the "crisis" facing "the security of Japan."[3] To resolve the crisis, he argued, drastic security measures ranging from collective self-defense to increased military spending would be indispensable. Thus, the DPJ's foreign policy "failures" take on increased significance: Not only did they contribute to the DPJ's own collapse, but they also helped justify the implementation of the so-called "Abe doctrine."[4]

But did the DPJ really fail at foreign policy? In the years since it fell from power, a body of media reporting and scholarly literature assessing the DPJ's time in office emerged.[5] Many details of the issues the DPJ had been struggling with have been clarified. Yet these insights did not change the narrative of the party's general failure. In this chapter I reexamine the DPJ's foreign policy record, focusing on the primary policy challenge faced by each of its three prime ministers. For Hatoyama Yukio (September 2009–June 2010) it was the "fiasco" of the Futenma base relocation.[6] For Kan Naoto (June 2010–September 2011), it was the "mishandling" of the Chinese trawler collision in the East China Sea,[7] and for Noda Yoshihiko (September 2011–December 2012), it was the purchase of some of the Senkaku/Diaoyu islets disputed with China and Taiwan. The fact that each prime minister faced one single major foreign policy challenge, and that three politicians rotated through the prime minister's office in three years, is an unfortunate fact for them, but fortunate for case selection here. I will combine theoretical insights from the growing literature on policy failures with Colin Hay's conception of crisis meta-narratives as outlined in the introduction to this book. Conceptually, I will break failure down in two categories: the subjective ascription of "failure" as an action with a political purpose, and failure, no quotation marks, as a judgment made after an objective assessment of a policy response and its outcomes. The attempt to combine the subjective "failure" and the objective failure in one study is in line with Hay's view on how objective failures can become identified and transformed into crisis meta-narratives.[8]

By examining both the narration of policy "failure" and the question of failure in terms of actual policy responses and outcomes, in this chapter I provide an alternative assessment of the DPJ's foreign policy record. It reveals that the attribution of "failure" to the DPJ and Abe's successful promotion of a "national security crisis" meta-narrative helped to return Japan to an LDP-style foreign policy even while the DPJ were still in office, and eventually to bring the LDP back to power. It discredited alternative courses of action, including a more "independent" foreign policy and a conciliatory approach to its nearest neighbors. Not least, it allowed for the strengthening of the US–Japan alliance's fundamental pillars and the loosening of the normative and constitutional constraints on Japan's military.

Failures and Crises in Foreign Policy

The invasion of Iraq in 2003 was a catastrophic failure, probably the greatest foreign policy blunder in the post–Cold War era. Today, few would disagree with this designation of failure. Yet for a time, it had been widely seen as a great success—the US had toppled Saddam Hussein with relative ease and were on track to set up a shiny new democracy in the Middle East. It was, as the banner on the aircraft carrier said, "Mission Accomplished." Although he later redefined the invasion as a "catastrophic success," George W. Bush was reelected for a second presidential term—after a campaign that had, of all things, focused on foreign policy.[9] This episode shows that the success or failure of a given foreign policy act is very much in the eye of the temporally, spatially, and/or politically located beholder. Indeed, many scholars have pointed to the contested nature of policy evaluation, be it in competition over the relevant facts or how these facts are to be interpreted.[10] The act of labeling a given foreign policy intervention or response a "failure" or a "success" is inherently political, even in apparently dispassionate scholarly journals. It has meaning far beyond the act—it can delegitimize a much broader policy or array of policies, and it can delegitimize a politician or even a government. "Failure" topples governments and loses elections. Years before the DPJ came to power, Prime Minister Nakasone Yasuhiro had been brought down by his "failed" consumption tax reform policy, while the responses to the Hanshin Awaji earthquake and the Aum Shinrikyo sarin gas attack in early 1995 contributed to the end of the Socialist-led Murayama Tomiichi government.

The preceding paragraph used the terms "foreign policy act," "foreign policy intervention," and "foreign policy response" apparently interchangeably. Yet these are not synonymous; each denotes a type of act under the umbrella of something much broader, which can be described as a "foreign policy." Even then, not every governmental action is consistent with either its stated (or practiced) foreign policy. The three cases examined in this chapter represent different orders of magnitude. Whereas Prime Minister Hatoyama's intervention on the Futenma base relocation signified a key element in a larger foreign policy shift, Prime Ministers Kan and Noda had to respond to situations thrust upon them. What makes them fit together is that they stand out in media and scholarly discourses as the three primary "failures" of the DPJ's foreign policy.

The key question is, how is a failure—in the objective sense—defined and/or identified to begin with? An obvious starting point in determining a foreign policy failure is to refer back to the stated goals: did the policy, or intervention, achieve what it set out to do?[11] Where these goals are not stated, they must be inferred from the general policy preferences of the actors involved. Even then, things are rarely clear-cut. Different actors in a ruling political party have fundamentally different foreign policy preferences, even at the cabinet level, and can compete to implement them (not to mention bureaucratic preferences). The cabinets of both David Cameron and Theresa May in the UK demonstrated this lack of unity on the most important British foreign policy issue of a generation, Brexit. Thus, Allan McConnell points out that we should consider other questions beyond the stated goals: Did the policy benefit those it was aimed at? Did it improve on what came before? Did it meet key ethical or moral standards? The existence of multiple standards for considering what exactly constitutes a foreign policy failure enables us to think more broadly about the consequences of a given intervention.[12]

A recent trend in constructivist scholarship is the problematization of the notion of "failure"—where "failure" is no longer an inherent attribute of a given foreign policy intervention, but rather a judgment about that intervention, a label that is applied following political debates.[13] In this view, a foreign policy intervention is what is made of it: when discursively powerful actors agree that a certain action was a success, this becomes the dominant understanding, and the reverse is likewise true. To be sure, this chapter does not deny the importance of either facts or truth, especially in this "post-truth" moment. Rather, it seeks to highlight the discursive nature of failure in the context of Japan's foreign policy. Positivist and discursive approaches ask different but often complementary questions. Where Hay seeks to synthesize materialist and discursive approaches to the state,[14] this chapter does not attempt to formulate a parsimonious synthesis of positivist and constructivist theories of foreign policy. Rather, it merely recognizes both the material and the ideational and combines the two approaches to problematize "common sense" evaluations of the DPJ's foreign policy record and the LDP's subsequent construction of a crisis.

For accomplishing the latter task, the chapter adapts Hay's conception of "crisis as a moment of decisive intervention."[15] That is to say, a crisis occurs when an accumulation of apparent failures is tied together in a single crisis meta-narrative that demands a "new trajectory" for the state. This crisis meta-narrative creates a moment where, rather than having their own individual logic or causality, disparate events become symptoms of a single, overarching crisis. In this case, the meta-narrative is the inexorable "decline" of Japan's economy, prestige, and national security during the apparently never-ending succession of "lost decades."[16] Thus, the "failures" that are identified and problematized in this chapter are, despite their fundamental differences, taken out of context and recombined to create the clear and present "national security crisis" as declared by Abe in his 2012 inaugural speech.[17] As Hay notes, the success of a crisis narrative stems not from its accuracy in describing complex webs of causation, but from its providing a simple and flexible account, where fault and responsibility are easily identified and assigned to Japan's postwar institutions and the opposition parties.

Three cases form the basis for the overarching crisis meta-narrative into which the "failures" are subsumed, where Japan's national security is threatened, a crisis that can only be resolved through, as Hay outlines, "decisive intervention" in the form of imposing a "new trajectory" for the future of the state.[18] Each of the following three sections contains two main parts: the first analyzes the discursive construction of "failure;" the second applies the criteria for policy failure outlined above, considering policy preferences, impact on target groups, and morality considerations. This highlights the contingent and specific nature of each event, and thereby problematizes the meta-narrative of a national (security) crisis facing Japan.

Hatoyama and the Futenma Base Relocation

The Futenma base issue was the first and most consequential policy intervention during the DPJ's three years in office. Marine Corps Air Station Futenma is located in densely populated Ginowan City on the main island of Okinawa. The base had become increasingly controversial due to a number of high-profile incidents since the 1990s, including aircraft crash-landings and crimes committed by members of the Marine Corps.[19] Tokyo and Washington had agreed to relocate the base to a newly developed area near the remote town of Henoko, in the northern part of the main island.[20] Hatoyama's decision to support local resistance and renegotiate this agreement so as to relocate the base outside of Okinawa was initially popular, both in Okinawa and across Japan. It was part of a broader foreign policy shift aiming at a more equal relationship with the United States and improved relations with Japan's Asian neighbors.[21] The official US response was spearheaded by Defense Secretary Robert Gates, who visited Tokyo in the October 2009, one month before US President Barack Obama himself was scheduled to arrive for a summit. At first, the US publicly appeared to be open to discussion. However, this public openness did not last long, and in private meetings it was made very clear from the beginning that there would be no renegotiation.[22] In Gates's own words, Henoko was "the best alternative, and it is time to move on."[23] Meanwhile, as Hatoyama struggled to find an alternative location, the narrative developed that he was damaging Japan–US relations. This contributed to the collapse of support for the renegotiation of the relocation plan and his administration more generally. With himself and the idea of the broader foreign policy change being discredited, Hatoyama fell back on the original agreement, and eventually resigned.

Thus, the conventional narrative is that Hatoyama's handling of the base issue precipitated a crisis in US–Japan relations, one which the prominent Japan hand and Center for Strategic and International Studies strategist Michael Green described as "the greatest period of political turmoil and confusion in the U.S.-Japan alliance since the mutual security treaty was signed in 1960."[24] Green's hyperbole and selective memory—he ignores *inter alia* the triple whammy of the Nixon shocks—exemplify the discourse around the policy shift in general and the Futenma base issue in particular. While these comments, published in the *Journal of Japanese Studies* in 2011, maintained academic decorum, his media commentary did not. In another article in *Foreign Policy* entitled "Tokyo Smackdown," he referred to Hatoyama as "dithering," his idea of regional cooperation through an East Asian Community as "half-baked," and the proposed investigation of the violation of Japan's three non-nuclear principles (not to possess, manufacture, or introduce nuclear weapons into Japan) through top-level secret US–Japan agreements as potentially a "big bore."[25] Other US-based analysts and columnists followed this pattern. Writing in the *Wall Street Journal,* Michael Auslin described Hatoyama as leaving Japan in "one of the most unstable and dangerous political periods in its postwar history."[26] Hatoyama was variously described as "wavering,"[27] "amateurish,"[28] and "loopy."[29] Even Joseph Nye, today a staunch defender of the liberal international order, dismissed the DPJ as "still in the thrall of campaign promises,"[30] an odd criticism of a democratically elected government. Victor Cha, another influential US academic, described Hatoyama's behavior as "cowboy diplomacy."[31] Thus, a wide selection of "scholar-officials" came out publicly to denounce Hatoyama.[32]

Much of the harsh criticisms were, according to Green himself, part of a deliberate move by US officials to undermine the foreign policy shift and discredit Hatoyama. In the aforementioned *Foreign Policy* article, Green wrote approvingly of the tactics employed by US Defense Secretary Robert Gates. "A shrewd judge," Gates knew that "a crisis in the U.S.-Japan alliance would split the DPJ and turn much of the media against Hatoyama."[33] He further enthusiastically noted that the next generation of Japanese leaders were realists who were not afraid to stand up to China. Green was right: the Japanese press became increasingly critical of Hatoyama's efforts, publishing articles peppered with quotes from US analysts and officials referring to a "crisis" in Japan–US relations. To be fair, the conservative *Yomiuri Shimbun*, the newspaper with the highest circulation rates worldwide, had been doing this even before the DPJ won the election, quoting none other than Green himself warning that there would be trouble for the alliance if the DPJ won.[34] A month later, the *Yomiuri* published a full interview with Green in which he labeled an article Hatoyama had written as "anti-American" and warned that if the DPJ continued on this path, it would precipitate a serious decline in US trust towards Japan.[35] Over time, the domestic criticisms of Hatoyama came to mirror US criticisms, and the left-leaning *Asahi Shimbun* joined in, blaming Hatoyama for making Washington "distrustful" of Tokyo.[36] In the words of Iimura Yoshisuke, the "Japanese media fell hook, line and sinker for the White House's media strategy."[37] After Hatoyama resigned, the focus turned to "restoring" the alliance. Green's prescience was impressive, as the "realist" Maehara Seiji was made foreign minister soon thereafter.

If we apply the questions from the preceding section to the failed Futenma relocation, the results are perhaps not surprising. Did the policy achieve what it set out to do? The short answer is no. Postmortems in scholarship and the media abound, and this does not need elaboration here. Aside from the aforementioned narrative of a "crisis" in US–Japan relations, scholars have also pointed to the new administration's inexperience, the failure to use the bureaucracy's expertise, the incompetence of Hatoyama himself, the lack of a unified position within the party, and factors inherent to the policy itself.[38] Indeed, it is very probable that the policy shift was doomed from the start, since it went beyond the limits of what is acceptable to both the US and Japanese foreign policy establishments, regardless of Hatoyama's competence or DPJ unity. However, applying two of the other criteria outlined above, we can problematize this ascription of failure. One of the problems is that, no matter how objective an approach one seeks to adopt, the definition of failure is always contested. For instance, one of the criteria is the "*failure to match moral, ethical or legal standards*."[39] The Futenma impasse existed long before Hatoyama took office, as consecutive LDP administrations had recognized the Henoko relocation's unpopularity and steered clear of it. Thus, despite the agreement entering its teens, the base remained where it was, adjacent to a highly populated urban area, increasing the risk of a serious accident endangering local residents.[40] Hatoyama's plan also sought to reduce the burden of the bases on Okinawa. Morality and foreign policy do not always mix well, but even proponents of the Futenma relocation plan recognized that the problems linked to the concentration of bases mean that the status quo can be seen as a "necessary evil" at best. Of course, whether it was the morally "right" thing to do or not, the plan failed, and the Futenma base remains at its current location. The Abe administration subsequently attempted to force the issue, and the construction of new runways at Henoko has begun, albeit in fits and starts.

McConnell's other criteria include the "*failure to improve on what went before*" and the "*failure to benefit particular interests or groups.*"[41] Once again, the line between objectivity and subjectivity is blurred. For some, Hatoyama's failure was absolute: not only was the policy a failure, but, in the words of Green, "it is much worse now because Hatoyama raised and then dashed expectations in a way that made a difficult problem even harder."[42] "Worse" is subjective. Viewed from the perspective of those opposed to the base move, the policy had positive unintended consequences. While the base remains, the failure rallied resistance against the relocation plan. The issue gained national and international attention and sympathy. It even reached the US Senate, with influential senators like John McCain coming out in favor of relocating the base out of Okinawa.[43] At the same time, the absolute opposition of other localities to the suggestions that they host the base—half of the population of Tokunoshima came out to protest the proposal—served to highlight the inequity of asking Okinawa to shoulder the burden of base-hosting.

In sum, Hatoyama's attempt to find an alternative was clearly a failure insofar as he reverted to the original Henoko plan and resigned, discredited. Yet questions of morality and unintended consequences—not to mention the causes of the failure—muddy the waters. Still, the whole affair was narrated not only as a singular "failure" on his part, but also as a major "crisis" in US–Japan relations. Thus, the controversy was not only used to tarnish the prime minister, but also served to discredit the idea of an alternative foreign policy direction for Japan. Perhaps most importantly, the reputation of the DPJ and its ability to handle foreign policy crises had been damaged, leading to a swing back to the traditional LDP-style approach such that, by the time Prime Minister Noda took office, there was little difference between the LDP and the DPJ. Before we reach Noda, however, we turn to the Kan administration and the continued undermining of the DPJ's foreign policy management.

Kan and the 2010 Senkaku/Diaoyu Trawler Collision Incident

On the long list of short-lived Japanese prime ministers, Kan Naoto stands out as one of the unluckiest. A former Socialist, a grassroots organizer and civil rights activist, Kan's administration was supposed to focus on domestic social and quality-of-life issues. This was not to be, and his term in office is mostly remembered for the March 11, 2011, triple disaster including the calamity of the Fukushima meltdowns. But while 3.11 dwarfs everything else that happened during his tenure, he faced a different "crisis"—the Senkaku/Diaoyu collision incident of 2010—shortly after taking office. Since its reemergence in the 1990s, the Senkaku/Diaoyu maritime territorial dispute has plagued Sino-Japanese relations. The dispute flared up with increasing severity during the 2000s, as China increased its presence in the surrounding seas, and the Koizumi administration responded with a more assertive stance. By the time the DPJ took power, the dispute had moved to center stage in bilateral relations.

The controversy began on September 7, 2010, when a Chinese trawler rammed two Japan Coast Guard (JCG) patrol ships that had been pursuing it in waters near the disputed islands. The captain and crew were arrested and brought to Okinawa. Within a few days, the crew was released, but the captain, Zhan Qixiong, was remanded and the Naha public prosecutor prepared a file in view of further legal proceedings (for obstruction of duty and illegal fishing). Beijing protested, and after his detention was extended by a further ten days on September 19, China raised the stakes, responding with a range of measures including the suspension of ministerial and civilian exchanges, the obstruction of rare earth exports, and the arrest of a number of Japanese business people in China on charges of espionage—in what has been described as "shock and awe diplomacy."[44] Although some of these measures may have been unconnected to the incident, due to the timing, they were construed as responses regardless of the original intentions.[45] Shortly after the extension of the captain's detention, on September 22, Premier Wen Jiabao raised the stakes once more with a statement at United Nations General Assembly (UNGA): "If Japan acts willfully despite advice to the contrary, China will take further actions, and Japan must accept full responsibility for all the severe consequences."[46] Two days later, on September 24, the local prosecutor in Naha, citing the need for peaceful bilateral relations, announced the cancellation of the proceedings and ordered the captain's release.[47]

This episode was narrated as a "failure" in the media and in scholarly analyses.[48] As Linus Hagström demonstrated, Japan's handling of the issue was depicted in both the domestic and international media as a "defeat" and "humiliating retreat."[49] Meanwhile, the Kan administration was seen as "weak-kneed," and as having "mishandled" the incident.[50] Comparisons were made with Hatoyama's "amateurism" during the Futenma crisis.[51] LDP representatives were particularly scathing, not only using budget deliberation time in the Diet to try to force the government to admit that it intervened in Zhan's release, but also presenting a flowchart for the media that outlined Japan's "diplomatic defeat."[52] Onodera Itsunori, who would later become Abe's first-choice defense minister, stated, with no shortage of hyperbole, that "I consider this our nation's biggest foreign policy blunder since the end of World War II, and I believe Prime Minister Kan is the one solely responsible for this failure."[53]

Analysts have largely followed the same line, with both Japanese and international scholars pulling no punches in their negative evaluations of the incident.[54] Illustrative is an Institute for Foreign Policy Analysis report that describes the initial response as "robust," but later moves as "indecisive" and seemingly caving in "to China's heavy-handed response."[55] Eventually, Chief Cabinet Secretary Sengoku Yoshito took responsibility for the affair and resigned. The overall narrative is, then, that Prime Minister Kan and his administration "mishandled" the issue, resulting in a Chinese "victory." Interestingly, Maehara Seiji, who, as we shall see, played a pivotal role in the controversy, somehow avoided critique, and is conspicuously absent in most later accounts of what happened.[56] Kan's "failure" was compounded a month later by the visit of Russian Prime Minister Dmitri Medvedev to the disputed Northern Territories/Kurile Islands. This provocative move, so the narrative went, was invited and made possible because of the "weakness" that Japan had demonstrated in the Senkaku incident.[57] The results were immediate, as Kan's approval ratings continued to slide.

However, Kan's failure in the Senkaku collision controversy is even less clear-cut than Hatoyama's in the Futenma relocation case. The obvious first question is whether the handling of the controversy had been conducive to achieving the goals that the government aimed at. As we have seen, the DPJ was far from unified on foreign policy. Kan's disinterest in foreign policy was not shared by his then Transport Minister Maehara Seiji, who happened to be in charge of the Japan Coast Guard at the time of the collision. Unlike Kan, who might best be described as a "pragmatic centrist"[58] on foreign policy, Maehara is generally considered a conservative China hawk.[59] It is no stretch to say that, rather than avoiding trouble with China, his principle motivation was to increase "awareness" of the issue, thereby stirring anti-China sentiment in Japan.

Importantly, Kan was attending the annual UNGA meeting in New York when the collision happened. In this context, it was Maehara himself who took the opportunity and intervened to ensure that the Chinese captain was arrested and taken into custody.[60] Maehara also traveled to Ishigaki and met the JCG officers involved in the incident. It is highly likely that Maehara and other China hawks in the DPJ administration were responsible not only for the arrest, but also for the prolongation of the detention. The latter act went against previous practice of arresting and then deporting Chinese (and Taiwanese) citizens arrested on or near the disputed islands—a practice to which even the nationalist Koizumi Junichirō had adhered to. Thus, Maehara's intervention meant a break with a secret agreement dating back to 2004.[61] Meanwhile, in Kan's absence, Chief Cabinet Secretary Sengoku Yoshito became the public face of the incident. Unaware of the agreement's existence, he announced that the case would be dealt with under domestic law and was not to be treated as a diplomatic issue. The bureaucracy had not informed him—the ongoing attempts to reform the bureaucracy had already led to very poor relations with the DPJ—and Maehara had already ordered the JCG to be more assertive with Chinese fishing vessels, up to and including their capture, long before the collision happened.[62]

Beijing's harsh reaction can therefore be understood in the overall context of the East China Sea dispute and the potential changes to the status quo that would result from the Japanese prosecution of a Chinese citizen for activities in the disputed zone.[63] Nevertheless, behind the scenes, Chief Cabinet Secretary Sengoku sought a diplomatic resolution with China.[64] Against this background, however, the Kan administration lacked credibility in its insistence that the local prosecutor's September 24 decision to release Zhan was, like the arrest and initial detention, made independently of Tokyo. Much as there was initial interference from Maehara and others like Foreign Minister Okada Katsuya that heated up the controversy, so was there interference from Kan and others like Sengoku to end it. As we shall see, this pattern mirrored Koizumi's handling of a similar incident in 2004.

Thus, the question of failure is far more complex than is allowed for in some of the commentary outlined above. Inferring from Kan's policy preferences, one can attribute failure to Kan insofar as he did not prevent Maehara from altering the status quo in the dispute to begin with. Yet, having made the original mistake not to react while at the UNGA, distancing himself from the issue and eventually releasing the captain was the least-worst option: the two alternatives were the over-ruling of Maehara and ordering the immediate release of the captain, or continuing the prosecution of the captain and risking intensified—potentially even military—conflict with China. We have seen that precedent did involve detainees being deported, but those cases were less serious—the Chinese crime in 2004 was tit-for-tat vandalism of a Senkaku shrine set up by right-wing Japanese activists who themselves had landed illegally on the islands. Koizumi intervened and ordered the prosecutor to release the individuals, "interfering" in domestic legal procedure just as Kan had done—but facing far less criticism.[65] Moreover, the critique focused on Kan's "weak-kneed" response, and how he seemed "to cave in" to China, without assessing the alternative: prosecution of the captain. This is unthinkable to most—with the exception perhaps of extreme China hawks of the likes of Tokyo Governor Ishihara Shintarō, to whom we will come presently—and the term "failure" hardly covers the potential outcome. There is one other clear alternative: immediate release. Given that the criticisms of Kan focused on the "weak-kneed" response, one can only imagine the reactions had the captain been released without any push-back. The argument could be made that the immediate deportation of the captain could have been seen as altering the status quo in China's favor.

Some analysts have suggested that, rather than a "loss," the incident may be seen as a "victory" for Japan insofar as China was widely perceived to have dramatically overreacted, and thereby damaged its reputation in a region where it has similar maritime and territorial disputes with multiple states.[66] Moreover, Maehara, who was promoted to head the foreign ministry on September 17, squeezed out an acknowledgment from the Obama administration that the US–Japan Security Treaty covered the disputed islands, something Washington had hitherto carefully avoided. This is part of the story, but the most important domestic effect of the incident—through its recruiting into the narrative of Kan's "weakness" and "failure"—was to further undermine the DPJ as a party, in particular on foreign policy. On the one hand, it strengthened those in the DPJ who sought to return to a more traditional US-centric policy and increased public support for a tougher stance on China. It is not surprising, then, that the "failure" strengthened Maehara. One might even suggest that, as with Ishihara and the 2012 island purchase controversy, this had been the intention all along. On the other hand, the collision incident provided another foreign policy "failure" to be recruited into the Japan-in-crisis meta-narrative: China was increasingly aggressive, the alliance was in trouble, Japan's security was at stake, and the DPJ was to blame.

Noda and the 2012 Senkaku/Diaoyu Island Purchase

The election of Noda Yoshihiko as prime minister, a hawk whose policy preferences and behavior most closely mirrored the LDP, is instructive for understanding the narration of the DPJ's mishandling of foreign policy and the emergence of the national crisis meta-narrative. As with his predecessors, Noda lasted only a year, as the DPJ's popularity continued to decline against the backdrop of the March 2011 Fukushima meltdowns, the global recession, and an increase of the consumption tax. Yet, while Noda's foreign policy did come in for criticism, attacks were far less pronounced than those against his predecessors. Noda was, after all, "one of us": a China hawk who, on taking power, publicly rejected the original DPJ foreign policy shift, confirmed his support for the Futenma relocation plan, acknowledged the centrality of the US–Japan alliance, and stated that the building of an East Asian Community could be postponed.[67] With this, whatever had been left of the DPJ foreign policy shift was eliminated. Moreover, during his tenure, typical LDP-style policies were implemented, including a return to the incremental lifting of restrictions on the overseas use of the military and the relaxation of limits on arms exports. Noda also made Maehara head of the DPJ policy research committee and installed "realists" such as Gemba Kōichirō as foreign minister and Nagashima Akihisa as his own top foreign policy advisor.[68]

The Senkaku dispute was to be the main issue on Noda's foreign policy agenda. As in Kan's case, the issue would be triggered by an aggressive third-party actor—this time not an inebriated Chinese fisherman, but Ishihara Shintarō, the then Governor of Tokyo and notorious nationalist provocateur, whose involvement with the dispute stretches back as far as the 1990s, and Kurihara Kunioka, the islands' owner. While in Kan's case the incident was surely unwelcome, that was not necessarily the case with Noda. Indeed, Noda had some history with the Senkakus. He had been among those critical of Koizumi's release of the protesters in a 2004 incident and, in response, had sponsored a Diet resolution on the "maintenance of inherent territory."[69] Two years earlier, in 2002, the Koizumi administration had leased several of the islets from Kurihara, apparently in order to prevent third-party purchase and allow for better control over nationalists' landings there.[70] Plans for the central government to purchase the islands had been discussed since 2006. Then, in 2011, Kurihara, deeply in debt, approached Ishihara. The two came to an oral agreement on the sale of three of the islets to the Tokyo Metropolitan Government.[71] Reports surfaced that Kurihara used the informal deal with Ishihara as a negotiating chip with the central government—he knew that the central government would pay more to avoid having the islets fall into Ishihara's hands.[72] Either way, Ishihara publicly announced that the Tokyo Metropolitan Government would purchase and develop three of the islets.[73] He backed up these plans by revealing a public fund that had already received over 1.4 billion yen in public donations for "protecting" the Senkakus from foreign takeover.[74]

The Chinese response was unsurprising. Foreign Ministry spokesman Liu Weimin described the attempt as "irresponsible" and reiterated China's claim. After much deliberation within the cabinet, Noda in July announced that the central government was considering purchasing the islands itself. The announcement coincided with the seventy-fifth anniversary of the Marco Polo Bridge incident, which is remembered in China as the beginning of the full-scale Japanese invasion. Against the backdrop of anti-Japanese protests and boycotts across China that August, Noda on September 9 met Chinese President Hu Jintao at an Asia-Pacific Economic Cooperation (APEC) summit in Vladivostok. Hu told Noda that any Japanese purchase would be "illegal and invalid."[75] Two days later Noda finalized the island purchase.

The Chinese response dwarfed that of 2010. Premier Wen Jiabao stated that China "will never budge even half an inch over the sovereignty and territorial issue."[76] Violent anti-Japanese protests broke out, forcing several Japanese companies to temporarily shut down operations in China.[77] The renewed boycott of Japanese goods led to falling sales of major brands, including Toyota and Nissan, and the Japanese tourism industry was hit hard when thousands of Chinese cancelled trips, eventually resulting in the discontinuation of a number of China–Japan flight-connections. By December, Noda and the DPJ were out of office following a comprehensive defeat in the lower house election. The LDP had considered including the island purchase in their manifesto, though this was obviously moot by the time of the election. Still, during the campaign Abe talked tough on the dispute, promising to station officials on the islands. Perhaps unsurprisingly, he did not follow up, but instead raised the rhetorical stakes in an interview with the *Washington Post*, where he called Chinese actions in the dispute as "coercion" and "intimidation" and described China's education policy as "anti-Japanese."[78] The longer-term Chinese reaction was a sustained program of coast guard vessels entering the islands' territorial seas on their regular patrols, naval vessels entering the contiguous zones, and surveillance planes entering the territorial airspace of the islands. This increased activity lasted until 2014, seriously challenging Japanese control over the disputed islands and surrounding waters.

As outlined below, the prevailing depiction of Noda's handling of the island purchase is that he played a bad hand as well as he could. However, the manner in which the nationalization went ahead did cause a major crisis in Sino-Japanese relations—the worst since the Koizumi era. Moreover, there were several missteps. The July announcement that the government was considering purchasing the islands was made precisely on the seventy-fifth anniversary of the Marco Polo Bridge incident. Hence, to soothe Chinese feelings, Yamaguchi Tsuyoshi, senior vice minister of foreign affairs, was sent to deliver a letter to Hu Jintao. It mentioned the importance of maintaining good relations and communication, but said nothing about the plan to nationalize the islands. The Chinese side interpreted this as meaning that there was still room for finding an alternative solution. On September 9, Noda met Hu at the APEC forum in Vladivostok, and again did not mention the decision to purchase the islands, instead speaking of the need to see the issue from "a broad perspective."[79] When the purchase was announced two days later, this left Hu with an egg on his face and precipitated the downward spiral in Sino-Japanese relations.

Thinking counterfactually, it is difficult to say whether the Chinese response would have been much different if the communication had been better and the timing more careful. The other counterfactual is what would have happened if Noda had not nationalized the islands: leaving them in the hands of Ishihara could have led to a much worse outcome. But this reading assumes that this was the only other option. Both the Japanese ambassador to China, Niwa Uichirō, and US Assistant Secretary of State Kurt Campbell had warned the Noda administration not to proceed with the nationalization. It does not appear that Noda was interested in exploring alternatives. Instead, in the Noda cabinet, Ishihara's gambit was seen less as a nuisance and more as an opportunity.[80] Rather than being stuck between a rock and a hard place, Noda was given a gift, a chance to alter the status quo in the dispute while appearing to be acting in everyone's best interest. This is consistent with Noda's and his fellow hawks' long-standing position on China. Viewed from this set of policy preferences, the purchase may have been a success. Though the Chinese response in the form of maneuvers in seas and airspace around the islands persisted for years, the impact on the "sovereignty game" of the dispute is debatable.[81] Perhaps most important for the discussion here is that, although the LDP, the US, and the Japanese media did not treat Noda as harshly as his predecessors, the collapse of Sino-Japanese relations *did* provide further fuel for the fire that Abe could draw from for constructing his meta-narrative of the crisis affecting the security of Japan.

Unlike Hatoyama or Kan, the criticisms of Noda were measured in both media and scholarly writing. Analyses tend to note one or two missteps, but, crucially, these missteps are excused, the general narrative being that Noda had an impossible situation forced upon him and did the best he could under difficult conditions. One assessment contrasted Kan, as "weak, inept, and soft on China," with Noda's purchase, which was "probably managed as successfully as possible."[82] US scholar-official Douglas Paal wrote that "historians will look back on his leadership and find missteps . . . but Noda's general intent to contain the issue seemed obvious."[83] Acclaimed scholar Gerald Curtis wrote in *Foreign Affairs* that "Noda, to his credit, looked for ways to defuse the crisis and restore calm between the two countries, but the Chinese would have none of it."[84] The general sense in policy analyses is that Noda was a relatively competent leader, one who made some mistakes and failed to prevent the crisis—but that we recognize that his intentions were good and he did his best.[85] This is particularly interesting for two reasons. First, 2012 had a far more severe impact on both Sino-Japanese relations and on Japan's control over the disputed islands and surrounding waters than did 2010, leading to a post-Koizumi nadir in Sino-Japanese relations. Secondly, the 2012 postmortems, unlike those of 2010, generally point to multiple moments where Noda could have acted differently.

In the Japanese media, too, criticism of Noda was far more circumspect than the hostility aimed at Hatoyama and Kan. *The Asahi Shimbun* was critical of Ishihara for triggering the crisis, and of the Chinese reaction, but published several editorials approving of Noda's response, stating that "there was no other way to stop the purchase by the Tokyo Metropolitan Government apart from nationalization."[86] The *Yomiuri Shimbun* took a slightly different position on Ishihara, but was no less approving of Noda. It praised Ishihara's actions and repeatedly called for the Tokyo and national governments to work together in the dispute.[87] Indeed, on Noda's inauguration, the *Yomiuri* breathed a public sigh of relief, publishing an approving editorial while criticizing both Hatoyama and Kan.[88] Tellingly, shortly before the DPJ fell from power, the *Yomiuri* published an article noting that despite

Noda having inherited a "negative legacy" from Hatoyama and Kan, he "could be evaluated as having left behind certain achievements," including the strengthening of the alliance, the relaxing of the constraints on arms exports, and showing a favorable stance to the Trans-Pacific Partnership free-trade agreement.[89]

Conclusion

Regardless of the mild praise Noda received from the conservative media, the overall story of the DPJ's handling of foreign policy was one of failure and of crisis. Even if Noda did manage to appear tough, the state of Japan's international relations when Abe came to power was troubled, to say the least. Aside from the three cases examined here, relations with South Korea and Russia had also deteriorated. Moreover, just days before the election, North Korea launched a satellite into space using ballistic missile technology. For Abe, the timing could not have been luckier. He described the rocket launch as "outrageous" and called on the UN to impose harsh sanctions.[90] Seen from the perspective of the meta-narrative of a national crisis, it was the cherry on top: Japan was surrounded by hostile and aggressive neighbors taking advantage of the DPJ's weakness. Worse, the DPJ had alienated Japan's only ally: the United States. Thus, Japan faced a national security crisis in the true sense of crisis as "a moment of decisive intervention."[91] Abe would make that intervention, and set Japan on a new path, enacting collective self-defense legislation, increasing military spending, continuing the erosion of the postwar constraints on Japan's military. The idea of a national security crisis would reach a climax in 2017.[92] The timing was again fortunate for Abe, with the LDP all-conquering in the 2017 election.

In retrospect, much of the rhetoric around the "crisis" was obviously a political attempt to discredit the DPJ and any alternative foreign policy for Japan. Michael Green referred to the "crisis" in Japan–US relations during the Hatoyama administration as the worst in the history of the alliance, leading to fears of abandonment in Japan. Yet the Hatoyama "crisis" barely resonates today. Rather, as we have seen, the crisis was created for the purposes of discrediting the DPJ's foreign policy. There is no evidence that the US was considering abandoning its ally. Note that Green is not on record as describing Trump's election as the greatest crisis in the history of the alliance, despite Trump's actual threats to withdraw from the Security Treaty. Indeed, even President Trump, who had been vocal in his criticism of Japan during the 2016 election campaign, seemed to have recognized just how valuable Japan and the current security arrangements are to the US.

It is worthwhile to reflect comparatively, and with the benefit of hindsight, on the attribution of failure and the construction of crisis during the DPJ years. The "crisis" in Japan–US relations, the "weak-kneed" response to China, and the lost ground in the territorial dispute were convincingly construed as posing a grave threat to Japan's security. And yet, thinking of failures, perhaps none stands out more clearly in recent years than Abe's dealings with Trump and North Korea. His vocal support for and diplomatic investment in the "maximum pressure" policy on North Korea saw him completely isolated and sidelined following the Trump–Kim détente. Trump even said that he was not "personally" bothered by North Korea's short-range missile tests.[93] But Abe slowly but surely softened his position and toed the US line, much as LDP administrations have done for decades. Indeed, Trump could not have hoped for a more accommodating ally than Japan under Abe. On a range of issues, from North Korea to Iran, trade to symbolic diplomacy, in both public and in private, Abe deferred to Trump again and again.[94] One might even argue that Abe sold out Japan's interests to a megalomaniac US president, though given the US-centric nature of mainstream policy discourse, this will unlikely earn the attribution of "failure." Rather, from a US perspective, it is a huge success.

Notes

1. Ellis S. Krauss and Robert J. Pekkanen, "The Rise and Fall of Japan's Liberal Democratic Party," *Journal of Asian Studies* 69, no. 1 (2010): 5–15; Steven R. Reed, Ethan Scheiner, and Michael F. Thies, "The End of LDP Dominance and the Rise of Party-Oriented Politics in Japan," *Journal of Japanese Studies* 38, no. 2 (2012): 353–376.

2. Prime Minister of Japan and His Cabinet (Kantei), "Press Conference by Prime Minister Shinzo Abe," December 26, 2012, https://japan.kantei.go.jp/96_abe/statement/201212/26kaiken_e.html. Unless otherwise stated, all online sources were accessed and available on September 30, 2020.

3. Ibid.

4. Sebastian Maslow, "A Blueprint for a Strong Japan? Abe Shinzō and Japan's Evolving Security System," *Asian Survey* 55, no. 4 (2015): 739–765; Christopher W. Hughes, *Japan's Foreign and Security Policy under the 'Abe Doctrine': New Dynamism or New Dead End?* (New York: Palgrave Macmillan 2015).

5. See, for example, Kobayashi Yoshiaki, *Seiken kōtai: Minshutō seiken to wa nan datta no ka* [Government Change: What was the Meaning of the DPJ Government] (Tokyo: Chūō Kōron Shinsha, 2012); Kenji E. Kushida and Philip Y. Lipcy, eds., *Japan under the DPJ: The Politics of Transition and Governance* (Washington, DC: Brookings Institution Press, 2013); Yoichi Funabashi and Koichi Nakano, eds., *The Democratic Party of Japan in Power: Challenges and Failures* (London: Routledge, 2016).

6. Jun Hongo, "Hatoyama Quits as Prime Minister," *Japan Times*, June 3, 2010, https://www.japantimes.co.jp/news/2010/06/03/national/hatoyama-quits-as-prime-minister/.

7. Mike Mochizuki, "China Over-Reached," *Oriental Economist* 78, no. 10 (2010): 6.

8. Colin Hay, "Crisis and the Structural Transformation of the State: Interrogating the Process of Change," *British Journal of Politics and International Relations* 1, no. 3 (1999): 317–344.

9. Associated Press, "Bush Calls Iraq Invasion a 'Catastrophic Success,' " *Fox News Network*, August 30, 2004, https://www.foxnews.com/story/bush-calls-iraq-invasion-a-catastrophic-success.

10. Mark Bovens and Paul 't Hart, "Revisiting the Study of Policy Failures," *Journal of European Public Policy* 23, no. 5 (2016): 653–666; Allen McConnell, "A Public Policy Approach to Understanding the Nature and Causes of Foreign Policy Failure," *Journal of European Public Policy* 23, no. 5 (2016): 667–684; Allen McConnell, "Policy Success, Policy Failure and Grey Areas In-between," *Journal of Public Policy* 30, no. 3 (2010): 345–362; Allan McConnell, "What Is Policy Failure? A Primer to Help Navigate the Maze," *Public Policy and Administration* 30, no. 3–4 (2015): 221–242; Kai Oppermann and Alexander Spencer, "Telling Stories of Failure: Narrative Constructions of Foreign Policy Fiascos," *Journal of European Public Policy* 23, no. 5 (2016): 685–701.

11. McConnell, "A Public Policy Approach."

12. McConnell, "What Is Policy Failure?"

13. Bovens and 't Hart, "Revisiting."

14. Hay, "Crisis."

15. Ibid., 323.

16. See Wirth and Maslow, this volume.

17. Kantei, "Press Conference."

18. Hay, "Crisis," 317, 320.

19. Glenn Hook, Ra Mason, and Paul O'Shea, *Regional Risk and Security in Japan: Whither the Everyday* (London: Routledge, 2015): 168–196.

20. For more details, see Paul O'Shea, "Overestimating the 'Power Shift': The US Role in the Failure of the Democratic Party of Japan's 'Asia Pivot,' " *Asian Perspective* 38, no. 3 (2014): 435–459; Paul O'Shea "Strategic Narratives and US

Military Bases in Japan: How 'Deterrence' Makes the Marine Base on Okinawa 'Indispensable,'" *Media, War & Conflict* 12, no. 4 (2018): 450–467.

21. Yukio Hatoyama, "A New Path for Japan," *New York Times*, August 26, 2009, https://www.nytimes.com/2009/08/27/opinion/27iht-edhatoyama.html.

22. O'Shea, "Overestimating."

23. Jun Hongo, "Guam Move Depends on Futenma: Gates," *Japan Times*, October 22, 2009, https://www.japantimes.co.jp/news/2009/10/22/national/guam-move-depends-on-futenma-gates/.

24. Michael J. Green, "The Democratic Party of Japan and the Future of the U.S.-Japan Alliance," *Journal of Japanese Studies* 37, no. 1 (2012): 91–116, here 91.

25. Michael J. Green, "Tokyo Smackdown," *Foreign Policy*, October 23, 2009, http://shadow.foreignpolicy.com/posts/2009/10/23/tokyo_smackdown.

26. Michael Auslin, "The Politics of Confusion," *Wall Street Journal*, June 3, 2010, https://www.wsj.com/articles/SB10001424052748704875604575281531543506628.

27. Victor Cha, "The New Renegade Ally?" *Chosun Ilbo*, December 10, 2009.

28. Green, "Tokyo Smackdown."

29. Al Kamen, "Among Leaders at the Summit, Hu's First," *Washington Post*, April 14, 2010.

30. Joseph S. Nye Jr., "An Alliance Larger than One Issue," *New York Times*, January 6, 2010, https://www.nytimes.com/2010/01/07/opinion/07nye.html.

31. Cha, "The New Renegade Ally?"

32. I use the term "scholar-officials" in the sense meant by Jerdén, i.e., security scholars who wield influence not only over debates and policy; see Björn Jerdén, "Security Expertise and International Hierarchy: The Case of 'The Asia-Pacific Epistemic Community,'" *Review of International Studies* 43, no. 3 (2017): 494–515.

33. Green, "Tokyo Smackdown."

34. Kawada Takuji, "Sentaku 09 shūin-sen: Nihon no anzen mamoremasu ka kokusai buchō" [Lower-House election 2009: Can they Protect Japan?], *Yomiuri Shimbun*, August 21, 2009.

35. Ogawa Satoshi, "[Minshu ni chūmon] Nichibeidōmei, shōrai-zō shimese Maikeru Gurīn-shi" [Michael Green request for the DPJ: Show a Vision for the Future of the Alliance], *Yomiuri Shimbun*, September 6, 2009.

36. O'Shea, "Overestimating."

37. Yoshisuke Iimura, "Seeking Deep Analysis," *The Oriental Economist* 78, no. 7 (2010): 10.

38. Ryo Sahashi, "The DPJ Government's Failed Foreign Policy," in *Looking for Leadership: The Dilemma of Political Leadership in Japan*, ed. Ryo Sahashi and James Gannon (Tokyo: Japan Center for International Exchange, 2015), pp. 135–158; Daniel Klausen, "Leadership, Strategy, and Policy Entrepreneurship in Japanese Security Politics: A Comparison of Three Prime Ministerships," *Electronic Journal of Contemporary Japanese Studies* 13, no. 1 (2013), https://www.japanesestudies.org.uk/ejcjs/vol13/iss1/clausen.html; Christopher W. Hughes, "The Democratic Party

of Japan's New (but Failing) Grand Security Strategy: From 'Reluctant Realism' to 'Resentful Realism'?" *Journal of Japanese Studies* 38, no. 1 (Winter 2012): 109–140; Green, "The Democratic Party of Japan."

39. McConnell, "A Public Policy Approach," 669, original emphasis.

40. Hook et al., *Regional Risk*.

41. McConnell, "A Public Policy Approach," 669–670, original emphasis.

42. Quoted in Josh Rogan, "State Department Japan Hand Loses Post as Campbell Goes on Tokyo Apology Tour," *Foreign Policy*, March 9, 2011, https://foreignpolicy.com/2011/03/09/state-department-japan-hand-loses-post-as-campbell-goes-on-tokyo-apology-tour/.

43. "US Senators Urge Rethink on Okinawa Base Plan," *BBC News*, May 12, 2011, https://www.bbc.com/news/world-asia-pacific-13372194.

44. Yoichi Funabashi, "Japan-China Relations Stand at Ground Zero," *East Asia Forum*, October 20, 2012, https://www.eastasiaforum.org/2010/10/20/japan-china-relations-stand-at-ground-zero/.

45. Linus Hagström, "'Power Shift' in East Asia? A Critical Reappraisal of Narratives on the Diaoyu/Senkaku Islands Incident in 2010," *Chinese Journal of International Politics* 5, no. 3 (2012): 267–297.

46. Ben Blanchard and Chisa Fujioka, "China's Wen Threatens to Step Up Japan Row," *Reuters*, September 22, 2010, https://www.reuters.com/article/us-china-japan/chinas-wen-threatens-to-step-up-japan-row-idUSTRE68L0B820100922.

47. Reinhard Drifte, "The Japan-China Confrontation over the Senkaku/Diaoyu Islands—Between 'Shelving' and 'Dispute Escalation,'" *Asia-Pacific Journal Japan Focus* 12, 30–3 (July 27, 2014), https://apjjf.org/-Reinhard-Drifte/4154/article.pdf.

48. With a few notable exceptions, see Peter Ennis, "Japan Blinked? Look Again," *Dispatch Japan: News and Views on the US, Japan and US–Japan Relations*, September 26, 2010, http://www.dispatchjapan.com/blog/2010/09/japan-blinked-look-again.html; Shogo Suzuki, "Japan and China's Masochists," *Diplomat*, November 11, 2010, https://thediplomat.com/2010/11/japan-and-chinas-masochists/; Hagström, "'Power Shift.'"

49. Hagström, "'Power Shift.'"

50. Maya Kaneko, "Kan Wins Points for Damage Control But Still Lacking Long-Term Strategies," *Japan Times*, November 15, 2010, https://www.japantimes.co.jp/news/2010/11/15/national/kan-wins-points-for-damage-control-but-still-lacking-long-term-strategies/; Alexei Anishchuk, "Japan in Diplomatic Row after Russia Isle Visit," *Reuters*, November 1, 2010, https://www.reuters.com/article/us-japan-russia-idUSTRE6A00AG20101101.

51. See Hagström, "'Power Shift.'"

52. Andy Sharp, "LDP Not Playing Ball," *Diplomat*, November 2, 2010, https://thediplomat.com/2010/11/ldp-not-playing-ball/.

53. Alex Martin and Masami Ito, "Parties Unite in Demanding Senkaku Video," *Japan Times*, October 1, 2010, https://www.japantimes.co.jp/news/2010/10/01/national/parties-unite-in-demanding-senkaku-video/; Sharp, "LDP."

54. Aside from those quoted directly, see also Giulio Pugliese and Aurelio Insisa, *Sino-Japanese Power Politics: Might, Money, and Minds* (New York: Palgrave Macmillan, 2017); Tobias Harris, "2010: Q&A on Politics," Néojaponisme, December 22, 2012, http://neojaponisme.com/2010/12/22/2010-qa-on-politics/; Sanaa Hafeez, "The Senkaku/Diaoyu Island Crises of 2004, 2010, and 2012: A Study of Japanese-Chinese Crisis Management," *Asia-Pacific Review* 22, no. 1 (2015): 73–99; Paul O'Shea, *Playing the Sovereignty Game: Understanding Japan's Territorial Disputes* (PhD diss., University of Sheffield, 2012); Sahashi, "The DPJ"; Yoshinori Kaseda, "The Japan-China Gentlemen's Agreement over the Senkaku Islands," in *Regional Institutions, Geopolitics and Economics in the Asia-Pacific*, edited by Steven B. Rothman, Utpal Vyas, and Yoichiro Sato (London: Routledge, 2017).

55. Weston S. Konishi, *From Rhetoric to Reality: Foreign-Policy Making under the Democratic Party of Japan* (Cambridge, MA: The Institute for Foreign Policy Analysis, April 2012), http://www.ifpa.org/pdf/fromRhetoricToReality.pdf.

56. See, for example, Konishi, *From Rhetoric to Reality*; Sahashi, "The DPJ." Even where his role in causing the escalation is recognized, such as in Hafeez, "The Senkaku/Diaoyu Island Crises," the criticism is still milder than that reserved for Kan or Sengoku.

57. Sahashi, "The DPJ," 168.

58. Konishi, *From Rhetoric to Reality*, 18.

59. Guibourg Delamotte, "Japan's Foreign Policy beyond Short-Term Politics," *Asia-Pacific Review* 19, no. 2 (2012): 46–61.

60. Hafeez, "The Senkaku/Diaoyu Island Crises."

61. The outline is of three main points: The Japanese side would not land on the islands, nor would they detain Chinese citizens to the point that it became a major diplomatic problem, and finally China would try to prevent Chinese protesters from landing; see O'Shea, *Playing the Sovereignty Game*.

62. Kaseda, "The Japan-China Gentlemen's Agreement."

63. O'Shea, *Playing the Sovereignty Game*.

64. Shin Kawashima, "The Senkaku Crisis in Perspective," interview with Sengoku Yoshito, *Nippon.com*, December 5, 2017, https://www.nippon.com/en/currents/d00365/?pnum=2.

65. O'Shea, *Playing the Sovereignty Game*, 205–207.

66. Suzuki, "Japan and China's Masochists"; Hagström, "'Power Shift'"; Ennis, "Japan Blinked?"

67. Konishi, *From Rhetoric to Reality*, 40.

68. Ibid., 40.

69. O'Shea, *Playing the Sovereignty Game*, 206.

70. Ibid., 194.

71. Antoni Slodkowski, "How Debts and Double-dealing Sparked Japan-China Islets Row," *Reuters*, November 11, 2012, https://www.reuters.com/article/us-china-japan-family/how-debts-and-double-dealing-sparked-japan-china-islets-row-idUSBRE8AA0EY20121111.

72. Ibid.

73. Kyodo, "Ishihara Seeking to Buy Senkaku Islands," *Japan Times*, 18 April 2012.

74. Kyodo, "Government Offering Senkakus Owner ¥2 Billion for Contested Isles," *Japan Times*, April 18, 2012, https://www.japantimes.co.jp/news/2012/08/27/national/government-offering-senkakus-owner-2-billion-for-contested-isles/.

75. Kiyoshi Takenaka and Sui-Lee Wee, "Japan Infuriates China by Agreeing to Buy Disputed Isles," *Reuters*, September 10, 2012: https://www.reuters.com/article/us-china-japan/japan-infuriates-china-by-agreeing-to-buy-disputed-isles-idUSBRE8890AU20120910;

76. Editorial, "Posturing over the Senkakus," *Japan Times*, September 14, 2012, https://www.japantimes.co.jp/opinion/2012/09/14/editorials/posturing-over-the-senkakus/.

77. "Broke out" also means "were allowed to break out." The CCP did not restrain the anti-Japanese demonstrators as they had on previous occasions.

78. "Transcript of Interview with Japanese Prime Minister Shinzo Abe," *Washington Post*, February 20, 2013, https://www.washingtonpost.com/world/transcript-of-interview-with-japanese-prime-minister-shinzo-abe/2013/02/20/e7518d54-7b1c-11e2-82e8-61a46c2cde3d_story.html.

79. James J. Przystup, "Japan-China Relations: 40th Anniversary: 'Fuggetaboutit!' " *Comparative Connections* 14, no. 3 (2013), http://cc.pacforum.org/2013/01/40th-anniversary-fuggetaboutit/.

80. Michael J. Green, Kathleen Hicks, Zack Cooper, John Schaus, and Jake Douglas, "Counter-Coercion Series: Senkaku Nationalization Crisis," CSIS Asia Maritime Transparency Initiative, June 14, 2017, https://amti.csis.org/counter-co-senkaku-nationalization/.

81. O'Shea, *Playing the Sovereignty Game*.

82. Hafeez, "The Senkaku/Diaoyu Island Crises," 83.

83. Douglas H. Paal, "Japan-China: Time to Climb Down," Carnegie Endowment for International Peace, September 29, 2012, https://carnegieendowment.org/2012/09/29/japan-china-time-to-climb-down-pub-49522.

84. Gerald L. Curtis, "Japan's Cautious Hawks: Why Tokyo Is Unlikely to Pursue an Aggressive Foreign Policy," *Foreign Affairs* 92, no. 2 (2013): 77–86, here 83.

85. The general sense, but not everyone; for example, Pugliese and Insisa state that Noda "wholly mismanaged" the issue. Pugliese and Insisa, *Sino-Japanese Power Politics*, 48.

86. Editorial, "Senkaku kokuyū-ka muyōna masatsu uchidome ni" [Nationalization of the Senkakus to Stop Unnecessary Friction], *Asahi Shimbun*, September 6, 2012; Editorial, "Senkaku to Chūgoku kyōkō shisei wa nani mo umanu" [The Senkakus and China: Not a Hard-Line Stance], *Asashi Shimbun*, September 13, 2012; Editorial "Jimintō sōsaisen—Koku ninau kakugo ga kikitai" [The Liberal Democratic Party Presidential Election: We Would Like to Hear the Resolution to Carry the Country's Burden], *Asahi Shimbun*, September 2012, 14.

87. Editorial, "Senkaku kokuyū-ka hōshin seifu to to wa antei kanri e kyōchō o" [The Senkaku Nationalization Policy: The National Government and the Capital Should Cooperate for Stable Management], *Yomiuri Shimbun*, July 10, 2012.

88. Editorial "Noda naikaku hossoku kokunan norikiru shohōsen o shimese" [The Inauguration of the Noda Cabinet: Provide a Prescription to Survive the National Crisis], *Yomiuri Shimbun*, September 3, 2011.

89. Editorial, "Minshutō seiken sōkatsu seiji no rekka o maneita 'datsu-kanryō'" [Review of the DPJ Administration: "De-Bureaucratization" Caused Political Deterioration], *Yomiuri Shimbun*, November 18, 2012.

90. Simon Tisdal, Justin McCurry, and Tania Branigan, "North Korea Rocket Launch Prompts International Condemnation," *Guardian*, December 13, 2013, https://www.theguardian.com/world/2012/dec/12/north-korean-rocket-launch-condemned.

91. Hay, "Crisis," 317.

92. See Mason and Maslow, this volume.

93. Associated Press, "Trump Says He Isn't Bothered by North Korea's Recent Missile Launches," *NBC News*, May 27, 2019, https://www.nbcnews.com/news/world/trump-says-he-backs-japan-s-efforts-talk-iran-n1010466.

94. Paul O'Shea and Sebastian Maslow, " 'Making the Alliance Even Greater': (Mis-)Managing U.S.-Japan Relations in the Age of Trump," *Asian Security* (2020), https://doi.org/10.1080/14799855.2020.1838486.

Chapter 8

From Ashes to New

The Delegitimization and Comeback of Japan's Official Development Assistance

RAYMOND YAMAMOTO

Introduction

With Japan's postwar constitution renouncing the right to belligerency and possession of military capabilities, Tokyo embraced Official Development Assistance (ODA) as a key instrument of foreign policy. Since the late 1980s, various administrations have therefore attempted to centralize the ODA decision-making process to gain control over the important tool. However, these efforts notwithstanding, the complex structure that had been set up in the 1950s remained largely in place. The implementation of reforms to streamline decision-making proved to be difficult, not least because of the large number of ministries involved in the vertically segmented bureaucratic process (*tatewari gyōsei*).[1] The Liberal Democratic Party (LDP)–led government under Prime Minister Abe Shinzō was the first to sufficiently control the process, allowing it to strategically use ODA for pursuing its own diplomatic, economic, and security political ends.

In hindsight, the increasingly negative public image of ODA in the 1990s was an important factor that enabled the Abe administration to eventually centralize ODA decision-making in the political executive.[2] However, questions about the increasing dissatisfaction among the Japanese public over their country's ODA policy at the time remain. Certainly, Japan's economic malaise and deepening debt crisis influenced public views on established practice. Yet ODA had been one of the most important policy instruments for steering the country's postwar economic growth. Why, then, did the public not consider using ODA as a means to overcome the economic crisis or "lost decades" that Japan has been stuck in since the early 1990s?

In this chapter I examine how "reform entrepreneurs" from within the LDP actively molded public opinion.[3] My analysis of elite discourses reveals that the reform entrepreneurs deliberately used crisis narratives to question bureaucracy-led decision-making by constructing a negative image of ODA. Through exposing the bureaucracy directly to public criticisms, often highlighting the negative consequences of providing ODA to China, the reform entrepreneurs weakened bureaucratic actors' position, enabling structural reforms that strengthened the role of the prime minister and his cabinet.

The burst of the bubble economy in the early 1990s shook Japan's self-confidence and provided the reform entrepreneurs with a rare opportunity for demanding decisive changes. Specifically, the increasingly alarmist narrative about Japan's financial and political instability amplified the public view that a restructuring of ODA decision-making was necessary. As such, the argument put forward in this chapter resonates with the scholarship on crisis narratives and policy change by Colin Hay, who defines crisis "as a moment of decisive intervention and not merely a moment of fragmentation, dislocation or destruction."[4] To illustrate the effect of crisis narratives on Japan's ODA policymaking, this chapter draws primarily on official speeches, government reports, and media coverage.

In the following pages, I briefly outline the origin and the expansion of ODA as a central instrument of Japan's foreign policy and the complex decision-making process that emerged from it. Building on these insights, I next analyze how LDP reform entrepreneurs aggravated crisis narratives to discredit bureaucracy-led ODA decision-making, thus facilitating the debate on comprehensive reforms of ODA policy. In the last part of this chapter I discuss the comeback of ODA as a tool in contemporary Japan's foreign policy after the LDP regained control over the decision-making process.

ODA and the Economic Success of Postwar Japan

The beginnings of ODA policy can be traced back to the signing of the San Francisco Peace Treaty in 1951. Then, it was agreed that "Japan should pay reparations to the Allied Powers for the damage and suffering caused by it during the war."[5] Although ODA had initially been launched to fulfill Japan's obligation to pay reparations, officials in Tokyo quickly understood how to utilize it for their own advantage, primarily for promoting Japanese business and trade. Seeking a speedy economic recovery and return to international society, ODA came as the perfect instrument for securing natural resources and for promoting peaceful relations through trade and economic assistance.

In theory, the Ministry of Foreign Affairs (MOFA) was invested with general policymaking authority, setting the framework for all other ministries. Yet, in reality, other ministries, most notably the Ministry of International Trade and Industry (MITI; since 2001 the Ministry of Economy, Trade and Industry, METI), the Ministry of Finance (MOF), and the Economic Planning Agency (EPA) pursued their own agendas. This constellation resulted in a vertically segmented structure that was difficult to control. In close cooperation with the private sector, MITI, MOF, and EPA pushed for an ODA strategy that focused on the maximization of Japan's economic benefit as the primary aim.[6] While MOFA did not pursue economic goals per se, it contributed to the neo-mercantilist orientation of Japan's ODA by emphasizing the principle of non-interference. This was indispensable for maintaining diplomatic relations with non-democratic countries in the region such as China.[7]

With the various ministries promoting their own agendas,[8] quantitative studies have shown that ODA disbursement from the late 1970s through to the 1990s was predominantly neo-mercantilist in nature.[9] Therefore, ODA can be understood as an inherent part of what some have described as the "developmental state."[10] That is, the postwar Japanese state has actively been intervening in markets with the goal of promoting economic growth and social development. Constrained by its pacifist constitution that banned the possession and use of armed forces, ODA quickly also became one of Japan's most important foreign policy tools. Subsequently, the ODA budget increased linearly ever since its beginnings. In 1989, Japan surpassed the United States and became the world's leading ODA donor in absolute terms. Tokyo's ODA spending reached its peak in 1997, when it disbursed 1.17 trillion yen (see figure 8.1).

Japan's neo-mercantilist strategy resulted in an ODA policy that is clearly distinct from the approaches of other Development Assistance Committee (DAC)[11] members, who have attached primary importance to poverty reduction. Comparing Japan's ODA policy to that of other donors, critical observers concluded early on that Japan lacked a "sense of international responsibility."[12] This argument is corroborated by the pattern of

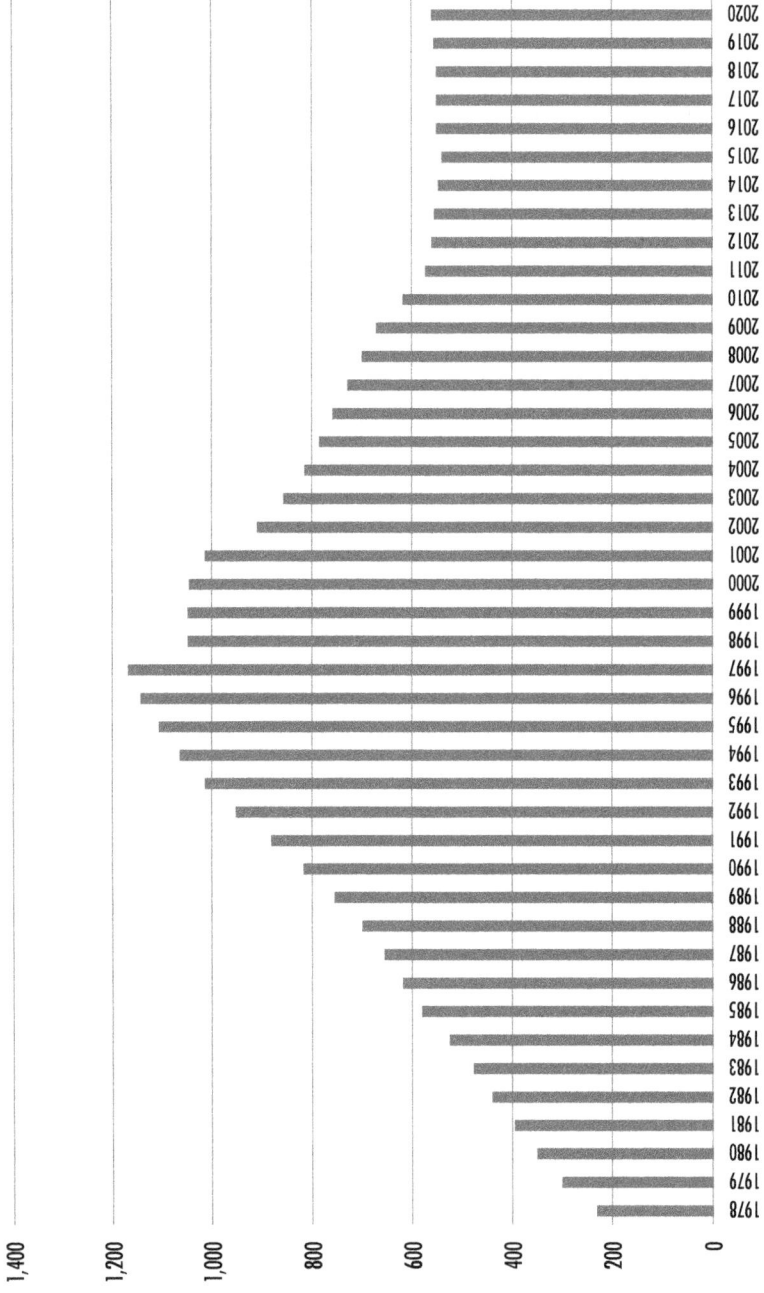

Figure 8.1. Japan's ODA budget (in billion yen). Source: Compiled by the author based on MOFA ODA budget data (2020), https://www.mofa.go.jp/mofaj/gaiko/oda/shiryo/yosan.html.

geographical allocation. Most of Japan's ODA has been directed to Asia, and not Africa, where the largest number of "least developed countries" would be located. From a financial point of view, moreover, the largest share of Japan's ODA was provided in the form of loans rather than grants. Not only did these require repayment, including interest, from the recipient countries, but, until the 1990s, they were often tied to the purchase of Japanese goods and services as well. Also, from a sectoral point of view, ODA focused primarily on large economic infrastructure and less on soft social infrastructure projects.[13]

Although Japan's ODA was often the target of international criticism, it is clear that it has been a highly successful tool for promoting Japan's (as well as the recipients') economic interest in achieving rapid economic recovery after the war. The public was well informed about these benefits. This resulted in strong domestic approval—a phenomenon some called "remarkable."[14] Unlike other OECD countries that primarily promoted the philanthropic aspect, Japanese ODA did not experience a decline in public support, or "aid fatigue," in the 1980s.[15]

Yet, concurrently, a number of politicians, including from the Japan Socialist Party, began demanding a substantial reform of ODA decision-making. They became very vocal in 1986 when it was revealed that Japan's ODA had, since the 1970s, systematically been used to bribe the kleptocratic ruler of the Philippines, Ferdinand Marcos, in order to win construction projects for Japanese contractors.[16] Regardless of such revelations, however, political and public support for ODA remained generally strong. It was not only beneficial to Japan's economy, but also came to symbolize the new power of the country in international relations. ODA was one of the few fields were Japan fulfilled the expectations as "Number One"[17] on the global stage.

The Delegitimization of Japan's ODA

As ODA was a highly successful postwar foreign policy instrument, unsurprisingly, few politicians called for its reform. This changed in the 1990s, when the political system in Japan experienced a fundamental crisis. The collapse of the "1955 system" characterized by the end of LDP one-party dominance, electoral reform, and the weakening of LDP factions had "loosened the LDP's control over far-right groups,"[18] who became more influential within the already conservative party. Equipped with great political expertise and entrepreneurial skills, the mostly young LDP members aimed to enhance the party's grip on foreign policy instruments.[19] The most influential foreign policy reform entrepreneurs in the case of ODA included Abe Shinzō, Asō Tarō, Etō Seishirō, Kōno Tarō, Ozawa Ichirō, Shiozaki Yasuhisa, and Takemi Keizō.[20] All of them had in common that they were opposed to the low-profile strategy of the postwar Yoshida Doctrine, which prioritized the maximization of Japan's economic gains over political or military ambitions. This dissatisfaction with the strategic posture of Japan also informed their attitudes toward ODA. The then LDP Secretary-General Ozawa Ichirō was a prominent voice of this movement. In 1993, he famously declared in his book *Blueprint for a New Japan* that both Japan's ODA and foreign policy lacked a "face" (*kao no nai Nihon*).[21]

The LDP's neoconservative wing supported the ensuing attempts by these and other entrepreneurs to strengthen political authority over the bureaucracy-led ODA decision-making process. Many reform entrepreneurs, including Abe and Asō, were active members of the Nippon Kaigi (Japan Conference), a powerful nationalist organization that emerged from the merger of the right-wing groups Nihon o Mamoru Kaigi (Conference to Protect Japan) and Gengō Hōsei-ka Jitsugen Kokumin Kaigi (Conference to Establish Reign Era Name Use as Law) in 1997.[22] According to the nationalists' view, Japan's low-profile foreign policy reflected a lack of national pride, which they saw as a legacy from the US occupation. In Abe's words, the primary goal of the reforms was to "release Japan from the confinement of its postwar history and once again place it into the hands of the Japanese citizens."[23] This nationalist discourse has framed the bureaucracy as a force constraining the political autonomy of Japan.

Given that ODA "is first and foremost . . . a budget issue, with voters paying attention to how their taxes are being spent, and to what end,"[24] an important precondition for strengthening the political influence was to tarnish the public and media's high confidence in the bureaucracy. Therefore, in order to achieve their objectives, the reform entrepreneurs had to portray ODA as a waste of taxpayers' money, despite being a highly cost-efficient foreign policy instrument. Here, MOFA emerged as their main target, as it was "inherently more susceptible to the country's public opinion."[25]

Against the background of the burst of the bubble economy in the early 1990s, the reform entrepreneurs faced a very favorable environment for their attempt. The economic downturn undermined public trust in the state's continued capacity to guarantee economic and social security, marking the beginning of Japan's "lost decades."[26] Other dramatic events such as the Great Hanshin earthquake and the Aum Shinrikyō gas attack on Tokyo's subway system in 1995 further aggravated the sense of national crisis.[27] Amid the unfolding lost decades, Prime Minister Hashimoto Ryūtarō in 1997 reduced the ODA budget by 10 percent. This was the first cut in ODA history, and it went through without facing any opposition.[28] Hashimoto also called for "bold revisions and reform" of the decision-making process to allow for better interministerial coordination of ODA projects in the future.[29] It was the first step in a series of reforms, at the end of which decision-making authority moved away from the bureaucracy to the executive.

Hashimoto's budget reduction and reform initiatives were proceeded by a declining public recognition of ODA as a meaningful foreign policy instrument. According to a survey conducted by the Prime Minister's Office, the number of people who supported the increase of ODA spending had dropped from 41.5 percent in 1991 to 19.2 percent in 2002, and the number of those in favor of a reduction had risen from 8 percent to 24.3 percent (see figure 8.2). While the decline of public support coincided with

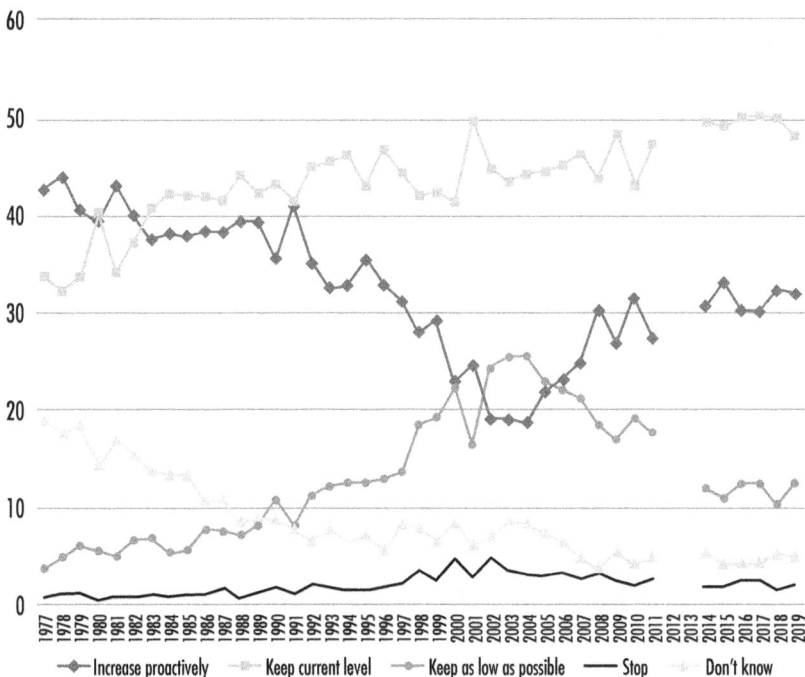

Figure 8.2. Japanese public support for ODA (in percent). Source: Compiled by the author based on Cabinet Office public survey data (various years), https://survey.gov-online.go.jp/h30/h30-gaiko/index.html.

the "lost decades," explanations that solely attribute the reason to growing public dissatisfaction with the country's economic situation remain insufficient. As shown above, ODA had played an important role in Japan's postwar economic growth. Never provided exclusively for philanthropic purpose, ODA clearly supported economic recovery and contributed to prolonged high growth rates. Therefore, the drastic decline of public support indicates a shift from understanding ODA as a tool beneficial to state interests toward the perception of it as a financial burden. Although the various crises of the 1990s were not solely responsible for the diminished public support, the reform entrepreneurs used them to facilitate the perceptional shift, or, in other words, to delegitimize the bureaucracy-led decision-making process.

A crucial document that assisted reform entrepreneurs in achieving their goal of de-legitimizing ODA was Japan's first ODA Charter of 1992. It is important to note that the Charter did not reflect a domestic consensus among the involved ministries and agencies, such as MOFA, MITI, MOF, and EPA. Rather, it was a reaction to strong external pressure (*gaiatsu*). Since the 1970s, and against the backdrop of a growing ODA budget, the international community, most notably the US, began to accuse Japan of being a free rider not willing to contribute to international security and stability. This pressure peaked in 1991 after Japan failed to contribute troops to the US-led international effort to liberate Kuwait from Iraqi forces. Shortly thereafter, Prime Minister Kaifu Toshiki pledged a greater Japanese international contribution (*kokusai kōken*) through ODA. Consequently, he announced new principles for Japan's development assistance, which later became the core of the 1992 ODA Charter. Thus, the Charter was a way to display the country's international commitment, especially to Japan's closest ally, the United States.[30]

The philanthropic wording of the Charter, including such values as freedom, human rights, and democracy, successfully reduced the pressure on Japan. As shown in the 1992 *Tokyo Declaration on Global Partnership with the US*, which highlighted Tokyo's efforts in promoting world peace and prosperity, it helped to assuage critique from Washington.[31] However, the Charter was not legally binding, and did not leave a statistically significant impact on the actual provision of ODA.[32] Nevertheless, it was an important document for the reform entrepreneurs in their pursuit of delegitimizing ODA. It provided them with an important reference point for criticizing the foreign policy approach promulgated by the ministries. In addition to the past successes as a foreign policy tool, the lack of a document specifying ODA principles would have made it very difficult to criticize current practice. Without specific normative criteria, few had questioned the purpose of ODA in the past. Clearly, it seemed to have served the economy well. In fact, even the DAC was perplexed by Japan's lack of identifiable principles and questioned its ODA philosophy, asking, "What is the basic rationale of Japan's aid programme and what are its objectives?"[33]

The Charter at last specified the ODA objectives and strategy. At the same time, it provided the reform entrepreneurs with the material for convincing criticism, especially regarding ODA provision to China. As the public's image of Japan's main ODA recipient and rising economic competitor had been deteriorating continuously in the 1990s, disapprovingly focusing on China was a crafty move. The reform entrepreneurs utilized primarily two aspects to make their case. First, they concentrated on the above-mentioned humanitarian language of the Charter that highlighted philanthropic goals such as the elimination of famine and poverty in the developing countries, and the spreading of freedom, human rights, and democracy. Second, the critics placed emphasis on a statement that stipulated the need to consider recipients' military spending.[34] By demonstrating that the bureaucracy in general and MOFA in particular had not been considering military spending and thus violated the principles, the reform entrepreneurs were able to portray the provision of ODA to China as an illegitimate act.

Conscious of the fact that the Charter was not a legally binding document, MOFA bureaucrats were aware of its primarily symbolic significance. They attempted to relativize the high standards of the 1992 Charter by stating, "There is no doubt that the principal motive of ODA is the humanitarian consideration to assist developing countries. At the same time, however, ODA plays a vital role in serving Japan's national interest and contributing to the lives of the Japanese people in many ways."[35] Yet such efforts proved insufficient and could not deflect the ever-increasing criticisms reform entrepreneurs were voicing throughout the 1990s.

Three Narratives of ODA Crisis and Reform

The Economic Argument

The most important aspect of the narrative the reform entrepreneurs promoted was that ODA was a charity. They based this argument on the 1992 Charter. In contrast to the reality, in which Japan's ODA ranked average when measured in relation to its GNP, they advanced the view that Japan had indeed been dispensing ODA over-proportionally. Framing ODA as charity also neglected the circumstances under which Japan was providing it not only to China but also to other countries as well.

In relation to the criticisms of ODA provision to China, it is important to highlight that Japan initiated the assistance following Beijing's renunciation of the right to war reparations in the 1972 Joint Communiqué, the document that provided the basis for reestablishing diplomatic relations between the two countries.[36] Japan was not required to pay reparations under the 1951 San Francisco Peace Treaty either. Nevertheless, it had strong economic incentives to provide ODA to China. Between 1979 and 2016, China received only 157.2 billion yen in the form of grants that do not require repayment. Meanwhile, 3.3164 trillion yen of ODA to China had been provided as loans, which China repaid with interest.[37] ODA loans were mainly intended for building economic infrastructure from which Japanese companies benefited directly as well as indirectly.[38] Only by the late 1990s, about 70 percent was used for infrastructure projects aiming to reduce environmental pollution, which had come to increasingly affect Japan as well.[39]

Concealing the mutual benefits of providing ODA to China in the public narrative, the reform entrepreneurs portrayed the expenditures as "wasted." Much of the criticism began focusing on the question why Japan actively provided ODA to China at a time when the Chinese economy was doing well, and Beijing even began to develop its own ODA program. This was a contradictory argument, as Japan itself had started its ODA program at a time, in 1951, when it was receiving loans from the World Bank.[40]

Lack of Appreciation

By presenting ODA as charity, the reform entrepreneurs constructed a hierarchy in the relationship of donor and recipient, a view Japan had previously attempted to avoid. The Fukuda Doctrine of 1977, in particular, emphasized relations among equal partners in Asia.[41] Yet, for the nationalists' troubled minds, hierarchy was important. They had long perceived Japan as superior to other Asian countries.[42] The creation of this hierarchy nurtured the expectation among the Japanese public that recipients should show appreciation (*kansha*) for the offered assistance, express a positive attitude, and devise friendly policies toward Japan—even more so in the context of the economic crisis Japan itself was experiencing.

According to the foreign policy scholar Iokibe Makoto, gratitude from China for the provided ODA was important for Japanese nationalists, whose pride the "lost decades" had undermined.[43] This view went hand in hand with the expectation that it would be an imperative for China as an ODA recipient to support Japan's foreign policy unconditionally. China, on the other hand, did not see the urge to express gratitude to Japan, since ODA was understood as a kind of war reparation and an instrument of mutual benefit.[44] The discrepancy between the expectations and demands on both sides attracted much attention when President Jiang Zemin came to Tokyo in 1998. This was the first time that a Chinese head of state visited Japan, and there were high expectations that he would officially thank the country for its continuous assistance provided through ODA. Jiang, however, did not cater to his Japanese hosts' expectations. Instead, he demanded a written "apology" for Japan's past military aggression. Prime Minister Obuchi Keizō refused to comply. Yet, despite the ensuing tensions, the Obuchi government designated a new package of 390 billion yen in loans for environmental, agricultural, and rural development projects in the fiscal year of 1999–2000.[45] Unsurprisingly, this agreement attracted strong criticisms.

Reform entrepreneurs repeatedly emphasized the lack of appreciation on China's part. Their attitude found further support after six upper house parliamentarians led by Konoike Yoshitada, an active member of the Nippon Kaigi, published a critical report in August 2004. The six politicians were sent to evaluate ongoing and past ODA projects in China and the Philippines. They expressed strong skepticism, especially regarding ODA to China, emphasizing Beijing's rapid economic growth and ever-increasing military capabilities. As a major issue, the report found that the Chinese government had not sufficiently promoted Japan's "generous" assistance, and thereby failed to counter anti-Japanese sentiments such as had broken out during the 2004 AFC Asian Cup soccer tournament. The authors dedicated much of their attention to a plaque acknowledging the Japanese "assistance" for building a new terminal at the Beijing International Airport. They found that it had not been displayed well enough to be seen by the public. Contradicting the Fukuda Doctrine's non-interference principle guiding Japan's development assistance, the report concluded that ODA needed to be used as a "weapon" (*buki*) of diplomacy to shape China's development.[46]

Strongly influenced by the reform entrepreneurs' reframing of ODA as an act of benevolence and charity, the public became increasingly sensitive to China's perceived lack of appreciation too. An opinion survey conducted by MOFA clearly illustrated the impact of this argument. The number of critics who referred to the lack of appreciation as the main reason for ODA reduction rose from 28.3 percent in 2004 to 37.8 percent in 2010.[47]

The Military Threat

The unfulfilled expectation of gratitude was not the only reason for criticism targeting ODA to China. The reform entrepreneurs were quick to raise the issue whenever Chinese actions appeared to take a direction contrary to Japan's national interests. Here, China's military modernization attracted much attention. Possibly the most influential criticism focused on the argument that Japan was supporting China's military build-up. The issue had also become a sensitive topic for the Japanese public due to various incidents that furthered the perception of China as a national security threat. These included China's nuclear weapon tests between 1994 and 1996, military exercises in proximity to Taiwan in 1996, and naval activities in the East China Sea and the vicinity of Japanese territory in 2000.[48]

Politicians employed two arguments to link Japan's ODA to the China military threat. Firstly, they argued that Japanese taxpayers' money had been used to finance the building of infrastructure, including highways, railroads, and airports that are indispensable for military mobilization. Here, a prominent example marshaled by the critics was the construction of the railway system in Fujian Province, which could potentially be used in an attack on Taiwan.[49] Secondly, the reformers argued that Japan's ODA enabled China to use funding originally designated for infrastructure development to strengthen the military. LDP Finance Minister and former Secretary-General Shiokawa Masajūrō called Japanese ODA to China "foolish," as China could attack Japan using an atomic bomb or missiles.[50]

The Comeback of ODA

As the media echoed and amplified their arguments, the reform entrepreneurs' criticisms of ODA gained strong influence over public opinion. A journalist of the conservative *Sankei Shimbun*, Komori Yoshihisa, described how shocked he was when he heard about the lack of Chinese appreciation for the provided ODA after he became correspondent in Beijing in 1998.[51] The conservative *Yomiuri Shimbun*, in 2000 criticized Japan's ODA by pointing to China's growing military budget.[52] Later, another article in *The Japan Times* offered a similar perspective, describing Japan's ODA to China as a "complete waste" because China did not support Japan's bid for a permanent seat in the UN Security Council.[53] Interestingly, liberal media outlets such as the *Asahi Shimbun* also expressed similar views and endorsed the ending of ODA.[54] Numerous nationalistic publications further influenced the public. These included titles such as *Owaranai taichū enjo* (*The Never-Ending Assistance toward China*) by Komori Yoshihisa and Aoki Naoto.[55] Unsurprisingly, the reform entrepreneurs' negative campaign in the mid-2000s resulted in the lowest public support for ODA ever since its initiation in the early 1950s (see figure 8.2).

The strong negative public sentiment against the bureaucracy strengthened politicians' influence over ODA policymaking, which in turn facilitated structural reforms. Increasing the political authority over the bureaucracy was crucial for the plan to elevate the Kantei, the Prime Minister's Office, to the core institution in the decision-making process. The first major structural change came in the form of the establishment of the Council of Overseas Economic Cooperation-Related Ministers during Prime Minister Abe Shinzō's first term in 2006. In the past, nine ministries coordinated policies. In contrast, the new council included only the prime minister, the chief cabinet secretary, and the central ODA ministries MOFA, MOF, and METI.[56] The Minister of State for Economic and Fiscal Policy, of Internal Affairs and Communications, of Education, Culture, Sports, Science and Technology, of Health, Labor and Welfare, of Agriculture, Forestry and Fishery, and of Land, Infrastructure and Transport all lost their seats in the new council.

At the same time, ODA policy formulation was transferred to MOFA to curtail interference by other ministries. Giving MOFA the primary authority was a strategic move, as the ministry, unlike METI, does not possess strong ties to domestic interest groups. However, that is not to say that MOFA gained autonomy in ODA policymaking. The control of the Prime Minister's Office over MOFA had been increasing drastically after the latter's China Division or "China School's" reluctance to adopt the anti-China position had backfired.[57]

Another important measure for weakening the bureaucracy's resistance to the strategic use of ODA and to enhance politicians' power was the establishment of the Personnel Affairs Bureau in the Cabinet Office (*naikaku jinji-kyoku*) in 2014.[58] This change allowed the prime minister to appoint not only vice ministers, but also their subordinate bureau and deputy bureau chiefs, while enabling him to marginalize and neutralize individual bureaucrats who deviated from the official line. Such far-reaching prime ministerial control over its staffing significantly curtailed MOFA's influence on policymaking. It forced the ministry to adopt a more conformist stance toward the Abe government's position on ODA matters.[59] This is equally the case for other ministries still involved in the ODA policymaking process.

Yet, while attempts at increasing politicians' control through discrediting the bureaucracy were ongoing, a diametrically opposite process of ODA relegitimization started to unfold, and highlighted the importance of ODA as a tool for furthering Japan's national interests. Taking office in 2001, Koizumi Junichirō was the first prime minister who embarked on this path. His first strategic decision aiming to recover public support for ODA was to revise the 1992 ODA Charter. Now enjoying greater influence over ODA policymaking, the LDP made certain that the previously strong philanthropic principle was toned down. In 2003, they added the phrase "to ensure Japan's own security and prosperity" as the primary objective to the revised Charter.[60] In 2015, a further revision under LDP tutelage would make this point even more explicit as it underlined ODA's direct contribution to Japan's security and economic growth.[61]

ODA and Japan's National Security

The aim to re-integrate ODA into the country's foreign- and security policymaking toolkit became even clearer in 2005, when Koizumi called for an increase of the ODA budget to 0.7 percent of the gross national income (GNI). His proposal came shortly after the LDP, on the grounds of Japan's tight fiscal circumstances, succeeded in forcing MOFA to announce the end of ODA to China by 2008.[62] Koizumi's demand was a clear contradiction to the past narrative that Japan could not afford to provide ODA. In 2005, the budget had amounted to a mere 0.28 percent of Japan's GNI.[63] In other words, had Koizumi's proposed increase to 0.7 percent been realized, this would have led to the highest ODA budget in history. Despite a slight economic recovery from 2003 onwards (predominantly due to growing trade with China),[64] the public remained skeptical about the utility of ODA for furthering the country's national interest. Therefore, it is hardly surprising that Koizumi's demand of a budget increase was unsuccessful.

Clearly, ODA's negative public image significantly complicated Koizumi's efforts to use it as a contribution to the US-led "global war against terror." With Japan's security role strictly limited by the constitution's Article 9, ODA was indispensable in promoting peace and stability through nonmilitary means and preventing a crisis in the US-Japan alliance.[65] In a 2004 speech at the Diet, Koizumi acknowledged that the Japan's Self-Defense Forces and ODA were an "inseparable pair"[66] in the field of humanitarian and reconstruction assistance. It was obvious that Koizumi needed to rebuild the tarnished ODA image before he could instrumentalize it for his own purposes. The selection in 2003 of one of Japan's most popular diplomats, the former UN High Commissioner for Refugees Ogata Sadako, as the new head of the Japan International Cooperation Agency (JICA), the main organization responsible for implementing ODA, illustrates Koizumi's intention. Public relations events such as "Global Festa JAPAN"[67] or the "Page for the Advancement of Visibility" (*me ni mieruka saito*),[68] an internet platform that served to draw public attention to the positive contributions of Japanese ODA, accompanied this effort.

The strategic relevance of ODA continued to increase across the terms of several successive prime ministers. Ironically, Abe, who had been very actively contributing to delegitimizing it, made the most active use of ODA following his return to the Prime Minister's Office in 2012. In the field of security, Abe integrated ODA into the country's first National Security Strategy, issued in 2013. Using ODA, he endorsed the export of patrol boats to those littoral countries of the South China Sea involved in maritime disputes with China. In 2013, the newly made loan agreement with the Philippines paved the way to providing ten boats to the Philippine Coast Guard.[69] Similar agreements were signed for six boats with Vietnam in 2014[70] and for two boats with Malaysia in 2016.[71] In line with the Free and Open Indo-Pacific strategy, which Abe announced in 2016,[72] Japan also began to expand its security-related ODA engagement to the Indian Ocean and donated two vessels to Sri Lanka.[73] Given that METI had categorized such boats as arms, it is thus possible to argue that the Abe government used ODA to provide "quasi-military" assistance to Southeast Asian littoral states for their fight against China's maritime expansion.[74]

ODA and the Return of Neo-mercantilism under Abe

While security political objectives undoubtedly represented an important new dimension, the most visible shift occurred through the inclusion of ODA into the Japan Revitalization Strategy, commonly known as "Abenomics."[75] Since the objective was to use ODA for supporting large infrastructure projects and thereby increase Japanese companies' profits, it can be argued that Abe reintroduced neo-mercantilist principles commonly attributed to the "Japan Inc." of the postwar era.[76] This change of strategy is intriguing because state intervention into the markets had largely been absent since the advent of the Koizumi administration in 2001.[77]

The idea to re-introduce neo-mercantilist elements into the ODA strategy can be traced back to 2009, when Hitachi, one of Japan's leading conglomerates, lost a large contract worth $20.4 billion for constructing four nuclear power plants in the United Arab Emirates to a Korean company that had no previous experience with building plants overseas.[78] Afterwards, the METI official and director of nuclear energy policy Mitsumata Hiroki summarized the disappointment and the consequences of losing the contract, arguing that "there is no growth for Japan unless we enhance exports. . . . No matter how superior our technology is, if it's confined within Japan, it will become obsolete like the species in the Galapagos."[79] This was a clear message from the private sector suggesting that Japan needed to increase its foreign engagement using ODA as in the past. It was a message that Prime Minster Abe, who sought to focus more on domestic issues, understood very well.

Following Abe's return to office in 2012, the growth of the Japanese economy became the matter of greatest importance. In his first term in 2006, Abe had experienced a great loss of public support after being primarily concerned with security political reforms. Therefore, aiming to gather strong public support, he now attributed the highest priority to economic policies. In his speech on Japan's growth strategy, Abe asserted that it was unavoidable for Japanese companies to expand internationally (*kaigai tenkai*) in a proactive manner.[80] As a result, the share of ODA spent on economic infrastructure significantly increased from 39.9 percent in 2011 (the year before Abe's comeback) to 49 percent in 2017. On the other hand, the share of Japan's ODA spent on social infrastructure declined from 25.2 percent to 16.1 percent during the same time period. In comparison, DAC members spent on average 17.1 percent for economic and 34.1 percent for social infrastructure projects, respectively, in 2017.[81]

The return of neo-mercantilism is also noticeable in the increased use of tied ODA, that is, loans given under the condition of their exclusive use for the purchase of Japanese goods and services. The DAC has been criticizing this practice because it increased the cost of projects by 15 to 30 percent on average.[82] Contrary to the principles adhered to by most DAC members, Japan extended the practice to heavily indebted poor countries (HIPCs) that are not classified as least developed countries (LDCs).[83] Tokyo provided 831 billion yen for a tied aid program called Special Terms for Economic Partnership in 2015, more than nine times as much as in 2014, when Japan allocated 90 billion yen to the same program. Although the amount decreased to 134 billion yen in 2016, the general trend clearly indicates a steady increase in loans directly benefiting Japanese companies.[84] This development led the DAC to criticize Japan in its 2014 review, urging Tokyo to "reverse the decline in the share of its aid that is untied"[85]—without much effect. According to a report by the European Network on Debt and Development, Japan in 2016 tied US$2.4 billion of its aid to the purchase of Japanese goods and services, the highest amount among the DAC group, making Japan's loans expensive in comparison to other donors.[86]

After being exposed to strong criticism in the 1990s, ODA regained its importance in various fields of Japan's foreign policy. The reform entrepreneurs, who had persistently labeled ODA a waste of resources in the past, gradually grew less critical as their control over ODA decision-making increased. Regarding public opinion, the increasing (political) use of larger amounts of ODA was promoted through the aforementioned campaigns that included "Global Festa JAPAN" and the "Page for the Advancement of Visibility." This resulted in a significantly more positive public attitude. The support for increasing ODA rose from 18.7 percent in 2004 to 30.4 percent in 2008 and remained relatively stable thereafter (see figure 8.2). Relying heavily on ODA as a foreign policy tool, Abe continued the previous efforts to restore ODA's domestic image by creating an appealing cartoon character branded "ODA-man."[87]

After gaining political control over the once bureaucracy-led ODA decision-making process, reform entrepreneurs stayed "silent," even when the economy suffered a significant setback in the wake of the Tōhoku earthquake, tsunami, and nuclear meltdown of 2011. Despite the ensuing economic hardships, the 2011 triple disaster did not lead to a decrease in support rates. The fact that the ODA budget has not seen any major cuts from 2011 onwards, and in 2016 even slightly increased for the first time in 17 years (see figure 8.1), shows that politicians saw no need to criticize ODA spending.

Even Kōno Tarō, one of the last outspoken reform entrepreneurs, later reversed his position. Kōno formerly claimed that ODA was a waste of financial resources without any positive benefits for the country's national interests. In 2009, he even demanded that the ODA budget be halved. Kōno's change of position can be regarded as the end of the reform entrepreneurs' strong opposition.[88] In his function as Foreign Minister, Kōno went into the opposite direction and requested a drastic increase of 11 percent for the 2018 ODA budget.[89] His proposal was driven by the fact that the budget could not meet the growing demand that resulted from Abenomics and from Abe's National Security Strategy.

Conclusion

The reform entrepreneurs who had emerged within the LDP in the 1990s demonstrated a remarkable ability to utilize the difficult socioeconomic circumstances of the 1990s' "lost decade" in their pursuit of tarnishing MOFA's authority over ODA policy formulation. Exploiting the philanthropic formulation of the 1992 Charter, they portrayed ODA as a charity provided to others amidst the internal economic crisis, thus downplaying its actual contribution to the pursuit of Japanese national interests. Their apt directing of public attention to many frictions in Sino-Japanese relations, in particular, played a pivotal role in the reform entrepreneurs' negative portrayal of ODA. Not only did reform entrepreneurs argue that ODA was inefficient in terms of securing national interests, they also framed it as harmful because it actively provided support to Japan's greatest economic rival and perceived military threat. This narrative contributed to the breaking of the bureaucracy's monopoly over ODA decision-making and heralded greater political control for the first time since the initiation of the ODA program in the early 1950s.

Once the bureaucracy submitted to the executive, the LDP reform entrepreneurs fell silent. They had gained the freedom to use ODA for their parochial economic and security political interests, and even made considerable efforts to restore its public image. The LDP leadership acknowledged the importance of ODA to advance national interests. Seeking to improve Japan's reputation in the international community, Koizumi utilized ODA to engage Japan in the US-led global war against terror. Later, Abe employed ODA for countering China's expansion in the South China Sea. Perhaps the most interesting role that ODA has acquired since its "comeback," however, is as part of "Abenomics." There, the use of ODA essentially represents the reintroduction of the old neo-mercantilist strategy that had been the core of Japan's ODA policy before the reforms of the early 2000s. Another intriguing development is the increased willingness to cooperate with China for the advancement of infrastructure in Asia.[90] Thus, at least in the field of ODA, the former reform entrepreneurs appear to be less driven by their ideological views than by pragmatism as they position themselves close to the very rationale of the bureaucracy that they had long criticized and striven to defame.

Notes

1. Iokibe Makoto, "Gaikō senryaku no naka no Nihon ODA" [Japan's ODA in the Foreign Policy Strategy], *Kokusai Mondai* 517 (2003): 3.

2. Saori N. Katada, "Old Visions and New Actors in Foreign Aid Politics: Explaining Changes in Japanese ODA Policy to China," in *Japanese Aid and the Construction of Global Development: Inescapable Solutions*, ed. David Leheny and Kay Warren (London: Routledge, 2010), 67; Paul Midford, "The Impact of Public Opinion on Japan's Aid Policy: Before and after the New Development Assistance Charter," in *Japanese Development Cooperation: The Making of an Aid Architecture Pivoting to Asia*, ed. André Asplund and Marie Söderberg (London: Routledge, 2016), 189.

3. Sheldon Garon, *Molding Japanese Minds: The State in Everyday Life* (Princeton, NJ: Princeton University Press, 1998).

4. Colin Hay, "Crisis and the Structural Transformation of the State: Interrogating the Process of Change," *British Journal of Politics and International Relations* 1, no. 3 (1999), 317; see also Wirth and Maslow, this volume.

5. Treaty of San Francisco art. 14; see https://treaties.un.org/doc/Publication/UNTS/Volume%20136/volume-136-I-1832-English.pdf. Unless otherwise stated, all online sources were accessed and available on September 1, 2020.

6. David Arase, *Buying Power: The Political Economy of Japan's Foreign Aid* (Boulder: Lynne Rienner Publishers, 1995), 32–33.

7. Tsukasa Takamine, "Domestic Determinants of Japan's China Aid Policy: The Changing Balance of Foreign Policymaking Power," *Japanese Studies* 22, no. 2 (2002): 195–197.

8. Arase, *Buying Power*, 6–7; William R. Nester, *Japan and the Third World: Patterns, Power, Prospects* (London: Palgrave Macmillan, 1992), 89.

9. John P. Tuman and Jonathan R. Strand, "The Role of Mercantilism, Humanitarianism, and Gaiatsu in Japan's ODA Programme in Asia," *International Relations of the Asia-Pacific* 6, no. 1 (2005): 61–80.

10. Chalmers Johnson, *Japan: Who Governs? The Rise of the Developmental State* (New York: Norton, 1995).

11. The DAC is an OECD forum that controls the ODA quality of its members in order to promote sustainable development in developing countries.

12. John White, *Japanese Aid* (London: Overseas Development Institute, 1964), 10.

13. Hiroshi Kato, "Japan's ODA 1954–2014: Changes and Continuities in a Central Instrument in Japan's Foreign Policy," in *Japan's Development Assistance: Foreign Aid and Post-2015 Agenda*, ed. Yasutami Shimomura, John Page, and Hiroshi Kato (London: Palgrave Macmillan, 2016), 6–14.

14. Robert M. Orr, *The Emergence of Japan's Foreign Aid Power* (New York: Columbia University Press, 1990), 25.

15. Dennis T. Yasutomo, "Why Aid? Japan as an 'Aid Great Power,'" *Pacific Affairs* 62, no. 4 (1989), 502.

16. Arase, *Buying Power*, 114–116.

17. Ezra F. Vogel, *Japan as Number One: Lessons for America* (Cambridge, MA: Harvard University Press, 1979).

18. Michael J. Green, *Japan's Reluctant Realism: Foreign Policy Challenges in an Era of Uncertain Power* (New York: Palgrave Macmillan, 2001), 84.

19. Ibid., 50–51; Tomohito Shinoda, *Contemporary Japanese Politics: Institutional Changes and Power Shifts* (New York: Columbia University Press, 2013), 77.

20. Midford, "The Impact of Public Opinion," 189; Tsukasa Takamine, *Japan's Development Aid to China: The Long-Running Foreign Policy of Engagement* (London: Routledge, 2006), 84–85.

21. Ozawa Ichirō, *Nihon kaizō keikaku* [Blueprint for a New Japan] (Tokyo: Kōdansha, 1993), 162–178.

22. Yuji Sasage, Keita Hayashi, and Kei Sato, "Japan's Largest Rightwing Organization: An Introduction to Nippon Kaigi," *Asia-Pacific Journal: Japan Focus* 13, no. 50 (December 2015), https://apjjf.org/-Mine-Masahiro/4410; Aoki Osamu, *Nippon Kaigi no shōtai* [The Autonomy of the Nippon Kaigi] (Tokyo: Heibonsha, 2016).

23. Abe Shinzō, *Utsukushii kuni e* [Toward a Beautiful Country] (Tokyo: Bungei Shunjū, 2013), 254.

24. Midford, "The Impact of Public Opinion," 178.

25. Katada, "Old Visions," 66–67.

26. Yoichi Funabashi and Barak Kushner, eds., *Examining Japan's Lost Decades* (London: Routledge, 2015).

27. Wirth and Maslow, this volume; see also David Leheny, *Think Global, Fear Local: Sex, Violence, and Anxiety in Contemporary Japan* (Ithaca, NY: Cornell University Press, 2006), 27–47.

28. Prime Minister of Japan and His Cabinet (Kantei), "Press Conference by Prime Minister Ryutaro Hashimoto on the Final Report of the Conference on Fiscal Structural Reform," June 3, 1997, https://japan.kantei.go.jp/0610fiscal.html.

29. Ministry of Foreign Affairs (MOFA), "Final Report of the Council on ODA Reforms for the 21st Century Final Report," Tokyo, January 1998, https://www.mofa.go.jp/policy/oda/reform/report21.html#section3.

30. Robert M. Orr, "The Aid Factor in U.S.-Japan Relations," *Asian Survey* 28, no. 7 (1988): 740–756.

31. MOFA, *Diplomatic Bluebook 1992*, Tokyo, April 1993, https://www.mofa.go.jp/policy/other/bluebook/1992/1992-contents.htm.

32. Tuman and Strand, "The Role of Mercantilism," 75.

33. DAC, *Aid Review 1990/1991: Report by the Secretariat and Questions for the Review of Japan* (Paris: OECD Publishing, 1991), 7.

34. MOFA, "Japan's Official Development Assistance Charter," Tokyo, June 30, 1992, https://www.mofa.go.jp/policy/oda/summary/1999/ref1.html.

35. MOFA, *Japan's ODA Annual Report (Summary) 1996*, Tokyo, 1997, https://www.mofa.go.jp/policy/oda/summary/1996/index.html.

36. Xianfen Xu, "Japan's Official Development Assistance (ODA) Policy towards China: The Role of Emotional Factors," *Journal of Contemporary China Studies* 2, no. 1 (2013): 78–79.

37. MOFA, "Overview of Official Development Assistance (ODA) to China," February 1, 2016, https://www.mofa.go.jp/policy/oda/region/e_asia/china/index.html.

38. Reinhard Drifte, "The Ending of Japan's ODA Loan Programme to China: All's Well That Ends Well?" *Asia-Pacific Review* 13, no. 1 (2006): 96.

39. Iwaki Shigeyuki, "Taichūgoku ODA minaoshi rongi" [Review of Japan's ODA towards China's ODA], Issue Brief No. 468 (February 2005), https://www.ndl.go.jp/jp/diet/publication/issue/0468.pdf.

40. Drifte, "The Ending of Japan's ODA," 103.

41. Sueo Sudo, "Japan-ASEAN Relations: New Dimensions in Japanese Foreign Policy," *Asian Survey* 28, no. 5 (1988): 509–525.

42. Kai Schulze, "Risks of Sameness, the 'Rise of China' and Japan's Ontological Security," in *Risk State: Japan's Foreign Policy in an Age of Uncertainty*, ed. Sebastian Maslow, Ra Mason, and Paul O'Shea (London: Routledge, 2016), 101–116; Taku Tamaki, "The Persistence of Reified Asia as Reality in Japanese Foreign Policy Narratives," *Pacific Review* 28, no. 1 (2015): 23–45.

43. Iokibe, "Gaikō," 2.

44. Xu, "Japan's Official Development Assistance."

45. Japan International Cooperation Agency (JICA), "Supporting China's Environmental Improvement Project and Inland Region Developments," March 28, 2000, https://www.jica.go.jp/english/news/jbic_archive/english/base/release/oec/1999/A06/nr99_29s.html.

46. House of Councillors, "Dai 1-kai Sangiin seifu kaihatsu enjo (ODA) chōsa haken hōkoku-sho" [1st House of Councillors Official Development Assistance (ODA) Survey Report], November 2004, https://www.sangiin.go.jp/japanese/kokusai_kankei/oda_chousa/h16/h16oda-houkoku.html.

47. Kantei, "Gaikō ni kansuru yoron chōsa" [Public Opinion Poll on Foreign Policy], October 2019, https://survey.gov-online.go.jp/index-gai.html.

48. Tsukasa Takamine, "A New Dynamism in Sino-Japanese Security Relations: Japan's Strategic Use of Foreign Aid," *Pacific Review* 18, no. 4 (2005): 440.

49. Komori Yoshihisa, "Taichū ODA, sengo saidai-kyū no shippai" [ODA to China, A Major Post-War Failure], *Sankei Shimbun*, October 26, 2018, https://www.sankei.com/world/news/181026/wor1810260002-n1.html.

50. "Shiokawa Calls ODA to China Foolish," *Japan Times*, July 17, 2001, https://www.asiaportal.info/database/japan-times-archives/.

51. Komori, "Taichū ODA."

52. "Shasetsu: Nitchū shunōkaidan fushin kaishō no guteiteki kōdō o motomeru" [Editorial: Japan-China Summit for Concrete Actions to Eliminate Distrust], *Yomiuri Shimbun*, October 14, 2000, https://database-yomiuri-co-jp.resources.asiaportal.info/rekishikan/.

53. Kiroku Hanai, "ODA Looks Wasted on China," *Japan Times*, October 25, 2004, https://www.japantimes.co.jp/opinion/2004/10/25/commentary/oda-looks-wasted-on-china/.

54. Drifte, "The Ending of Japan's ODA," 109–110; Green, *Japan's Reluctant Realism*, 83.

55. Komori Yoshihisa and Aoki Naoto, *Owaranai taichū enjo* [The Never-Ending Assistance towards China] (Tokyo: PHP Kenkyūjo, 2009).

56. MOFA, "Council of Overseas Economic Cooperation-Related Ministers," Tokyo, August 24, 1993, https://japan.kantei.go.jp/policy/index/oda/konkyo_e.html; MOFA, "Council of Overseas Economic Cooperation," April 28, 2006, https://japan.kantei.go.jp/policy/index/kaigai/index_e.html.

57. Joel Rathus, *Japan, China and Networked Regionalism in East Asia* (New York: Palgrave Macmillan, 2011), 63–65.

58. Makihara Izuru, *Abe ichi-kyō no nazo* [The Mystery of Abe's Strength] (Tokyo: Asahi Shimbun Shuppan, 2016).

59. Raymond Yamamoto, "The Trajectory of ODA's Strategic Use and Reforms—from Nakasone Yasuhiro to Abe Shinzō," *Australian Journal of International Affairs* 72, no. 6 (2020): 633–648.

60. MOFA, "Japan's Official Development Assistance Charter 2003," Tokyo, November 30, 2004, https://www.mofa.go.jp/policy/oda/reform/charter.html.

61. Masaaki Ohashi, "NGOs and Japan's ODA: Critical Views and Advocacy," in *Japan's Development Assistance: Foreign Aid and Post-2015 Agenda*, ed. Yasutami Shimomura, John Page, and Hiroshi Kato (New York: Palgrave Macmillan, 2016), 327–343; Hiroshi Kato, "Japan's ODA 1954–2014: Changes and Continuities in a Central Instrument in Japan's Foreign Policy," in *Japan's Development Assistance*, 1–18.

62. MOFA, "Press Conference by Prime Minister Junichiro Koizumi on the Occasion of the Asian-African Summit 2005 and the Commemoration of the Golden Jubilee of the Asian-African Conference 1955," April 23, 2005, https://www.mofa.go.jp/region/asia-paci/meet0504/press.html.

63. OECD, "Net ODA," 2019 (n.d.), https://data.oecd.org/oda/net-oda.htm.

64. Jun Tsunekawa, "Toward a Stable Relationship between Japan and China: From a Bilateral to a Multilateral Approach," in *China's Shift: Global Strategy of the Rising Power*, edited by Masafumi Iida, NIDS Joint Research Series 3 (Tokyo: NIDS, 2009), 111.

65. Iokibe, "Gaikō," 4.

66. MOFA, "MOFA: Statement by Prime Minister Junichiro Koizumi (Decision on the Extension of the Basic Plan Regarding Humanitarian and Reconstruction Assistance of the Self Defense Forces in Iraq)," December 9, 2004, https://www.mofa.go.jp/region/middle_e/iraq/issue2003/announce_pm/state0412.html.

67. MOFA, "The 50th Anniversary of Japan's International Cooperation," 2004, https://www.mofa.go.jp/policy/oda/cooperation/anniv50/index.html.

68. JICA, "ODA mieruka saito" [ODA Visualization Page], n.d., https://www.jica.go.jp/oda/index.html.

69. MOFA, "Firipinkyōwakoku ni taisuru enshakkan ni kansuru kōkan kōbun no shomei ni tsuite" [About the Signature of the Yen Loan to the Republic of the

Philippines], December 13, 2013, https://www.mofa.go.jp/mofaj/gaiko/oda/data/zyoukyou/h25/y131213_1.html.

70. MOFA, "Betonamu ni taisuru non purojekuto mushō shikin kyōryoku ni kansuru kōkan kōbun no shomei ni tsuite" [About the Signature of the Non-Project Grant Aid Exchange with Vietnam], August 1, 2014, https://www.mofa.go.jp/mofaj/gaiko/oda/data/zyoukyou/h26/140801_2.html.

71. MOFA, "Marēshia ni taisuru junshisentō no zōyo oyobi mushō shikin kyōryoku ni kansuru shokan no kōkan" [Exchange of Notes on Donations and Grant Aid for Patrol Boats to Malaysia], November 16, 2016, https://www.mofa.go.jp/mofaj/press/release/press4_003936.html.

72. MOFA, "India and Japan: Confluence of Maritime Democracies," October 7, 2016, https://www.in.emb-japan.go.jp/itpr_ja/00_000123.html.

73. MOFA, "Suriranka ni taisuru mushō shikin kyōryoku 'kaijō anzen nōryoku kōjō keikaku' ni kansuru shokan no kōkan" [Exchange of Notes on the Grant Assistance for the 'Maritime Safety Capacity Improvement Plan' to Sri Lanka], June 30, 2016, https://www.mofa.go.jp/mofaj/press/release/press4_003444.html.

74. Raymond Yamamoto, "The Securitization of Japan's ODA: New Strategies in Changing Regional and Domestic Contexts," in *Japanese Development Cooperation: The Making of an Aid Architecture Pivoting to Asia*, ed. André Asplund and Marie Söderberg (London: Routledge, 2016), 72–89.

75. See Shibata, this volume.

76. Hidetaka Yoshimatsu, "Japan's Export of Infrastructure Systems: Pursuing Twin Goals through Developmental Means," *Pacific Review* 30, no. 4 (2017): 494–512.

77. Ulrike Schaede, "From Developmental State to the 'New Japan': The Strategic Inflection Point in Japanese Business," *Asia Pacific Business Review* 18, no. 2 (2012): 167–185.

78. Nikkei, "Abe's 'New Mercantilism' Bears Fruit for Japan," *Nikkei Asian Review*, January 4, 2016, https://asia.nikkei.com/Economy/Abe-s-new-mercantilism-bears-fruit-for-Japan.

79. Yuka Hayashi, "Japan Inc. Once Again Starts to Seek Growth Overseas," *Wall Street Journal*, April 29, 2010, https://www.wsj.com/articles/SB10001424052748703648304575211902891469786.

80. Kantei, "Abe sōri 'seichō senryaku supiichi' " [Prime Minister Abe 'Growth Strategy Speech'], April 19, 2013, https://www.kantei.go.jp/jp/96_abe/statement/2013/0419speech.html.

81. Calculations based on statistics in OECD, "Query Wizard for International Development Statistics," 2019 (n.d.), https://stats.oecd.org/qwids/.

82. Edward J. Clay, Matthew Geddes, and Luisa Natali, *Untying Aid: Is It Working? An Evaluation of the Implementation of the Paris Declaration and of the 2001 DAC Recommendation of Untying ODA to the LDCs* (Copenhagen: Danish Institute for International Studies, 2009), 1.

83. OECD, *OECD Development Co-Operation Peer Reviews: Japan* (Paris: OECD Publishing, 2014), 60–61.

84. JICA, "Honpō gijutsu katsuyō jōken" [Special Term for Economic Partnership], 2017 (n.d.), https://www.jica.go.jp/activities/schemes/finance_co/about/step.html.

85. OECD, *OECD Development*, 18.

86. Polly Meeks, "Development, Untied: Unleashing the Catalytic Power of Official Development Assistance through Renewed Action on Untying," October 16, 2018, 15, https://eurodad.org/files/pdf/5ba3a41be1899.pdf.

87. Wrenn Yennie Lindgren, "WIN-WIN! With ODA-Man: Legitimizing Development Assistance Policy in Japan," *Pacific Review* (2020): 1–31, https://doi.org/10.1080/09512748.2020.1727552.

88. Kōno Tarō, "ODA wo hangen seyo" [Decrease ODA by Half!], Kōno Tarō Official Website, February 9, 2009, https://www.taro.org/2009/02/post_509.php.

89. Sankei, "Kōno Tarō gaishō 'hantai' datta no ni ODA yosan zōgaku e" [Although Foreign Minister Kōno Tarō was against it, Demand for ODA Increase], *Sankei Shimbun*, August 24, 2017, https://www.sankei.com/politics/news/170824/plt1708240021-n1.html.

90. Oki Nagai, "China and Japan Kick Off Joint Effort on Foreign Infrastructure," *Nikkei Asian Review*, September 26, 2018, https://asia.nikkei.com/Politics/International-relations/China-and-Japan-kick-off-joint-effort-on-foreign-infrastructure.

Chapter 9

A State of Crisis

North Korean Missiles, Abductions,
and the Transformation of Postwar Japan

RA MASON AND SEBASTIAN MASLOW

Introduction

With US President Donald J. Trump threatening "fire and fury" in response
to missile launches by the Democratic People's Republic of Korea (DPRK,
henceforth North Korea), by late 2017 the Korean Peninsula was, once more,
"on the brink" of war.[1] In April and May that year, North Korea launched
intermediate-range ballistic missiles (IRBM) of the Hwasong-12 type. In
July, tests of the Hwasong-14, an intercontinental ballistic missile (ICBM)
with an estimated range of 6,700–10,000 kilometers, followed. In August,
Kim Jong Un fired a salvo of short-range missiles into the Sea of Japan, and
another Hwasong-12 missile flew across Hokkaido at a maximum height of
550 kilometers before splashing down in the Pacific Ocean. Demonstrating
its technological advances, on September 3, North Korea finally tested a
thermonuclear device. This brought the number of nuclear tests to a total
of six since 2006.

The growing tensions meant that the Japanese public was put on high
alert throughout 2017. Local municipalities conducted civilian missile evacuation drills in schools and communities,[2] train services were temporarily
halted, and the government used the J-Alert early warning system to send
messages on incoming North Korean missiles to all mobile phones and

television sets. As North Korea threat perceptions grew in response, Prime Minister Abe Shinzō on September 25 declared a national crisis (*kokunan*). He dissolved the lower house of the Diet, stating that "With the successive launches of ballistic missiles flying over Japan and the conducting of a nuclear test, the provocations by North Korea have quickly escalated and the threat has truly become something *real.*"[3] In the following snap elections, Abe's Liberal Democratic Party (LDP) secured a landslide victory. Reflecting on this success, Finance Minister Asō Tarō concluded that "it's the government that decides how to address the series of threats from North Korea, so I believe the Japanese people chose the government or the combination of political parties that can best respond"; hence, support for the Abe government is "clearly partly thanks to North Korea."[4]

Following the 2002 Pyongyang Summit revelations of state-sponsored abductions and ongoing advances in missile and nuclear weapons technology, North Korea has presented a key national security concern for Japan.[5] In this chapter, we reexamine the process by which North Korean threats have been recruited into an overall crisis narrative that enabled a major transformation in Japan's security policy and "peace state" (*heiwa kokka*) identity.[6] We argue that conservative policymakers have instrumentalized North Korea as a frame for the construction of a national crisis meta-narrative, and to subsequently impose the transformation of Japan's postwar peace state. This meta-narrative highlights the contradictions and malfunctions of the old state and its institutions, and has served to delegitimize the liberal elites that had been supporting it. Here, we follow Colin Hay and conceptualize crisis as "a moment of decisive intervention" and deliberate "strategic restructuring" of state institutions.[7] The construction of crisis narratives is understood as a "politically mediated" process of ideological and political contestation.[8] Successful crisis narratives, therefore, do not rely on accounts of complex causalities but hinge on the ability to narrate simplistic accounts of contradictions, failure, and responsibility.[9] Thus, we illustrate how the Japanese state's inability to protect its citizens from North Korea is narrated as a symptom of a "failing" and "weak" postwar state.[10] As such, the narrative redraws the boundaries of the national security discourse and thereby demands a decisive "departure from the postwar regime."

In response to this redrawing, we address the limited presence of effective counter-narratives. This illustrates how alternate courses of action—such as the promotion of Japan as a "peace state"—have been marginalized to the point where the crisis narrative with North Korea at its core has become overwhelmingly dominant. Concomitantly, we sketch out the extent to which this is a function of postwar liberal elites' declining influence, and show how the resulting changes in the national security discourse narrated a transformation in the state's institutional structure during the Abe administration. In so doing, we reveal new contradictions in the former prime minister's policy of transforming the old state and constructing a new crisis narrative. This highlights the misleading portrayal of an increasingly vulnerable Japan whose defense capabilities—relative to those of its regional rivals—are seen to be in decline.[11]

Understandings of Japan's Response to North Korea

Scholars tracing Japan's transformation toward "normal state" status have typically focused either on external and internal balancing or on changes in Japan's "pacifist" identity allowing for new discourses on proactive security practice in response to a belligerent North Korea.[12] Analyzing the impact of state-level military developments, for example, realists observe that "North Korea, even relegating China to a secondary position, has elbowed itself to the front of Japan's declared security anxieties, and apparently took up the preeminent role once occupied by the Soviet Union."[13] While China was not portrayed openly as an imminent security threat, North Korea became a "perfect excuse"[14] and "catch-all proxy"[15] for Japanese policymakers to argue for their country's remilitarization. Thus, realist scholarship itself articulates the crisis discourse when authors point to the drastically changing security environment as reason for "redesigning" Japan's response capabilities.[16] Implicitly, these arguments assume a temporally indefinite crisis without a shot being fired toward Tokyo from Pyongyang (or Beijing for that matter).

In contrast, constructivist and critical interpretations of Japan's relations with North Korea engage with the discourses that articulate threat perceptions. However, they often stop short of identifying specific actors and narratives, particularly from within the Diet itself. Peter J. Katzenstein, for instance, refers elusively to a Japanese population "unnerved by North Korea."[17] Others focus on Tokyo's North Korea policy in terms of the mismatch between capability and threat perception, and contend that "if there were ever an issue with the potential to turn Japan into a 'military power,' transcending mere capability, this would be it."[18] By pointing to the influence of public opinion, social movements, and perceptions of victimhood, scholars have also looked to the North Korea issue as a means by which to deconstruct the notion of an "abnormal" Japan.[19] Such analyses revealed that Tokyo has

constantly pushed its agenda on the abduction issue, even when it contradicted multilateral approaches to solve the North Korean nuclear and missile
crisis, such as the six-party talks.[20] Yet, within the range of constructivist
interpretations of Japan–North Korea relations,[21] the explicit role of the Diet
in the social construction of North Korea–centered crises is notably absent.
In a similar vein, critical literature, which approaches Japan's North Korea
policy from (neo-)Marxist or (neo-)Gramscian perspectives, leans toward
critique of structural conditions, particularly US hegemony and the various
threat perceptions that the United States is deemed to promote.[22] Complicit
in these, Japan is described as a "client state" (*zokkoku*), but the key agency
of Japanese lawmakers is neglected.[23] While many scholars have argued
that Japan's institutional "immobilism" is rooted in the US-led post-1945
system,[24] few have developed explicit analysis of the discursive construction
of the state-in-crisis narrative that emerged as a result.[25]

Moreover, in all of these approaches, the significance of temporality
remains underappreciated. In this regard, we unpack a range of statements
in Diet and public discourses. These point to critical junctures at which
perceptions of state failure in response to a belligerent North Korea emerged.
The focus on "crisis, discourse and temporality"[26] allows us to demonstrate
why greater emphasis needs to be placed on the institutionally transformative
effects of crisis narratives in shaping the postwar state as a whole, thereby
adding value to accounts limited to explaining the trajectory of post–Cold War
Japan's security policy. Using this lens, we revisit Japan's response to North
Korea's missile and nuclear programs, and the unfolding of the abduction
issue since the early 1990s. We demonstrate that emerging narratives, first,
in principle subject the North Korean state to the possibility of preemptive
strikes and other punitive measures and, second, mandate the Japanese
state to become stronger militarily, economically, and socially by means of
constitutional change, military build-up, and economic structural reform.

Japanese Security Narratives in Response to
North Korea's Missile Threat

On May 29, 1993, North Korea launched a medium-range Nodong missile—designed for potential use against Tokyo—into the Sea of Japan.[27]
In the current climate, this act would surely have drawn a dramatic and
vociferous response.[28] At the time of the launch and in the following weeks,

however, barely twenty direct mentions of the incident were made across all Diet chambers.[29] Given this discrepancy within the discourse, then, at what point were North Korean actions rendered as a crisis of the postwar Japanese state, and how were discursive interventions that demanded a departure from Japan's postwar pacifism toward a militarily potent Japan justified? These questions can be answered by identifying the initiation of narrative shifts across Diet discourse thereafter. Statements such as the following by LDP representative Mihara Asahiko illustrate such attempts:

> When a neighboring country tries to extend its adventurism by launching a Nodong 500 miles, as the only country to be the victim of nuclear war, our people feel greater uncertainty than any other. . . . I believe we must work hard to stop their adventurism and exhaust all means to get them to become a more peaceful and open country.[30]

Mihara does not claim that North Korea's actions have thrown the Japanese state into crisis (yet), but rather that North Korea has become the source of unknown but undeniable concerns. This makes it a potential source of crisis that requires a response by "all means" necessary in order to mitigate it. With security concerns further heightened after allegations of a North Korean nuclear program surfaced, the 1994 Higuchi Report concluded that Japan required offensive military capabilities to address the threat of North Korean ballistic missiles.[31] This assessment coincided with the debate over Japan's participation in US-led theater missile defense.[32] Notwithstanding these subtle changes in the security discourse, it was the 1998 launch of a Taepodong missile over Japanese air space into the Western Pacific that led to the explicit identification of a crisis and gave rise to decisive security policy responses.[33] The irony here is that while the Nodong missile was built with ambitions to target Japan, the Taepodong was not. Still, the latter received far greater attention, with some twenty-six direct references including specific mentions of crisis made by lawmakers across party lines.

The 1998 "Taepodong Shock" marked a shift in mainstream policy positions and the depiction of North Korean defense activities. Representative of a new breed of assertive revisionist foreign policymakers from across the political spectrum, the Democratic Party of Japan's (DPJ's) Maehara Seiji asserted that "these North Korea problems are extremely serious."[34] He linked the Taepodong missile test to concerns about advances in North

Korea's nuclear weapons program and promoted the development of a more effective crisis management system (*kiki kanri taisei*) in order to deal with such regional threats. Preceding Maehara's postulations, Nukaga Fukushiro (LDP), then head of the Japan Defense Agency, effectively confirmed the two parties' convergence on this issue when he asserted that "of course with that purpose in mind we are tackling this with a sense of crisis."[35] Thereafter, policymakers justified interventions in response to Pyongyang's actions with the need to counter the proliferation of weapons of mass destruction.[36]

The subsequent failure of Tokyo's attempts to normalize diplomatic relations with Pyongyang foreshadowed the development of the North Korea threat narrative into a state-in-crisis narrative. A focus on the pacifist postwar state's insufficient responses to the North Korea threat precluded the pursuit of conciliatory policy lines.[37] This resulted in concrete measures such as Japan's push for joining the US-led ballistic missile defense (BMD) system. Indeed, Administrative Vice-Minister of Defense Akiyama Masahiro considered such a policy shift "impossible without the DPRK firing the [Taepodong] missile."[38] Further steps included the strengthening of the US–Japan alliance. New legislation, introduced in 1999 for that purpose, enabled Tokyo to provide rear area support to the United States in "situations in areas surrounding" Japan, including contingencies on the Korean Peninsula. This discursive shift emphasized the gravity of potential losses in Japan's security if the crisis was not dealt with decisively. In the following section we show how the recruitment of the politically and socially sensitive issue of North Korean agents' abduction of Japanese citizens into this crisis narrative played an additional key role.

The Abduction Issue and the (Re)Framing of the Japanese State

As early as January 1980, the *Sankei Shimbun* reported the mysterious vanishing of several individuals from coastal areas of Japan. In 1987, the exiled North Korean agent Kim Hyon Hui identified one of these as Taguchi Yaeko. However, it was not until 1988 that the LDP's Kariyama Seiroku declared in a Diet debate that "strong indicators exist that North Korea was probably involved in the criminal cases of vanishing couples since 1978."[39] Nevertheless, the "abduction allegations" (*rachi giwaku*) failed to mobilize the public and it was only from 1996 that the debate about the kidnappings would rapidly gain traction. This was the result of a report about the 1977 abduction of thirteen-year-old Yokota Megumi. In the following years, the

Yokota case moved to the center of public interest in what became the "abduction problem" (*rachi mondai*) in Japan–North Korea relations.[40]

By early 1997, the authorities officially identified six Japanese abductees[41] and the issue triggered the formation of a powerful political movement that demanded the rescue of the victims from their North Korean prison. At the center of this movement was the Association of the Families of Victims Kidnapped by North Korea (*Kitachōsen ni yoru rachi higaisha kazoku renraku kai: Kazokukai*). The Kazokukai was supported by the National Association for the Rescue of Japanese Abducted by North Korea (*Kitachōsen ni rachi sareta nihonjin o kyūshutsu suru tame no zenkoku kyōgikai: Sukuukai*). The movement received strong political support from the Assembly Members Alliance for the Speedy Rescue of Japanese Kidnapped by North Korea (*Kitachōsen ni rachisareta nihonjin o sōki ni kyūshutsu suru tame ni kōdō suru giin renmei: Rachi giren*).[42] This powerful advocacy coalition, in combination with substantive evidence unearthed by the Japan National Police Agency,[43] turned the abduction issue into the public's greatest concern. Ahead of nuclear and missile tests, more than 80 percent of the Japanese public considered it key in bilateral relations with North Korea (figure 9.1).[44] Particularly after the 2002 Kim–Koizumi Summit, during which Kim Jong Il admitted to a number of the abductions,[45] prominent revisionists seized upon this issue as a means to rally public support for wider reforms of Japan's national security system.[46]

A recurrent pattern in public and political narrative formed that linked the abductions to a supposedly weak Japan unable to protect its citizens. The blame was put on those in support of the old postwar pacifist regime, including the media and liberal intellectuals. These assertions gave rise to demands for broad and swift changes to the postwar state.[47] After the 2002 summit, North Korea was framed as a "terror state" (*tero kokka*), a "spy state" (*kōsaku kokka*), and a "lawless state" (*muhō kokka*). In contrast, Japan was portrayed as an "incapable state" (*munō kokka*).[48] Meanwhile, the liberal elites who, supporting the peace state, had long advocated dialogue with North Korea were defamed as "traitors" (*kokuzoku*)[49] and members of a "North Korea (policy) clique" (*Kitachōsen-zoku*).[150] Although known for more than a decade, the date of the abductions' official revelation was termed as Japan's "9.17." Likening it to the US's 9/11, this naming was meant to underscore the scale of the national trauma incurred.[51] Hence, key proponents of regime change in North Korea declared that the abduction issue "forces us to completely reassess the state of Japan's postwar politics, society, debate, and thought."[52] The chief questions they asked were "why it has taken the Japanese state 25 years to rescue the abductees?"[53] and "why

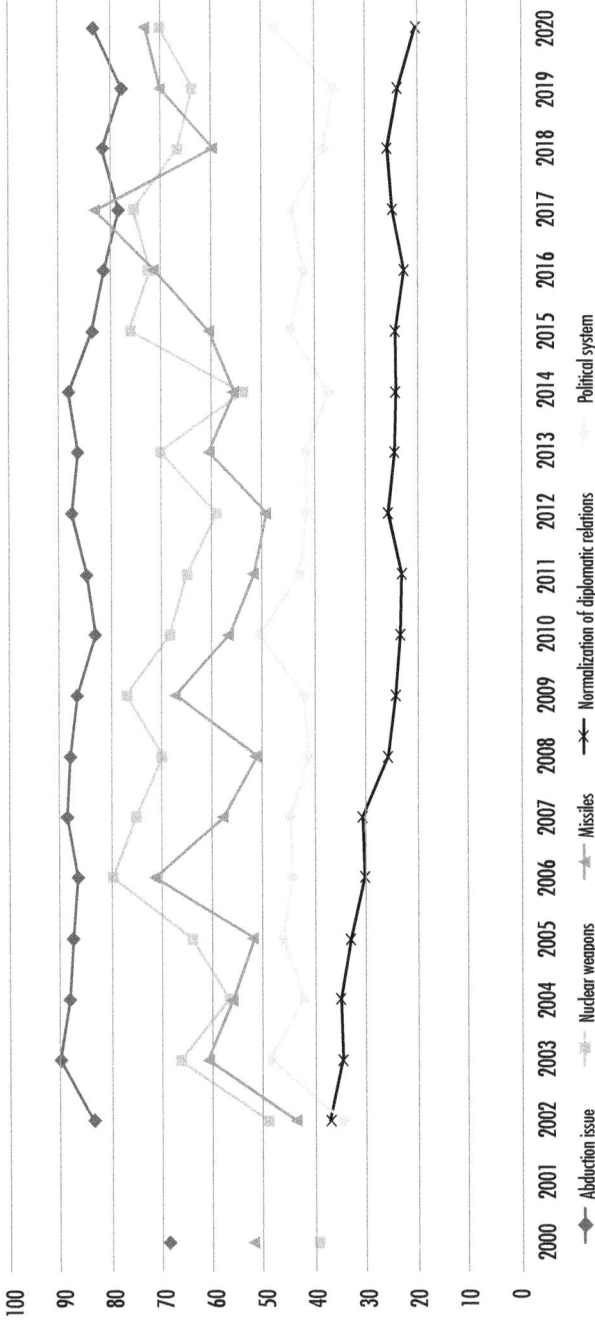

Figure 9.1. Public opinion on Japan's relations with North Korea, 2000–2020 (in percent). Source: Compiled by the authors based on Cabinet Office (various years), https://survey.gov-online.go.jp/index.html.

was Japan unable to prevent the abductions from happening?" In response, they blamed a malfunctioning Japanese police and intelligence apparatus for failing to prevent the crimes followed.[54]

Japan's neoconservatives recognized the great utility of the failing postwar state narrative for advancing their political agenda. For example, Kitaoka Shinichi, a key security adviser to Prime Minister Abe, wrote that "in the past [leftist] intellectuals and magazines have idealized North Korea and criticized South Korea. . . . Japan is located next to a dangerous state that only understands the language of military force. I can't understand why people would think it is unnecessary to strengthen Japan's defense capabilities."[55] Former Tokyo Governor Ishihara Shintarō even argued that Japan should "go to war with North Korea to rescue the abductees." For Ishihara, Japan's dealings with North Korea revealed that the "diplomacy of a country that lacks an army and a defense ministry will be humiliated."[56] The LDP's Hirasawa Katsuei opined that "if Japan would have been a 'normal state' the abductions would definitely not have happened," and that Tokyo's lack of resolve to deal with the abduction issue is a "sign of how Japan wants to preserve its pacifism at any price."[57] Meanwhile, members of the now politically powerful abduction movement argued that the postwar constitution's "Article 9 [prohibiting Japan from possessing and using armed forces] hinders the solution of the abductions."[58]

The abduction issue was recruited into a meta-narrative that purported the failing of the postwar state and mandated comprehensive reform. The subsequent analysis shows how those controlling political power for most of the twenty-first century's first two decades have drawn on this meta-narrative to mobilize overwhelming support to restructure the postwar national security system.

Contradictions of a "Weak State"

Leading the way were Japan's arguably most prominent post–Cold War prime ministers, Koizumi Junichirō and Abe Shinzō. Koizumi made direct references to abductions (*rachi*) and crisis (*kiki*) in his Diet statements on a total of twenty-three separate occasions, spanning from the first half of 2001 to late 2005. Koizumi claimed that he and his administration were "raising security issues, which include the abduction issue and nuclear development, as the topic of highest priority."[59] In the same speech, he went on to refer directly to "maritime spy-boat incursions," other "immoral acts," and "the issue of missiles and such like," as well as alluding specifically to his "regret" for being unable to protect Japan from these external aggressions. Here, the postwar state's failure to prevent the abductions, and the rationale for intervention in response to this perceived state failure, are molded into a cohesive state-in-crisis narrative.

By conflating multiple security issues and highlighting Japan's vulnerability to an elevated and comprehensive North Korean threat, Koizumi was able to prime a security environment predisposed to strengthening defense capabilities. In the years following the failed 2002 Japan–North Korea summit, Koizumi asserted that "the abductions by North Korea are a major problem that impacts upon our citizens' lives and security."[60] He not only advocated domestic policy reform, but also urged international action in response to North Korean provocations, most explicitly when contending that, "in order to comprehensively resolve the problem of [North Korean] abductions, nuclear development and missiles, we must work closely with the countries involved to negotiate a hard line."[61] Koizumi thereafter leveraged the North Korean threat to (re)frame the parameters of national security discourse, including a more proactive military posture, greater integration with US defense forces, and multi-billion-dollar investment in their BMD system. These measures purportedly addressed the perceived crises on the Korean Peninsula.[62] As Koizumi's chief cabinet secretary, Abe partly guided this process; as his successor, he drove it forward decisively.

Abe came to prominence through his advocacy of a hardline stance against North Korea.[63] This included declaring the return of surviving victims and an inquiry into the fate of the deceased a precondition for the reopening of talks over diplomatic normalization. Thereafter, he championed the abduction issue to mobilize public opinion and deepen the sense of national crisis by including social and ideological elements.[64] In his 2006 political manifesto *Towards a Beautiful Country*, Abe defined the "abductions as a violation of Japan's sovereignty," which urges "reflection on the fifty-eight years of the Japanese postwar state."[65] According to Abe, "Japan has neglected the abduction issue. There was no awareness and sincere effort to think about national security. The state had lost its will to protect its citizens. We need to seriously reflect on this."[66] In the Diet, he made full use of the newly created Special Committee on Abductions by North Korea and Related Affairs to promote tough sanctions against North Korea, take measures against alleged North Korea supporters in Japan, and adopt a robust defense posture.[67] Abe also successfully proposed the "Law Concerning Measures to Address the Abduction Issue and Other North Korean Human

Rights Violations," featuring an annual North Korean Human Rights Abuses Awareness Week. As prime minister, Abe established the Headquarters for the Abduction Issue, which, over the years, received a growing budget.[68] With this institutional backing, Abe's cabinets raised the kidnapping issue at various domestic and international events, including the G7 summits, and at the United Nations. Later, the Headquarters also offered school children the chance to experience the "abduction moment" of Yokota Megumi themselves, employing cutting-edge virtual reality technology.[69] Thus, in its efforts to "raise awareness," the government made North Korea a nightmarish experience for its citizens. Adopted by succeeding cabinets, including those of the DPJ, these measures enabled Abe and other conservative politicians to entrench the North Korean issue into broader domestic and international political discourses.

Nevertheless, while Abe's stance is often characterized as particularly extreme in this regard, his tone in public was measured during both terms in office (2006–2007 and 2012–2020). This subtlety facilitated the framing of the abduction issue, coupled with missile development and nuclear proliferation, as an indefinite continuation of moments of national crisis. Indeed, in an address to the Diet in January 2007, Abe stated, "I'm pushing strongly for real action towards getting North Korea to give up its nuclear program, and will continue to tackle the abduction issue."[70] This statement confirmed the entrenchment of the crisis narrative and reiterated the demand for tough responses.

The abductions were now depicted by the majority of political leaders as a failure that stemmed from Japan's particular vulnerability and military impotence in the postwar era. Hence, security-related political reforms were easily justified through the emotive issue of abductions, which remained conceptually coupled to the potential threat posed by North Korea's increased military capabilities. Specifically, the psychologically powerful concept of nuclear weapons, compounded by the general sense of vulnerability, led to the conflation of the missile threat with the humiliation and outrage about the abductions. This was then used to crystallize the framing of North Korea and the Korean Peninsula as a place in need of decisive (military) intervention. Thereby Abe and his supporters appropriated the North Korea–related national crisis narrative to justify not only individual one-time measures, such as sanctions and increased funding for BMD systems, but also bringing about tangible policy shifts at the institutional level.

The removal of political opposition was a particularly significant step in the consolidation of the national crisis narrative and its effective use for imposing institutional change. The convergence of political views came as a result of the above-mentioned naming and shaming of Japan's liberal elites as well as the increasingly converging rhetoric offered from parties supposedly opposing the LDP. In contrast to long-standing opposition narratives, few politicians now argued for preserving Japan as a "peace state." The ensuing departure from the previous posture of an exclusively "defense-orientated defense" provoked a new debate about preemptive strike capabilities that the LDP had recommended in its 2004 proposal "A New Japanese Defense Policy: Towards a Secure and Safe Japan."[71] Proponents of such policy change, including the LDP's defense policy hawk Ishiba Shigeru, rejected criticisms by framing opponents as "utopian pacifists" (*kūsōteki heiwashugisha*).[72] Furthermore, controversial decisions such as supporting the 2003 US-led Iraq campaign were linked to the North Korea threat to justify Japan's new role and de facto participation in constitutionally prohibited collective self-defense operations. Ishiba was most explicit in this:

> When it comes to North Korea most have the same perception. But then some say "Don't send the Jieitai [SDF] to Iraq. America is bad." I don't understand these people who say in the case of North Korea "that America should deal with it." I don't see how it is possible to separate the Iraq problem from the North Korea problem. . . . Both states share the nature of being terror states.[73]

Concomitantly, leading opposition figures started to adopt this narrative. In response to Pyongyang's multiple missile launches in 2006, for instance, DPJ spokesman Nagashima Akihisa, a long-time proponent of engagement with North Korea, asserted that "this is a grave security crisis that puts at risk the lives and property of our people. In relation to this crisis, as confirmed by our leader, Hatoyama, there is no [division between] ruling and opposition party as far as this goes."[74] Nagashima's concern shows very clearly how the state-in-crisis meta-narrative, in addition to North Korea, also made Japan an object of decisive intervention. There, political opposition must be minimized in order for the legislature and executive to act united in response to outside threats.[75]

Thereafter, following Abe's return to power in 2012, more and more references to "changes in Japan's security environment" can be found throughout security debates and policy documents. Outlining Japan's new doctrine of "proactive pacifism" (*sekkyokuteki heiwashugi*), the 2013 National Security Strategy made twenty references to North Korea and its missile and nuclear weapons development to argue for change in Japan's corresponding posture.[76] Abe also added urgency to his agenda of restoring a strong state through the strengthening of the Japan Self-Defense Forces (SDF), claiming that "[t]he security environment surrounding Japan is becoming increasingly severe. North Korea is developing weapons of mass destruction and ballistic missiles. And provocations against our sovereignty are there. This is reality."[77] In response, during 2013 and 2014, Abe implemented broad changes to the security system, including the introduction of a National Security Council, the lifting of Japan's virtual ban on arms exports, the passing of state secrecy legislation, the granting of successive defense budget increases, the modernization of defense forces, and the reinterpretation of the constitution that permits Japan to participate in collective self-defense operations alongside the United States.[78]

In addition, after North Korea's 2017 missile and nuclear tests, Defense Minister Onodera Itsunori further elevated the threat to an "unprecedented, critical and imminent" level.[79] In a cabinet statement of December 2017, the Abe government also declared that "North Korea's nuclear and missile development has become a greater and more imminent threat for Japan's national security, and we need to drastically improve our ballistic missile defense capability to protect Japan continuously and sustainably."[280] To that end, justifying Japan's decision to purchase the US Aegis Ashore BMD system, Onodera added that "North Korea's nuclear missile development poses a new level of threat to Japan and as we have done in the past we will ensure that we are able to defend ourselves with a drastic improvement in ballistic missile defence."[81] Such statements show how the second Abe administration juxtaposed North Korea with a vulnerable Japan and thereby tasked itself with strengthening nation and state to deal with this newly narrated crisis.

Making Japan Strong Again

In the early post–Cold War years, members of the Japan Communist Party (JCP),[82] independent academics, and journalists on the left of Japan's political spectrum formed a pro-engagement advocacy nexus toward North Korea. Their approach was anchored in the residual "peace state" narrative propagated by left-leaning political actors and the 1960s student protests against the formal establishment of the US–Japan alliance.[83] This narrative starkly contrasts to the now-dominant state-in-crisis narrative, which advocates proactive pacifism through containment and military intervention. The latter narrative was able to gain hegemonic status through the discrediting of the former's progressive voices and the exploitation of the political convergence between those who sought military strength to defend against North Korean threats, those who strove to strengthen the US–Japan alliance, and those who sought to increase Japan's international status in general.[84] In other words, high-level political debate in Japan over North Korea became contested not over what level of threat should be identified (if at all!), but rather over a given administration's ability to successfully and responsibly intervene to address the predesignated, supposedly grave crisis requiring decisive intervention according to most of the major parties' manifestos.[85]

This transformation confirms the mechanism outlined in Hay's framework, in that it reveals the discursive reconstitution of the state via narratives of national crisis. The response to North Korean missile testing in 2009, for example by the LDP's Tanigawa Shūzen, epitomizes this process. After having referred specifically to the "crisis," Tanigawa posed a rhetorical question:

> Are we to overlook the repeated aberrations of North Korea, beginning with the abductions of our fellow citizens, missile launches, nuclear tests and the like? The role of the state is to protect the lives and property of the people. If we do not question North Korea's means, as the country which poses the greatest threat to ours, that amounts to an abandonment of our responsible state role and dignity.[86]

The historic transfer of ruling power from the LDP to the DPJ in 2009 did not alter the discursive process. Leading DPJ lawmakers reiterated these basic sentiments. They even took the unprecedented step of identifying the North Korean threat as a primary reason for revising Japan's periodic National Defense Program Guidelines, as well as for promoting further military cooperation with the US and investing additional funds in sophisticated BMD systems.[87] Justifying these moves, former DPJ leader Banri Kaeda, for instance, reflected that "I am filled with anxiety concerning North Korea's continuing behavior, including abductions, nuclear testing, and missile launches, which threaten the peace and stability of the region."[88]

In addition, start-up parties such as the Japan Restoration Party (JRP, *Nippon ishin no kai*), which temporarily replaced the weakening left as political opposition,[89] went as far as expressing the desire to restore Japan's standing in their party name, and openly promoted this in the Diet by resorting to North Korean threat narratives.[90] For example, in response to

Pyongyang's 2017 missile tests, former JRP representative Yoshida Toyofumi, asserted that "as a country and a people we share the sense of crisis in the same way. . . . We must continue to deal with these various problems with the sense of crisis."[91] Correspondingly, having once again made discursive reference to abduction, nuclear, and missile issues in the same statement, the Party of Hope's (*Kibō no tō*) Tamaki Yuichirō explicitly advocated more fundamental institutional changes to the defense apparatus:

> Our party, in addition to providing immediate full support in cooperation with our alliance partner in the sphere of defense, will seek to clarify the extent of deterrence. For that purpose, we will aim for revision to the existing Security Related Laws [*anpokanrenhō*] in terms of specifying the established three principles of crisis situations. We will also consider the establishment of legislation to allow the full deployment of cautionary defense facilities and missile defense systems on outlying islands. By all means, won't you join us in constructive debate that goes beyond the division of ruling and opposition parties?[92]

In this case too, the reference to the bridging of party-political divides evinces the convergence of security policy positions vis-à-vis the belligerent North Korea.

Conversely, the reality of North Korea's official military objectives and in fact declining capabilities has largely been absent from the debate. As noted by North Korea analyst Shigemura Toshimitsu,[93] for example, Pyongyang barely has sufficient oil to engage in the most basic military operations, let alone to fight any kind of sustained campaign. Rather, North Korea consistently emphasizes its right to self-determination and self-defense, and openly accuses Tokyo's leaders of double standards for having constructed a crisis narrative in order to justify Japan's own military expansion.[94] In contrast, mainstream Japanese discourses highlight the country's vulnerability vis-à-vis Pyongyang, despite its overwhelming advantage in military power. While Japan ranks seventh among the world's military spenders, North Korea enters most leading indexes at approximately twenty-third. And despite an impressive-sounding million-strong standing army, the "Hermit Kingdom" has highly limited forward power-projection capabilities and aging equipment.[95] North Korea also lacks the kind of state-of-the-art BMD and other US-backed defense systems such as the F-35 stealth fighter jet, Global Hawk surveillance drones, and aircraft carriers that the SDF can expect to rely upon.[96] In that sense,

Japan's leaders have disproportionately deployed North Korean threats to fuel a public discourse that "reassesses its might and rights."[97]

The North Korea Crisis as "Lived Experience"

As we have shown, reform agents such as Abe and his supporters within the LDP have been proclaiming that the postwar state's institutions failed to respond to the North Korean ballistic missile and nuclear weapons threat. Thus, in his 2012 reelection campaign, Abe pledged to "take back Japan" (*Nippon o torimodosu*) from the constraints of postwar pacifism (and thus return its rightful standing in international affairs). Indeed, the LDP-led government has subsequently blended this rhetoric of change with the already established North Korean crisis narrative. For instance, one official poster distributed across the country reads that the Abe government will "definitely bring back the abductees" (*Rachi kanarazu torimodosu*). The LDP's Ishiba Shigeru also employed this language and titled his 2013 book *Nippon o torimodosu. Kenpō o torimodosu (Take Back Japan. Take Back the Constitution).*[98]

Abe implemented the first steps of this agenda in 2014 when his cabinet approved the reinterpretation of Article 9 of Japan's constitution to nominally legalize collective self-defense under specific circumstances. The election of Donald Trump in 2016 and the crisis on the Korean Peninsula in 2017 then provided Abe with new momentum to push even further in pursuing his agenda of bringing back a "strong state" through constitutional revision. To make the existential levels of threat and crisis tangible among the general population, and break down abstract geopolitics into "lived experience," local authorities in early 2017 started to conduct evacuation drills, including at elementary schools, in preparation for the impact of missiles or debris thereof.[99] This was followed by a cabinet decision in April to use the J-Alert system (introduced in 2007 to alert the public of natural disasters) to warn the population of incoming North Korean missiles.[100] On August 29, the first such warning was issued. Consequently, echoing the elites' narrations of crisis from below, local officials, people on the street, and school children were quoted as saying, for instance, that "I get the impression that the crisis level has gone up. . . . Prefectural residents are very concerned."[101] The second warning was issued on September 15,[102] immediately before Abe dissolved the lower house with direct reference to the national crisis spurred by North Korea. Interestingly, while some observers pointed to the political instrumentalization of J-Alert, these warnings were not linked to defense measures such as the actual use of Japan's BMD. After all, possession of a high-quality and precise missile defense system targeted at North Korea raises the question why blanket warnings needed to be issued through large parts of Japan.[103]

At the institutional level, the crisis meta-narrative resulted in moves toward the further integration of the SDF with the US military, presented as the only effective means to alleviate the apparently escalating crisis unfolding in Kim Jong Un's North Korea.[104] This imperative had already been made tangible through joint Japan–US military drills in August 2017. In response to Pyongyang's November 2017 missile test, Prime Minister Abe asserted that he would "do everything to tackle missile, nuclear and, most importantly of all, the grave issue of abductions." In the same address, he confirmed that "we will continue to sustain a high degree of precautionary capability, based on a foundation of strong alliance between the United States and Japan, and provide the appropriate supply of information to our people, ensuring the peace and security of our country."[3105] Thus, explicitly linking crisis alleviation with a tighter US–Japan alliance, North Korea became part and parcel of Abe's agenda to restore a "strong Japan."

Conclusion

In line with Hay's conceptualization of crisis and state transformation, the discourses analyzed in this chapter showed how North Korea's abduction of Japanese citizens, and its missile and nuclear testing, were recruited into the construction of a state-in-crisis narrative. This process combined a variety of different security issues into the meta-narrative of state failure, thereby suppressing counter-narratives, delegitimizing political opponents, and mandating the reconstitution of the postwar state. In particular, selected statements by leading Diet members and their coverage in the mass media elucidate how Japan has been portrayed as being increasingly vulnerable, and in need of stronger offensive military capabilities. This highlights how changes at the level of security policy have justified the need for decisive (military) interventions against supposedly imminent threats. Crystalized in a state-in-crisis narrative by Abe from 2012, the North Korea threat enabled policymakers in Tokyo to redesign postwar security institutions in an attempt to install a militarily active Japan that is even more deeply embedded in the US alliance.

Rather than identifying or priming single moments of decisive intervention, as Hay suggests, an ongoing crisis narrative, which makes these moments repetitious and indefinite, has been created. In this context, the specific recruiting of North Korea into a key meta-narrative for the transformation of Japan's postwar state has important implications for Tokyo's North Korea policy. The emphasis on the North Korea threat as an imperative for accelerating the departure from postwar pacifism made it increasingly difficult for Japan to adjust its foreign policy to an unfolding détente. This became clear when the US engagement of North Korea from early 2018 onwards stirred Japanese fears of becoming isolated and abandoned.[106] These concerns increased as the United States refrained from endorsing key Japanese positions, including on North Korea's firing of short-range missiles. By advocating an "abduction issue first"[107] policy, Abe introduced immobilism into Japanese foreign policy and thus contradicted his vision for a proactive Japan. This approach increases the risk of rifts in the alliance, and Japan's relations with South Korea and China may also suffer further from overuse of the North Korean crisis narrative, as both neighboring countries are invested in mediating détente on the Korean Peninsula. Japan, therefore, used North Korea to restore its international standing, but—whether by strategic design or unintended consequence—reproduced an enduring state of crisis.

In 2014, amid tensions on the Korean Peninsula, Abe was forced to show a degree of flexibility in his dealings with North Korea. Partially departing from his hardline approach, this resulted in the "Stockholm agreement" and the (temporary) lifting of some sanctions in response to North Korea's reopening of investigations on the abduction issue. Perhaps, then, Abe was aware of a growing sense of foreign policy failure. In his 2018 speech at the UN General Assembly, too, he omitted references to "pressure" when discussing North Korea.[108] Moreover, in October, Japan reached out to North Korea to launch new talks. In April 2019, it was revealed that Japan's "Diplomatic Bluebook" would also drop references to "maximum pressure," thus signaling a softening approach toward North Korea. In a radical departure from his framing of North Korea as cause for Japan's "national crisis" requiring decisive intervention, Abe in May 2019 even expressed his desire for unconditional talks with Kim Jong Un.[109] However, while the public remains largely focused on the abduction issue (see figure 9.1), a sudden policy change would raise questions as to why the government failed to facilitate progress much earlier, thus exposing the contradictions of Abe's strong state agenda. Following Abe's abrupt resignation in August 2020, his successor as prime minister, Suga Yoshihide, has also declared resolution of the abduction issue to be a foreign policy priority. Yet diplomatic failure risks exposing Suga's Japan to precisely the criticisms of remaining an "abnormal" state under weak leadership that Abe and the

LDP have been seeking to overcome. Unable to impose transformation of Japan's postwar state, Suga and his LDP-led government might then find themselves the object of a newly unfolding state-in-crisis narrative.

Notes

1. Van Jackson, *On the Brink: Trump, Kim, and the Threat of Nuclear War* (Cambridge: Cambridge University Press, 2018); Peter Baker and Choe Sang-Hun, "Trump Threatens 'Fire and Fury' Against North Korea if It Endangers U.S.," *New York Times*, August 8, 2017, https://www.nytimes.com/2017/08/08/world/asia/north-korea-un-sanctions-nuclear-missile-united-nations.html. Unless otherwise stated, all online sources were accessed and available on October 27, 2020.

2. Hyun Oh, "Sirens Blare as Japan, Fearing North Korea, Holds First Missile Drill," *Reuters*, March 17, 2017.

3. Prime Minister of Japan and His Cabinet, "Press Conference by Prime Minister Shinzo Abe," September 25, 2017, https://japan.kantei.go.jp/97_abe/statement/201709/_00011.html, emphasis added; see also Yasuhiro Izumikawa, "The North Korea Factor in the 2017 Election," in *Japan Decides 2017: The Japanese General Election*, ed. Robert J. Pekkanen, Steven R. Reed, Ethan Scheiner, and Daniel M. Smith (New York: Palgrave Macmillan, 2018), 313–327.

4. Kyodo, "Taro Aso Explains Comments Crediting Snap Election Win to North Korea," *Japan Times*, October 28, 2017, https://www.japantimes.co.jp/news/2017/10/28/national/politics-diplomacy/aso-seeks-clarify-comments-attributing-election-win-north-korea-crisis/.

5. Suzuki Kazuto, "Japan's View of the North Korean Threat," *IAI Commentary*, March 22, 2018.

6. For example, Linus Hagström and Ulv Hanssen, "The North Korean Abduction Issue: Emotions, Securitisation and the Reconstruction of Japanese Identity From 'Aggressor' to 'Victim' and From 'Pacifist' to 'Normal,'" *Pacific Review* 28, no. 1 (2015): 71–93.

7. Colin Hay, "Crisis and the Structural Transformation of the State: Interrogating the Process of Change," *British Journal of Politics and International Relations* 1, no. 3 (1999): 317–344; Colin Hay, "Rethinking Crisis: Narratives of the New Right and Constructions of Crisis," *Rethinking Marxism* 8, no. 2 (1995): 60–76.

8. Hay, "Crisis," 323–324.

9. Ibid., 335.

10. Ibid., 330–331.

11. Barry Buzan, Ole Wæver, and Jaap de Wilde, *Security: A New Framework for Analysis* (Boulder, CO: Lynne Rienner, 1997).

12. Along the structural realist/social constructivist divide in International Relations, this scholarship includes Richard J. Samuels, *Securing Japan: Tokyo's Grand Strategy and the Future of East Asia* (Ithaca, NY: Cornell University Press,

2007); Christopher W. Hughes, *Japan's Remilitarisation* (London: Routledge, 2009); Andrew L. Oros, *Japan's Security Renaissance: New Policies and Politics for the Twenty-First Century* (New York: Columbia University Press, 2017); Karl Gustafsson, Linus Hagström, and Ulv Hanssen, "Japan's Pacifism Is Dead," *Survival* 60, no. 6 (2018): 137–158.

13. Christopher W. Hughes, " 'Super-Sizing' the DPRK Threat: Japan's Evolving Military Posture and North Korea," *Asian Survey* 49, no. 2 (2009): 291–311, here 291.

14. Linus Hagström and Christian Turesson, "Among Threats and a 'Perfect Excuse': Understanding change in Japanese Foreign Security Policy," *Korean Journal of Defense Analysis* 21, no. 3 (2009): 297–314.

15. Hughes, " 'Super-Sizing,' " 294; Kenneth B. Pyle, "Japan's Return to Great Power Politics: Abe's Restoration," *Asia Policy* 13, no. 2 (2018): 69–90. Explicit references to China's military expansion and ambitions have only gradually become prominent in recent official publications in Japan; see, for example, *National Institute for Defense Studies East Asian Strategic Review 2017* (Tokyo: NIDS, 2017): 71–94.

16. Eric Heginbotham, and Richard J. Samuels, "Active Denial: Redesigning Japan's Response to China's Military Challenge," *International Security* 42, no. 4 (2018): 128–169.

17. Peter J. Katzenstein, "Japan in the American Imperium: Rethinking Security," *Asia-Pacific Journal: Japan Focus* 6, no. 10 (2008), https://apjjf.org/-Peter-J.-Katzenstein/2921/article.html.

18. Linus Hagström and Marie Söderberg, "Introduction: Japan, the Great Powers, and the Coordination of North Korea Policy," in *North Korea Policy: Japan and the Great Powers*, ed. Linus Hagström and Marie Söderberg (London: Routledge, 2006), 1–18, here 5.

19. Linus Hagström, "Critiquing the Idea of Japanese Exceptionalism: Japan and the Coordination of North Korea Policy," *European Journal of East Asian Studies* 7, no. 1 (2008): 131–154; Linus Hagström, "The 'Abnormal' State: Identity, Norm/Exception and Japan," *European Journal of International Relations* 21, no. 1 (2015): 122–145.

20. Linus Hagström, "Normalizing Japan: Supporter, Nuisance, or Wielder of Power in the North Korean Nuclear Talks?" *Asian Survey* 49, no. 5 (2009): 831–851; see also Yoichi Funabashi, *The Peninsula Question: A Chronicle of the Second Korean Nuclear Crisis* (Washington, DC: Brookings Institution Press, 2007).

21. For example, Key-young Son, "Constructing Fear: How the Japanese State Mediates Risks from North Korea," *Japan Forum* 22, no. 1 (2010): 169–94; Ra Mason, *Japan's North Korea Relations and the Recalibration of Risk* (London: Routledge, 2014).

22. Misato Matsuoka, *Hegemony and the US-Japan Alliance* (London: Routledge, 2019).

23. Gavan McCormack, *Client State: Japan in the American Embrace* (London: Verso, 2007).

24. Kenneth B. Pyle, "Japan's Immobilism," *NBR Analysis* 9, no. 4 (1998); H. Richard Friman, Peter J. Katzenstein, David Leheny, and Nobuo Okawara, "Immovable Object? Japan's Security Policy in East Asia," in *Rethinking Japanese Security: Internal and External Dynamics*, ed. Peter J. Katzenstein (London: Routledge, 2008), 147–168.

25. Umeda Masaki, *"Kitachōsen no kyōi" to shūdanteki jieiken* [The North Korea Threat and Collective Self-Defense] (Tokyo: Kōbunken, 2007); Handa Shigeru, *"Kitachōsen kyōi" no karakuri: Henshitsu suru Nihon no anpo seisaku* [The Trick of the "North Korea Threat": Japan's Changing Security Policy] (Tokyo: Iwanami Shoten, 2018).

26. Hay, "Crisis," 319.

27. Mason, *Japan's North Korea Relations*, 55.

28. For politically contrasting public commentaries of the 2017 "Korean Peninsula Crisis," see, for example Sakurai Yoshiko, "Kitachōsen kiki no saki ni machiukeru akumu no sujigaki, Chūgoku shihai no Chōsen hantō e mamorikata towareru Nippon" [The Nightmare at the End of the North Korea Crisis, Japan Must Prepare to Protect the Korean Peninsula from Chinese Dominance], October 28, 2017, https://yoshiko-sakurai.jp/2017/10/28/7113; Japan Communist Party, "Kitachōsen no dandō disairu hassha o kibishiku kyūdan suru: Kikidakai no tame no chokusetsu taiwa ha iyoiyo kyūmu" [We Censure North Korea for its Missile Launch: Direct Talks to Mediate the Crisis are Necessary], November 30, 2017, https://www.jcp.or.jp/akahata/aik17/2017-11-30/2017113001_02_1.html.

29. For all committee reports cited here we use the Kokkai kaigiroku kensaku shisutemu (Diet Minutes Research System), available at http://kokkai.ndl.go.jp/.

30. Security Committee, November 25, 1993.

31. Issued by the Advisory Group on Defense Issues with Higuchi Kotaro as chairman; the report's official name is "The Modality of the Security and Defense Capability of Japan: The Outlook for the 21st Century."

32. Jimbo Ken, "Dandō misairu bōei (BMD) to Nichibei dōmei: Nichibei kyōdō kaihatsu no seisaku katei to dōmei no 'senryaku chōsei'" [Ballistic Missile Defense and the Japan–US Alliance: The Policy Process of Japan–US Joint Development and "Strategic Coordination"], *Kokusai Anzenhosho* 29, no. 4 (2002): 40–58.

33. For specific and explicit, trans-party references to the North Korean Taepodong missile launch as representing a "crisis," see Diet debate between Minister of Defence Kōmura Masahiko, Maehara Seiji and others, Lower House Main Session, September 3, 1998.

34. Security Committee, December 18, 1998.

35. Diplomacy and Defence Committee, October 15, 1998.

36. Ibid.

37. Hay, "Rethinking Crisis," 64.

38. Cited in Hisae Masahiko, *Nihon no kokubō: Beigunka suru Jieitai/meisō suru seiji* [The Defense of Japan: The Americanization of the SDF and the Disoriented Politics] (Tokyo: Kodansha, 2012), 112.

39. 112th Diet Session Upper House Budget Committee, March 26, 1988.

40. Ōtake Hideo, *Koizumi Junichirō popyurizumu no kenkyū: Sono senryaku to shuhō* [A Study of Koizumi Junichirō's Populism: Strategy and Methods] (Tokyo: Tōyō Keizai Shinposha, 2006), 234.

41. Lower House Main Session, February 7, 1997.

42. For a detailed account of the movement's formation and its consecutive activities see Araki Kazuhiro, *Rachi kyūshutsu undō no 2000 hi: 1996-nen—2002-nen* [2000 Days of the Abductees Rescue Movement: From 1996 to 2002] (Tokyo: Soshisha, 2002); Aoki Osamu, *Repo rachi to hitobito: Sukuukai, kōan keisatsu, Chōsensōren* [Reportage: Abductions and the People: Sukuukai, Police, and Chōsensōren] (Tokyo: Iwanami Shoten, 2011); Celeste L. Arrington, *Accidental Activists: Victim Movements and Government Accountability in Japan and South Korea* (Ithaca, NY: Cornell University Press, 2016), chapter 5.

43. Ministry of Foreign Affairs, "Abductions of Japanese Citizens by North Korea," Tokyo, 2012, http://www.mofa.go.jp/region/asia-paci/n_korea/abduction/pdfs/abductions_en.pdf.

44. See also Seung Hyok Lee, *Japanese Society and the Politics of the North Korean Threat* (Toronto: University of Toronto Press, 2016).

45. North Korea admitted the abduction of thirteen Japanese, five of whom were returned and eight declared dead. Japan officially identifies seventeen abduction victims. See the Japanese government's official homepage for the abduction issue at https://www.rachi.go.jp/jp/ratimondai/index.html.

46. Araki Kazuhiro, Itō Sukeyasu, Araya Takashi, and Yobiyaku Burū Ribon no Kai, eds., *Jieitai gensō: Rachi mondai kara kangaeru anzen hoshō to kenpō kaisei* [The Illusion of the Self-Defense Forces: Thinking About National Security and Constitutional Revision from the Perspective of the Abduction Issue] (Tokyo: Sankei Shimbun, 2016); Richard J. Samuels, "Kidnapping Politics in East Asia," *Journal of East Asian Studies* 10, no. 3 (2010): 363–396.

47. See Araki Kazuhiro, *Kitachōsen no hyōchakusen: Umi kara yattekuru aratana kyōi* [North Korea's Ships Drifting Ashore: A New Threat from the Sea] (Tokyo: Soshisha, 2018); and Abe Masami, *Media wa shinde ita: Kensho Kitachōsen rachi hōdō* [The Media Was Dead: Investigation of the Media Coverage of North Korean Abductions] (Tokyo: Sankei Shimbun Shuppan, 2018). Abe Masami was the *Sankei Shimbun* journalist who broke the abduction story in January 1980.

48. Hasuike Tōru, *Dakkan: Hikisakareta 24nen* [Recapture: Separated 24 Years] (Tokyo: Shinchōsha, 2003); also David Leheny, *Think Global, Fear Local: Sex, Violence, and Anxiety in Contemporary Japan* (Ithaca, NY: Cornell University Press, 2006).

49. Hirasawa Katsuei, "Kokuzoku 'Tanaka Hitoshi' no bōsō" [The Reckless Action of the 'Traitor' Tanaka Hitoshi], *Shokun!* 11 (2002).

50. Inagi Takeshi, "'Kitachōsenzoku' no danmatsuma" [The death throes of the North Korea clique], *Shokun!* 12 (2002).

51. Yamagiwa Sumio, *Rachi no kairyū: Kojin mo kokka mo utta seiji to media* [The Current of Abductions: Politics and Media Selling the State and its People] (Tokyo: Fusosha, 2004), 15.

52. Satō Katsumi, "Kōen rachimondai de towareru 'sengo no Nihon' to iu kokka" [Speech: The State of 'Postwar Japan' Put in Question by the Abduction Issue], *Gekkan Jiyū Minshu* 597 (2002).

53. Shigematsu Toshimitsu, *Kitachōsen dētabukku: Sengun seiji, kosaku kara kaku kaihatsu, posuto Kim Jong Il made* [North Korea Databook: From Military-first Policy and Spying to the Development of Nuclear Weapons and the Post-Kim Jong Il regime] (Tokyo: Kodansha, 2002), 17.

54. Kawabe Katsurō, *Rachi ha naze fusegu koto ga dekinakatta no ka: Nihon keisatsu no jōhō haiboku* [Why Were the Abductions not Prevented: The Intelligence Defeat of Japan's Police] (Tokyo: Chikuma Shinsho, 2004); Richard J. Samuels, *Special Duty: A History of the Japanese Intelligence Community* (Ithaca, NY: Cornell University Press, 2019), 155–159.

55. Kitaoka Shinichi, "Sengo Nihon gaikōshi ni nokoru seikō de aru" [A Success in Japan's Postwar Diplomacy], *Chūō Kōron* 11 (2002): 46–52.

56. Ishihara Shintarō and Nishimura Shingo, "'Rachi sōsa' yare! [Investigate the Abductions!]," *Shokun!* 11 (2002): 24–37.

57. Hirasawa Katsuei, *Rachi mondai: Taikitachosen gaikō no arikata o tou* [The Abduction Issue: Revisiting the State of Japan's North Korea Policy] (Tokyo: PHP Kenkyusho, 2004), 133; authors' interview with Hirasawa Katsuei, Tokyo, May 10, 2013.

58. Hasuike Tōru, *Rachi: Sayu no kakine o koeta tadakai e* [Abduction: Towards a Bipartisan Struggle] (Tokyo: Kamogawa Shuppan, 2009), 85.

59. Upper House Main Session, October 23, 2002.

60. Lower House Main Session, October 13, 2004.

61. Upper House Main Session, January 20, 2006.

62. Hisae, *Nihon no Kokubō*, 110–114.

63. Nogami Tadaoki, *Dokyumento Abe Shinzō: Kagureta sugao o ou* [Documentary Abe Shinzō: Tracing the Hidden Face] (Tokyo: Kodansha, 2006).

64. Hasuike Tōru, *Rachi higaishatachi o migoroshi ni shita Abe Shinzō to reiketsu na menmen* [The Cold-Hearted Abe Shinzō Who Left the Abduction Victims to Their Own Fate] (Tokyo: Kodansha, 2015).

65. Abe Shinzō, *Utsukushii kuni e* [Towards a Beautiful Country] (Tokyo: Bungei Shunju, 2006), 46.

66. Ibid., 46.

67. Aoki, *Repo rachi*; Wada Haraku, *Abe Shushō wa rachi mondai o kaiketsu dekinai* [Prime Minister Abe is Unable to Solve the Abduction Issue] (Tokyo: Seitosha, 2018).

68. Aoki, *Repo rachi*.

69. "VR de Yokota Megumi san 'rachi shunkan' o saigen naikakufu" [Experiencing the "Abduction Moment" of Yokota Megumi Using VR Cabinet Office], *TV Asahi*, August 7, 2019, https://news.tv-asahi.co.jp/news_society/articles/000161524.html.

70. Upper House Main Session, January 30, 2007.

71. Liberal Democratic Party (Defence Working Group), "Teigen: Atarashii Nihon no bōei seisaku: Anzen/anshin na Nihon o mezashite" [A New Japanese Defense Policy: Towards a Secure and Safe Japan], Tokyo, March 30, 2004.

72. Ishiba Shigeru and Kiyotani Shinichi, *Gunji o shirazu shite heiwa o kadaruna* [Don't Talk About Peace if You Don't Know About the Military] (Tokyo: KK Bestsellers, 2006), 142.

73. Ishiba Shigeru, *Kokubō* [Defense] (Tokyo: Shinchosha, 2005), 42–43.

74. Lower House Security Committee, July 6, 2006.

75. Emma Chanlett-Avery, "North Korea's Abduction of Japanese Citizens and the Six-Party Talks," *CRS Report*, March 19, 2008, https://fas.org/sgp/crs/row/RS22845.pdf, 3–9.

76. Cabinet Secretariat, "National Security Strategy," December 17, 2013, https://www.cas.go.jp/jp/siryou/131217anzenhoshou/nss-e.pdf.

77. Prime Minister of Japan and His Cabinet, "Address by Prime Minister Shinzo Abe at the 2013 Troop Review for the Anniversary of the Establishment of the Self-Defense Forces," October 27, 2013, https://japan.kantei.go.jp/96_abe/statement/201310/27kunji_e.html.

78. Sebastian Maslow, "A Blueprint for a Strong Japan? Abe Shinzō and Japan's Evolving Security System," *Asian Survey* 55, no. 4 (2015): 739–765.

79. James Griffiths, "Japan's Abe Remains Trump's Best Ally Against 'Unprecedented' North Korea Threat," *CNN*, October 24, 2017, https://edition.cnn.com/2017/10/24/politics/japan-north-korea-trump-abe/index.html.

80. Mari Yamaguchi, "Japan Approves Missile Defense System Amid NKorea Threat," *Associated Press*, December 19, 2017, https://apnews.com/article/39f053831e4f449c9be4186e7a0863a4.

81. Justin McCurry, "Japan Buys US Missile Defence System to Counter North Korean Threat," *Guardian*, December 19, 2017, https://www.theguardian.com/world/2017/dec/19/japan-buys-us-missile-defence-system-to-counter-north-korean-threat.

82. Tomohiro Osaki, "Japanese Communist Party Says Dialogue, Not Pressure Will Work on North Korea," *Japan Times*, October 16, 2017, https://www.japantimes.co.jp/news/2017/10/16/national/politics-diplomacy/japanese-communist-party-says-dialogue-not-pressure-will-work-north-korea/.

83. Wada Haruki, *Heiwa kokka no tanjō: Sengo Nihon no genten to henyō* [Birth of the Peace State: Origins and Transformation of Postwar Japan] (Tokyo: Iwanami Shoten, 2015).

84. As part of this process, a number of more localized counter-narratives were also effectively disabled via stigmatization through association with *socialist*

policies, or, as in the case of Okinawa, by combining this with an undermining of local political and media forces, as well as their own self-stereotyping as oppositional. This is exemplified by news sources such as the "Shushō, kyūjō kaisei hyōmei/kiki ni binjō yatō kakuran" [Prime Minister Wants to Revise Article Nine/Sensing Crisis Opposition in Disarray], *Okinawa Times* (morning edition), May 4, 2017, 5; and "Heiwa kokka no sonzaikan shimese" [Peace State Must Show Its Presence], *Ryukyu Shimpo* (morning edition), August 15, 2017, 8.

85. It is noteworthy that in recent decades, even the JCP, which had traditionally been staunchly opposed to the over-vilification of North Korea, has moved its public rhetoric substantially in the direction of such a convergence. See, for example, Japan Communist Party, "Editorial: North Korea's 'Brinkmanship' Brings Instability into Asia," *Akahata*, June 25, 2006.

86. Upper House Main Session, July 14, 2009.

87. Ministry of Defense (MOD), "National Defense Program Guidelines for FY 2011 and Beyond," Tokyo, 2010, https://www.mod.go.jp/e/d_act/d_policy/pdf/summaryFY2011.pdf.

88. Lower House Main Session, January 30, 2013.

89. For discussion, see Takemasa Ando, *Japan's New Left Movements: Legacies for Civil Society* (London: Routledge, 2014), 146–52.

90. Many of the party's leading Diet members were formerly affiliated with the LDP or DPJ. The party disbanded in 2014.

91. Security Committee, March 10, 2017.

92. Lower House Main Session, November 20, 2017.

93. Toshimitsu Shigemura, "Nihonteki orientarizumu to kokusai kankei" [Japanese Orientalism and International Relations], *Waseda Asian Review* 9 (2011): 24–29.

94. Tom O'Connor, "North Korea Says Japan Wants War in 2018 as Both Gather New, More Powerful Weapons," *Newsweek*, December 27, 2017, https://www.yahoo.com/news/north-korea-says-japan-wants-211245504.html.

95. "Comparison Results of World Military Strengths: Military Power Comparison Results for Japan vs. North Korea," *Global Firepower*, 2018, https://www.globalfirepower.com/countries-comparison-detail.asp?form=form&country1=japan&country2=north-korea&Submit=COMPARE.

96. MOD, "The Guidelines for Japan-U.S. Defense Cooperation," Tokyo, 2015, http://www.mod.go.jp/e/d_act/anpo/shishin_20150427e.html.

97. Motoko Rich, "North Korea's Threat Pushes Japan to Reassess its Might and Rights," *New York Times*, September 15, 2017, 3.

98. Ishiba Shigeru, *Nippon o torimodosu. Kenpō o torimodosu* [Take Back Japan. Take Back the Constitution] (Tokyo: PHP Kenkyusho, 2013).

99. Kyodo, "Japan Holds First-Ever Evacuation Drill Simulating North Korean Missile Strike into Waters Nearby," *Japan Times*, March 17, 2017, https://www.japantimes.co.jp/news/2017/03/17/national/japan-holds-first-ever-evacuation-drill-simulating-north-korean-missile-strike-waters-nearby/. These drills were continued until December 2017; Kyodo, "Fukuoka conducts J-Alert drill to brace

for North Korean missile launch," *Japan Times*, December 1, 2017, https://www.japantimes.co.jp/news/2017/12/01/national/fukuoka-conducts-j-alert-drill-brace-north-korean-missile-launch/.

100. Prime Minister of Japan and His Cabinet, "Press Conference by the Chief Cabinet Secretary," April 21, 2017, https://japan.kantei.go.jp/tyoukanpress/201704/21_a.html.

101. "Northern Japan Wakes up to 'J-Alert' as N. Korean Missile Flies Over Japan," *Mainichi*, August 29, 2017, https://mainichi.jp/english/articles/20170829/p2a/00m/0na/014000c.

102. Justin McCurry, " 'Duck and Cover': In Japan, North Korean Missile Alerts are Becoming a Fact of Life," *Guardian*, September 15, 2017, https://www.theguardian.com/world/2017/sep/15/duck-and-cover-in-japan-north-korea-missile-alerts-becoming-fact-of-life.

103. For an example see Handa, *"Kitachōsen kyōi."*

104. "North Korea: US, Japan Step Up Cooperation in Face of Nuclear Threat," *Asian Correspondent* August 18, 2017, https://asiancorrespondent.com/2017/08/north-korea-us-japan-step-cooperation-face-nuclear-threat/.

105. Upper House Main Session, December 5, 2017.

106. Motoko Rich, "Japan Worries It'll Be Forgotten as Its Allies Talk to North Korea," *New York Times*, April 25, 2018, https://www.nytimes.com/2018/04/25/world/asia/japan-north-korea-talks.html.

107. Wada, *Abe Shushō*.

108. Yuki Nikaido, "Abe's Speech Omits 'Pressure' in Referring to North Korea," *Asahi Shimbun*, September 26, 2018, http://www.asahi.com/ajw/articles/AJ2018092 60032.html.

109. Kyodo, "Abe Determined to Seek Unconditional Talks with Kim: Spokesman," *Mainichi*, May 7, 2019, https://mainichi.jp/english/articles/20190507/p2g/00m/0na/057000c.

Chapter 10

"The World Is Marveling at Japan!"

Japanese Strategies to Avoid its "Crisis of Confidence"

SHOGO SUZUKI

Introduction[1]

In 2017, a minor controversy erupted in Japan over a patriotic poster produced by the Association of Shinto Shrines (Jinja Honchō), which is frequently associated with conservative lobby groups with links to the ruling Liberal Democratic Party (LDP). Originally issued in 2011 to encourage Japanese citizens to fly the national flag on national holidays, the poster showed a woman smiling, with the caption "How lucky I am to be Japanese" (*Watashi Nihonjin de yokatta*). The rising sun of the Japanese flag was in the background, and even the blusher on the woman's cheeks was based on the symbol.[2]

Apart from asking citizens to fly the national flag, the poster was clearly designed to impress Japanese people that they were a very special nation, and that it was a privilege to be part of this exceptional community. However, there were red faces all around when it emerged that the model posing in the poster was actually Chinese. In recent years, conservative nationalists in Japan have been anxious that Japan is in decline relative to China and South Korea, and thus losing its status as leading state of Asia and in the world. They have attempted to halt Japan's decline by producing a patriotic, unified nation that is not overawed by its neighbors, and the irony that they had inadvertently used a Chinese model to propagate their message was not lost on Japanese citizens.

This incident also occurred in the context of a broader trend among certain political forces that seek to reinforce the notion of Japan as a great country. This is partly linked to a long-standing concern that Japanese citizens do not love their country enough and fail to sacrifice themselves for the collective. There is also an underlying sense of insecurity that Japan—facing multiple issues of a contracting economy and a rapidly aging society—is being surpassed by its neighbors. Japan has, since the late nineteenth century, been a—if not *the*—great power of Asia. In 2011, however, Japan was overtaken by the People's Republic of China (PRC) as the world's second largest economy. The days of its "economic miracle" seem a distant memory. Worse still, as China's and South Korea's importance in the international community increased, Japan found itself on the back foot when faced with repeated Chinese and South Korean criticisms over its alleged lack of contrition for its imperialist past. This led some to perceive, in addition to material decline, a weakening of Japanese moral authority within the international community.[3]

If we are to understand "crisis" as a "politically mediated moment of decisive intervention and structural transformation,"[4] then clearly Japan has yet to suffer from a "crisis." We have not witnessed any moment of decisive intervention and structural transformation, despite some quarters arguing that Japan is facing pervasive state and economic failure. Arguably, the Japanese state has yet to take decisive action, such as beefing up its military capacity to match that of the PRC, adopting radical economic policies designed to escape its long-term economic stagnation, or promoting pro-natal policies that would radically boost childbirth. This could be because this sense of "failure"—"an accumulation or condensation of contradictions"—is not broadly shared (yet) among Japanese citizens.[5] But another reason could be that some quarters of Japan have found some "coping strategies" that serve to deny that Japan is facing imminent decline. It is therefore worth examining the dynamics of how a state and its populace manage to bury their heads in the sand, even if this may ultimately risk "catastrophic equilibria," where "the symptoms of failure are readily apparent and widely perceived, yet no sense of crisis is mobilised and no decisive intervention is made."[6] Not all states intervene to address effectively their accumulated "failures." It is too early to say whether or not the various "failures" that Japan faces will result in a crisis, but the various social dynamics in Japan play a role in deciding how the Japanese state will act in the future. In this chapter I explore one of these dynamics: the generation of somewhat narcissistic narratives that counter the growing anxieties of an impending accumulation of failures.

The Coming Decline of Japan

Japan is a country that has arguably been able to punch above its weight and carve out for itself the identity of a regional great power. The traditional regional hegemon was the Chinese empire. China claimed to be the center of civilization, and its emperor to be the "son of heaven." Polities along China's periphery were deemed culturally inferior. This all changed in the late nineteenth century, when the European international order expanded to East Asia. Transforming itself into a Westernized state, Japan escaped its "inferior" status vis-à-vis China by becoming the first non-European polity to abolish the unequal treaties foisted upon it by the European powers, attaining sovereign equality with the "civilized" European powers. The Japanese also embarked on their own "civilizing missions" to demarcate themselves from "backward" Asia, invading and colonizing Taiwan, and annexing Korea as well. Institutional recognition of Japan's equality with the European great powers came in the form of permanent membership of the Executive Council of the League of Nations, as well as being designated a mandatory power to govern former German colonies in the South Pacific until the latter were deemed to be capable of self-government.

Despite its defeat in World War II and the loss of its empire, Japan was able to regain its status as a regional power by becoming the second largest economy in the world. While it did not become a military power, it became the only Asian member of the G7 group of developed countries. As Iokibe Makoto notes, when the Cold War came to an end,

> Japan held 15 percent of the world's GDP . . . the economic world was a bipolar one between the U.S. and Japan, and to this we could add Europe and call it a tripolar world. While East Asia, including China, was economically rising rapidly, it was not a major presence.[7]

Japan's rise was also confirmed—somewhat ironically—by a growing number of "Japan threat" discourses that saw Japan as the next challenger to American hegemony. "One does not have to argue that Japan is preparing for war," thundered one of the more sensationalist works to emerge around this time. "It is sufficient to note that Japan would be insane not to prepare for war."[8] Such populist discussions spilled over into academic debates as well. International relations scholar Christopher Layne asserted in 1993 that Japan was starting to "develop the capability to gather and analyze politico-military and economic intelligence independently of the United States"—a sure sign of its wish to "acquire the full spectrum of great power capabilities and its desire to seek international recognition of its great power status."[9] Samuel P. Huntington also cautioned against American appeasement of Japan, insinuating that an empowered Japan would seek to overturn American primacy.[10]

Japan's position (actual or perceived) as the next challenger to *Pax Americana* did not last very long, however. The Japanese economic bubble burst in 1991, plunging the country into a long-term recession. Japanese scholars such as Iokibe were left observing that the "speed by which Japan has fallen [since the hubris of the 1980s] is enough to remind one of the Buddhist teaching that everything is evanescent [*shogyō mujō*]."[11] Japan's sense of failure was not limited to economic decline. In addition to the long-term recession, Japan is also facing a long-term demographic problem.[12] The birthrate has remained stubbornly low, and, as life expectancy is increasing, Japan is now one of the most rapidly aging societies in the world. According to Yoshikawa Hiroshi,[13] already 25 percent of the Japanese population is over 65 years old, and the ratio between those of working age (15–64) and the aged (above 65) is projected to reach 1.8:1 by 2030. This could spell the further contraction of the Japanese economy. Other signs of Japan's "stagnation" are already visible in rural areas, where there are a significant number of dwindling, isolated communities inhabited almost exclusively by elderly people that are destined to become extinct once their remaining members pass away.

If these phenomena are internal indicators of decline, changes in the international environment have served as external signs for Japan's diminishing strength. The contracting economy and demographic problems, as well as the political constraints epitomized by Article 9 of the postwar constitution, have limited Japan's capacity to play a proactive role in Asia-Pacific security affairs and beyond. This has prompted its key ally, the United States, to openly question whether or not Japan desires "to continue to be a tier-one nation, or is she content to drift into tier-two status."[14] Most important was the rise of Japan's neighbors China and, perhaps to a lesser extent, the Republic of Korea (ROK). The economically rising China enjoys political privileges as a great power (such as a permanent seat in the UN Security Council), and has substantially increased its military spending. The Japanese have little chance of matching the PRC's military power. With its aging and declining population, Japan's ability to increase its military personnel is limited. While population size in itself is not necessarily a problem with regard to military power, Japan's aging population has shrunk its tax base and increased social security spending. This, coupled with Japan's ballooning national debt, means that funds for military spending are limited.

The relative importance of Japan for the ROK has been in long-term decline, too. South Korea has enjoyed strong economic growth and a growing international presence. Since its democratization in the late 1980s and the ending of the Cold War, the ROK's international standing has rapidly improved, and its foreign relations have become diversified and less dependent on the US and Japan. Globalization has also reduced the costs of interacting with distant countries, further diminishing Japan's influence.[15] Meanwhile, the ROK's economy is fast catching up with that of Japan. In 1960, Japan boasted a GDP per capita three times that of South Korea. In 2019, however, this gap had shrunk, with Japan's GDP per capita only 1.26 times that of its Korean neighbor.[116] South Korea also competes successfully with Japan in producing goods such as cars and televisions, which were once considered the latter's forte.

Consequently, both the PRC and the ROK have become less hesitant in challenging Japan with regard to political disputes that were previously swept under the carpet for the sake of stable bilateral relations. Japan has thus become increasingly embroiled in bitter arguments over the interpretation of its imperialist past ("the history issue," usually known in Japanese as *rekishi ninshiki mondai*), as well as territorial disputes over Takeshima/Dokdo Island and the Senkaku/Diaoyu Islands. The message of Japan's diminishing international influence is not lost on the Japanese. As Iokibe notes,

In September 2010, a Chinese fishing boat rammed a Japanese patrol boat in the waters surrounding the [disputed] Senkaku Islands . . . two months later, Russian President Medvedev landed on the Northern Territories [claimed by Japan]. In August 2012, South Korean President Lee Myung-bak landed on [the contested] Takeshima Island. Such behavior is unthinkable between states that share a forward-looking bilateral relationship. Even if friendly relations do not exist, if there were some sense of fear or respect towards Japan, this would not have happened. The twenty-year recession and the resulting fall of Japan's international presence has played a part in this.[17]

Coping with Decline

But how can this "fall of Japan's international presence" be halted? Changes in national fortunes can give rise to the perception that the state is facing a growing number of failures. Ready examples of fears of "national decline" can be found in the United States, which has a powerful sense of exceptionalism that entitles it to lead the world, but nevertheless goes through almost cyclical periods of anxiety over its decline.[18] The rise and fall of the "Japan threat" thesis in the late 1980s and early 1990s is a case in point. More recently, Japan's place has been taken over by China, and Americans are now fretting over the "China threat" and the decline of the US.[19]

While it is noted that "the gradual accumulation of unresolved contradictions and steering problems and the eventual precipitation of a fully-fledged condition of state and economic failure" are "liable to be narrated as a structural crisis of the state regime,"[20] this may not be inevitable. In the case where a state's perceived "decline" has the potential to be seen as "failure," there are a number of strategies that can be followed in order to cope with this. The first is to accept this "decline," but then take measures to address the shortcomings that are causing it. If this takes place in the absence of a crisis, this is known as a "conjunctural mode of political rationality."[21] The second is to simply accept this decline and make a virtue out of it. The third is to deny outright that any "decline" has taken place, insist that all indicators for one's greatness remain intact, and take measures to discredit all discourses that point to the state's "decline." The fourth response is to accept some aspects of "decline" but nevertheless look for alternative social markers of "greatness," and claim one's identity on this basis (put simply, "new wine, old bottles"). The last three responses are, to varying degrees, coping strategies that deny the existence of problems that are causing the decline of the state. When faced with narratives of its own decline/weakness, the state acts agilely to acknowledge that the perimeters of its past greatness have indeed been eroded. However, a new identity narrative of greatness is expressed through another trait that is constructed as positively exceptional. Although greatness is lost in one area, it can be resurrected and secured in other regards. The state may therefore "decline" temporarily, but by constructing a new identity narrative, it can secure its previous image of "greatness"—however temporarily—once more.[22]

These are of course ideal types, and in practice we can expect a variety of strategies to be deployed at the same time. The US, for instance, relies on a number of coexisting strategies. Joseph S. Nye's 1990 thesis of "soft power," which was written in the context when "half the [American] public believe[d] the country [was] in decline" faced with a rising Japan,[23] can be interpreted as a coping strategy that accepts that even though the US may be "less powerful at the end of the twentieth century than it was in 1945,"[24] it had a non-material power—soft power—to maintain its pre-eminence. Here, Nye accepts a degree of American decline, but nevertheless suggests that a state's "greatness" no longer lies in military power alone. He then looks for an alternative, non-material power that the US is believed to have abundance, and claims greatness on the basis of this alternative social marker. This agenda becomes clearer when Nye concludes that the "United States retains more traditional hard power resources than any other country. It also has the soft ideological and institutional resources to preserve its lead in the new domains of transnational interdependence."[25] G. John Ikenberry, on the other hand, seems to adopt a coping strategy close to "denial." His main thesis is that the US has constructed a highly institutionalized, stable international order based on liberal principles that not only makes the US exercise strategic restraint, but also gives non-hegemonic states a stake in this order. As a result, Ikenberry argues that the interests of the world essentially coincide with those of the United States.[26] As Richard K. Betts puts it, "The United States is daddy, but the world is one big happy family, gratefully educated and disciplined by his standards of proper behavior."[27]

Japan's Coping Strategies

Japan's national identity has long been split between those who wanted Japan to remain a pacifist state with a relatively isolationist/insular foreign policy and those who wished for Japan to regain greater strategic and political prestige and autonomy and regain its position as a "great power" in the more traditional (military) sense.[28] For the former, talks of Japan's "decline" are arguably not a pressing political issue, and one could argue that for this group, the strategy of "accepting" Japan's decline is not necessarily an unattractive option, provided that the economy is robust enough to alleviate social problems such as unemployment or domestic poverty.

For the latter, however, Japan's economic stagnation or Chinese and South Korean challenges to Japanese territorial claims are all signs of a failure to protect Japan's claim to great power status. The problem is that Japan does not have the luxury of being able to possess a massive military force like the US or China. Furthermore, given its shrinking economy, it is difficult to adopt the tactic of outright denial to shore up the belief of Japan's "greatness"—often expressed by terms such as "the first-rate country in Asia" (*ajia no ittōkoku*) or "economic great power" (*keizai taikoku*)—along traditional lines of military and/or economic might. Instead, the main focus of Japan's coping strategy seems to be mainly to look for alternative sources of "greatness" that do not rely on economic prowess alone. This strategy of relying on alternative markers of "greatness" has been used frequently in Japan at times of an identity crisis. In the context of the 1930s, Japan's increasing international alienation for its invasion of China, coupled with the vetoing of the Racial Equality Clause in the 1919 Versailles Peace Conference, had given rise to the suspicion that Japan had never been (and would never be) accepted as a great power equal to the Western powers because its ethnic makeup was not White. This came as a shock to many Japanese, who had believed that Japan had achieved equality with the other "great powers" in the international community through the fulfilling of the "standard of civilization" and the abolition of the unequal treaties, only to see this status withdrawn because they were seen as inferior Asians.[29]

As a result, attempts were made in some quarters to claim "greatness" on the basis of something that the peoples of the West (i.e., Europeans and North American Caucasians) did not possess: hairless bodies. In a special issue of the journal *Hinode* entitled "Shining in the World: This is Japan's Greatness" published in 1933, Adachi Buntarō, an anatomist at the prestigious Kyoto Imperial University, wrote in an essay titled "The Japanese Body that is Superior to the Foreign Body" (*Gaijin ni suguru Nipponjin no karada*):

> Animals are furry. Humankind has shed its fur as it has evolved. When we compare Westerners and Japanese, which is hairy though? It is shocking to see how hairy Westerners are: not only are they hairy on the arms and legs, but also the chest and back. When one sees this, we feel a sense of pride, and think: "Westerners haven't shed their hair enough, that means they are closer to animals than us!" It becomes tempting to show off our [hairless] Japanese bodies to them.[30]

In the post–World War II world, however, overt expressions of racial superiority based on physical attributes have become taboo. One cannot claim "greatness" on the basis of lesser body hair, and neither does it help that the "hairy" Westerners managed to inflict a humiliating military defeat on Japan in 1945. Contemporary proponents of Japan's "greatness" have had to look elsewhere for alternative sources of "greatness" that would halt the perception that Japan is in "decline."

Discovering Japanese "Soft Power"

One particular coping strategy that has been embraced enthusiastically by the Japanese is the use of the concept of "soft power." As noted above, with the US in mind, the notion of "soft power" was arguably coined to highlight alternative sources of "greatness." It is thus not particularly surprising that it has been a readily available source for inspiration to resurrect Japan's "greatness." As noted by Alexander Bukh, soft power has "created an important caveat in the context of the ever-growing literature on China's rise and Japan's decline, by suggesting that . . . Japan's power and influence are not limited to its economy."[31] By using soft power effectively, it was believed, Japan could "enhance its political influence, counter the rising influence of China, and generate a political power shift in Asia and beyond,"[32] and mark the "return to its rightful place: a country not just respected but also loved."[33]

Within official circles, Japan's soft power is argued to emanate from its liberal democratic values,[34] foreign policy (particularly Overseas Development Aid and participation in peacekeeping operations),[35] and culture (traditional and popular).[36] Political values and an "attractive" foreign policy are certainly useful sources to claim superior "soft power" vis-à-vis the PRC, which has persistently challenged Japan's sense of superiority. With China being a one-party authoritarian state holding an unsavory record of human rights abuses, Tokyo has increasingly sought to highlight its credentials as a liberal democracy whenever it is embroiled in a diplomatic dispute with the PRC. Such moves may also enjoy a certain degree of domestic resonance, given that fears of Japan's economic failure and decline have resulted in anti-Chinese (and anti-Korean) nationalist emotion in certain quarters.[37] Japan's morally superior political system and values therefore allow Japan to take a leading role within Asia and the global order, thus resisting the notion that its power and influence are on the wane. Such thinking was clearly visible in initiatives such as the "Arc of Freedom and Prosperity" among liberal democracies in the Asia-Pacific region.[38]

This theme has continued to this day. Shortly after his second inauguration as prime minister, Abe Shinzō launched the concept of an Asian "democratic security diamond" consisting of Japan, the US, Australia, and India as a means to contain the rising power of China. Crucially, Japan was positioned "as one of the oldest sea-faring democracies in Asia" and that it "should play a greater role . . . in preserving the common good in both regions."[39] There was a clear—albeit indirect—aspiration to deny China a leading role in the regional politics of the Asia-Pacific. The more recent "Free and Open Indo-Pacific Strategy" similarly makes references to "universal values as freedom, democracy, and the rule of law" that Japan possesses.[40] Again, this form of soft power was seen as something that could be used to bring Southeast Asian and South Asian states to Japan's side in its attempts to counter China's growing influence in the region.

Claiming Soft Power through Uniqueness: Dealing with the Korea "Threat"

Japan's fears of decline, however, do not appear to have been dispelled by its claims to be the upholder of universalistic values of liberal democracy and human rights, despite their potential efficacy against China. Part of the reasons for this is related to the rise of South Korea, with whom Japan has had a difficult relationship because of its history of colonizing the Korean peninsula.[41] Since its democratization in the late 1980s, the ROK has established itself fully as a member of the liberal democratic camp. Japan therefore cannot demarcate itself from, and claim superiority over, South Korea on the basis of universal liberal democratic values. As Bukh notes, "Japan's embrace of Western-style liberal democracy has constrained its ability to assign any normative values to its culture besides those associated with the West."[42] Given that the same dynamic will apply to South Korea, it becomes harder to differentiate Japan from South Korea and claim "greatness" or "superiority" on this basis.

     In addition, South Korea's persistent criticism of Japan's lack of contrition for the historical wrongs it committed toward the Korean people poses a threat to Japan's attempts to claim "greatness" on the basis of "universal values." In particular, the "comfort women" issue, which refers to the imperial Japanese military's abuse of women during World War II, has proved to be highly damaging to Japan's global image, and with it, to its soft power.[43] The "comfort women" issue has been framed by South Korea as an issue pertaining to broader universal women's rights, and this serves to highlight (regardless of whether or not this is actually the case) the moral failure on the part of the Japanese state to redress this wrongdoing. Japan has thus found itself facing criticisms from a broader international audience, and this has the potential to damage the basis for Japan's claim to possessing sufficient soft power that can make up for its decline in the economic realm.

So how can Japan overcome the "Korea threat" to its soft power, which is so critical for halting its perceived "decline"? Part of the answer—provided primarily by the government—has been to claim that the country boasts significant global attraction for its culture. Claims by foreign observers that "from pop music to consumer electronics, architecture to fashion, and food to art, Japan has far greater cultural influence now than it did in the 1980s, when it was an economic superpower" have undoubtedly spurred this move.[44] While it is difficult to ascertain if the Japanese political elite conceives the competition for soft power in zero-sum terms, South Korea's success in popular culture (as epitomized by the global hit of "Gangnam Style") is also said to have "stirred neighboring countries including Japan to extend their cultural diplomacy activities, thereby contributing to the soft power competition that has been intensifying across the whole of East Asia."[45] Consequently, the Japanese government has recently spent US$883 million to promote Japanese creative industries, and also sponsored an international *manga* (comic) prize. Moreover, demonstrating Tokyo's seriousness in boosting Japan's soft power, Prime Minister Abe appointed Inada Tomomi as minister in charge of "Cool Japan." Inada subsequently made appearances dressed " 'as a GothLoli,' or 'Gothic Lolita,' in the fashion of the iconic teens of Harajuku."[46]

However, placing one's eggs in the basket of creative arts is a risky business. For a start, it is questionable as to whether politicians can serve as effective ambassadors for "Cool Japan" to promote Japanese soft power. Inada, for instance, is known for her sympathies to conservative political groups who espouse historical revisionism. She has taken part in rallies that question the narratives surrounding the Nanjing Massacre,[47] which sends out an image that is far from "cool" and damages Japan's international image. Japanese artists can send out messages that are critical of Japan, and at odds with the government's agenda, too. Some are also reluctant to being recruited for state-sponsored attempts to promote Japanese soft power, and it was reported that "Takashi Murakami, a famous artist and sculptor, begged the government last year [2013] to stop inviting him to its events."[48] Furthermore, Japan faces a tough battle for soft power based on popular culture, because the ROK is also a formidable rival for soft power derived from cultural products: Korean dramas and K-pop boy and girl bands have been hugely popular in Asia and beyond.

Consequently, much effort has been put into looking for culture that is considered uniquely "Japanese" (and therefore inaccessible to Korea or China) and claiming "greatness" on the basis of these qualities. Such thinking was reflected in an official publication entitled *Sekai ga odoroku Nippon!* (The Japan that Impresses the World!), produced by the Ministry of Economy, Trade and Industry (METI), which has taken "the lead in [cultural policy] by establishing the Cool Japan promotion office in June 2010."[49] Japan, the publication stated, has a "Brand" based on the "idea of Japan's traditional sensitivity and values, continuing on through the generations." Moreover, this "spirit is unique to the Japanese people, to get close, sympathize, cooperate, and act in harmony with others. And this individuality is cultivated by Japan's abundant nature."[50] The publication declares that this results in the production of world-renowned artisanal products of high quality, an almost obsessive pursuit for perfection, and an ability to show respect and consideration for others. This spirit allegedly comes from the way the Japanese live in harmony with nature (*wa*). The METI pamphlet proceeds to produce a convoluted, vague argument asserting that Japanese pursue this *wa* "by unifying their mind (inner nature), environment (outer nature), and body."[51] This process, called *michi*, can allegedly be observed to this day. Blithely ignoring the bullying, physical violence, and overworking of schoolchildren that have dogged Japanese extracurricular activities (particularly in sports), the pamphlet states,

> For example, boys and girls engaged in school club activities go all out in their practice, and even more importantly, they do so with manners, taught by coaches and trainers. The spirit of *michi* underlies this approach of training that goes beyond mere improvement of skills. . . . The spirit of *michi* still survives within the DNA of Japanese people on a subconscious level.[52]

Of course, there are plenty of other states that are known for both their natural beauty and high-quality products, and one would think that respect and consideration for others is a quality highly prized and cultivated in other cultures; however, this does not seem to be the case. One of the reasons highlighted in the METI pamphlet is that the Japanese brain is somehow wired differently from those of foreigners. This allows Japanese to live and appreciate harmony in a very unique way. Non-Japanese, according to this publication, hear the sound of insects using the right brain just as they listen to the sound of music or machinery or some random noise, whereas Japanese speakers listen to the sound of insects using the left brain. This unique brain structure that interprets "sound" as "voice" has enabled Japanese people to listen to subtle changes in the natural environment and create abundant linguistic expressions.[53]

The implication is that, due to these biological attributes that can only be found in Japanese people, only the Japanese are able to live in perfect harmony with nature, and this allows them to cultivate the qualities that make their products great, and create a national psyche characterized by respect and courtesy toward others.

At this point, one cannot help but draw parallels with the aforementioned prewar claim about the superiority of the Japanese people based on supposedly unique physical attributes of being less hairy than "Westerners." In similar fashion to its prewar counterpart, the discourse on display in the METI pamphlet is full of sweeping ethnocentric claims based on rather dubious assertions that are hardly going to be taken seriously internationally. While the pamphlet tries to overcome this by listing positive appraisals of Japan by foreigners (interestingly, Westerners are quoted by name, while Asians are merely quoted as "foreign students"), the main thrust of the argument is decidedly inward-looking, and (despite the fact that it is also written in English) seems more like a narcissistic discourse of "compensation for greatness" that is targeted to a Japanese audience.

National Narcissism as a Coping Strategy for "Greatness"

Fears of "national decline" are a pervasive sentiment shared by "Japanese writers, officials, and academics," who often talk about Japan's "lost decades."[54] Economic stagnation, "reports of crime and disorder, concerns about longer-term demographic challenges, and representations of the experiences of a new generation of young people with shaky job prospects and precarious economic circumstances" have produced a sentiment that Japan "in the 1990s and 2000s was not the future Japan imagined back in the 1960s, 1970s, and 1980s, when people were encouraged to believe that Japan's future would be better, richer, and more successful that its past."[55] But beyond these concerns, there also exists frustration toward Japan's so-called "economic giant, political pygmy" status that has long been held by conservative revisionists. Their frustrations and fears of Japanese decline have taken on an increasing sense of urgency because of Japan's economic stagnation and the rise of China and South Korea.

Japan's conservative revisionists believe that Japan has been not only militarily stifled through the constitution and US–Japan Security Treaty, but also placed under American spiritual occupation since 1945.[56] They have called for constitutional change and radical social change to reintroduce traditional Japanese values to counteract the rampant individualism that has influenced postwar Japan. They have also sought to revise the historical narrative of modern Japanese history, which they claim depicts Japan unfairly as an aggressor. This group has an additional concern that is not always shared by all of the political/intellectual elite: the fear of Japan's moral standing in the international community declining, and the idea that Japan has been forced to maintain an artificially low international profile by the Allies ever since the end of World War II. Nowadays, China and South Korea, the two states most vocal about Japan's historical wrongdoing, are seen as the main protagonists of this anti-Japan conspiracy.[57] As such, the latter two's attempts to further besmirch the honor of the Japanese state are—as can be seen from the *Sankei Shimbun's* use of words such as "the history wars" (*rekishi-sen*)—understood as something that needs to be vigorously combated.

Given the various fiscal and demographic constraints noted above, there seems to be very little scope for Japan to rearm itself and become a "political giant" to make up for its loss of economic power. Furthermore, despite the rising military threat from China, the Japanese public has shown limited enthusiasm for rapid rearmament independent of the US–Japan Security Alliance, making the realization of the conservative revisionists' dream of "greatness" politically difficult. The latter are also limited in their ability to appeal to "greatness" on the basis of "universal" values such as democracy and respect for human rights. This is because of their historical revisionism,[58] which includes the refusal to acknowledge the past abuse of women as "comfort women" or the Nanjing Massacre.[59] This denial of Japanese wrongdoing is deeply connected to conservative revisionists' agenda of restoring Japan's honor that is being sullied by China and South Korea. However, given that the Japanese government has officially accepted wrongdoing in the San Francisco Peace Treaty, and has not denied the existence of the Nanjing Massacre or the "comfort women" issue, such discourses cannot gain much traction. While the appeal to democratic values and respect for human rights may have some resonance in any propaganda aimed at China, it will not work against the ROK, which is also a liberal democracy. Instead, the denial of Japanese war crimes is more likely to be seen as fundamentally reactionary and antithetical to the respect of human rights. This means that conservative revisionists' attempts to protect Japan's "greatness" by appealing to "universal values" have fallen flat.

Conservative revisionists have therefore increasingly turned to inward-looking discourses that have a decidedly narcissistic undertone to them. Such sentiments, which have "an inflated view of the importance and deservedness of one's own nation," have been dubbed as "national narcissism" by Huajian Cai and Peter Gries.[60] In the case of the Japanese conservative revisionists' "national narcissism," the emphasis is on Japanese uniqueness making the country great. Satō Yoshinao, for instance, states that even though Japan may appear to be in the economic doldrums, the rest of the world will soon wake up to the unique qualities that make Japan stand out from the rest, and they will copy Japanese ways of doing things. This will mean the restoration of Japan's importance in the world. Satō, who interestingly departs from the narrative of "uniqueness" espoused in the METI pamphlet, argues that all countries

> will pursue quality over quantity once they become a developed country. Japan is ahead of the pack in terms of specializing in making things of high quality. Once you start chasing after a quality life, you will inevitably meet Japan. . . . All nations will encounter Japan once they start pursuing quality. This is why "the world will Japanize."[61]

If one were to accept this argument, it would most certainly be worthwhile knocking on Japan's door to find out what one could learn from Japan and get oneself "Japanized" as soon as possible. However, there appear to be some tough barriers to achieving this goal, because the qualities required to "Japanize" seem to be so unique to Japan that only the Japanese can attain it. Satō claims that the reasons for Japan's success are the Japanese people's abilities to think about the "bigger picture," "the collective good," and their "capacity to act for the collective."[62] This is only possible because the Japanese have allegedly lived in a "stable and continuous agrarian, settled society" (*nōkō teijū gata no antei keizoku shakai*). Collective action was essential in agriculture (particularly during times of planting and harvesting), and egoistic behavior would be punished by social isolation.[63] In contrast, in a hunting society (which Satō effectively conflates with "the West"), those with "good eyes and quick athletic skills" were prized, and, given the difficulty of storing meat for a long time, emphasis was placed on short-term, immediate gains. This mentality is reflected in Western ways of running enterprises.

Given that the historical background of one's society's development is (mysteriously) passed down through generations without intervening external influences, it seems almost impossible for Westerners, with their hunter backgrounds, to "Japanize." Satō seems to insinuate this when he argues that Japan's success has aroused intense jealousy among Westerners, who have conspired to prevent Japan from becoming great again. He claims that "Western ways" of management—with their criticisms of "Japanese" ways of collective decision-making and lifelong employment—were forced on the Japanese by Westerners. The Japanese were naïve enough to embrace Western ways of doing things, and this has resulted in Japan's economic stagnation.[64]

The quest for "Japanese greatness" has even extended to the animal world. In his book *Sensei, Nippontte sugoi ne* (Teacher, Isn't Japan Wonderful)—which comes with a glowing recommendation by former Education Minister Nakayama Nariaki—Hattori Takeshi sees Japanese honeybees epitomizing the qualities of the Japanese nation. Whereas Western honeybees are unable to withstand a hornet's attack,[65] Japanese honeybees are able to ward off these predators. How is this done? Hattori asserts that the Japanese honeybees "fight in a *very Japanese way.*"[66] They typically swarm the hornet, creating a bee cluster. The rising inner temperature of the bee cluster effectively roasts the hornets to death. The fact that the honeybees are not available for interview or psychological analysis to confirm if they have the Japanese nation in mind when fighting hornets does not discourage Hattori from identifying a unique national quality of "unity" that is shared by both the Japanese honeybees and the Japanese people. He goes on to state how, in a splendid display of Japanese "unity," passengers on a busy commuter train near Tokyo all helped in the rescue of a woman trapped between the platform and the train. This news is accompanied with claims by foreigners that this would *never* happen in their respective countries; that "Japan has impressed the world again" through its actions; and "this is why Japan is among the top countries."[67]

Another popular theme of the conservative revisionists is to blunt the PRC and ROK's alleged attempts to discredit Japan's status in the international community by emphasizing the moral backwardness of the two states. This is contrasted with Japan's unique qualities that make it stand head and shoulders above China and South Korea. Such claims seem to be regarded as even more credible if they come from individuals with non-Japanese backgrounds. Shi Ping (Seki Hei), a former Chinese national who is now a naturalized Japanese citizen and the conservative revisionists' favorite critic of China, posted on social media a photo of a sign calling on hotel guests not to kill any insects that have entered the room (and whose sounds, we may recall, the Japanese allegedly hear very differently), and stated, "I do not think that the Japanese, who cherish the lives of insects, will kill hundreds of thousands of civilians in another country. The so-called 'Nanjing Massacre' must surely be a fabrication."[68] Such claims are no doubt aimed at combating the "anti-Japan conspiracy" that seeks to weaken Japan's moral authority and international standing.

Another foreign citizen who has had a significant impact in debates of Japan's greatness is Kent Gilbert. His book *Jukyō ni shihai sareta Chūgokujin to Kankokujin no higeki* (The Tragedy of the Chinese and Koreans, Who Are Trapped in Confucianism) has been a national bestseller. The book's general thrust is to portray the Chinese and Korean people as immoral and selfish due to their inability to escape the pernicious influences of Confucianism. Gilbert goes as far as claiming that recent research had revealed that "there are big differences between the DNA of Chinese, Koreans, and Japanese."[69] Despite this assertion, Gilbert believes that cultural difference is what accounts for Japan's uniqueness, and makes them morally superior to the Chinese and Koreans. While the Japanese may also have been influenced by Confucianism at some point in their history, they allegedly only absorbed the best parts, and fused it with indigenous traditions to invent a new normative code, *bushidō*, or the way of the samurai. This apparently made Japan different from China or Korea, who are, to this day, unable to shake off the shackles of Confucianism. Ignoring the rather obvious point that all states in East Asia have, to different degrees, absorbed a wide variety of cultures and ideologies (such as Buddhism, liberalism, or communism), Gilbert goes on to argue that Japan's unique culture, coupled with the unique tradition of valuing harmony and the uninterrupted existence of the imperial family, has created a nation with qualities such as "endurance" and "self-sacrifice."[70] It is because of this, Gilbert asserts, that scandals such as the 2014 "nut rage incident"—where the vice president of Korean Air threw a tantrum for not being served nuts on a plate and ordered the aircraft she was boarding to turn back to the gate and eject the offending flight attendant—are unthinkable in Japan.[71] Such discourses are part and parcel of the conservative nationalists' attempts to discredit the moral standing of the PRC and (particularly) the ROK, and address their own fears that Japan's normative standing is in decline because of persistent attempts by the two states to dredge up the "history issue" and dishonor the Japanese state.

Conclusion

An increasing fear that the West is in decline has resulted in discourses that remind the people of the "greatness" of one's country. In the US, President Trump's catchphrase was (and continues to be) "Make America Great Again." In the UK, those who have been campaigning for a complete severing of institutional links between Britain and the European Union argue that Brexit will result in the emergence of a global, powerful, and independent nation that represents a truly "Great" Britain. In the case of the latter, one can often observe thinly veiled references to the age of Empire, where Britain established itself as a powerful trading nation, taking advantage of its "splendid isolation" from the European continent.

In this chapter I have suggested that there are a number of potential avenues by which a state can deal with its "decline": acceptance; initial acceptance and correction (to restore "greatness"); outright denial of decline; and partial acceptance of decline followed by a search for alternative markers of "greatness." Although it is likely that all strands of coping strategies are used simultaneously in most states, in Japan, the emphasis has been on the last option. This is dictated by Japan's own circumstances. Richard Ned Lebow, while acknowledging the importance of non-material factors, noted that "for the time being great power status is still based on the combination of economic power and military might."[72] The political constraints Japan faces mean that seeking greatness through military power is not an option. Furthermore, the sheer size of the China market and its workforce means that matching the PRC's economic power is looking increasingly unviable for Japan, with its rapidly aging and shrinking population.

The key alternative marker of greatness that has been utilized by Japan is "soft power," as it has emphasized its credentials as a liberal democracy with close relations to the West, as well as its unique cultural attributes that make the "rest of the world" marvel at Japan. It is interesting that there is considerable emphasis on the latter, even among the political elite, despite the fact that the often-narcissistic undertones of "Japanese uniqueness" likely do not have broad international appeal. If we are to accept that a state's status of "greatness" needs external recognition by other members of the international community, claims of greatness based on how one hears the calls of insects or the behavior of indigenous honeybees are hardly going to be taken seriously. Unfortunately for METI, their pamphlet extolling the "greatness" of Japan came under ridicule even by the supposedly "great" Japanese people themselves. Netizens came up with scathing comments about it, stating that the pamphlet was "decidedly uncool and un-Japanese to praise yourself as cool" or "you can tell we're on the decline when we start doing things like this." The section on Japanese hearing was derided as a "neuromyth" that was an "embarrassment that should not be aired to the whole world."[73]

Why, then, would Japan choose to claim "greatness" on seemingly narcissistic narratives that have limited international resonance and cannot "provide Japan with any sense of direction in the international realm" or "function as an ideational basis for Japan's cultural diplomacy?"[74] It seems that part of the answer lies in long-standing tensions within debates on Japan's national identity. Bukh has noted that "the choice and form of communication strategies, which are the main tools of exercising soft power, will depend on the socially constructed view of reality that the wielder of soft power holds—in other words, its identity."[75] While Japan's use of its identity as a liberal democracy may make it morally "superior" to the PRC, this tactic cannot differentiate Japan from other liberal democracies. The rise of South Korea as an established liberal democracy only heightens fears that reliance on liberal democratic values alone is insufficient, and will only make Japan one among many other states in Asia.[76]

Hence, Japan has turned increasingly toward emphasizing Japanese uniqueness, which has a long-standing tradition within Japanese debates of national identity. Yet the fact that voices extolling the "greatness" of Japan are written mainly in Japanese for a domestic audience perhaps suggests a hidden resignation (even among the conservative nationalists) that claims to greatness no longer carry much international resonance in the context of a rising China. The best that the conservative nationalists can hope for (through the publication of works praising Japan) is to create a populace that will not meekly acquiesce to Chinese power or accept Chinese and Korean attempts to sully Japanese national honor. At the same time, however, the insular nature of these "coping strategies" may also reflect a certain degree of domestic demand for such discourses. Some authors have noted that the growing sense of unease toward Japan's economic failures and the subsequent loss of social security seems to have produced a nationalism that looks for external enemies.[277] There also exists a considerable sense of fatigue toward the seemingly never-ending arguments over the "history issue." Such social dynamics do create a ready domestic market for discourses that "prove" Japan's greatness—even more so if this "greatness" is contrasted to the alleged inferiority of China and South Korea.

It is highly unlikely that Japan can ever regain its previous position as a great power that it enjoyed prior to World War II. Its claims to greatness, while perhaps effective in soothing anxieties of decline to a certain extent within the domestic context, are unlikely to convince the rest of the world, and will have limited effect on the social hierarchies of International Society. With a growing national debt and rapidly shrinking populace, it is questionable as to whether Japan can continue its role as a "civilian power" that provides development aid or contributes to peacekeeping operations to the extent that it does now.[78] It remains to be seen whether or not these accumulative "failures" are seen to be so large that they will trigger a sense of "crisis" which demands intervention. But the general inertia for change currently visible in Japan may suggest that the narcissistic coping strategies are effective to a degree.

Notes

1. The author would like to acknowledge the collaborative research with Linus Hagström that has informed parts of this chapter.

2. The image is available at BBC News Japan, "'Watashi Nihonjin de yokatta'—Posuta o meguru giron futtō" ["How Lucky I am to be Born Japanese": A Heated Controversy over a Poster], *BBC News*, May 12, 2017, https://www.bbc.com/japanese/features-and-analysis-39893086.

3. Iokibe Makoto, *Nippon wa suitai suru no ka* [Will Japan Decline?] (Tokyo: Chikura Shobō, 2014), iv.

4. Colin Hay, "Crisis and the Structural Transformation of the State: Interrogating the Process of Change," *British Journal of Politics and International Relations* 1, no. 3 (1999): 317–344, here 323.

5. Hay, "Crisis," 323.

6. Ibid., 327.

7. Iokibe, *Nippon*, iii.

8. George Friedman and Meredith Lebard, *The Coming War with Japan* (New York: St. Martin's Press, 1991), 12.

9. Christopher Layne, "The Unipolar Illusion: Why New Great Powers Will Rise," *International Security* 17, no. 4 (1993): 5–51, here 37–38.

10. Samuel P. Huntington, "Why International Primacy Matters," *International Security* 17, no. 4 (1993): 68–83, here 76.

11. Iokibe, *Nippon*, iii.

12. See the chapters by Chivacci and Takeda in this volume.

13. Yoshikawa Hiroshi, *Jinkō to Nippon keizai: Chōju, inobeeshon, keizai seichō* [Population and the Japanese Economy: Longevity, Innovation, Economic Growth] (Tokyo: Chūō Kōron Shinsha, 2016).

14. Richard L. Armitage and Joseph S. Nye, *The U.S.-Japan Alliance: Anchoring Stability in Asia* (Washington, DC: Center for Strategic and International Studies, 2012), 1.

15. Kimura Kan, "Ryōdo mondai, ianfu mondai no kōzō wa koerareru no ka?" [Is it Possible to Overcome the Structure of Territorial Disputes and the Comfort Women Issue?], in *Tettei kenshō Kankokuron no tsūsetsu, zokusetsu: Nikkan tairitsu no kanjō vs. riron* [A Thorough Examination of the Mainstream and Popular Explanations of Korea: Emotions vs. Theories of Japan-Korea Disputes], ed. Asaba Yūki, Kimura Kan, and Satō Daisuke (Tokyo: Chūō Kōronsha, 2016), 265–268.

16. Figures calculated from World Bank, March 16 2021, https://data.worldbank.org/indicator/NY.GDP.PCAP.CD.

17. Iokibe, *Nippon*, v.

18. Michael Cox, "Is the United States in Decline—Again? An Essay," *International Affairs* 83, no. 4 (2007): 643–653.

19. Christopher Layne, "This Time it's Real: The End of Unipolarity and the Pax Americana," *International Studies Quarterly* 56, no. 1 (2012): 203–213.

20. Hay, "Crisis," 330.

21. Ibid., 329.

22. See Rebecca Adler-Nissen, "Stigma Management in International Relations: Transgressive Identities, Norms, and Order in International Society," *International Organization* 68, no. 1 (2014): 143–176, here 153.

23. Joseph S. Nye Jr., "Soft Power," *Foreign Policy* 80 (1990): 153–171, here 153.

24. Ibid., 153.

25. Ibid., 171.

26. G. John Ikenberry, *Liberal Leviathan: The Origins, Crisis, and Transformation of the American World Order* (Princeton, NJ: Princeton University Press, 2011).

27. Richard K. Betts, "Institutional Imperialism," *National Interest* 113 (May/June 2011): 85–96, here 88.

28. See Soeya Yoshihide, *Nippon no "midoru pawaa" gaikō: Sengo Nippon no sentaku to kōsō* [Japan's "Middle Power" Diplomacy: The Choices and Visions for Postwar Japan] (Tokyo: Chikuma Shobō, 2005), 17.

29. See Konoe Fumimaro, "Eibei hon'i no heiwashugi o haisu" [Rejecting the Anglo-America-centric pacifism], in *Seidanroku*, ed. Itō Takeshi (Tokyo: Chikura Shobō, 1936), 240–241.

30. Cited in Hayakawa Tadanori, *"Nippon sugoi" no disutopia: Senjika jiga jisan no keifu* [The Dystopia of "Japan is Great": Genealogy of Self-Congratulation during the War] (Tokyo: Seikyūsha, 2016), 21.

31. Alexander Bukh, "Revisiting Japan's Cultural Diplomacy: A Critique of the Agent-Level Approach to Japan's Soft Power," *Asian Perspective* 38, no. 3 (2014): 461–485, here 463.

32. Ibid.

33. David Leheny, *Empire of Hope: The Sentimental Politics of Japanese Decline* (Ithaca, NY: Cornell University Press, 2018), 94.

34. For a discussion of how claims to soft power on the basis of Japan's political values interact with international ideational structures, see Bukh, "Revisiting."

35. See Yamamoto, this volume.

36. See Kurata Yasuo, "Sofuto pawaa no katsuyō to sono kadai: Riron, waga kuni no gensen no jōkyō o fumaete" [The Utilization of Soft Power and Its Challenges: Theory, and Examining the Sources of Soft Power in Japan], *Rippō to chōsa* 320 (September 2011): 119–138; Hanscom Smith, "Toward a Universal Japan: Taking a Harder Look at Japanese Soft Power," *Asia Policy* 15 (January 2013): 115–126, here 119–120.

37. Takahara Motoaki, *Fuan gata nashonarizumu: Nikkanchū no netto sedai nikumiau hontō no riyū* [Nationalism of Anxiety: The Real Reason for the Mutual Hate Between the Japan-Korea-China Internet Generation] (Tokyo: Yōsensha, 2006), 88–89.

38. See Ministry of Foreign Affairs of Japan (MOFA), "Speech by Mr. Taro Aso, Minister for Foreign Affairs on the Occasion of the Japan Institute of International Affairs Seminar: 'Arc of Freedom and Prosperity: Japan's Expanding Diplomatic Horizons,'" November 30, 2006, http://www.mofa.go.jp/announce/fm/aso/speech0611.html, emphasis added. Unless otherwise stated, all online sources were accessed and available on October 10, 2020.

39. See Shinzo Abe, "Asia's Democratic Security Diamond," *Project Syndicate*, December 27, 2012, http://www.project-syndicate.org/commentary/a-strategic-alliance-for-japan-and-india-by-shinzo-abe.

40. MOFA, "Priority Policy for Development Cooperation FY2017," April 2017, https://www.mofa.go.jp/files/000259285.pdf.

41. This section draws on Shogo Suzuki, "Japanese Revisionists and the 'Korea Threat': Insights from Ontological Security," *Cambridge Review of International Affairs* 32, no. 3 (2019): 303–321.

42. Bukh, "Revisiting," 481.

43. See Kimura Kan, *Nikkan rekishi ninshiki mondai to wa nani ka: Rekishi kyōkasho, "ianfu," popyurizumu* [What is the Japan-Korea History Issue: History Textbooks, "Comfort Women," and Populism] (Kyoto: Mineruva Shobō, 2014).

44. Douglas McGray, "Japan's Gross National Cool," *Foreign Policy* 130, no. 1 (November 2009), http://foreignpolicy.com/2009/11/11/japans-gross-national-cool/. See also Warren A. Stanislaus, "Japan House: Tokyo's New Public Diplomacy Push," *Diplomat*, July 22, 2017, https://thediplomat.com/2017/07/japan-house-tokyos-new-public-diplomacy-push/; and Leheny, *Empire of Hope*, 99–107.

45. Koichi Iwabuchi, "Pop-Culture Diplomacy in Japan: Soft Power, National Branding and the Question of 'International Cultural Exchange,'" *International Journal of Cultural Policy* 21, no. 4 (2015): 419–432, here 423. This point is also confirmed by "Squaring the Cool: Japan's Soft Power," *Economist*, June 17, 2014, https://www.economist.com/blogs/banyan/2014/06/japans-soft-power.

46. *Economist*, "Squaring the Cool." The image is available at Livedoor News, "Furansu ni 'ima no Nihon' urikomi, Inada daijin mo gosuri ishō de norinori" [Selling France "the Japan of Today," an Enthusiastic Minister Inada Dressed as GothLoli], *Livedoor News*, September 24, 2013, https://news.livedoor.com/article/detail/8092481/.

47. See " 'Nankin-sen no shinjitsu o tsuikyū suru kai' shūkai Inada Tom-omi moto-bōeisho-ra ga kōen 'Iwarenaki hinan ni danko hanron suru,' " *Sankei Shimbun*, December 14, 2017, http://www.sankei.com/politics/news/171214/plt171 2140010-n1.html.

48. *Economist*, "Squaring the Cool."

49. Iwabuchi, "Pop-Culture Diplomacy," 423; see also Leheny, *Empire of Hope*, 106.

50. Ministry of Economy and Industry (METI), *Sekai ga odoroku Nippon!* [The World is Marveling at Japan!], Tokyo, February 2017, http://www.meti.go.jp/press/2016/03/20170308001/20170308001-1.pdf, 1.

51. Ibid., 37.

52. Ibid.

53. Ibid., 33.

54. Leheny, *Empire of Hope*, 11.

55. Ibid., 12.

56. Mike M. Mochizuki, "Japan's Search for Strategy," *International Security* 8, no. 3 (1983–4): 152–79, here 167; see also Richard J. Samuels, *Securing Japan: Tokyo's Grand Strategy and the Future of East Asia* (Ithaca, NY: Cornell University Press, 2007), 120–23.

57. Suzuki, "Japanese Revisionists," 314.

58. This is not to say that they do not try: see, for instance, Sakurai Yoshiko ed., *Nippon to Indo: Ima musubareru minshushugi kokka: Chūgoku "fūjikome" wa kanō ka* [Japan and India: The Democracies Now Being Joined Together—Is It Possible to "Contain" China?] (Tokyo: Bungei Shunjū, 2012).

59. For instance, Seki Hei, *Chūgokujin no shōtai* [The Real Chinese] (Tokyo: Takarajimasha, 2011), 148.

60. Huajian Cai and Peter Gries, "National Narcissism: Internal Dimensions and International Correlates," *PsyCh Journal* 2, no. 2 (2013): 122–132, here 123.

61. Satō Yoshinao, *Naze sekai wa Nihonka suru no ka* [Why Will the World Japanize] (Tokyo: Ikuhōsha, 2017), 5.

62. Ibid., 87.

63. Ibid., 89.

64. Ibid., 132.

65. Hattori Takeshi, *Sensei, Nippontte sugoi ne* [Teacher, Isn't Japan Wonderful!] (Tokyo: Takagi Shobō, 2015), 222.

66. Ibid., 223, emphasis added.

67. Ibid., 229–233.

68. See @liyonyon, https://twitter.com/liyonyon/status/979852748786028545 ?s=12, posted 6:47 pm, March 30, 2018.

69. Kent Sidney Gilbert, *Jukyō ni shihai sareta Chūgokujin to Kankokujin no higeki* [The Tragedy of the Chinese and the Koreans, Who Are Trapped in Confucianism] (Tokyo: Kōdansha, 2017), 6.

70. Ibid., 140–144.

71. Ibid., 144.

72. Richard Ned Lebow, *A Cultural Theory of International Relations* (Cambridge: Cambridge University Press, 2008), 489.

73. See "Keisanshō kara Nihon zessan hon ga tōjō 'Sekai ga odoroku Nippon!' " [The Ministry of Economy, Trade and Industry Issues a Book Lauding Japan: "The World is Marveling at Japan!"], Excite.co.jp, March 13, 2017, https://www.excite.co.jp/News/smadan/E1489390986586/.

74. Bukh, "Revisiting," 477.

75. Ibid., 465.

76. Ibid., 476.

77. See, for instance, Kayano Toshihito, *Seichō naki jidai no nashonarizumu* [Nationalism under Stagnation] (Tokyo: Kadokawa, 2015), 16–17.

78. Hanns W. Maull, "Germany and Japan: The New Civilian Powers," *Foreign Affairs* 69, no. 5 (1990): 91–106.

Conclusion

Narrating Japan's Crisis, Narrating Japan's Rebirth

SEBASTIAN MASLOW AND CHRISTIAN WIRTH

What Crisis, What Decline?

Japan finds itself at the forefront of dealing with a rapidly aging society, post-disaster recovery, mounting public debt, and tectonic geopolitical shifts. These compound challenges are elevated by the country's struggle against the COVID-19 pandemic. In view of the still-deepening sense that Japan faces an existential crisis, and the ensuing drive to bring about national rejuvenation through a comprehensive overhaul of its social, economic, and political institutions, we started out with the question, "What really is in crisis and declining?" It was our endeavor to gain greater clarity about the problems at hand and the solutions available by distinguishing between "real" failures of social, economic, and political institutions and narrated failures or crises. This clarification allows for an assessment of the policies that have been designed to resolve Japan's problems, and it generates insights into the dynamics of institutional change and the transformation of the Japanese state in historical perspective. Given that Japan has been leading the postwar East Asian development and modernization drive, these findings also contribute to a better understanding of global transformations that sociologists, economists, and political scientists have been debating for some time.[1]

The analyses of "real" failures, narrations of crisis, and concomitant interventions through policy changes in various fields lead us to the conclusion that there has indeed been a discursive process that steered Japan toward a greater unification of the diverse array of independent agencies, apparatuses, and institutions that compose the state. This enhanced agency is most visible in the Liberal Democratic Party's (LDP's) unchallenged rule. Yet, as the contributions to this volume also reveal, the selective identification of crises at specific levels gave rise to numerous piecemeal interventions in the respective policy fields. While these often signify drastic policy changes that deeply affect society, economy, and politics, they do not (yet) amount to the "decisive" interventions that would be required to address the failures that gave rise to the postwar state-in-crisis narrative. To the contrary, despite the fact that writings on the nation's "lost decades,"[2] its "decline" and "collapse,"[3] or "eternal defeat"[4] display a consensus about the existence of an enduring national crisis, these narratives were often employed to stave off fundamental reforms of failing institutions and prevent, or roll back, incipient political change. As such, the net effect of the national crisis meta-narrative has not only been to further the long-standing bipartisan elite project of economic liberalization, but also to cement the LDP's grip on the ever-more-centralized ruling power.[5]

While the contributing authors differ in their assessments of the severity of the problems facing Japan, they overwhelmingly agree that the observed institutional changes represent mere recalibrations or "minor tinkering" with failing systems.[6] Consequently, we conclude that Japan is heading toward a "catastrophic equilibrium" where the "old cannot die, and the new cannot be born"[7] until a more drastic "decisive intervention" occurs, or the existing structures die away altogether. As the country is failing to resolve social and gender inequalities, and moving slowly in transforming into a sustainable and open society, those who have argued that Japan under the leadership of Abe Shinzō has reached its "peak" may eventually be proven correct in their pessimistic forecasts.[8] This path-dependent development becomes visible when we first analyze long-term socioeconomic trends and then compare them with actual institutional changes.

Examining the condition of the Japanese society, David Chiavacci probed the narratives of the "equal middle-class society" and emerging "gap society" against the available scientific evidence for equality and inequality. He found that inequality has risen less dramatically than the latter crisis narrative suggests, mainly because Japanese society has never been as equal as the preceding frame or narrative of a middle-class society made it appear.

Chiavacci argued that the end of Japan's rapid growth phase in the early 1990s meant that the pie ceased to grow, and that the consequently intensifying struggles over how to divide the remaining wealth largely arrested the middle classes' social mobility and threatened—but not (yet) significantly diminished—its members' social status. Importantly, the Democratic Party of Japan (DPJ) under Ozawa Ichirō was able to capture the ensuing sense of crisis over declining rural areas to temporarily win ruling power. Yet, the eventually "failing" DPJ rule became itself recruited into the meta-narrative of a Japan in crisis, and the LDP under the reborn Abe returned to power with the promise of turning back the time (and policies) to the seemingly more stable era before the onset of the recent privatization and liberalization drive. While things are not as bad as the crisis narrative suggests, Chiavacci nevertheless concludes that Japan's social, economic, and political crisis is much more fundamental and cannot be solved by trying to bring back the good old days; Japan needs to go beyond the postwar paradigm of a work- and growth-oriented society.

Such transition, however, is difficult to achieve, as Japan's fertility rate plummeted to a low of 1.42 in 2019.[9] Confronted by this decline, Abe declared a crisis of the family and, as part of his economic growth agenda, set the new target for Japan's birthrate to 1.8 by 2026. Hiroko Takeda illustrated that this intervention in the private realm of the family served as an attempt to rectify a perceived loss of "a middle-class society standard family" long heralded as core of the Japanese postwar political-economic fabric and basis of the LDP's legitimacy. Recovering the state-in-crisis through traditional family values resembles what Takeda described as Japan's brand of authoritarian populism. Here, the solution to Japan's demographic and family crises goes hand in hand with the disempowerment of the female body to achieve the political objectives of a neoliberal agenda. This emphasis on family values failed to reconcile the contradictions in the agenda of Abe's Japan. After all, it is neoliberal labor market deregulations and—despite long-standing official rhetoric—the persistent lack of social welfare provision, for example for childcare, that led to the disintegration of the family in the first place. Thus, the authoritarian populist return to traditional values has only served to conceal the effects of economic liberalization, such as the LDP has been promoting even at the expense of its own legitimacy.

Similarly, Saori Shibata, in her examination of the seemingly "decisive intervention" that Abenomics stands for, showed that the comprehensive economic strategy failed to alleviate the many ills it was meant to. Thus, the numerous "arrows" shot to reinstate sustainable economic growth, supporting rural areas and women, clearly missed their targets. While Abenomics' effects remained limited to temporarily boosting approval ratings, they have disguised the fact that the Abe government often simply continued to promote decades-old policies, at times in more intensified ways, and under new slogans. To the contrary, prioritizing the creation of a business-friendly climate for big corporations, Abenomics 2.0 furthered precarious working conditions. At the same time, "womenomics" cemented women's role as cheap labor. And the liberalization of the agricultural sector for the sake of concluding international free-trade agreements put additional strain on the aging rural communities. Thus, Abenomics generated resistance in various corners of the society. Hence, Japan, Shibata argued, remains stuck within a path-dependent neoliberal policy framework that leads to economic failure, exacerbates social instability, and deepens the crisis of the capitalist state. It represents a further move toward turning Japan into a disorganized market economy.

Although Iris Wieczorek evaluates the paradigm shift in the field of science, technology, and innovation policy in a positive light, her findings do not contradict more critical accounts of socioeconomic change. This is because the partially self-imposed imperative to boost GDP growth rates facilitated interventions that are entirely in line with the neoliberal agenda. With reference to an idealized Silicon Valley model, Prime Minister Koizumi sought to break the historically conditioned dominance of large corporations in science, technology and innovation. Yet only Prime Minister Abe, upon returning to power in 2012, succeeded in bringing about this major paradigm shift toward the creation of a start-up–friendly ecosystem. Still, Japan has not fully taken over the Silicon Valley model. After all, the conditions in the two countries differ widely, and innovation and entrepreneurship in Japan happen in many places. The questions that remain, though, is to what extent this push for innovation will benefit the entire society, and to what extent it may just be a shift of the responsibility for national and individual well-being toward the individual, in line with the liberal promise of a better common life in the future in return for individual sacrifice of the present. So, what effect did Japan's multiple national crises have on some of the principal institutions underpinning the state?

Crisis and the Recovery of Institutions

Has the pervasive sense of crisis led to a sufficiently strong unification of the diverse array of independent agencies, apparatuses, and institutions that would allow for a decisive intervention to fundamentally transform the state? The present findings must lead to the conclusion that the LDP's and cabinet's enhanced agency has facilitated drastic policy measures, but has not effected any decisive changes that would alleviate the current institutions' underlying failures. This is because their agency was not strong enough and, more importantly, because it did not provide a sufficiently unified and accepted view of an alternate *future* state regime. Its vision for a new Japan is in fact an amalgam of nostalgic images of Japan in the prewar Meiji period and the postwar Japan Inc. Therefore, it remains fundamentally incompatible with the socioeconomic conditions outlined above.

Due to the dramatic demographic decline, the university system and the student have become narrative objects in the struggle for the future of the Japanese society. Jeremy Breaden found that "education is the crisis of choice in Japan," but that no decisive intervention that would fundamentally change the failing system has taken place. This is because a "discursive unification" has not yet occurred; it has been "short-circuited" as the various crisis narratives gave rise to countless "piecemeal remedial actions" instead. This also resulted from the fact that the student as the most powerful device for linking these systemic problems to people's everyday experiences is not easily appropriated for the narration of a crisis meta-narrative. Breaden noted that student-centered narratives show several specific features that work against the progression into a full-blown Hayesian Crisis. Student-centered narratives tend to be highly nostalgic, romanticizing a time in the past when things worked more satisfactorily—even if they never really did. This nostalgia makes for a peculiar articulation of forward- and backward-looking discourses and generates "solutions" that actually reference the very "problems" they originally sought to solve.

In the narrative about Japan's "lost decades" and "precarious future," demographic shifts and the associated social and economic problems represent long-term trends. However, the event that most dramatically revealed the fatal consequences of a state-in-crisis was the March 2011 triple disaster. The 3.11 disaster was instantly framed as Japan's "worst crisis since defeat in World War II."[10] Yet, as Koichi Hasegawa demonstrated, political and bureaucratic infighting forestalled effective crisis management. And because the nuclear disaster itself resulted from the postwar state's inability to impose effective safety regulations on its nuclear industry, the triple disaster exposed the so-called nuclear village's enduring power tying the LDP to the parochial interests of the bureaucracy and the electric power industry. Therefore, post-Fukushima politics betrayed hopes for a radical shift in Japanese political institutions. While some new regulatory measures were implemented and civil society activism increased, Hasegawa showed that social movements failed to trigger a transition toward the phasing-out of nuclear energy production as happened in Germany, South Korea, and Taiwan. To the contrary, even before its return to power in 2012, the LDP had skillfully reengineered the 3.11 narrative to redirect public attention to deflect its responsibility for the nuclear meltdowns toward the DPJ's failure in crisis management.

Complementing such accounts of how political elites used crisis narratives for discrediting their opponents, Paul O'Shea demonstrated how the ascription of foreign policy failures to the DPJ decisively contributed to the party's fall from power only three years after its historic electoral victory. His discussion of three controversies surrounding Sino–Japanese and Japan–US relations revealed how ousted LDP figures, combining power with DPJ politicians close to the mainstream LDP position of supporting the US–Japan alliance and opposing rising China, joined forces with influential US-alliance managers and successfully portrayed prime ministers Hatoyama and Kan as inept and endangering national security. The narrative of failure and crisis blamed them for inviting further Chinese, Korean, and Russian aggression against the weakened Japan by allegedly caving in to Chinese pressure and at the same time questioning the long-standing status quo of the US–Japan alliance. O'Shea concluded that the narration of a general national security crisis not only enabled the Abe-led LDP to regain power, but also allowed it to make a "decisive intervention" for steering Japan's security politics away from the pacifism of the postwar era.

Contrary to what this ending of the Yoshida Doctrine would suggest, Official Development Assistance (ODA), the classical foreign policy tool of the postwar era, has also seen a revival. As Japan joined others and redoubled its efforts to rebuild a twenty-first-century version of a "rich nation and strong army," thereby blurring the boundary between politics and economics, ODA reemerged as an important instrument of foreign *and* security politics. A precondition for this new usefulness, however, has been that the decision-making process be centralized in the hands of the executive. Here, Raymond Yamamoto showed that discursive references to China proved very effective in first delegitimizing ODA spending as a waste of tax-money, only to switch back and justify increased spending with the need to push back against China's growing influence once decision-making had been centralized in the Prime Ministers' Office. Most, if not all, of the outspoken critics who sought to stop ODA spending in the 1990s and 2000s morphed into advocates of the increasingly strategic use of higher amounts of ODA, such as for supporting Vietnam and the Philippines in protecting disputed waters against Chinese incursions. Thus, despite largely successful efforts to differentiate Japanese from Chinese infrastructure construction projects across the Indo-Pacific region, the Abe government returned to a neo-mercantilist use of ODA as well.

Yet, as Ra Mason and Sebastian Maslow concluded, it was the North Korea threat that emerged as the main catalyst for the reform of Japanese defense and security political institutions. Since around 2002, political elites, scholars, and the media have woven North Korea–threat arguments into a meta-narrative of national crisis that mandates the revision of Japan's postwar security system toward a militarily potent nation capable of protecting its citizens. In 2017, Prime Minister Abe went as far as calling general elections to confirm his leadership in overcoming Japan's national crisis—implicitly revealing his own failure to do so since regaining power five years earlier. Throughout 2017, Japanese authorities had conducted unprecedented evacuation drills and issued emergency warnings preparing the public for missile strikes. Confirming Hay's theory, these moves embedded abstract geopolitics in the lived experience. In light of an ever-more-belligerent North Korea, constitutional revision and increased defense spending became thinkable and reasonable. Yet, deeply locked into Abe's agenda to revise Japan's national security system, the state-in-crisis narrative, with the resolution of the abduction issue as priority, limited Tokyo's ability to adjust to changes in international North Korea diplomacy. Enthusiastically embracing the US "maximum pressure" approach, President Trump's sudden engaging of the DPRK left Japan isolated, disoriented, and powerless. Incapable of playing an active role in international security affairs, the Abe government's approach to foreign and security politics therefore risked contradicting its agenda of restoring a "strong nation," exposing its failure to overcome Japan's postwar predicament.

Returning to the source of Japan's deepening sense of crisis and heightening fears of decline, Shogo Suzuki showed how China's and South Korea's relative to Japan prospering economies, have profoundly shaken conservative elites' self-confidence. This effect was compounded by the global resonance that increasing calls for redress of Imperial Japan's wartime atrocities received, especially from South Korean activists. Consequently, Suzuki observed a tendency among conservatives and nationalists to rediscover various facets of the Japanese nation's and the Japanese people's uniqueness. Similar to liberal US scholars in the 1990s, these circles seek to cope with their inevitable decline relative to the populous and vast Chinese state through the rediscovery of Japan's "soft power." In addition to drawing on newly discovered credentials as a democracy characterized by the "rule of law" and provider of "high-quality" ODA, officials have also attempted to use popular culture. Many of these coping strategies appear particularly inward-looking and are therefore unlikely to boost Japan's image beyond its borders. Yet Japanese elites are not alone in the (vain) quest for past greatness. What inferences about the transformation of the Japanese state can we draw from these findings?

Embracing Crisis for the Transformation of the State

In April 2019, Japan marked the end of the imperial Heisei era and the beginning of the Reiwa era. Since the former is often seen as synonymous with the nation's "lost decade(s)," many saw this transition as a juncture in the national quest for bringing Japan back on track toward prosperity, stability, and security. In his January 2020 address to the Diet, Prime Minister Abe consequently declared, "Our country is no longer the Japan it used to be. . . . We were able to completely smash 'the wall of resignation.' With that confidence and pride, everyone, let us carve out Japan's new Reiwa Era together from now on."[11]

Clearly, strong political leadership allowed successive Abe cabinets to implement coherent strategies in various policy fields. Yet the use of crisis narratives for creating this agency and for justifying drastic but ultimately ineffective measures, suggests the continuation of both the instrumental management of a sense of national crisis and the concomitant centralization of power in the prime ministerial executive for its own sake.

The Abe government is not the first to have mobilized support for its policies through references to national decline and crisis. Japan witnessed similar debates in the heydays of its economic miracle. In the aftermath of the 1973 global oil crisis, a group of influential public intellectuals published an essay in the widely read monthly *Bungei Shunju* titled "Nihon no jisatsu" (Japan's suicide).[12] They highlighted the limits of Japan's consumption-oriented growth model and called for a return to pre-modern Japanese values and traditions. The essay's authors later contributed to a 1979 policy report presented to the cabinet of Prime Minister Ōhira Masayoshi (1978–1980). In an attempt to provide Japan with a vision for the twenty-first century, the Ōhira Report emphasized the strength of Japan's culture as an intrinsic feature of the nation's economic recovery and future growth. In the 1990s, then, prominent economists were not convinced by the effects of financial restructuring and market reforms to resolve the post-bubble crisis and predicted the "fall" of postwar Japan's growth model.[13] As we have seen in the introduction, the Obuchi cabinet in 2000 issued yet another report to this end, titled "The Frontier Within: Individual Empowerment and Better Governance in the New Millennium," with a very similar message. Out of a "sense of urgency" that "Japan is heading for decline," the nation's "catch up and overtake" development model was diagnosed as having run its course. Acknowledging the malfunctioning of Japan's egalitarian society, "individual empowerment" was now embraced in terms of "human vitality" and "prosperity through dynamism" as the basis for Japan's recovery as a "beautiful country."[14] In December 2011, prompted by another decade of economic stagnation and the impact of the nation's largest natural disaster in modern times, the DPJ came up with its own vision for the "rebirth of Japan," too,[15] Given the pervasive presence of the sense crisis in everyday politics, the LDP after its return to power in 2012 adopted this very "rebirth" rhetoric and promised a "new Japan."[16]

As seen from the recurrent references to the Meiji era in contemporary debates,[17] however, the LDP's intervention to reconcile the many contradictions within the state-in-crisis narrative, in many ways, constituted a return to the past and not a transformation toward the future. This circular logic of national, that is, top-down narrations of crisis and rebirth exacerbates old institutional and policy failures and leads to additional ones, risking recruiting Abe and the LDP themselves into a new crisis meta-narrative. This includes major foreign and security political failures. The Abe administration's continued inability, despite strong determination, overwhelming political dominance, and nationalist credentials, to restore public confidence in the economy, field a renewable energy strategy, and resolve Japan's territorial dispute with Russia to sign a World War II peace treaty, are just as telling as the continued failure to address problems of historical recognition with the Koreas.

At the micro-level of everyday politics, a lack of progress in closing the gaps in social and gender inequality,[18] and series of political scandals and blunt political interventions in judicial procedures, overshadow official calls for Japan's "rebirth" as a beautiful country where everyone can thrive. Thus, in glaring contradiction to the Abe governments' enthusiasm for freeing Japan from its postwar constitutional shackles, economic doldrums, and societal decay, legal scholars and political scientists diagnosed the end of democracy and a shift toward an illiberal state.[19] In particular, Abe's high-handed approach in ramming through a new state secrecy law and new anti-conspiracy legislation, curtailing civil liberties and preventing undesirable institutional change, fanned fears over the backsliding of Japan's postwar democracy.[20]

At the macro-level of economic policies, "minor tinkering" not only falls short of the promised radical changes; in many ways, it returns to past paradigms and practices. Abe's reform agenda remains committed to large-scale spending on public works projects.[21] As a result, Japan's public debt is ballooning. Meanwhile, the deregulation of the labor market continues and the share of irregular (and thus disposable) labor is further increasing. In this vein, Abe's pledge of a "rebirth" has failed to restore Japan's strength.

One decade after Japan suffered the triple disaster of 3.11, the sense of uncertainty and insecurity that was molded into Japan's national crisis narrative is once again visible in the battle against COVID-19.[22] Early into the pandemic, the conservative leadership interpreted the low death rate as evidence for their successful crisis management and proof of Japan's "cultural superiority" (*mindo*).[23] Designed to limit economic damage, the "Japan model,"[24] however, by late 2020, lost its credibility in the face of spiking infection numbers and a healthcare system at breaking point. The failed response also risked derailing the rescheduled 2021 Tokyo Olympics and Paralympics, the very marker for Japan's "rebirth." With Japan's public debt already reaching 266 percent of its GDP, the LDP-led government, now under Prime Minister Suga Yoshihide, approved record budgets to mitigate the crisis at hand.[25] And those who had for years been promoting the neoliberal restructuring of Japan's economic institutions did not miss the opportunity and called for more of the same medicine. They renewed their calls for a "blueprint for a new Japan" to make the country fit for the post-COVID world.[26] Yet this way of identifying, or narrating, failures, and prescribing remedies is not unique to Japan.

Despite considerable differences in their stages of economic development and political superstructures, the Japanese, Korean, and Chinese political economies' common origins and, in principle, similar socioeconomic trajectories, may allow for some generalization of the larger phenomenon discussed here. It is particularly intriguing that the continuously strong and, compared to the 1980s and 1990s, recentralized state continues to wield superior power over both the deindustrializing economies and the fragmenting and rapidly shrinking urbanized societies. Undergoing transformations toward post-developmental or even post-modern forms, these states are increasingly reliant on social mobilization through ethno-nationalistic ideologies. Unlike what well-known macro-sociological theorizing has been suggesting, we therefore witness neither cosmopolitan momentums nor the decentralization of power across the local, national, regional, and global levels—nor the general liquefaction, that is the dissolution, of political power. To the contrary, despite the absence of a decisive intervention, Japan and its East Asian neighbors may well be on the way to a greater transformation that includes the re-embedding of political power in a few urban centers. But while the consequences for national and international politics remain to be seen, crisis meta-narratives have already set the course.

Notes

1. See, for example, Mark T. Berger, *The Battle for Asia: From Decolonization to Globalization* (Abingdon: Routledge, 2004); Sang-Jin Han, and Young-Hee Shim, "Redefining Second Modernity for East Asia: A Critical Assessment," *British Journal of Sociology* 61, no. 3 (2010): 465–488; Prasenjit Duara, *The Crisis of Global Modernity: Asian Traditions and a Sustainable Future* (Cambridge: Cambridge University Press, 2015).

2. Andrew Gordon and Takii Kazuhiro, eds., *Sōhatsu suru Nihon e: Posuto "ushinawareta 20-nen" no dessan* [Towards an Emerging Japan: A Post-"Lost Decades" Sketch] (Tokyo: Kōbundō, 2018); Yoichi Funabashi and Barak Kushner, eds., *Examining Japan's Lost Decades* (Abingdon: Routledge, 2016).

3. Iokibe Makoto, *Nippon wa suitai suru no ka* [Will Japan Decline?] (Tokyo: Chikura Shobō, 2014); Kitaoka Shinichi, *Nihon seiji no hōkai: Dai-san no haisen o dō norikoeru ka* [The Collapse of Japanese Politics: How to Overcome the Third Defeat] (Tokyo: Chūō Kōron Shinsha, 2012).

4. Shirai Satoshi, *Eizoku haisenron—sengo Nihon no kakushin* [Eternal Defeat: The Essence of Postwar Japan] (Tokyo: Ōta Shuppan, 2013).

5. Makihara Izuru, *"Abe ikkyō" no nazo* [The Puzzle of Abe's Dominance] (Tokyo: Asahi Shimbun Shuppan, 2016); Nakakita Kōji, *Jiminto: "Ikkyō" no jitsuzō* [LDP: The Real Image of One-Party Dominance] (Tokyo: Chūō Kōron Shinsha, 2017).

6. Colin Hay, "Crisis and the Structural Transformation of the State: Interrogating the Process of Change," *British Journal of Politics and International Relations* 1, no. 3 (1999): 317–344.

7. Colin Hay, "Rethinking Crisis: Narratives of the New Right and Constructions of Crisis," *Rethinking Marxism: A Journal of Economics, Culture & Society* 8, no. 2 (1995): 60–76, here 61.

8. Brad Glosserman, *Peak Japan: The End of Great Ambitions* (Washington, DC: Georgetown University Press, 2019).

9. Kyodo, "Number of Newborns in Japan Fell to Record Low while Population Dropped Faster than Ever in 2018," *Japan Times*, June 7, 2019, https://www.japantimes.co.jp/news/2019/06/07/national/number-newborns-japan-fell-low-918397-2018-government-survey/. Unless otherwise stated, all online sources were accessed and available on December 22, 2020.

10. Justin McCurry, "Japan PM Calls Tsunami the Worst Crisis Since WWII," *PRI*, March 13, 2011, https://www.pri.org/stories/2011-03-13/japan-pm-calls-tsunami-worst-crisis-wwii.

11. Satoshi Sugiyama, "In Policy Speech, Abe Vows to Establish 'New Era of Japanese Diplomacy,'" *Japan Times*, January 20, 2020, https://www.japantimes.co.jp/news/2020/01/20/national/politics-diplomacy/policy-speech-shinzo-abe-new-era-japanese-diplomacy/.

12. Interestingly, "Japan suicide" was prominently republished in the March 2012 issue of *Bungei Shunju*, suggesting that the DPJ had mismanaged the country in the aftermath of 3.11. The entire essay was later published as a book; see Group 1984, *Nihon no jisatsu* [Japan's Suicide] (Tokyo: Bungei Shunju, 2012). A detailed discussion of the essay's context and content is provided by Andrew Gordon, "Kōdō seichō kara 'ushinawareta 20-nen' e: Kokka, shijō, jendaa no ideorogii [From High-Growth to 'Lost Decades': Ideologies of State, Market and Gender]," in *Sōhatsu suru Nihon e: Posuto "ushinawareta 20-nen" no dessan* [Toward an Emerging Japan: A Post–"Lost Decades" Sketch], ed. Andrew Gordon and Takii Kazuhiro (Tokyo: Kōbundō, 2018), 1–42, here 8–12.

13. Morishima Michio, *Naze Nihon wa botsuraku suru no ka* [Why is Japan Falling?] (Tokyo: Iwanami Shoten, 1999).

14. The Prime Minister's Commission on Japan's Goals in the 21st Century, "The Frontier Within: Individual Empowerment and Better Governance in the New Millennium," January 2000, https://www.kantei.go.jp/jp/21century/report/pdfs/index.html.

15. Prime Minister's Office of Japan, "Nihon saisei ni mukete" [Toward the Rebirth of Japan], n.d., https://www.kantei.go.jp/jp/headline/saisei.html.

16. Abe Shinzō, *Atarashii kuni e* [Towards a New Country] (Tokyo: Bungei Shunju, 2013).

17. Tomohiro Osaki, "150 Years on, Abe Calls for 'Emulation' of Meiji Era Bravery to Overcome Japan's Modern Crises," *Japan Times*, October 23, 2018, https://www.japantimes.co.jp/news/2018/10/23/national/150-years-abe-calls-emulation-meiji-era-bravery-overcome-japans-modern-crises/.

18. Gill Steel, ed., *Beyond the Gender Gap in Japan* (Ann Arbor: University of Michigan Press, 2019); Tamura Tetsuki ed., *Nichijō seikatsu to seiji: Kokka chūshinteki seijizō no saikentō* [Politics and Everyday Life: Rethinking Methodological Statism in Political Science] (Tokyo: Iwanami Shoten, 2019).

19. Makihara Izuru, *Kuzureru seiji o tatenaosu—21-seiki no Nihon gyōsei kaikakuron* [Repairing Japan's Broken Politics: Administrative Reform for a 21st-

Century Japan] (Tokyo: Kodansha, 2018); Yamaguchi Jirō, *Minshushugi wa owaru no ka: Setogiwa ni tatsu Nihon* [Is Democracy Dead? Japan at the Crossroads] (Tokyo: Iwanami Shinsho, 2019); Higuchi Yōichi, *Riberaru demokurashi no genzai: "Neo-riberaru" to "iriberaru" no hazama de* [The State of Liberal Democracy: Between the "Neoliberal" and "Illiberal"] (Tokyo: Iwanami Shinsho, 2019).

20. Arthur Stockwin and Kweku Ampiah, *Rethinking Japan: The Politics of Contested Nationalism* (Lanham: Lexington Books, 2017).

21. Robin Harding, "Abe's Stimulus Brings Back 'Bridges to Nowhere' Spectre in Japan," *Financial Times*, December 6, 2019, https://www.ft.com/content/e4044976-1812-11ea-9ee4-11f260415385.

22. Rintaro Oba, "Births Set to Drop 10% in Japan and US in COVID Baby Bust," *Nikkei Asia*, August 23, 2020, https://asia.nikkei.com/Spotlight/Society/Births-set-to-drop-10-in-Japan-and-US-in-COVID-baby-bust.

23. "Aso: Low Virus Death Rate Thanks to Japanese Superiority," *Asahi Shimbun*, June 5, 2020, http://www.asahi.com/ajw/articles/13432875.

24. Paul O'Shea, "Sweden and Japan are Paying the Price for COVID Exceptionalism," *Conversation*, December 18, 2020, https://theconversation.com/sweden-and-japan-are-paying-the-price-for-covid-exceptionalism-151974.

25. Yuko Takeo and Emi Urabe, "Japan Approves Record $1 Trillion Budget for Next Year," *Bloomberg*, December 21, 2020, https://www.bloomberg.com/news/articles/2020-12-21/japan-approves-record-1-trillion-budget-for-next-year; Ministry of Finance, Central Government Debt, November 2020, https://www.mof.go.jp/english/jgbs/reference/gbb/e202009.html.

26. Takenaka Heizō, *Posuto-korona no "Nihon no kaizō keikaku": Dijitaru shihonshugi de kyōsha to naru bijon* [A Post-Corona "Blueprint for a New Japan": A Vision for Becoming Stronger through Digital Capitalism] (Tokyo: PHP Ken-kyūsho, 2020).

Contributors

Jeremy Breaden, Associate Professor in Japanese Studies, School of Languages, Literatures, Cultures and Linguistics, Faculty of Arts, Monash University, Australia.

David Chiavacci, Professor in the Social Sciences of Japan, University of Zurich, Switzerland.

Koichi Hasegawa, Specially Appointed Professor, Graduate School of Comprehensive Human Sciences, Shokei Gakuin University, Japan, and Professor Emeritus of Tohoku University, Japan.

Sebastian Maslow, Senior Lecturer in International Relations, Department of Global Studies, Sendai Shirayuri Women's College, Japan.

Ra Mason, Associate Professor in International Relations and Japanese Foreign Policy, University of East Anglia, United Kingdom.

Paul O'Shea, Senior Lecturer, Centre for East and South-East Asian Studies, Lund University, Sweden.

Saori Shibata, University Lecturer, Leiden University Institute for Area Studies, Netherlands.

Shogo Suzuki, Senior Lecturer, School of Social Sciences, University of Manchester, United Kingdom.

Hiroko Takeda, Professor of Political Analysis, Graduate School of Law, Nagoya University, Japan.

Iris Wieczorek, Senior Research Fellow, German Institute for Global and Area Studies, Germany.

Christian Wirth, Research Fellow, German Institute for Global and Area Studies, Germany, and Adjunct Research Fellow, Griffith University Asia Institute, Australia.

Raymond Yamamoto, Associate Professor, Department of Global Studies, Aarhus University, Denmark.

Index

Photos and figures are indicated by *italicized* page numbers.
Tables are indicated by t.